Business Taxation

CIMA

Published in association with
the Chartered Institute of
Management Accountants

Other titles in the CIMA series

Stage 1

Economics for Accountants
Keith West

Quantitative Methods
Kevin Pardoe

Stage 2

Accounting Information Systems and Data Processing
Krish Bhaskar and Richard Housden

Management
Cliff Bowman

Financial Accounting
Peter Taylor and Brian Underdown

Cost Accounting
Mark Lee Inman

Stage 3

Management Accounting Techniques
David Benjamin and Colin Biggs

Advanced Financial Accounting
Peter Taylor and Brian Underdown

Company Law
Julia Bailey and Iain McCallum

Stage 4

Management Accounting: Control and Audit
Jeff Coates, Ray Stacey and Colin Rickwood

Management Accounting: Strategic Planning and Marketing
Patrick McNamee

Financial and Treasury Management
Paul Collier, Terry Cooke and John Glynn

Revision Guides

Quantitative Methods Revision Guide
Paul Goodwin

Cost Accounting Revision Guide
Colin Drury

Company Accounting Revision Guide
Peter Taylor and Brian Underdown

Economics Revision Guide
Rob Dixon and Keith West

Business Law Revision Guide
Stan Marsh

Advanced Accounting Techniques Groups and Special Transactions Revision Guide
Peter Taylor and Brian Underdown

Business Taxation

Stage 3

Neil Stein

Heinemann Professional Publishing

Heinemann Professional Publishing Ltd
Halley Court, Jordan Hill, Oxford OX2 8EJ

OXFORD LONDON MELBOURNE AUCKLAND SINGAPORE
IBADAN NAIROBI GABORONE KINGSTON

First published 1989

British Library Cataloguing in Publication Data
Stein, Neil D
Business taxation. – (CIMA series stage 3).
1. Great Britain. Business firms. Taxation.
I. Title II. Series
336.2′07′094′

ISBN 0 434 91873 3

Printed in Great Britain by
Redwood Burn Limited, Trowbridge, Wiltshire and
bound by Pegasus Bookbinding, Melksham, Wiltshire.

Contents

Preface

This book has been written with the needs of the CIMA Business Taxation syllabus primarily in mind. It provides a clear exposition of all aspects of that syllabus, as amplified by the Guidance Notes from the Examination Committee reproduced in the Introduction.

However, tax syllabuses contain many common features, and the book will also be helpful for students preparing for the taxation examinations of other professional bodies:

- Institute of Chartered Accountants in England and Wales
- Institute of Chartered Accountants of Scotland
- Institute of Chartered Accountants in Ireland (Northern Ireland syllabus)
- Chartered Association of Certified Accountants
- Association of International Accountants
- Society of Company and Commercial Accountants
- Institute of Chartered Secretaries and Administrators
- Association of Accounting Technicians

Although mainly intended as a student text, its clarity of explanation and wealth of examples make it useful to anyone wanting a guide through the UK tax maze.

The book is divided into five parts. Parts one to four comprises the study text and cover income tax, corporation tax, capital gains tax and value added tax. Each chapter concludes with a useful summary of its contents and a set of progress questions to test absorption of the material in the chapter.

Part Five contains over fifty questions, many of them from past examinations, to provide the practice without which examination success is almost impossible.

We are grateful to the professional bodies who gave permission for their examination questions to be reproduced – the Chartered Institute of Management Accountants (CIMA) the Chartered Association of Certified Accountants (CACA) and the Society of Company and Commercial Accountants (SCCA). Some of the questions have been updated to reflect the inevitable changes in taxation over the years.

Neil Stein

Introduction

Taxation as a source of revenue for the Government

Taxation is the means by which the Government raises revenue to meet its expenditure. It may also be used as a means of influencing or controlling the economy.

The three largest sources of revenue are *income tax*, charged on income and profits of individuals, *corporation tax*, charged on profits of companies, and *value added tax* suffered by consumers on a wide range of goods and services.

The Chancellor of the Exchequer introduces his or her proposals to raise the revenue needed to finance government expenditure in an annual Budget, usually presented to Parliament in March each year. The Budget proposals, after debate and amendment in the House of Commons, become the Finance Act imposing the taxes for the current year.

We may divide these taxes into *direct* taxes, levied on income and profits and administered by the Inland Revenue, and *indirect* taxes, charged on consumption in one way or another.

The forecast revenue for 1988/89 from the various taxes is:

	£million	*£million*	*% of total*
Direct taxes (Inland Revenue)			
Income tax	42,100		33
Corporation tax	19,800		15.5
Capital gains tax	1,950		1.5
Miscellaneous	4,150		3
		68,000	53
Indirect taxes and sundry items			
(mainly Customs and Excise)			
Value added tax	26,200		20.5
Petrol and other fuel taxes	8,400		6.5

	£million	*£million*	*% of total*
Cigarettes, tobacco	5,000		4
Alcoholic drinks	4,500		3.5
Miscellaneous	16,100		12.5
		60,200	47
		128,200	100

Taxes within the Business Taxation syllabus

The CIMA Business Taxation paper is mainly concerned with direct taxes, with particular reference to tax on business profits. The only indirect tax covered is value added tax, of which an introductory knowledge only is required.

The syllabus is reproduced below together with the Guidance Notes issued by CIMA.

Business Taxation – syllabus

Aim

To test the candidate's ability to:

(a) advise managers on the application of the principles of taxation to decision making;
(b) apply the rules of case and statute law through computation;
(c) apply taxation knowledge to the process of formulating corporate plans.

Content	*Ability required*
1 Principles and practice (weighting 5%)	
Introduction to public finance and principles of taxation	2
Administration: structure and procedures; returns, assessments, appeals, collection	2
2 Income tax matters affecting businesses (weighting 20%)	
Assessments; statutory income	2
Scope of all schedules: basis of assessment, deductions and reliefs including loss relief (preparation of personal tax computation will not be required)	2
Rules for Cases I and II of Schedule D (excluding changes in accounting date)	3
Capital allowances	3
Deduction of tax at source: payments without deduction of tax	3
Schedule E: Emoluments, Pay-as-you-earn (PAYE), expenses and benefits	3
3 Corporation Tax (weighting 35%)	
Scope	2
Taxation of profits; relief for losses	3
Close companies; distributions	3
Groups, including treatment of losses	3
Periods of account and changes in accounting date	3

Capital allowances; plant, Industrial Buildings Allowance (IBA), others; methods of granting relief	3
Payment of dividends: Advanced Corporation Tax (ACT) rules	3
Taxation of international businesses; position of companies trading internationally; overseas subsidiaries; double taxation relief; controlled foreign companies	2
4 Capital Gains Tax (weighting 15%)	
Scope	2
Exemptions, relief and losses	3
Groups of companies; inter-company transactions	3
Shares and securities	3
5 Value Added Tax (weighting 10%)	
Scope	2
Registration and deregistration	2
Exemptions and zero rating	2
Tax point; taxable value; payments and refunds	3
Application in groups of companies	3
6 Tax planning (weighting 15%)	
Applications, including loss strategy, maximising group relief, ACT management, capital allowances, company takeovers	4
Integration of tax planning into the budgeting process	4
Tax avoidance and evasion	2

The numbers alongside each syllabus item indicate the level of ability required:

Ability level	*Requirement*
1	*Appreciation* To understand a knowledge area at an early stage of learning or outside the core of management accounting, at a level which enables the accountant to communicate and work with other members of the management team.
2	*Knowledge* To advise on such matters as laws, standards, facts and techniques at a level of detail appropriate to a management accounting specialist.
3	*Skill* To apply theoretical knowledge, concepts and techniques to the solution of problems where it is clear what technique has to be used and the information needed is clearly indicated.
4	*Application* To apply knowledge and skills where candidates have to determine from a number of techniques which is the most appropriate and select the information required from a fairly wide range of data, some of which might not be relevant; to exercise professional judgement and to work with members of the management team and other recipients of financial reports.

Guidance notes on syllabus

Aims and objectives
While the aims of the Business Taxation course are stated clearly in the syllabus document, it might be helpful to expand on these rather brief statements.

In devising the syllabus it was intended that management accountants acquire an awareness of the importance and consequences of taxation implications inherent in the decision making process rather than that they become taxation specialists.

Outline approach
The style of the paper will be that,

1 In contrast with the papers set under the previous syllabus, less emphasis will be placed on intricate calculations within computations; rather, candidates will be required to demonstrate a practical understanding of principles.
2 Under this current syllabus, emphasis will be placed on candidates' ability to comment on figures produced by computations; in having an understanding of the rationale underlying recent legislation, and in showing that they can recommend to management the most tax efficient course of action from a number of alternatives.
3 Candidates will be required to demonstrate their ability to communicate knowledge by means of reports, letters and memos.

Specific topic areas
1 Principles and practice
Examples of the type of knowledge required would be

(a) time limits for appeals and claims,
(b) date of payment of taxes,
(c) deferment of taxation.

2 Income tax matters affecting businesses
This section of the syllabus requires most clarification, particularly the role of personal taxation.

(a) While personal taxation computations will not be called for, a sound knowledge is necessary of the method of compiling statutory income and the role of personal allowances as they relate to claims for the relief of trading losses. Candidates will be expected to demonstrate the ability to maximise personal allowances in loss situations (including allowances available to married couples).
(b) Knowledge is required of assessing income under all schedules and of relieving losses under Schedules A and D Cases I and II. No detailed questions will be set on Schedule B or losses in aggregation.
(c) Candidates should be conversant with the basis of assessment under Schedule D Cases I and II including opening and closing

businesses but excluding change of accounting date. The ability to choose an optimum cessation date would be expected. Candidates will be expected to adjust trading profits for taxation purposes and to quote relevant case law.

(d) Questions relating to capital allowances will, unlike papers under the previous syllabus, be less likely to call for detailed computations but will concentrate upon core areas and recent legislation. No questions will be asked on

  (i) dwelling houses,
  (ii) agricultural land and buildings,
  (iii) mines, oil wells, dredging.

  A sound knowledge of case law relating to capital allowances will be required.

(e) A knowledge is expected of the role played in the computation of statutory income by annual charges, expenses and payments to secure personal pensions.

(f) For employee taxation a full knowledge of all aspects of the PAYE and benefits systems is required.

  In relation to income tax, it should be noted that no questions will be set on

  1 personal taxation of husband and wife (ss. 283 and 287)
  2 any aspects of partnership taxation.

3 Corporation tax

Since this area of the syllabus has the greatest weighting, an extensive knowledge of all aspects of corporation tax is expected.

The following is an expansion of the brief statements contained in the syllabus.

(a) Taxation of profits:
  Detailed knowledge of the method of computing the Schedule D Case I income is essential, including relevant case law.

(b) Loss relief problems will be set, including the use of trading losses against surplus FII – s. 242. An understanding of choices and the interaction between charges and losses is expected.

(c) Close company identification and the consequences of close company status, including the apportionment process, is required knowledge.

(d) Detailed knowledge of group situations with particular regard to

  1 minimization of tax within a group by best use of a loss,
  2 group income elections,
  3 differing accounting dates,
  4 surrender of ACT

(e) Full knowledge of all aspects of ACT and its interaction with FII.

(f) In relation to overseas matters the following knowledge is required

  (i) the impact of a foreign subsidiary on a UK group of companies,

(ii) maximisation of double tax credits and interaction with ACT,
(iii) the nature of controlled foreign companies and the consequences of this status.

Detailed knowledge of double taxation treaties with other countries is not required.

4 Capital gains tax
The part of the syllabus covering capital gains is reasonably clear and little expansion is required. It should be noted that questions involving individuals will be restricted to situations where the individual is involved in a business, e.g. is disposing of a business or shares in a family company or assets used in a business. Again, the position of groups presents planning opportunities. In relation to indexation, candidates will be given the indexation factor between two dates rather than the RPI figures.

5 Value added tax
In addition to the items specified, a knowledge of the system of statutory penalties (Keith Report) is required. Questions on both computations and reports can be expected. Planning aspects inherent in group registration arrangements may be examined.

6 Tax planning
As a general rule students would be advised not to consider tax planning as a freestanding area of the syllabus. Rather they should consider tax planning opportunities as they work through each area of the syllabus. It should be noted that detailed questions on tax avoidance as dealt with in the *Ramsay* and *Furniss* v. *Dawson* cases will not be asked.

Note: Section references are to the Income and Corporation Taxes Act 1988.

Tax legislation

The rules relating to each major tax are covered in statutes. Those relevant for CIMA Business Taxation are:

1 Income and Corporation Taxes Act 1988 (ICTA 1988)
2 Capital Gains Tax Act 1979 (CGTA 1979)
3 Value Added Tax Act 1983 (VATA 1983)
4 Taxes Management Act 1970 (TMA 1970)
5 Capital Allowances Act 1968 (CAA 1968)

In addition to these, we have annual Finance Acts with amend these main Acts. As the ICTA 1988 has so recently consolidated all income tax and corporation tax statutes up to 1988, the only Finance Act relevant for these taxes in the Finance Act (FA) 1988. It may be necessary to refer to earlier Finance Acts for capital gains tax and VAT amendments to the main Acts listed above.

In general, it is not necessary for you to be aware of precise section references in these statutes. There are, however, a few occasions when it is customary to refer to a claim available to a taxpayer using the relevant section reference. This is indicated in the text where necessary. Section references in the text are to the ICTA 1988 unless otherwise stated.

Structure of the book

Study text

- Part One (Chapters 1–10) Income tax
- Part Two (Chapters 11–18) Corporation tax
- Part Three (Chapters 19–24) Capital gains tax
- Part Four (Chapter 25) Value added tax

Parts One to Three each include a chapter on tax planning for the tax covered in that section. The administration of income tax and corporation tax is introduced in Chapter 1 and dealt with in detail in Chapter 9. Further aspects peculiar to capital gains tax and value added tax are explained in the relevant sections.

Each chapter concludes with a summary of its contents and a set of progress questions to be worked through before proceeding to the next chapter.

Practice questions

In Part Five of the book are practice questions, many of them from past CIMA examinations. As explained in the study hints below, it is vital for you to practise these questions – *without* looking at the answers first – to develop speed, accuracy, and familiarity with the type and level of questions you are likely to meet in the examination.

Study hints

Approach to study

The emphasis in most taxation examinations is on tax computations of various kinds. It is absolutely essential for you to practise working through the questions in Part Five of the book.

Your approach to study will vary depending on whether you are attending a course of lectures or working on your own. Whichever approach you are adopting, *repeated study* of the material is the key to absorption of it. *Always* glance through the chapter to be covered before attending a lecture on it, and *always* consolidate by studying it in detail afterwards. Do *not* expect to be able to pass examinations by merely attending lectures.

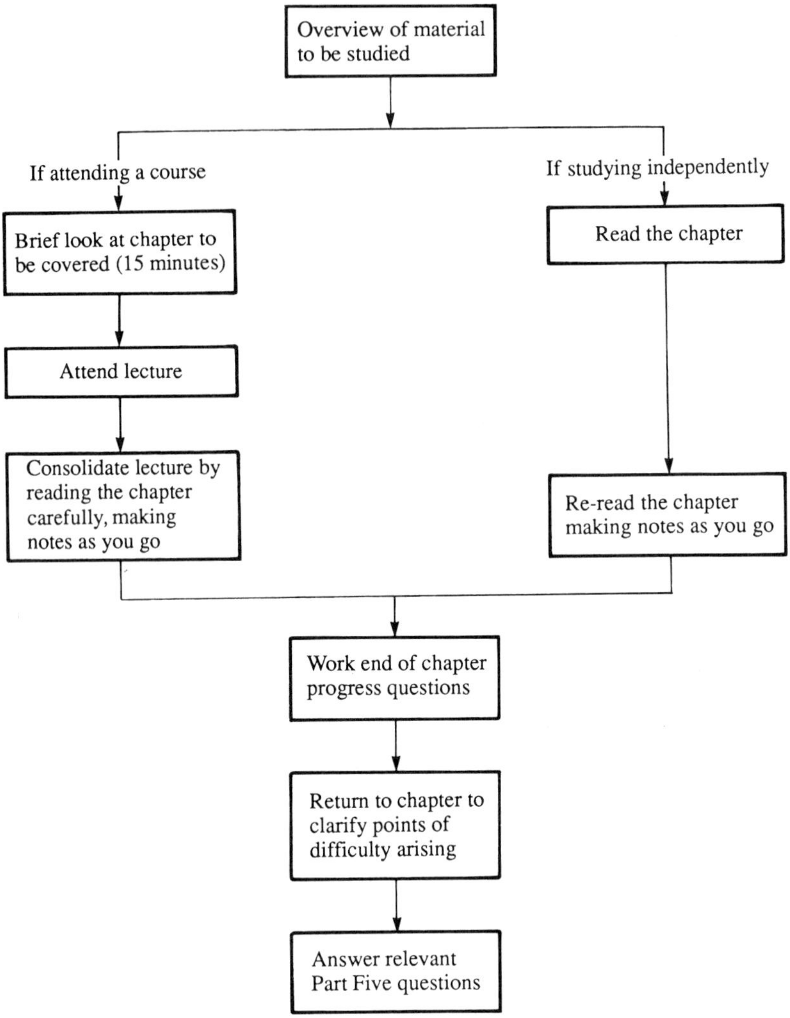

Figure 1

Your programme of study for each chapter or topic should be something like that shown in Figure 1.

If attending lectures, you will, of course, be given practical work to be done in the session, but that will be supplemented by homework along the lines indicated.

Time required

You will probably need to spend about 100 hours per subject to prepare for your CIMA examinations – that means that you have to work for about as long outside the lecture room as you do inside it.

Revision

Revision during your study
Build some revision sessions into your programme. It is useful to *rework* both end of chapter progress questions and Part Five questions from time to time.

Pre-examination revision
Aim to complete your studies about a month before the examination, so that you have that final month for revision. About 50 per cent of your revision time should be practising past examination questions (a set of questions for revision purposes appears in Part Five of the book), the remainder picking up points revealed as weaknesses as you attempted the questions. It is useful to *rework* both progress questions and Part Five questions at this time.

Part One Income Tax

1 Income tax – basic principles

Persons liable to income tax

In general, all individuals resident *in* the UK, or deriving income *from* the UK even if not resident, are liable to income tax. There are the inevitable minor exceptions for people like ambassadors and their foreign staff, members of visiting armed forces and officials of the United Nations.

It is important to realize, as we saw in the Introduction, that limited companies do not pay income tax on their profits but instead are liable to parallel corporation tax.

Some organizations are also exempt from income tax and corporation tax. The most important examples of these are registered charities and approved pension funds.

The income tax year

If we are to tax income, it will be useful to define a period of time for which to measure that income. For income tax purposes, we use the year ending on 5 April* each year. We refer to this year as the 'income tax year' or 'fiscal year' and identify each one by naming the two calendar years into which it enters – '1988/89' for example means the year ending on 5 April 1989.

* This odd date arose for historical reasons – in the Middle Ages the legal year in England was the year to 25 March. When the Gregorian calendar was adopted in England in 1752, it was necessary to omit eleven days from the year. To avoid having a year for revenue purposes of less than 365 days, eleven days were added at the end of the year, bringing us on from 25 March to 5 April!

What is income?

Having defined the persons liable to income tax, and the period for which we shall measure income, it is now necessary to define what income is to be regarded as within the charge to income tax. There is no short statutory definition of income or taxable income, but the main types of taxable income are defined in ICTA 1988 as explained below.

The Schedules and Cases

The Income and Corporation Taxes Act 1988 (ICTA 1988) defines the rules to be followed in calculating the income for tax purposes from different sources. The study of income tax is very largely the study of these statutory rules, though case law is also important in interpreting the meaning of statutes and dealing with borderline areas.

The Act classifies income according to its type using five main headings (referred to as 'Schedules'), some with subheadings referred to as 'Cases'.

This rather archaic terminology derives from a statute enacted in 1803 shortly after the introduction of income tax by William Pitt in 1799 to help pay for the Napoleonic wars.

For each Schedule and Case the tax legislation defines:

(a) Rules for calculating the amount of income for tax purposes (e.g. what expenses if any may be deducted as costs incurred in obtaining that income).
(b) Rules for relating income to the income tax years to 5 April – the so-called 'basis of assessment'. For some types of income we adopt the 'actual' basis of assessment – that is, we tax the actual income arising in the income tax year. For other types of income we adopt the 'preceding year' basis of assessment – the income charged to tax in a given tax year is that arising in the previous tax year. (If you are beginning to think that there are some odd features in the UK income tax system, you are quite right!)

Table 1 summarizes the Schedules and Cases. The Schedules are designed by capital letters A to F, the Cases by Roman numerals – I, II, III, etc.

Rates of income tax

The Chancellor of the Exchequer presents his Budget to Parliament each year, usually in March or April, fixing among other things the rates of tax and personal reliefs for the forthcoming year. When approved by Parliament, the Finance Bill embodying the Budget proposals becomes the Finance Act for that year.

The rates fixed for 1988/89 by the Finance Act 1988 are:

Basic rate	25%
Higher rate (on taxable income over £19,300)	40%

Table 1 The schedules and cases of income tax

Schedule and case	*Income assessable*	*Normal basis of assessment*	*Normal due dates for payment* (basic rate tax)*	*Chapter references*
A	Rents and other income derived from landed property in the UK, less allowable expenses	Actual (Rent *due* in tax year less expenses paid)	1 January in tax year of assessment	6
(B)	(Commercial woodlands) Abolished by Finance Act 1988 – profits from the operation of commercial wood-lands now tax free		–	–
C	Interest on UK Government securities plus interest on overseas government securities if paid through a UK paying agent. No allowable deductions	Actual	–	8
D Case I	Profits of trade or business less allowable expenses	Preceding year-profit shown by profit and loss account for year ending in preceding income tax year)	1 January in tax year of assessment and following 1 July in two equal instalments	3 to 5
D Case II	Profits of profession or vocation less allowable expenses			
D Case III	Interest etc. not taxed at source	Preceding year (income arising in preceding tax year)	1 January in tax year of assessment	8
D Case IV	Income from foreign securities	Preceding year (income arising in preceding tax year)	1 January in tax year of assessment	8
D Case V	Income from foreign possessions			8
D Case VI	Any income not falling under another Schedule or Case	Actual	1 January in tax year of assessment	6 and 8
E	Income from employments	Actual	Monthly on 19th of each month	7
F	Dividends paid by UK companies	Actual	–	8, 12 and 13

* In all cases an alternative due date if later than that shown, is thirty days after the date of issue of the notice of assessment.
The classification of income into Schedules and Cases also operates for corporation tax purposes, though the basis of assessment is different, as explained in Chapter 11.

A taxpayer does not have to pay tax on the whole of his or her income, however. Personal reliefs are given which have the effect of exempting from tax the first few thousand pounds of a taxpayer's income. The most important of these is the *Personal allowance*, fixed for 1988/89 at £2,605 for a single person and £4,095 for a married couple. (Full details of allowances available for 1988/89 are given in Appendix 1 to this Chapter.) Here is a basic illustration.

Illustration 1.1

Adam, a single man, has the following income in 1988/89:

	£
Salary	18,000
Profits from part-time business	4,000
Interest on Government securities (all taxed at source)	1,000

To calculate Adam's tax liability we have to proceed in three stages:

(a) Compute *total* income
(b) Deduct personal reliefs from total income to arrive at *taxable* income
(c) Charge tax on taxable income

Adam
Income tax computation 1988/89

	£
Salary	18,000
Profit from part-time business shown by accounts for year to 31 December 1987	4,000
Interest on Government securities	1,000
Total income	23,000
Less: Personal reliefs	
Single allowance	2,605
Taxable income	£20,395
Tax payable	
£	
19,300 @ 25%	4,825
1,095 @ 40%	438
£20,395	£ 5,263

The means by which this £5,263 is collected by the Revenue is explained below.

Collection of income tax at source

The Inland Revenue try to make the collection of income tax as easy as possible – for themselves. With this thought in mind, they arrange where possible to collect tax *at source* – that is to say, by deduction at the point when income first comes into existence. Many of us are familiar with this process in relation to our salaries – we receive them after deduction of tax under the Pay As You Earn (PAYE) procedure. The Revenue require employers to deduct tax from wages and salaries as they are paid, and pay over the total amount collected each month. That has obvious advantages from the Revenue point of view:

(a) The tax revenue is received more quickly
(b) The trouble and expense of assessing every employee's tax liability at the end of the tax year are saved
(c) Little or no tax is lost through bad debts – employees do not have to find a substantial lump sum after the end of the tax year to pay their tax bill.

The same principle is applied to most interest received by individuals:

(a) *Interest on UK Government securities* – tax on the interest on most UK Government securities is deducted at source by the paying agent and paid over to the Treasury.
(b) *Interest paid by UK companies* – tax on debenture interest and the like paid by UK companies is deducted at source – the net amount is paid to the debenture holder and the tax deducted is paid over to the Revenue quarterly.
(c) *Dividends paid by UK companies* – Although the concept here is a little more complex than for interest paid by UK companies, the practical effect is once again that the shareholder receives an amount which is net of basic rate of income tax (see Chapter 12 for more details).
(d) *Bank interest and building society interest* – once again the amount actually received by the taxpayer is treated as net of basic rate tax.

There is one important difference between tax deducted at source from wages and salaries and tax deducted, or treated as having been deducted, from interest and dividends. This is that the deduction from interest and dividends is always at basic rate (25 per cent) on the full amount, whereas the PAYE procedure applied to wages and salaries will allow for the taxpayer's personal reliefs and may also collect higher rate tax if the taxpayer's income is high enough.

Let us apply what we have just learnt to the Adam example above. How will Adam pay the £5,263 due to the Revenue for 1988/89?

First of all, PAYE deductions from his salary will collect tax on £18,000 less personal reliefs £2,605. Secondly, tax at basic rate will have been deducted from the interest on Government securities. That leaves the profit from the business. It is not practicable to tax this at source because the final profit cannot be arrived at until accounts covering the period have been drawn up. (That is the logic for adopting the preceding year basis of assessment, leaving time for the preparation of accounts.)

Adam will submit his business profit and loss account to the Revenue with a computation adjusting the profit for any expenses charged there which are not allowed for tax purposes.

The Revenue will then raise an assessment to tax on the agreed amount (here £4,000 at 25 per cent or £1,000). Adam's position for 1988/89 becomes:

	Gross income £	*Tax* £	*Notes*
Salary	18,000	3,848.75	Tax deducted under PAYE (Schedule E) (£18,000–£2,605) @ 25%
Profits from part-time business	4,000	1,000.00	Tax assessed under Schedule D Case 1
Interest on Government securities	1,000	250.00	Tax @ 25% deducted at source (Schedule C)
	£23,000	£5,098.75	

We still haven't finished. Considering each source of income in isolation, tax at basic rate only is dealt with. When all the income is aggregated, it becomes clear that taxable income exceeds £19,300 and some higher rate tax is payable.

Adam will accordingly be assessed to higher rate tax on the £1,095 by which his taxable income exceeds £19,300:

	£
Tax at basic rate as above	5,098.75
Higher rate tax	
£1,095 @ (40%–25%)	164.25
	£5,263.00

As the higher rate tax liability can only be ascertained when all income is ascertained and aggregated, the due date for its payment is 1 December after the end of the tax year concerned or thirty days after the date of issue of the notice of assessment, whichever is later.

Tax returns

The next point to turn to in this introduction to income tax principles is the basic means of communication between the Revenue and the taxpayer. Each year the Revenue may require a taxpayer to complete a Return of Income and Claim for Allowances. This has to state all income for the year, with supporting information where necessary, and give details of personal reliefs claimed. (The single allowance is given automatically but the married allowance and the rest must be specifically claimed.) The Return of Income is the basis on which the Revenue determine and issue assessments.

Revenue officials and appeal procedures

Fuller coverage of tax administration is given in Chapter 9. Basic details of two points are introduced here because they are necessary to an understanding of basic taxation.

Revenue officials

The tax returns described in above are submitted to the local *Inspector of Taxes*. For tax assessment purposes, the country is divided into tax districts, each under the control of an Inspector of Taxes, whose main task is to assess and agree tax liabilities of the businesses in his or her area and their employees.

Once a tax liability is agreed between the Inspector of Taxes and the taxpayer, the task of collecting the tax is handled by the Collectors of Taxes, operating in parallel with the Inspectors of Taxes.

Appeal procedure

If the taxpayer and the Inspector of Taxes cannot reach agreement on the amount of tax payable, it is open to the taxpayer to initiate an appeal procedure which can lead through the High Court to the House of Lords (see Chapter 9 for more details).

Repayment claims

The principle of deduction of tax at source could mean that a taxpayer suffers tax by deduction amounting to more than his or her eventual tax liability. If this happens the taxpayer can make a *repayment claim*, supported by the dividend vouchers etc., which provide evidence of the tax deducted.

Illustration 1.2

Eve, a single woman, has a total income for 1988/89 of £15,000, derived entirely from dividends and interest:

	Amount received	*Basic rate tax 25%*	*Gross equivalent*
	£	£	£
Dividends from UK companies	7,500	2,500	10,000
Interest on UK Government securities (all taxed at source)	3,750	1,250	5,000
	11,250	3,750	15,000

Eve's tax position for 1988/89 will be:

	£
Dividends from UK companies	10,000
Interest from UK Government securities	5,000
Total income	£15,000
Less personal reliefs	
Single allowance	2,605
Taxable income	£12,395
Tax payable	
£12,395 @ 25%	3,098.75
Tax suffered by deduction	
£15,000 @ 25%	3,750.00
Repayment to be claimed	£ 651.25

Summary

Persons liable to income tax

All individuals resident *in* the UK, or deriving income *from* the UK while not resident, are liable to UK tax on that income. There are minor exceptions.

The income tax year

For income tax purposes, income is measured for the income tax year ending 5 April each year and identified by naming the two calendar years involved – 1988/89 for example.

The schedules and cases of income tax

The statutory rules governing the assessment of income tax (and corporation tax) are based on the classification of income into types and referred to as 'schedules' and 'cases'. It is essential for you to learn Table 1 above really thoroughly – this is the most important point in the chapter.

Rates of income tax

Rates of income tax and allowances are fixed by the Chancellor of the Exchequer and enacted in the annual Finance Act. Income tax rates for 1988/89 are:

(a)	Basic rate	25%
(b)	Higher rate (on taxable income over £19,300)	40%

Personal reliefs

In calculating an individual's income tax liability several reliefs may be deducted which have the effect of exempting part of the taxpayer's income from tax (see above and Appendix 1 below).

Collection of tax at source

Where possible, the Revenue collect income tax by deduction of tax at source. This applies particularly to salaries and wages (taxed under PAYE) and to most interest received.

Tax returns

The taxpayer may be required to make an annual Return of Income and claim for allowances to the Revenue, forming the basis for the assessment of his or her tax liability.

Revenue officials

The two main Revenue officials handling income tax, corporation tax and capital gains tax are:

(a) Inspectors of Taxes, responsible for assessing and agreeing tax liabilities
(b) Collectors of taxes, responsible for collecting the tax assessed.

Appeals

If the taxpayer does not agree an assessment raised by the Inspector of Taxes, and agreement cannot be reached by negotiation between them, an appeal procedure exists which enables the case to be taken through the courts (see Chapter 9).

Repayment claims

If a taxpayer has paid too much tax, a repayment claim may be submitted and a refund obtained.

Progress questions

Attempt the following questions to test your absorption of the material to date.

Use these questions for revision by re-working them from time to time. Answers are on page 392.

1 Are the following statements true or false?

	True	*False*
(a) In general, UK income tax applies to all individuals deriving income from UK, whether resident in the UK or not		
(b) Income derived from overseas by UK residents is not liable to UK tax but may be subject to overseas tax in the country of origin.		
(c) Registered charities are exempt from UK income tax and corporation tax.		
(d) Individuals pay income tax on their income, partnerships and limited companies pay corporation tax on theirs.		

2 Which schedules or cases of income tax are assessed on the preceding year basis?

3 For the following schedules and cases of income tax state:

(a) Income assessed under them
(b) Normal basis of assessment
(c) Normal due date for payment of tax:

Schedule A
Schedule D Case I
Schedule D Case VI

4 What is the higher rate of tax?

5 (a) What are the advantages to the Revenue of collecting tax at source where possible?
(b) Give four examples of income normally taxed at source.

Appendix 1 Rates of personal reliefs 1988/89

	£
Single allowance	2,605
Married allowance	4,095
Single allowance (taxpayer or spouse aged 65 to 79)*	3,180
Married allowance (taxpayer or spouse aged 65 to 79)*	5,035
Single allowance (taxpayer or spouse aged 80 or over)*	3,310
Married allowance (taxpayer or spouse aged 80 or over)*	5,205

* These 'age' reliefs only apply when the taxpayer's total income is below defined limits. Once a taxpayer's total income exceeds £10,600 (1988/89) the age reliefs are progressively reduced so that eventually a taxpayer aged over 65 merely claims the normal single or married allowance.

Wife's earned income relief (limited to amount of wife's earned income)	2,605
Additional relief in respect of children (available to an individual not entitled to the married allowance but who has care of one or more children, or to a married man whose wife is totally incapacitated and who has care of one or more children)	1,490
Widow's bereavement allowance (available to widows (not widowers) in the tax year of their husband's death and, if they have not remarried before the beginning of it, the next tax year)	1,490
Blind persons relief	
single person, or one spouse of married couple registered as blind	540
Married man, if both his wife and himself are registered as blind	1,080

2 Income tax Schedule D Cases I and II – adjustment of profit

Introduction

We saw in Chapter 1 that income is classified in Schedules and Cases according to its type.

Cases I and II of Schedule D are the most important for examination purposes. This chapter covers them from an income tax point of view, though many but not all of the rules apply for corporation tax purposes also – see Chapter 11.

Case I covers profits derived from *trade*, while Case II covers profits from a *profession* or *vocation*. In fact the rules for the two cases are exactly the same, though it is worth an extra half mark or so in the exam if you are alert enough to notice that the question deals with a profession of some kind (fairly unlikely in the CIMA tax examination, but possible).

The words 'trade', 'profession' and 'vocation' are not clearly defined in statute. Generally speaking, we might say that a trade involves *buying and selling*, with or without manufacturing, while a profession is more likely to relate to the provision of a *service* requiring the exercise of intellectual skill. A vocation is even more difficult to define exactly. Case law has held racing tipsters, jockeys and dramatists all to be carrying on a vocation.

The most difficult point in this area is to define exactly when a series of isolated purchases and sales begins to constitute a trade. To help us solve this problem the Royal Commission on Taxation set up in 1955 six so-called 'badges of trade'. The word 'badge' is used here in its sense of 'mark' or 'indication'.

The six badges of trade are:

(a) *The subject matter of the realization* – a taxpayer might find it easier to argue against the contention that he or she was conducting a trade if there could be some other reason, such as personal enjoyment, for the purchase and sale. The classic case in this area is

Rutledge V CIR 1929, in which the purchase and sale of $1\frac{1}{4}$m. toilet rolls at a profit of £10,000 was held to be trading even though it was an isolated transaction. Also, in *Cape Brandy Syndicate* v. *CIR* 1921, it was held that a joint venture in brandy constituted trading.

(b) *Length of period of ownership* – the longer an item is retained before its sale the less likely it is that the courts will regard the operation as trading.

(c) *Frequency of similar transactions* – the more often you engage in similar transactions, the more likely it becomes that you will be held to be trading.

(d) *Supplementary work* – if you repair or improve the goods, engage in marketing or advertising or open up offices, you are more likely to be conducting a trade.

(e) *Circumstances responsible for the realization* – if you can show some special reason for the transaction apart from the wish to make a profit, you have more chance of escaping assessment as a trader. For example, if a sudden emergency calling for ready money arose, that could provide an alternative explanation justifying a sale and tending to negate the presumption that it was in the course of trade.

(f) *Motive* – evidence as to the motive for a purchase and sale could either support or negate the presumption that a trade was being carried on.

Allowable and disallowable expenditure; adjustment of profits

The starting point for calculating tax on business profits is going to be the business profit and loss account, but a lot of adjustments are usually needed to arrive at taxable profit. For example, the proprietor may have drawn a salary out of the business and charged that as an expense in the profit and loss account. (I know this is against the rules of accounting, but in taxation exams these rules are frequently broken so that you may have the pleasure of adjusting for such items.) For income tax purposes, the salary has to be added back to the profit in arriving at the amount charged to income tax under Schedule D Case I.

We actually have to go through a list of possible profit and loss account items and consider whether they are allowable or not.

(a) Income outside the scope of Schedule D Case I or II

These have to be *deducted* from the profit. Examples are:

(i) Income taxable under another Schedule or Case:

- Rents receivable – taxed under Schedule A
- Dividends receivable – taxed under Schedule F
- Interest receivable – taxed under Schedule D Case III or Schedule C

(ii) Items not liable to income tax at all:

- Gains on sale of fixed assets (may be subject to capital gains tax – see Chapter 19, or dealt with in capital allowances computations – see Chapter 4)
- Tax-free Government grants

(b) Allowable and disallowable expenditure

The basic rule for expenditure is in s.74 ICTA 1988 – expenditure may not be deducted unless it is '*wholly* and *exclusively* laid out or expended *for the purposes of the trade, profession or vocation.*' Case law assists in interpreting the meaning of the rule and there are one or two statutory provisions which modify the basic rule by specifically allowing or disallowing certain items as we shall see. Please learn that rule and especially the words underlined.

To illustrate the application of the rules we shall go through the main items likely to be found in a profit and loss account and consider the status of each:

(i) Purchases
Most or all of this item will be allowable. The only likely exceptions are items not 'for the purpose of the trade'. For example the cost of purchases which were for the personal use of the proprietor would be disallowed.

(ii) Stock
Items taken *from stock* for the proprietor's own use are disallowed and the market value (selling price), *not cost* must be adjusted for. This is based on the decision in *Sharkey* v. *Wernher* 1955, one of the more important tax cases. Note the distinction between purchases specifically for the proprietor (disallowed at cost), and items taken from stock for the proprietor (disallowed at selling price).

(iii) Wages and salaries
Wages and salaries will be allowed, subject to being for the purpose of the trade. Special points are:

- salary or wage to proprietor. Always disallowed
- salary or wage to proprietor's spouse. This *is* allowed provided the amount is actually paid and is reasonably commensurate with the duties performed (*Copeman* v. *Flood* 1940).

(iv) National Insurance contributions
National Insurance contributions for *employees* whose wages are allowed are obviously allowed. Self-employed people pay two types of National Insurance:

- Class 2 contributions (flat rate) – *not* allowed
- Class 4 contributions (based on percentage of profit) – 50 per cent allowed (s. 617 (5) ICTA 1988)

The 50 per cent allowance of Class 4 contributions is deducted in computing total income (see Chapter 1). Thus the whole of Class 4 contributions are disallowed in computing the amount assessable under Schedule D Cases I or II, and the 50 per cent is then deducted in computing total income in the course of arriving at the overall tax liability.

(v) Rent, rates, lighting, heating and similar costs

These will be allowed, provided they are for business purposes. A problem arises when premises are used partly for business purposes and partly for private purposes, as when a person operates a business from home. In that case it is usual to agree with the Inspector of Taxes the proportion of such expenses which can be allowed.

(vi) Depreciation

Any amount provided for depreciation is always disallowed, and capital allowances, where available, deducted instead. See Chapter 4 for details.

(vii) Repairs

This is a problem item. Repairs to business assets are allowed but any element of improvement is disallowed. Two important cases apply in this area:

- *Law Shipping Co. Ltd* v. *CIR* 1923
- *Odeon Associated Theatres* v. *Jones* 1971

In the Law Shipping case, a second-hand ship was purchased in a dilapidated condition. A few months later, extensive repairs were made. It was held that most of the expenditure related to the pre-acquisition period. £12,000 out of the total expenditure of £51,558 was allowed and the rest had to be treated as capital expenditure.

The Odeon Theatres case related to cinemas bought in a dilapidated condition and subsequently repaired over a number of years. The Revenue naturally contended that the Law Shipping decision applied, but the Court of Appeal held that the case could be distinguished. The judgement attached importance to the following points:

- Evidence that normal accounting practice treated the expenditure as revenue
- The cinemas were capable of being used without the repairs (unlike the ship in the Law Shipping case)
- The state of disrepair had not reduced the purchase price.

These two partially conflicting cases leave us with the problem of what to do in the examination. It is suggested that unless the question actually tells you the three points listed above as the basis for distinguishing the Odeon Theatres case, *disallow* any improvement expenditure and cite the Law Shipping case as your authority.

(viii) Bad and doubtful debts
This is another problem item. To be allowable bad debts written off have to relate to the trade. Loans to staff or customers written off will thus not be allowed unless they are connected in some way with the trade, for example if the business involved the making of loans.

Provision for doubtful debts are only allowable if they relate to *specific* trade debts. General provisions not related to specific debts will be disallowed.

Any amounts recovered from debtors whose balance has previously been written off must be brought to credit if the original write-off was allowed as a deduction.

In an examination question information about bad and doubtful debts is frequently given in the form of a ledger account. Here is an illustration.

The Bad and Doubtful Debts Account of a trader was as follows:

Bad and Doubtful Debts

	£		£
Debts written off		Balances brought forward	
Trade	760	General provision	850
Loan to employee	100	Specific provision	700
Loan to customer	200		
		Bad debts recovered	250
Balances carried forward		(previously allowed)	
General provision	1,000		
Specific provision	800	Profit and Loss account	1,060
	2,860		2,860

What adjustment is required for tax purposes?

See if you can sort that out before proceeding to the answer.

The easiest way to proceed is to cross out (in pencil lightly) the disallowable items on both sides of the account and recalculate the profit and loss account transfer. That gives us:

Bad and Doubtful Debts

	£		£
Debts written off		Balances brought forward	
Trade	760	General provision	~~850~~
Loan to employee	~~100~~	Specific provision	700
Loan to customer	~~200~~		
		Bad debts received	250
Balances carried forward		(previously allowed)	
General provision	~~1,000~~		610
Specific provision	800	Profit and Loss account	~~1,060~~
	~~2,860~~		~~2,860~~
	1,560		1,560

The profit and loss account item must be *reduced* by £450–from £1,060 to £610. This represents the disallowance of:

	£
Loan to employee	100
Loan to customer	200
Increase in general provision	150
	£450

We therefore add back £450 in the computation of taxable profit. Note that the adjustment can be to *increase* the profit and loss account debit, in which case the profit shown by the profit and loss account must be increased.

(ix) Legal expenses
Yet another awkward one to sort out. Legal expenses can relate to three main types of matter:

- Revenue items connected with the trade, like expenses of debt collecting or staff service contracts. These are normally *allowed*.
- Capital items connected with the trade, like costs of acquiring fixed assets. These are normally *disallowed*. An exception to this rule is the costs of *renewing* a short lease (one for less than fifty years). These are *allowed*. See also (xvi) below.
- Items not connected with the trade. These are obviously going to be *disallowed*. Examples are expenses connected with a tax appeal (not connected with trade because relating to the business as taxpayer – hard but true), or with the formation of the business. In *Strong and Co of Romsey Ltd* v. *Woodifield* 1906 it was held that damages paid to a guest staying in a hotel for injuries sustained were not made 'for the purpose of earning the profits and were disallowed.

(x) Other professional fees
Audit and accounting services are allowable, provided as always they relate to the business. Costs in connection with tax appeals are disallowed as explained in (ix).

(xi) Fines
Fines for breaking the law are virtually always disallowed. The only exception is parking fines paid for employees.

(xii) Amounts paid under deduction of tax
If a taxpayer pays something under deduction of tax – a deed of convenant say – this must *always* be disallowed in the Schedule D Case I or II computation. *Some* payments of this kind qualify for deduction in calculating the taxpayer's total income. The purpose of the disallowance is to ensure that the tax deducted is accounted for to the Revenue. If profit is insufficient to cover such payments, an assessment under s. 350 will be raised to collect the tax deducted.

(xiii) Subscriptions and donations
Subscriptions to trade associations are allowable, provided they are on the Revenue approved list (most are). Donations to a political party are

not allowable. Charitable donations are generally not allowable, unless the 'wholly and exclusively' rule is complied with. Thus donations to charities from which the staff could benefit are normally allowable. Small amounts given to local charities are usually allowed.

Donations by deed of covenant are never allowable – see (xii) above.

(xiv) Entertainment costs and gifts to customers
Entertaining *customers* is disallowed, and this includes, from 15 March 1988, overseas customers.

Entertaining *staff*, surprisingly enough *is* allowed. Thus a staff Christmas party, for example, would be allowable.

The allowability of gifts to customers is limited by statute. They are allowed only if:

- Not more than £10 per donee
- Not food, drink or tobacco
- Prominently marked with an advertisement for the donor.

(xv) Removal expenses
Cost of removal are *allowed*, provided there is no element of expansion. In practice, normal removal expenses are allowed. If removal costs for plant and machinery are disallowed, they may be added to the value of the plant for capital allowances purposes.

(xvi) Patents and trade marks
The costs of obtaining a patent or trade mark are allowed by s. 83 ICTA 1988.

(xvii) Defalcations
Losses through defalcations by *staff* are allowed, but not, obviously enough, defalcations by a proprietor or, in the case of a company, a director.

(xviii) Interest payable
Interest payable will be allowed (unless paid under deduction of tax).

Hire purchase interest and charges on the acquisition of business assets will be allowable. Any reasonable basis of spreading the total over the years will be accepted.

(xix) Redundancy payments to employees
We have three possible types of redundancy payment.

- Payments *up to the statutory limit* either from a continuing business or on discontinuance. These are made allowable by s. 579 ICTA 1988.
- Payments above the statutory limit or not under statute from a *continuing* business. These are normally allowable.
- Payments above the statutory limit on *discontinuance*. These are allowable provided they do not exceed three times the statutory redundancy limit, and provided they would have been allowable but

for the discontinuance. Note that the 'three times' rule allows the statutory amount *plus* a further three times that amount.

(xx) Travelling expenses
Travelling expenses within the basic definition are allowable, but *not* travel from home to work, except in very unusual circumstances.

(xxi) Cost of obtaining loan finance
The cost of obtaining a loan to assist in financing the business is allowable. This is surprising, as it sounds rather like capital expenditure but it is specifically provided by s. 77(1) ICTA 1988 that it is allowable.

(xxii) Income tax
As you would expect, income tax itself can never be an allowable expense.

(xxiii) Value added tax (VAT)
A business doesn't normally suffer VAT, but if VAT is incurred it is then allowed as an expense. See Chapter 25 for more details.

(xxiv) Pre-trading expenditure – s. 401
If expenditure is incurred in the three years before trading commences, for income tax purposes it is treated as a trading loss arising in the year of assessment in which the trade actually commences. See Chapter 5 for more details.

Examination approach

The normal examination question on this topic presents a profit and loss account (often not prepared according to approved accounting standards) and asks you to calculate the adjusted profit for tax purposes.

The format of your answer should be something like this (figures are invented):

Computation of adjusted profit for year ended 31 December 19X8

	£	£
	+	–
Profit per profit and loss account	10,000	
Entertainment expenses	2,160	
General provision for doubtful debts	300	
Depreciation	1,200	
Dividends received		350
Interest received		200
Profit on sale of plant		
	13,660	550
	550	
Adjusted trading profit	£13,110	

In other words, set up two columns headed + and −, enter in the + column the profit shown in the profit and loss account (loss goes in − column) then go line by line through the profit and loss account adjusting as necessary. Items to be added back are entered in the + column, items to be deducted go in the − column. There may also be matters not in the profit and loss account but given elsewhere in the question to be adjusted for – goods taken from stock by the proprietor for example. Add both columns, subtract the smaller from the larger, and the answer is the adjusted profit or loss.

Experience shows that a class of thirty students will initially produce thirty different answers, but with practice the majority gradually home in on the correct answer.

Here is a comprehensive illustration.

Illustration 2.1

Jane has been in business for many years as a florist. Her profit and loss account for the year ended 31 December 19X8 was as follows:

		Reference to notes	£	£
Sales				368,620
Less:	Cost of sales	1		261,280
	Gross profit			107,340
Less:	Expenses			
	Salaries and wages	2	56,790	
	Shop expenses (rent, rates, lighting heating)	3	21,360	
	Printing and stationery		1,120	
	Motor van expenses	4	4,150	
	Depreciation of motor van		1,200	
	Loss on sale of van		450	
	Bad and doubtful debts	5	560	
	Redundancy payment to staff dismissed		580	
	Legal expenses	6	1,240	
	Sundry expenses (all allowable)		1,810	89,260
				18,080
	Dividend received			1,280
	Net Profit			£19,360

Notes

1 *Cost of sales* – Cost of sales include flowers taken from stock by Jane for herself. The cost of the flowers was £360 and they had a selling value of £500.

2 *Salaries and wages* – Jane's salary of £18,000 per annum is included here.

3 *Shop expenses* – Jane has a flat over the shop. Expenses totalling £2,860 are agreed to relate to the flat.

4 *Motor van* – private use of motor van by Jane is agreed to be 20 per cent.

5 *Bad and doubtful debts* – the ledger account for bad and doubtful debts for the year shows:

Bad and Doubtful Debts

	£		£
Debts written off		Balances brought forward	
Customers	390	General provision	180
Staff	20	Specific provision	270
Balances carried forward		Bad debts recovered	50
General provision	300	(previously allowed)	
Specific provision	350	Profit and loss account	560
	£1,060		£1,060

6 *Legal expenses* – legal expenses consist of:

	£
Debt collection	470
Tax appeal	480
Advice on staff service contracts	290
	£1,240

Compute Jane's adjusted profit or loss for Schedule D Case I for the year.

Go through the question now and decide on the treatment of each item. Then prepare your own calculation along the lines indicated with + and – columns.

Jane
Computation of adjusted profit, year ended 31 December 19X8

	Reference to tutorial notes	£ +	£ –
Net profit per profit and loss account		19,360	
Flowers for private use	1	500	
Jane's salary	2	18,000	
Expenses relating to private flat		2,860	
Motor van expenses 20%		830	
Depreciation of motor van	3	1,200	
Loss on sale of van	3	450	
Bad and doubtful debts (see working)	4	140	
Legal expenses – tax appeal	5	480	
Dividend			1,280
		43,820	1,280
		1,280	
Adjust profit		£42,540	

Working
Bad and doubtful debts

	£		£
Debts written off		Balances brought forward	
Customers	390	General provision	~~180~~
Staff	~~20~~	Specific provision	270
Balances carried forward		Bad debts recovered	50
General provision	~~300~~	(previously allowed)	
Specific provision	350		420
		Profit and loss	~~560~~
	~~1,060~~		~~1,060~~
	740		740

Adjustment is to disallow £140 (£560 less £420).

Tutorial notes

1 The decision in *Sharkey* v. *Wernher* requires the selling price of items from stock to be used. If the point comes up in a question, state the name of the case if you can.

2 Jane's salary must be added back. No information is given about her insurance contributions. If these had been paid by the business they too would have had to be added back, though not, of course, contributions for employees.

3 Depreciation and loss on sale of van are both added back *in full*. The part relating to the personal use is disallowed as personal use and the remainder is disallowed because replaced by capital allowances. Note that the capital allowances themselves *do not* form part of the calculation of the adjusted profit for income tax. The capital allowances are deducted *from* the adjusted profit. This point is explained in detail in Chapter 4.

4 *Bad and doubtful debts* – it is really necessary to show a working for this adjustment even though you may work it out directly on your calculator.

5 *Legal expenses* – The debt collection and preparation of staff service contracts are allowable as revenue items but the cost of the tax appeal is not.

Summary

Importance of Schedule D Cases I and II

Questions based on Cases I and II of Schedule D are likely to form a major part of most taxation examination papers.

This chapter has dealt with two main points – the six badges of trade and the adjustment of profit for tax purposes.

The six badges of trade

These are the criteria to be applied in determining whether a trade is being carried on:

(a) Subject matter
(b) Length of ownership
(c) Frequency
(d) Supplementary work
(e) Circumstances responsible for realisation
(f) Motive

Adjustment of profit

The most important thing to master here is the ability to decide on the allowability of expenses.

The general rule given in s. 74 ICTA 1988 is that to be allowable, expenditure must be 'wholly and exclusively for the purposes of the trade, profession or vocation'. Case law interprets and statute law modifies the effect of the general rule. Experience at answering a range of questions is the only way to develop your skill here.

Progress questions

Attempt the following questions to test your absorption of the material to date. Rework the questions at intervals for revision purposes. Answers are on pages 392–3.

1 What are the six badges of trade?

2 What is the general rule for allowability of expenses for Schedule D Cases I and II?

3 The following expenses incurred by businesses are generally allowable in full. True or False? Give details of exceptions.

	True	*False*
(a) National Insurance contributions for:		
(i) Staff working in the business	✓	
(ii) Proprietors of business		✓
(b) Depreciation of assets used in the business		✓
(c) Bad debts written off	✓?	
(d) Legal expenses relating to the acquisition of fixed assets	✓	
(e) Entertainment of customers		✓

3 Income tax Schedule D Cases I and II – basis of assessment

The normal basis of assessment

We saw in Chapter 1 that the normal basis of assessment for Schedule D Case I is the so-called *preceding year* basis – the profits taxed in a tax year to 5 April are those shown by the business profit and loss account made up for a year ending in the *preceding* tax year (ICTA S60).

Thus if the regular accounting date of a business is 31 December the adjusted profits of the year ended 31 December 1987 will be assessed in 1988/89, and the tax will be due in two equal instalments on 1 January 1989 and 1 July 1989 (see Figure 2).

You can see from this that it might make a considerable difference if a business chose 30 April as its regular accounting date rather than say 31 March. The postponement of one month would mean that the accounting period ended in the next tax year, thus moving the basis forward by one year and so postponing the due dates for the tax by one year – a useful contribution to cash flow.

It is vital for you to become really familiar with this rule. It is very easy to make a careless mistake here. Try these:

	Accounting date	*Assessed in?*
Year ended:	30.9.88	....
	31.10.89	....
	30.6.88	....
	28.2.89	....
	31.12.87	....
	31.1.88	....
	30.4.89	....

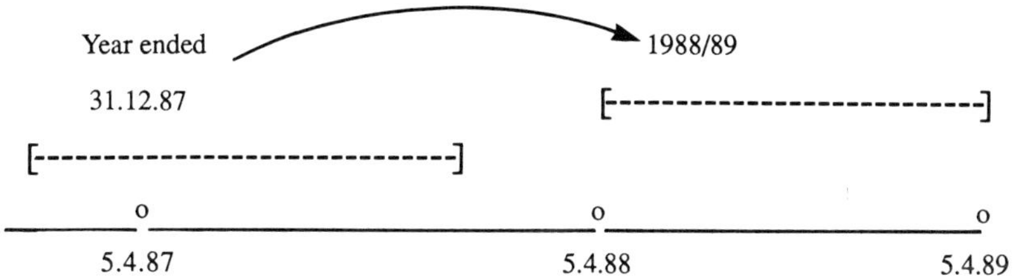

Figure 2

Accounting date 31 March 1988:

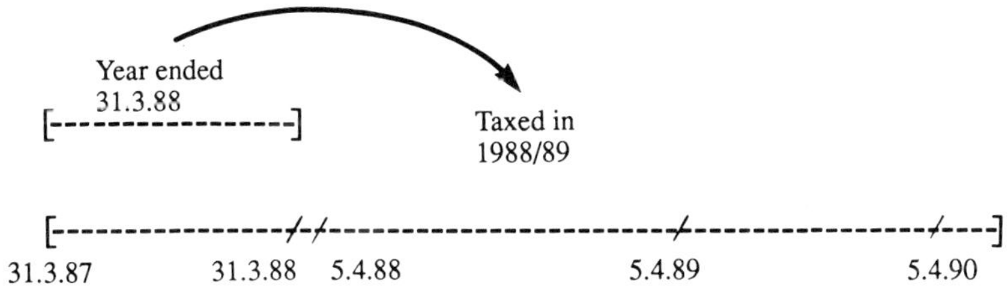

Figure 3

Accounting date 30 April 1988:

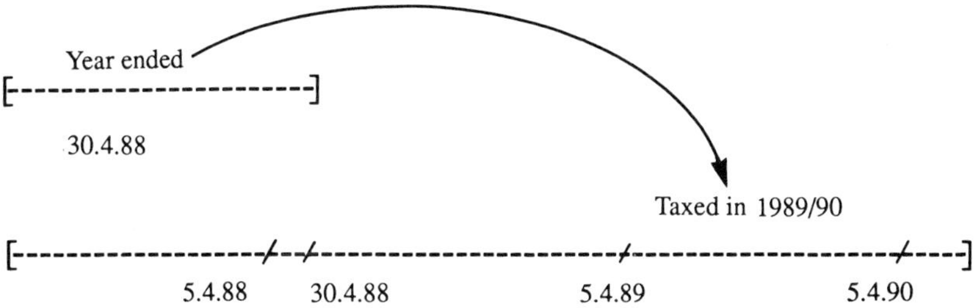

Figure 4

Your answers should be as follows:

	Accounting date	*Assessed in?*
Year ended	30.9.88	1980/90
	31.10.89	1990/91
	30.6.88	1989/90
	28.2.89	1989/90
	31.12.87	1988/89
	31.1.88	1988/89
	30.4.89	1990/91

Opening years

The preceding year basis is all very well once a business has been established for a few years, but what about the first year of operation? In fact there are some rather strange rules for the first *three* years of a business. The application of these rules can lead to some peculiar results and it is amazing that they have lasted so long without reform.

The rules are detailed in s. 61 ICTA 1988 and they work like this:

(a) *First tax year in which the business exist* – there can clearly be no preceding year in this case. The basis we take is to tax the *actual profit in the tax year* – the profit of the period from commencement to the following 5 April.

(b) *Second tax year in which the business exists* – it is unlikely that there will be a complete preceding year here either (unless the business began 6 April). The arbitrary rule here is to tax *the profits of the first twelve months' trading.*

(c) *Third tax year in which the business exists* – in the third tax year we shall usually find accounts made up for a year ending in the preceding tax year and we adopt the *preceding year* basis for the first time. In a few cases this will not be possible as we shall see below, and then it is not until the fourth year that the preceding year basis gets under way. (See Table 2 for a summary.)

Table 2

Tax year	*Basis of assessment*
First	Actual profit from commencement to following 5 April
Second	First 12 months
Third	Preceding year (usually)
Fourth and subsequent	Preceding year

Here is an illustration.

Illustration 3.1

Keith commenced trading on 1 January 1988 making up accounts regularly to 31 December each year. His adjusted profits were:

Year ended	£
31.12.88	12,000
31.12.89	18,000
31.12.90	24,000

To calculate the assessments based on these profits we must first identify the tax year in which the business *commenced*. Very easy to make a careless mistake here. The answer is . . . 1987/88. Yes? Yes.

The assessments are:

	Basis	*Amount* £
Year 1 1987/88	Actual profit 1.1.88 to 5.4.88: 3/12 × £12,000	3,000
Year 2 1988/89	Profit first 12 months 1.1.88 to 31.12.88	12,000
Year 3 1989/90	Preceding year: 1.1.88 to 31.12.88	12,000
Year 4 1990/91	Preceding year: 1.1.89 to 31.12.89	18,000
Year 5 1991/92	Preceding year: 1.1.90 to 31.12.90	24,000

This result can be represented in diagrammatic form as shown in Figure 5.

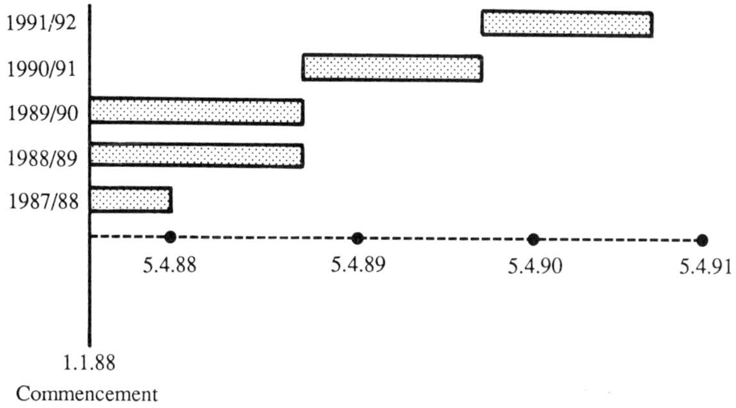

Figure 5

The assessments for the first three years are all based on the same profits. How can this be acceptable to the taxpayer? Remarkably enough it often works out to the taxpayer's advantage, because the profits of the first year are likely to be less than those of later years. If we accept that there has to be a tax liability for each tax year, it will be better for the taxpayer if the low opening profits are used as the basis.

But supposing the profits start high and fall later. That could be very bad news for the taxpayer. Fortunately the taxpayer has an option given by s. 62 ICTA 1988 in that situation. The taxpayer may elect to have the profits of the second *and* third years assessed on the basis of the actual profits of those years. This election must be made within seven years of the end of the second year of assessment and may be revoked within six years of the end of the third. This arrangement allows the taxpayer to make an election when the results of the second year are known, but to revoke it if it turns out not to be beneficial when the results of the third year are available.

Illustration 3.2

Keith began business on 1 January 1988 as before but his profits were:

Year ended	£
31.12.88	12,000
31.12.89	6,000
31.12.90	4,800

The assessments based on these profits will be:

Year	*Normal Basis*	£	*Taxpayers election under s. 62*	£
1987/88	1.1.88 to 5.4.88 3/12 × £12,000	3,000		
1988/89	1.1.88 to 31.12.88	12,000	6.4.88 to 5.4.89 9/12 × £12,000 + 3/12 × £6,000	10,500
1989/90	1.1.88 to 31.12.88	12,000	6.4.89 to 5.4.90 9/12 × £6,000 + 3/12 × £4,800	5,700
		£24,000		£16,200
1990/91	1.1.89 to 31.12.89	18,000		
1991/92	1.1.90 to 31.12.90	24,000		

The taxpayer's election would have to be made within seven years from 5 April 1989, the end of the second year of assessment.

The taxpayer's s. 62 election applies to 1988/89 *and* 1989/90.

We first calculate the assessments on the normal basis, then calculate alongside the revision the *actual* basis for these two years. In practice the apportionment of profit is made exactly, allowing for the odd five days of April, but for examination purposes the apportionment is done in months as shown in the illustration. The assessments on the revised basis are clearly lower in total, and so they would be adopted.

It may well be that the effect of the taxpayer's election is to increase the assessment for one of the two years but to reduce the assessment for the other. If the taxpayer makes the election he must accept the higher assessment in order to get the benefit of the lower assessment in the other year.

Closing years

The rules for the closing years of a business are defined in s. 63 ICTA 1988. In the tax year of permanent cessation, the basis of assessment is the *actual* profits from 6 April to the date of cessation. All previous assessments initially stay the same.

Illustration 3.3

Louise, after making up accounts regularly to 31 December, ceases trading on 30 September 1988. Her adjusted profits have been:

Period		£
Year ended	31.12.85	24,000
	31.12.86	15,000
	31.12.87	48,000
Nine months to	30.9.88	18,000

Assessments based on these profits, working backwards, will be:

	Basis	Amount
1988/89 (year of cessation)	*Actual profits* 6.4.88 to 30.9.88 6/9 × £18,000	12,000
1987/88	Preceding year	15,000
1986/87	Preceding year	24,000

Note that the effect is to exclude from the tax the fat £48,000 profit of the year ended 31.12.87. In the crazy logic of income tax, this 'balances' the fact that when the business began the profits of one period were taxed several times.

Such an effect could suggest an obvious tax avoidance scheme – if after trading for some years, your profit is very high in one year, cease trading in the next tax year and the high profits will escape tax. To block this elementary device, the *Revenue* have an option which is similar to that of the taxpayer in the opening years. It gives them the right to adjust to actual the assessments for the two years immediately before the year of cessation – the penultimate and antepenultimate years.

The effect on Louise would be:

Year	*Normal basis*	£	*Revenue election under s. 63*	£
1988/89	6.4.88 to 30.9.88 6/9 × £18,000	12,000		
1987/88	Preceding year	15,000	6.4.87 to 5.4.88 9/12 × £48,000 + 3/9 × £18,000	42,000
1986/87	Preceding year	24,000	6.4.86 to 5.4.87 9/12 × £15,000 + 3/12 × £48,000	23,250
		£39,000		£65,250

Clearly the Revenue will make the election under s. 63, but like the corresponding election for the taxpayer in the opening years, it must be for *both* years. The Revenue must accept the reduction in the assessment for 1986/87 in order to get the benefit of the increase in 1987/88.

Summary

Basis of assessment

(a) Normal basis of assessment
This is defined in s. 60 ICTA 1988: the profits assessable in a tax year are those of the business profit and loss account made up for the twelve months ending in the *preceding* tax year.

(b) Assessment in opening years
Section 61 defines the rules for the opening years. Section 62 gives the taxpayer an election which applies in the second *and* third years:

	Normal basis s. 61	*Taxpayer's election s. 62*
Year 1	*Actual profits* from commencement to following 5 April	
Year 2	Profits of first twelve months	*Actual profit* 6 April to 5 April
Year 3	Preceding year (usually – see below)	*Actual profit* 6 April to 5 April
Year 4	Preceding year	

(c) Assessment in closing years
Section 63 defines the normal basis and gives an election to the Revenue which applies to the penultimate *and* antepenultimate years:

	Normal basis on cessation	*Revenue election*
Year of cessation	*Actual profits* from 6 April to cessation	
Penultimate year	Preceding year	*Actual profits* 6 April to 5 April
Antepenultimate year	Preceding year	*Actual profits* 6 April to 5 April

ICTA 1988 section references

It is not essential to remember section numbers in most cases, but this Chapter does include four which most people know:

(a) Section 60 The normal preceding year basis of assessment
(b) Section 61 The basis of assessment for opening years
(c) Section 62 The taxpayer's option in opening years
(d) Section 63 The basis of assessment in closing years, including the Revenue option.

Advanced points

There is really only one advanced point we need to cover and that is the situation as regards the opening years when the first accounts of a new business are made up for a period other than one year.

In principle the rules are unchanged, but the way they operate causes a slight difference.

Here is a three part illustration to cover the matter.

Illustration 3.4 – Part 1

Malcolm commenced business on 1 January 1988 and made up his first accounts for the nine months to 30 September 1988.

His adjusted profits were:

	£
9 months ended 30.9.88	27,000
Year ended 30.9.89	40,000
Year ended 30.9.90	30,000

The normal basis of assessment for the opening years will be:

Year	*Basis*	*Amount* £
1987/88	Actual 1.1.88 to 5.4.88 3/9 × £27,000	9,000
1988/89	First 12 months 1.1.88* to 31.12.88 – £27,000 + 3/12 × £40,000	37,000
1989/90	1.1.88 to 31.12.88** As 1988/89	37,000
1990/91	Preceding year	40,000
1991/92	Preceding year- year ending 30.9.90	30,000

Two differences arose compared with the simpler situation where the first accounts were made up for twelve months:

*(a) In 1988/89 it was necessary to apportion profits to find the profits for the first twelve months' trading.

**(b) In 1989/90 there was not yet a proper preceding period of one year, because the first accounts were made up for nine months only, and these were the ones ending in the preceding year 1988/89. The rule here is to take the assessment for Year 2 (1988/89 first 12 months' trading) and repeat it.

The taxpayer's election under s. 62 is calculated exactly as before:

	Original assessment £	*Revised assessment s. 62*	£
1987/88	9,000		
1988/89	37,000	6/9 × £27,000 + 6/12 × £40,000	38,000
1989/90	37,000	6/12 × £40,000 + 6/12 × £30,000	35,000
	74,000		73,000
1990/91	40,000		
1991/92	30,000		

In this case the election will increase the 1988/89 assessment by £1,000, but reduce that for 1989/90 by £2,000. The election should therefore be made in an examination question.

Illustration 3.4 – Part 2

Malcolm commenced business on 1 January 1988 and made up his first accounts for the fifteen months to 31 March 1989.

His adjusted profits were:

	£
15 months ended 31 March 1989	30,000
Year ended 31 March 1990	40,000
Year ended 31 March 1991	50,000

The calculations here will be almost exactly as in Part 1, and the fact that the accounting date is 31 March makes them all the easier.

	Original assessment	£	*Revised assessment*	£
1987/88	1.1.88 to 5.4.88			
	3/15 × £30,000	6,000		
1988/89	1.1.88 to 31.12.88		6.4.88 to 5.4.89	
	12/15 × £30,000	24,000	12/15 × £30,000	24,000
1989/90	1.4.89 to 31.3.90*		6.4.89 to 5.4.90	40,000
	12/15 × £30,000	24,000		
		48,000	No election	64,000
1990/91	1.4.89 to 31.3.90	40,000		
1991/92	1.4.90 to 31.3.91	50,000		

Illustration 3.4 – Part 3

Malcolm commenced business on 1 January 1988 and made up his first accounts for the 18 months ended 30 June 1989.

His adjusted profits were:

	£
18 months ended 30 June 1989	27,000
Year ended 30 June 1990	30,000
Year ended 30 June 1991	40,000

There is one point of difference with the previous illustration – the first period of account of 18 months crosses 5 April twice, as it includes

*You may wonder why the basis period for 1989/90 is taken as 1.4.89 to 31.3.90, rather than as 1.1.89 to 31.12.89. It makes no difference to the calculation, which is 12/15 of £30,000 in both cases. It is Revenue practice to do this, and its only effect is on basis periods for capital allowances (see Chapter 4).

5 April 1988 and 5 April 1989. The effect of this is to leave the fourth year of assessment without a normal basis.

	Original assessment	£	Revised assessment	£
1987/88	1.1.88 to 5.4.88			
	3/18 × £27,000	4,500		
1988/89	1.1.88 to 31.12.88		6.4.88 to 5.4.89	
	12/18 × £27,000	18,000	12/18 × £27,000	18,000
1989/90	1.7.88 to 30.6.89		6.4.89 to 5.4.90	
	12/18 × £27,000	18,000	3/18 × £27,000 +	
			9/12 × £30,000	27,000
		£36,000	No election	£45,000
1990/91	1.7.88 to 30.6.89 (still no accounts for 12 months ending 1989/90)			
	As 1989/90	18,000		
1991/92	1.7.89 to 30.6.90	30,000		
1992/93	1.7.90 to 30.6.91	40,000		

Progress questions

Attempt the following questions to test your absorption of the material to date.

Rework these questions from time to time for revision. Answers are on page 393.

1 Explain the normal basis of assessment for income tax Schedule D Cases I and II.

2 Established businesses make up their accounts to the following dates. State for each one the income tax year in which the profits would be assessed:

	Assessment in tax year
(a) 31 December 1989	....
(b) 30 June 1988	....
(c) 31 March 1989	....
(d) 30 April 1988	....
(e) 31 May 1989	....

3 A business commences on 1 January 1988, making up accounts for the calendar year. Ignoring any elections, its income tax assessments for the first years of its existence will be based on the periods:

	Period	*Tax year of assessment*
(a)	Year 1	....
(b)	Year 2	....
(c)	Year 3	....
(d)	Year 4	....

4 What election is available to the taxpayer in 3 above?

(a) ICTA 1988 reference ....

(b) Effect of election

4 Capital allowances

Introduction

We saw in Chapter 2 that any depreciation provided in accounts is always disallowed for tax purposes and replaced by a standard deduction available for most, but not all, types of capital expenditure. The reason for this is that taxpayers can adopt a wide range of different depreciation percentages and accounting policies. A standard deduction common to all taxpayers is fairer for tax purposes, and can also be used to provide investment incentives to businesses – generous allowances encourage capital expenditure. The statutory rules relating to capital allowances are to be found in the Capital Allowances Act 1968, (CAA 1968), as amended by later Finance Acts.

Capital allowances are granted for most but not all types of business capital expenditure. The main categories of qualifying expenditure are listed below and dealt with in detail in the sections which follow:

- Plant and machinery (very broady defined – see below)
- Industrial buildings
- Patents
- Know-how
- Scientific research.

Allowances are also available for agricultural land and buildings, mines and oil wells, dredging and the provision of dwelling houses for letting on assured tenancies, but these are all excluded from the Business Taxation syllabus. Note that relief is *not* given for expenditure on non-industrial buildings like office blocks, except for new commercial buildings in enterprise zones – see page 50. (Office accommodation normally only qualifies if it is up to 25 per cent of a building otherwise qualifying as an industrial building.) Relief is granted for expenditure on certain types of hotel. This is dealt with along with the relief for industrial buildings below.

The rules governing capital allowances are broadly the same for income tax and corporation tax. This chapter is based on the *income tax* rules. Changes for corporation tax are explained in Chapter 11.

Capital allowances are mainly relevant in relation to tax on the profits of a trade or profession under Schedule D Cases I and II. They may also be deductible from income under Schedule A or Schedule E, provided the asset concerned qualifies for relief under the rules of those schedules. The chapters on Schedule A and Schedule E briefly pick up this point.

Plant and machinery

Expenditure qualifying

One's first reaction on seeing the words 'plant and machinery' is to think of a factory full of equipment. For capital allowances purposes, however, the term means more than this. For example, a lawyer's library of books is regarded as his or her 'plant and machinery', motor vehicles of all kinds qualify, as do office furniture and equipment.

So what are the criteria? As there is no statutory definition we have to find the answer in case law.

Plant and machinery must be:

(a) 'Apparatus used by a businessman in carrying on his business.' (*Yarmouth* v. *France* 1887)
(b) *Not* part of the fabric of the building or of the setting in which the business is carried on. Relevant decisions on this point are:
    (i) *Dixon* v. *Fitch's Garage Ltd* 1975 – canopy of a petrol station *not* plant (part of the setting)
    (ii) *Jarrold* v. *John Good and Sons Ltd* 1963 – *movable* office partitions *are* plant (not part of the building or setting because movable)

Note that alterations to building in the course of installing plant are allowable as plant and machinery because they are necessary to enable the plant to be used. This is specifically provided by s. 45 CAA 1968. The following special categories of expenditure also attract capital allowances as if they were expenditure on plant and machinery:

(a) Fire safety
(b) Heat insulation of industrial buildings
(c) Expenditure on sports grounds necessary to comply with the requirements for the issue of a safety certificate.

Allowances available

The main allowance is a 25 per cent annual write-down, calculated on the *reducing balance basis* and referred to as the Writing Down Allowance (WDA). The taxpayer may elect to claim less than the full 25 per cent in any given year. (We shall see how this could be beneficial later – see the tutorial note to the example on page 54.)

In the year in which extra plant is acquired, the full 25 per cent is available, regardless of the date in the accounting period in which the expenditure is incurred.

The allowance is restricted by reference to *the length of the basis period* if the basis period is less than one year, as will normally be the case for income tax in the opening year of the business. The special problems of capital allowances for income tax in the opening years of a business are considered on page 51.

In some situations a *balancing allowance* or a *balancing charge* (a kind of negative allowance) will arise. See page 41.

The allowance is given on the full cash price of items acquired on hire purchase terms, in the tax year in the basis period of which the contract is entered into.

The basic capital allowance computation

The calculation of capital allowances is *fairly* simple. As we have a standard 25 per cent allowance on all types of plant and machinery, most of the expenditure is pooled into a single calculation, as shown in the illustration below:

Illustration 4.1

Caesar has been in business for many years, making up accounts to 31 December each year. In the year ended 31 December 1987 (assessable in 1988/89) the position was as follows:

Balance of expenditure brought forward from 1987/88		£20,000
Expenditure during 1987:		
15 February	New plant	8,000
15 March	Second-hand lorry	4,500
14 July	Office equipment	3,500

All of this expenditure, including the balance brought forward, qualifies for the 25 per cent WDA.

The format of the computation can be:

		Pool £	*Allowances* £
1987/88 balance brought forward		20,000	
1988/89	expenditure		
	New plant	8,000	
	Second-hand lorry	4,500	
	Office equipment	3,500	
		36,000	
	WDA 25%	9,000	
			9,000
Balance carried forward to 1989/90		27,000	

Notes

1 We are calculating the allowances for 1988/89. Expenditure qualifying is that incurred in the income tax basis period for 1988/89, in this case the year ended 31 December 1987.
2 No distinction is made between new and second-hand items. All qualifying expenditure received the full 25 per cent allowance regardless of the date of purchase.
3 It is convenient to set out the computation as shown. In later examples we shall introduce more columns to deal with items which are not merged into the pool.
4 The £9,000 allowance is deducted from the adjusted profit to be assessed in 1988/89.
5 The balance carried forward from year to year is normally called the 'written down value', often abbreviated to 'WDV'.

Sales of plant and machinery in the pool

When plant etc. in the pool is sold, we must obviously make some adjustment to the pool, or the computation would become meaningless.

In making the adjustment, simplicity and convenience prevail over strict arithmetical accuracy.

What we do is to deduct *sale proceeds* from the opening pool balance plus additions for the year before calculating the WDA for the year. That means that no WDA is given in the year of sale on the plant sold.

The amount deducted for sale proceeds cannot exceed the original cost of the item concerned. In other words we must not take out of the pool more than the amount put into it in the first place.

This procedure can cause a problem. What if the amount to be deducted exceeds the pool balance? In this case we should have a negative balance to form the basis of the WDA for the year. To correct this we restore the negative balance to zero by means of an adjustment called a *balancing charge*.

Illustration 4.2

Facts as Illustration 4.1 except that some plant which had cost £50,000 was sold for £40,000 on 8 June 1987. The computation would become:

Capital allowances 1988/89

		Pool	*Allowances*
		£	£
1987/88	balance brought forward	20,000	
1988/89	expenditure		
	New plant	8,000	
	Second hand lorry	4,500	
	Office equipment	3,500	
		36,000	

	Pool	Allowances
	£	£
Proceeds of sale of plant	40,000	
	(4,000)	
Balancing charge	(4,000)	
		(4,000)
Balance carried forward to 1989/90	nil	

The £4,000 balancing charge is added to the profit to be assessed in 1988/89. There would be no writing down allowance in 1988/89 as there is no pool balance on which to calculate it.

Items excluded from the pool

The following types of plant and machinery are excluded from the pool and have to be dealt with separately.

(a) Motor cars costing less than £8,000 with no private use
These are kept in a separate pool. The computation takes exactly the same form as that for the general pool described on page 39.

(b) Motor cars costing over £8,000
These are dealt with *individually* in the computation, because the maximum annual WDA on such cars is £2,000 per annum. A separate column is therefore needed for *each* car. When such a car is sold, a balancing allowance or charge is made so that over the whole period of ownership the capital allowances granted equal the difference between cost and sale proceeds (subject to any restriction for private use). The problem does not arise if the business of the taxpayer is hiring cars or providing a taxi service.

(c) Plant and machinery with an element of private use
When there is an element of non-business use of an asset by the *proprietor*, the capital allowances granted are restricted to the proportion of business use, which must be negotiated with the Revenue. (Note that this restriction does *not* apply to private use by employees, for whom completely different arrangements, explained in the chapter on Schedule E, are made in order to charge tax on the benefit they derive.) To permit the restriction, we must keep such assets completely separate and deal with them individually. Balancing charges or allowances are made in the year of sale of such assets.

This point can arise with any asset, though the most common assets concerned are, of course, motor cars.

(d) Short-life assets which are excluded from the pool at the taxpayer's option
The WDA at 25 per cent on the reducing balance basis does not provide a sufficiently fast write-off for assets with a life of (say) three to five years.

To allow for this, the Finance Act 1985 introduced provisions allowing the taxpayer to elect within two years of the end of the accounting period of acquisition, to have such assets excluded from the pool ('de-pooled'), and the capital allowances calculated separately. If the asset is sold within five years, a balancing charge or allowance is made. If at the end of five years the asset has not been sold, the written down value is transferred into the main pool. The effect is that specific allowance is obtained for the full cost within the life of the asset. The benefit is shown in illustration 4.4 below. Once made, the election is irrevocable.

The de-pooling election cannot be made for all types of asset. The exceptions relevant for your examination are:

(a) Motor cars (vans and lorries *do* qualify)
(b) Assets with an element of private use.

Illustrations

The illustrations in this section cover all the points made so far. Illustration 4.3 brings in everything except de-pooling and should be studied really carefully so that you master thoroughly the order in which items are dealt with and the format used. Illustration 4.4 shows the effect of the de-pooling election.

Illustration 4.3

Hamlet has been in business for many years, making up accounts to 30 June each year. In the year ended 30 June 1988 the following transactions took place:

(a) Purchases

1987	14 Aug	Motor car £6,500 (no private use)
	1 Sept	Plant £27,000
	4 Dec	Motor car £12,000 (private use 20%) as replacement for car sold on 10 November.
1988	6 Mar	Plant £8,000

(b) Sales

1987	10 Nov	Motor car sold for £8,100 (private use 25%)
1988	5 Apr	Plant sold for £8,800 (original cost £18,000)
	6 June	Plant sold for £1,000 (original cost £800)

(c) Balances brought forward from 1988/89

General pool plant	£28,000
Car pool	£13,500
Motor car over £8,000 (sold 10 November)	£11,100

Compute capital allowances due for 1989/90

Discussion

1 It is first necessary to set up an appropriate format. This will be:

General pool	*Car pool*	*Car > £8,000*		*Total allowances*
£	£	£		£

Extra space is left to the right of the car >£8,000 column to allow for the computation of the restricted allowance.

2 A balancing adjustment will arise on the sale of the car on 10 November. This needs to be calculated and it is then possible to use the same column to deal with the replacement car.

Capital allowances 1989/90

	General pool	*Car pool*	*Car > £8,000*		*Total allowances*
	£	£	£		£
WDV bought forward from 1988/89	28,000	13,500	11,100		
Additions in 1989/90	35,000	6,500			
	63,000	20,000			
Disposals in 1989/90	9,600				
			8,100		
	53,400	20,000			
Balancing allowance			3,000	× 75%	2,250
New car			12,000		
Writing down allowance 25%	13,350	5,000	2,000 (max)	× 80% £1,600	21,950
WDV carried forward	40,050	15,000	10,000		£24,200

Tutorial notes

1 On the disposal of the 'expensive' car a balancing charge or allowance will arise. Note the method for handling the 'private use' restriction. The *full* amount of the allowances is dealt with in the main column, then the allowable percentage is calculated and extended into the total allowances column.

2 The purchase of the new 'expensive' car leads to an allowance of the maximum of £2,000, which is deducted in the main column. The private use restriction reduces the allowable amount to £1,600, and this amount is included in the crosscast of WDAs.

Illustration 4.4

Ophelia has been in business for many years making up accounts to 30 September each year.

In the year ended 30 September 1987 she purchased for £12,000 some new plant which had a useful life of four years. A friend has told her that there is a way in which she may obtain accelerated relief for the new plant. Prepare computations showing the benefit of the election available to tax-payers under Finance Act 1985. The written down value of pooled plant brought forward from 1987/88 is £20,000, and the new plant is expected to be sold as scrap for £500 in 1991/92.

(a) No election

	Pool £	*Total allowances* £
1988/89		
WDV brought forward	20,000	
New plant	12,000	
	32,000	
WDA 25%	8,000	8,000
	24,000	
1989/90		
WDA 25%	6,000	6,000
	18,000	
1990/91		
WDA 25%	4,500	4,500
	13,500	
1991/92		
Proceeds of sale	500	
	13,000	
WDA 25%	3,250	3,250
WDV carried forward	9,750	

(b) With the election

	Pool £	*Short-life assets* £	*Total allowances* £
1988/89			
WDV brought forward	20,000		
New plant		12,000	
	20,000	12,000	
WDA 25%	5,000	3,000	8,000
	15,000	9,000	
1989/90			
WDA 25%	3,750	2,250	6,000
	11,250	6,750	
1990/91			
WDA 25%	2,812	1,688	4,500
	8,438	5,062	
1991/92			
Proceeds of sale		500	
Balancing allowance		£4,562	4,562
WDA 25%	2,110		2,110
WDV carried forward	6,328		£6,672

The effect of the election, which must be made by 30 September 1989 (two years after the end of the basis period in which the expenditure occurred), is to increase capital allowances in 1991/92 by £3,422, with an equal reduction in the WDV being carried forward into 1992/93.

2.7 Leasing or hiring of cars costing over £8,000

One obvious way to circumvent the restriction on WDA of cars costing over £8,000 would be to lease or hire them instead of buying them outright. To prevent this a restriction is placed on the allowability for tax purposes of leasing and hire charges for such cars.
The restriction works like this:

Allowable leasing/hiring costs are restricted to:

$$\text{Lease costs} \times \frac{\text{£8,000} + \tfrac{1}{2}(\text{cost} - \text{£8,000})}{\text{Cost}}$$

Illustration 4.5

The two directors of Casca Limited, Mark and Antony both have leased cars at their disposal. Mark's car has a cost of £12,000 and is leased at £3,000 per year, while Antony's car has a cost of £20,000 and is leased at £5,000 per year. How much will be allowed to Casca Limited for tax purposes?

Allowable amounts:

$$\text{Mark £3,000} \times \frac{\text{£8,000} + \tfrac{1}{2}(\text{£12,000} - \text{£8,000})}{\text{£12,000}} = \text{£2,500}$$

$$\text{Antony £5,000} \times \frac{\text{£8,000} + \tfrac{1}{2}(\text{£20,000} - (\text{£8,000})}{\text{£20,000}} = \text{£3,500}$$

Industrial buildings

Introduction

The capital allowances granted for industrial buildings are calculated in an entirely different way from those for plant and machinery. There is no pooling (each building is considered separately), balancing charges and allowances arise on sales, and the writing down allowance is calculated on the straight line basis, usually at 4 per cent per annum. Allowances on second-hand buildings are calculated on a different basis from those on new buildings.

What is an industrial building?

The fundamental characteristic of an industrial building qualifying for capital allowances is that it must be used in some manufacturing trade, but other buildings can also qualify.

The CAA 1968 provides us with a basic definition, and case law has clarified its precise meaning.

The following buildings will qualify for the allowance, if used for the purpose of a manufacturing trade:

(a) Mills or factories used in a manufacturing trade, mining, oil exploration or fisheries
(b) Storage buildings holding raw materials for manufacture or finished goods. (Wholesale and retail warehouses will *not* qualify – the building must be used in connection with manufacturing)
(c) Drawing offices associated with an industrial operation (*CIR* v. *Lambhill Ironworks* 1950)
(d) Canteens and other welfare buildings used by employees in a trade as in (a)
(e) Sports pavilions used by employees in *any* trade (not required to be manufacturing)

Other trades which can qualify include transport, docks, tunnels, bridges, agriculture, fisheries, mining, oil wells.

Expenditure on the thermal insulation of an industrial building qualifies for allowance as if it were expenditure on plant and machinery, as noted above.

The whole cost of an industrial building can qualify even though it contains some non-industrial accommodation. The limit is 25 per cent of total cost. Thus an industrial building containing offices not exceeding 25 per cent of total cost will qualify in full. If the cost of the office content slightly exceeds 25% the whole allowance is lost – there is no marginal concession, and the allowance will only be given on the industrial part.

Note that expenditure on the land does *not* qualify. Expenditure on tunnelling, foundations, and the installation of approach roads for a factory etc. does qualify, however.

What allowances are available?

On a new building the allowance is a writing down allowance of 4 per cent, calculated on the straight line basis. For buildings new before 6 November 1962 the allowance is 2 per cent.

Until 31 March 1986 there was also an additional allowance granted in the year of expenditure as well as the writing down allowance. Although his allowance is no longer granted, it is relevant when dealing with balancing adjustments (see below).

Rates of this allowance, called the 'initial allowance', were:

13 November 1974 to 10 March 1981	50%
11 March 1981 to 13 March 1984	75%
14 March 1984 to 31 March 1985	50%
1 April 1985 to 31 March 1986	25%
1 April 1986 onwards	nil

If needed in the examination these rates will be given to you. Note that, unlike the corresponding allowance for plant and machinery, the writing down allowance is given only when the building has been *brought into use,* whereas the initial allowance was given by reference to the year of *expenditure.*

When a building is sold a balancing charge or allowance is made on similar lines to those for some types of plant and machinery. The calculation on the sale of a building is described in Illustration 4.6.

The sale of an industrial building

When an industrial building is sold, a balancing adjustment has to be made. No writing down allowance is given in the year of sale.

Illustration 4.6

Brutus makes up accounts to 31 December each year. On 1 June 1987 he sold an industrial building to Cassius for £380,000 (including land £70,000). The building had originally cost £200,000 new on 1 June 1982 (including land £50,000), on which date it was brought into use.

Show the capital allowances for all years affected.

Discussion

The building was purchased in 1982 and thus qualifies for industrial building allowance in 1983/84. In 1982 there was an initial allowance of 75 per cent on cost. As the building was new it qualifies for this and writing down allowances will be at 4 per cent. The sale took place in 1987 (tax year 1988/89). Writing down allowances are thus available from 1983/84 to 1987/88 inclusive – five years in all.

Answer

	£	£
1983/84		
Cost (£200,000 minus £50,000)		150,000
IA 75%	112,500	
WDA 4%	6,000	118,500
		31,500
1984/85 to 1987/88		
WDA 4% × 4 years		24,000
Residue before sale		7,500
1988/89		
Proceeds of sale (£380,000 minus £70,000)		310,000
Balancing charge		302,500
Limited to total allowances granted		£142,500

The balancing charge cannot exceed the total allowances granted.

The next question is – what allowances will the purchaser of that building get? We answer that in the next section.

Buying a second-hand building

Allowances for second-hand buildings are quite different from those for new ones. First of all, the rate of writing down allowance is not 4 per cent, second the allowance may not be based on the second-hand price paid, and third, for purchases before 1 April 1986, no initial allowance was available.

The calculation is done in a rather peculiar fashion. We need to work out two things – the rate of allowance available and the figure on which the allowances will be based.

(a) Calculating the rate of allowance available

To calculate the rate of allowance available we need to establish the date when the building was first brought into use, and how much remains, at the date of purchase, of the period of twenty-five years beginning at that date. If the building was first brought into use before 5 November 1962 the period is fifty years. (These periods of twenty-five years and fifty years reflect the WDA rates of 4 per cent and 2 per cent.)

Let us do that for the situation dealt with in the previous example.

The building was first brought into use on	1 June 1982
The building was purchased second-hand on	1 June 1987

Therefore there remains twenty years of the original period of twenty-five years. The second-hand purchaser 'takes over' the remainder of the twenty-five years and writes off the allowable cost over that period. The write-off will accordingly be over twenty years.

Note that we use the *dates of bringing into use and purchase*, not accounting dates or tax years.

(b) Calculating the amount on which the allowance is based

Regardless of the price paid by the second-hand purchaser, he or she cannot obtain relief on a figure greater than the *original* cost of the building when new. Thus in our example the second-hand purchaser cannot obtain relief on a figure greater than £150,000.

Putting (a) and (b) together, the annual writing down allowance available to Cassius will be:

$$\frac{\pounds 150{,}000}{20} = \pounds 7{,}500 \text{ for 20 years}$$

No relief will be available for the excess of the actual purchase price over the original cost.

In normal cases the amount on which the second-hand purchaser obtains relief is the *lower* of the actual price he pays and the original price when new. To be strictly accurate we should arrive at the figure by referring to the industrial building allowance calculation of the seller for the year of sale and adding the balancing charge made to the residue of expenditure before the sale. In the illustrations we have just been looking at this would give us:

	£
Residue before sale	7,500
Balancing charge	142,500
	£150,000

Here is a further illustration of the calculation of industrial building allowances.

Illustration 4.7

Rosencrantz bought a new factory on 1 May 1980 and brought it into use on that day. The cost was £120,000 (including land £30,000). Rosencrantz makes up accounts to 31 March each year. On 1 March 1986 he sold the building to Guildenstern for £180,000 (including land £50,000). Guildenstern makes up accounts to 31 December each year. What industrial buildings allowances will be obtained by them in all years affected up to 1988/89?

Allowances to Rosencrantz

		£	£
Qualifying expenditure			90,000
1981/82	Initial allowance 50%	45,000	
	Writing down allowance 4%	3,600	48,600
			41,400
1982/83 to			
1985/86	Writing down allowance 4 × 4%		14,400
Residue of expenditure			27,000
1986/87	Sale proceeds		130,000
	Surplus on sale		103,000
	Balancing charge limited to allowance obtained		63,000

Allowances to Guildenstern	£
1987/88	
Residue of expenditure before sale	27,000
Balancing charge	63,000
	90,000

At 1 March 1986 there remains nineteen years and two months of the original period of twenty-five years beginning 1 May 1980. Accordingly, the industrial building allowance Guildenstern will receive in 1987/88 is:

$$\frac{£90,000}{19\ 2/12} = £4,696$$

This amount will also he claimable in each of the next eighteen years (1988/89 to 2005/06) if Guildenstern continues to own and use the building. In 2006/07 the final balance of £776 will be claimable.

Hotels

Expenditure on a qualifying hotel can attract allowances on a similar basis to industrial buildings.

To qualify, the hotel must have at least ten letting bedrooms, be open for at least four months during the period April to October, and must provide meals and service as well as accommodation.

Expenditure up to 31 March 1986 qualified for an initial allowance of 20 per cent and WDA 4 per cent. Expenditure after this date attracts the 4 per cent WDA only.

Commercial buildings in enterprise zones

Expenditure on new *commercial buildings* in enterprise zones continues to attract a generous allowance of 100 per cent in the year of expenditure. Note that the relief extends to shops, offices and hotels as well as industrial buildings.

On the sale of a commercial building in an enterprise zone, balancing charges will arise for the seller and the allowances for the second-hand purchaser will be calculated exactly as for industrial buildings.

In general, enterprise zones are small designated areas in Scotland, Northern Ireland, Wales and the North of England, though there are one or two in the South of England, the Isle of Dogs in London's Dockland, for example.

Patents

The capital cost of *acquiring* a patent can qualify for capital allowances. For expenditure up to 31 March 1986 there is an annual WDA of one-seventeenth of cost (straight line) or, if the remaining life of the patent is less than seventeen years, the cost is written down over that shorter period. Expenditure on patents after that date qualifies for a 25 per cent WDA (reducing balance) just like plant and machinery. There will be a balancing allowance equal to the unrelieved balance of expenditure in the year in which the patent expires.

Sale of patent

On the sale of a patent by a trader there is a balancing charge or allowance. A balancing charge cannot exceed the total allowances previously granted.

Know-how

'Know-how' is defined as industrial information and techniques likely to assist in manufacturing or processing goods or materials or in working (or searching for) mineral deposits or in agricultural, forestry or fishing operations.

Expenditure up to and including 31 March 1986 is written off over six years (straight line) beginning with the tax year in the basis period of which the expenditure was incurred.

Expenditure after 31 March 1986 qualifies for a 25 per cent WDA (reducing balance).

Scientific research

Capital expenditure on scientific research related to a trade attracts 100 per cent allowance. In other words, the whole of the expenditure is written off in the year in which it is incurred.

Capital allowances in the opening and closing years of a business (income tax)

Introduction and basic rules

We have seen that, in general, capital allowances for income tax purposes are granted by reference to the expenditure in the basis period of the tax year concerned. In the opening years of a business the profits of the same period are subjected to tax more than once, while in the closing years there is a period which escapes tax altogether if the business has been in existence for some years.

1 *Overlaps (opening years)* – when there is an overlap between income tax basis periods, the period common to both counts in the first period only for capital allowance purposes.
2 *Gsps (closing years)* – when there is a gap between income tax basis periods, for capital allowance purposes it is carried *forward* and added to the following period, *unless* that following period is the year of permanent cessation, in which case the gap is carried *back* and included in the previous period.

Studying the application of these rules will provide a useful revision of income tax basis periods in opening and closing years.

Opening years

Let us have an immediate illustration.

Illustration 4.8

Miranda began business on 1 January 1987 and made up her accounts to 31 December each year. Her profits in the first four years of trading were:

Year ended	£
31 Dec 1987	8,000
31 Dec 1988	12,000
31 Dec 1989	16,000
31 Dec 1990	20,000

Show the assessments for 1986/87 to 1989/90.
The rising trend of profits means that we do not need to consider the taxpayer's election under s. 117.

The assessments will be as shown in Figure 6.

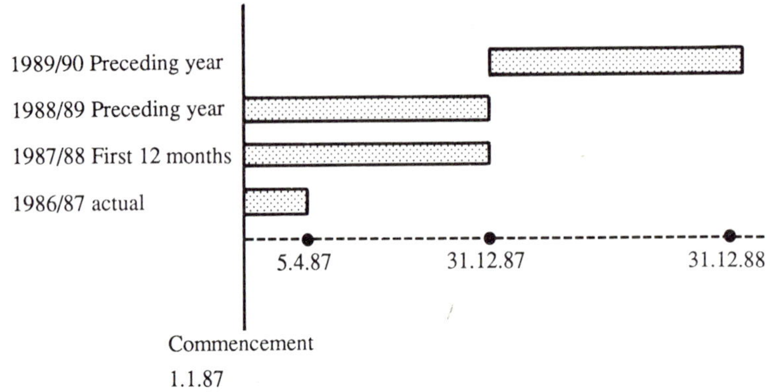

Figure 6

The assessments will be:

1986/87:	3/12 × £8,000	£ 2,000
1987/88:	1st 12 months	£ 8,000
1988/89:	Preceding year (year to 31.12.87)	£ 8,000
1989/90:	Preceding year (year to 31.12.88)	£12,000

So far nothing we didn't know already.

Let us now insert some capital expenditure on plant and machinery and see how we proceed.

Capital expenditure of plant and machinery:

1987		
6 Feb	Office equipment	£10,000
4 Apr	Motor car	£ 9,000 (1/4 private use agreed)
10 May	Office equipment	£ 1,000

We must first allocate this expenditure to basis periods. 1986/87 is on an actual basis and therefore the expenditure on 6 February and 4 April relate to 1986/87. Is there any special point? Yes, the profit basis period is three months only. Therefore it is fair that we should receive only 3/12 of a year's WDA, and this is exactly what happens.

The expenditure on 10 May is in the basis period for 1987/88 (first 12 months' trading). We may restate Figure 6 to show the capital allowance position (see Figure 7).

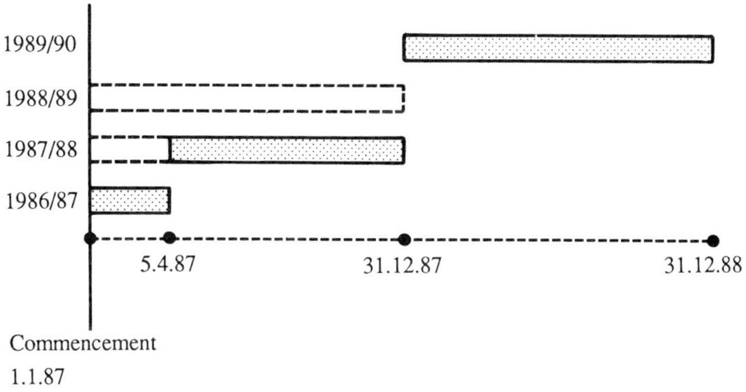

Figure 7

The dotted lines in Figure 7 indicate the basis periods for profit purposes which cannot count for capital allowances as they have already been included in earlier periods.

That means that there can be no fresh capital expenditure qualifying for relief in 1988/89 because there is no basis period for it to happen in. But – for 1987/88 and 1988/89 we get a *full* year's writing down allowance, because a *full* year's profit is being taxed in these years. It is only in 1986/87 that the allowances are restricted because of the length of the basis period.

The capital allowances computation is:

	Pool £	*Car with private use* £	*Total allowances* £
1986/87			
Expenditure	10,000	9,000	
WDA 3/12 × 25%	625	500 × 9/12 £375	1,000
	9,375	8,500	
1987/88			
Expenditure	1,000		
	10,375	8,500	
WDA 25% (no restriction because a full year's profit is being taxed)	2,584	2,000 × 9/12 £1,500	4,094
	7,781	6,500	
1988/89			
WDA 25% (no fresh expenditure can qualify,			

	Pool £	*Car with private use* £		*Total allowances* £
but full 25% on balance brought forward, as a full year's profit is being taxed)	1,946	1,625	× 9/12 £1,219	3,165
	5,835	4,875		
1989/90				
WDA 25%	1,459	1,219	× 9/12 £914	2,373
WDV c/fwd	4,376	3,656		

The net assessments after deducting capital allowances will be:

	1986/87 £	*1987/88* £	*1988/89* £	*1989/90* £
Adjusted profit	2,000	8,000	8,000	12,000
Capital allowances	1,000	4,094	3,165	2,373
	£1,000	£3,906	£4,835	£9,486

Tutorial notes

1 Notice how careful you have to be with the car in 1986/87. The allowance is first of all limited to £2,000 per annum. This then becomes £500 because it applies in a three-month basis period. (For examination purposes we make apportionments in months, ignoring the odd five days). Then we have to take nine-twelfths of the £500 because of the private use restriction.

2 For 1986/87 the adjusted profit is below the single personal allowance. That means there is no point in claiming the capital allowances as there is no tax liability. The taxpayer would therefore benefit by *renouncing* them. The effect would be that allowances for 1987/88 would be calculated on the basis of the unreduced balances brought forward – £10,000 in the pool and £9,000 for the car.

Closing years

In the closing years, there will be a gap, the profits of which are never taxed (unless the business is in existence for so short a time that the years affected by the Inland Revenue election for actual on cessation overlap with the years affected by the taxpayer's election for actual on commencement). Our rule for coping with gaps in the capital allowances computation was stated on page 51 – carry them forward unless the year into which they are then carried is the year of permanent cessation, in that case carry them back. This means that if the Revenue election for the penultimate and antepenultimate years is exercised the expenditure in the gap is carried *forward,* while if it is not the gap expenditure is carried back.

Illustration 4.9

Cleopatra ceased trading on 30 June 1988 after having been in business for many years, previously making up accounts to 30 September each year. Her adjusted profits in recent periods have been:

Period ended		*Profit* £
30 September	1985	20,000
	1986	12,000
	1987	24,000
30 June	1988	18,000

(a) Show the original and final assessments for all years affected
(b) Show how relief for the following capital expenditure would be granted (all pooled):

	£
Balance brought forward from 1985/86	20,000
Expenditure:	
1 March 1985 (ignore first year allowance)	4,000
4 February 1986 (ignore first year allowance)	6,000
10 November 1986	12,000
4 July 1987	2,000
6 May 1988	1,000

On 30 June 1988 when the business ceased, all the plant was sold for £40,000. No item realized more than its cost.

(c) Show how the capital allowances calculations would be affected if the adjusted profit for the year ended 30 September 1987 had been £2,000 instead of £24,000.

Figure 8 shows the basis periods with no Revenue election and those if the Revenue makes their election under s. 118.

It also shows the treatment for capital allowances purposes of the gap which opens up because of the cessations.

Original assessment – no Revenue election	£	*Revised assessment with Revenue option under s. 118*		£
1986/87 Preceding year –		Actual 6.4.86 – 5.4.87		
year to 30.9.85	20,000	6/12 × £12,000	6,000	
		6/12 × £24,000	12,000	18,000
1987/88 Preceding year –		Actual 6.4.87 – 5.4.88		
year to 30.9.86	12,000	6/12 × £24,000	12,000	
		6/9 × £18,000	12,000	24,000
1988/89 Actual –		Actual 6.4.88 – 30.6.88		
6.4.88 – 30.6.88				
3/9 × £18,000	6,000	3/9 × £18,000		6,000

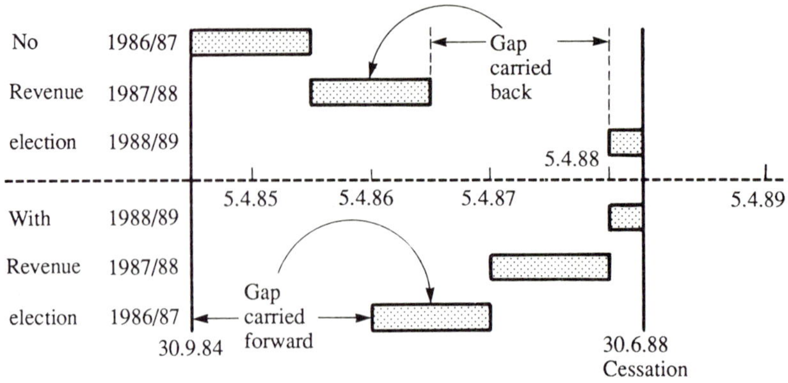

Figure 8

Clearly the Revenue election will be made, the assessments will be as shown, and for capital allowances purposes the expenditure during the period 1 October 1984 and 5 April 1986 will be counted as for 1987/88, the capital allowances basis period for which will then become 1 October 1984 to 5 April 1987.

		Pool	*Allowances*
	£	£	£
Capital allowances			
Brought forward from 1985/86		20,000	
1986/87 (basis period treated as 1.10.84 to 5.4.87)			
Expenditure			
1.3.85	4,000		
4.2.86	6,000		
10.11.86	12,000	22,000	
		42,000	
Writing down allowance 25%		10,500	10,500
		31,500	
1987/88 (basis period 6.4.87 to 5.4.88)			
Expenditure			
4.8.87		2,000	
		33,500	
Writing down allowance 25%		8,375	8,375
		25,125	
1988/89 (basis period 6.4.88 to 30.6.88)			
Expenditure		1,000	
		26,125	
Proceeds of sale		40,000	
Balancing charge		£13,875	(13,875)

The net assessments for the years concerned would be:

	1986/87	*1987/88*	*1988/89*
	£	£	£
Adjusted profit	18,000	24,000	6,000
Capital allowances	(10,500)	(8,375)	13,875
	£7,500	£15,625	£19,875

If the adjusted profit for the year ended 30 September 1987 had been £2,000, the Revenue election under s. 118 would no longer have been beneficial, and the basis periods for capital allowances purposes would have been:

1986/87	Year ended 30 September 1985
1987/88	1 October 1985 to 5 April 1988
1988/89	6 April 1988 to 30 June 1988

The capital allowance computation would then have been:

		Pool	*Allowances*
	£	£	£
Balance brought forward from 1985/86		20,000	
1986/87 (basis period 1 October 1984 to 30 September 1985)			
Expenditure			
1.3.85		4,000	
		24,000	
Writing down allowance 25%		6,000	6,000
		18,000	
1987/88 (basis period 1 October 1985 to 5 April 1986)			
4.2.86	6.000		
10.11.86	12,000		
4.7.87	2,000	20,000	
		38,000	
Writing down allowance 25%		9,500	9,500
		28,500	
1988/89 (basis period 6.4.88 to 30.6.88)			
Expenditure		1,000	
		29,500	
Proceeds of sale		40,000	
Balancing charge		£10,500	(10,500)

The net assessments would become

	1986/87	*1987/88*	*1988/89*
	£	£	£
Adjusted profit	20,000	12,000	6,000
Capital allowances	(6,000)	(9,500)	10,500
	£14,000	£2,500	£16,500

Summary

Capital allowances are granted on a wide range of business capital expenditure in place of the depreciation charge in the profit and loss account, which is always disallowed. They may also be allowed against income from property taxed under Schedule A, or against income from employments taxed under Schedule E.

For the purpose of the Business Taxation examination the two most important types of allowance are those for plant and machinery (including cars) and for industrial buildings. Brief coverage of other capital allowances is also given.

The rates of the main capital allowances are now:

(a) 25% writing down allowance (reducing balance basis):

- Plant and machinery
- Fire safety expenditure
- Thermal insulation of industrial buildings
- Safety expenditure at sports grounds
- Patents
- Know-how

(b) 4 per cent writing down allowance (straight line basis):

- Industrial buildings
- Hotels
- Agricultural land and buildings

(c) 100 per cent

- New commercial buildings in enterprise zones
- Scientific research

Progress questions

Attempt the following questions to test your absorption of the material in this Chapter. Rework them from time to time for revision. Answers are on pages 393–4.

1 Which of the following items qualify as plant and machinery or are treated for capital allowances purposes as if they were expenditure on plant and machinery?

	Yes	*No*
(a) A lawyer's library of reference books	✓	
(b) A canopy over a petrol station		✓
(c) Movable office partitions	✓	
(d) Fixed office partitions		✓

	Yes	*No*
(e) False ceilings		
(f) A swimming pool at a caravan park		
(g) Fire safety expenditure		
(h) Thermal insulation of offices		
(i) Thermal insulation of industrial buildings		

2 What allowance is granted for allowable expenditure on plant and machinery and how is it calculated?

3 In a capital allowances computation we have to include purchases and sales of allowable items.

(a) Which comes first in the computation, additions during the year or sales during the year?
(b) What deduction is made in respect of a sale?
(c) What happens if sale proceeds exceed the pool balance?

4 In the computation of capital allowances for plant and machinery expenditure on most allowable items is *pooled*. Name three items excluded from the general pool and explain how they are treated.

5 What restriction is placed on the allowability of charges for leasing or hiring cars?

6 What is the fundamental characteristic of industrial buildings for capital allowances purposes?

7 Give four examples of buildings which qualify as industrial buildings.

8 Fill in the gaps:

If an industrial building contains some office accommodation, the cost of the whole building can still qualify for industrial buildings allowance provided the office accommodation does not exceed... per cent of the cost. If this percentage is exceeded allowances are only granted on ...

9 What allowance is normally granted for allowable expenditure on new industrial buildings? Is there any exception to this?

10 What happens on the sale of an industrial building?

11 How is the allowance for second-hand industrial buildings calculated?

12 What allowance is granted for:

(a) Qualifying hotels
(b) Patents

(c) Know-how
(d) Scientific research?

13 In the opening and closing years of a business there may be overlaps and gaps between basis periods. How are these treated for capital allowances?

5 Income tax – relief for trading losses

Introduction

If a business makes a loss, it is only reasonable that some relief should be available. For a continuing business there are two main ways to obtain relief – to carry the loss forward and offset it against future profits of the same trade (s. 385 ICTA 1988) and to set it against other income of the same tax year or the following year (s. 380 ICTA 1988).

If the loss is in the early years of business, the loss can be carried *back* for three years (s. 381 ICTA 1988). This is a useful concession to new businesses, and may enable the taxpayer to obtain a refund of tax paid in earlier years before the business began.

All these loss-relieving provisions are available for *pre-trading expenditure,* expenditure of an allowable nature incurred in the three years before commencement of a business. Such expenditure is counted as a loss incurred in the year of assessment in which the business actually commences. A separate claim must be made for loss relief for pre-trading expenditure.

If a loss arises in the last twelve months of trading, this too may be carried back for up to three years (s. 388 ICTA 1988).

It is usual to refer to these loss claims by their section references, so you will need to learn them.

A basic point about loss relief is that the assessment for the tax year in the basis period of which the loss was made is *nil.* We then have to try to get relief for the loss by making the most beneficial claim or combination of claims under the sections metioned above.

Carrying forward losses – s. 385

This is the easiest form of loss claim to understand. The amount of the loss, as adjusted for tax purposes and increased by capital allowances if any, is used to reduce the first available adjusted profits of the same trade in future years. Any capital allowances of those future years are first deducted from the profits.

Illustration 5.1

Justin has been trading for a number of years. His recent results have been:

Year ended	*Adjusted profit or loss* £	*Capital allowances*
31 August 1987	10,000 profit	2,000
31 August 1988	21,000 loss	1,400
31 August 1989	12,000 profit	1,500
31 August 1990	18,000 profit	2,100

Show the net assessments based on these results, including the effect of a claim under s. 385 ICTA 1988 for the loss.

	£	£
1988/89	10,000	
Less: Capital allowances	2,000	8,000
1989/90		NIL
1990/91	12,000	
Less: Capital allowances	1,500	
Less: s. 385 loss claim	10,500	
	10,500	NIL
1991/92	18,000	
Less: capital allowances	2,100	
	15,900	
Less: s. 385 loss claim (balance)	11,900	4,000

	£
The loss in 1989/90 is:	
Loss	21,000
Capital allowances	1,400
	22,400
Claimed 1990/91	10,500
	11,900
Claimed 1991/92	11,900

The claim has to be made against the first available profits and to the full extent of those profits. It is not open to Justin to claim (say) £7,000 of the loss in 1990/91 so as to retain some profit to offset personal reliefs.

There is no time limit for the carry-forward, but a claim must be made within six years of the end of the tax year in the basis period of which the loss arose – in this case by 5 April 1996.

Transfer of business to a limited company – s. 386

This relief is really an extension of s. 385. If a sole trader sells his business to a limited company at a time when he is making losses, the sole trader business obviously ceases and the trader could make a terminal loss claim under s. 388 (see below). But if the trader transfers the business to a company in exchange for shares in that company, any unclaimed losses may be claimed against the income the taxpayer derives from the company.

Note that there is never any possibility of transferring the benefit of the losses of the loss relief *to the company*. The claim is only in respect of *income derived from the company*, earned or unearned, and claiming against the earned income first in any given year.

The relief is available as long as at least 80 per cent of the consideration is received in the form of shares, and as long as the taxpayer continues to hold these shares.

Illustration 5.2

Kate has carried on business for some years as a sole trader. At 30 June 1988 she converts her business to a limited company, Kate Limited, in which she owns the whole of the share capital. At that time she has unrelieved losses of £18,000 from her business.

After the formation of the company she derived the following income from it.

	Directors' fees	*Dividends (including tax credit)*
Year ended 5 April	£	£
1989	8,000	4,000
1990	12,000	6,000

A claim under s. 386 will mean that relief for the £18,000 loss will be obtained as follows:

		£	£
1988/89	Directors' fees	8,000	
	Dividends	4,000	
		12,000	
Less: s. 386 Claim		12,000	NIL
1989/90	Directors' fees	12,000	
	Less: s. 386 claim (balance)	6,000	
		6,000	
	Dividends	6,000	12,000

As with a s. 385 claim, relief must be claimed against the first available income.

Relief against other income – s. 380

I said in the introduction to this chapter that a claim under s. 380 could apply to two tax years – the tax year of the loss and the following year. This is true, but it is important to understand exactly which two years the relief can apply to. 'The tax year of the loss' normally means the tax year *in which the accounts showing the loss ended*, and 'the following year' is the year after that.

Illustration 5.3

Leonard has been trading for many years and in the year ended 30 June 1988 he made an adjusted loss of £18,000 after having made a profit of £7,000 in the previous year. He has other income from investments amounting to £10,000 gross per annum. He is considering making a claim for relief under s. 380 against his other income. For which two years are claims available?

The claims are available for *1988/89*, the year in which the accounts showing the loss ended, and 1989/90, the following year.

Leonard may claim for 1988/89 only, 1989/90 only, or for both years.

We may next ask ourselves what income is available in these years to offset the loss:

(a) 1988/89 – in 1988/89 we have investment income of £10,000, but also the £7,000 profit of the year ended 30 June 1987, falling to be assessed in 1988/89.
(b) 1989/90 – in 1989/90 we merely have the £10,000 of investment income.

The interesting point is that a s. 380 claim effectively allows us to claim relief for a loss against the profit of the previous year, as well as against any other income of the two years involved.

Loss claims under s. 380 would therefore be:

1988/89		£
	Schedule D Case I	7,000
	Dividends	10,000
		17,000
	Less: s. 380 claim	17,000
		NIL
1989/90		£
	Schedule D Case I	NIL
	Dividends	10,000
		10,000
	Less: s. 380 claim (balance)	1,000
		£9,000

Any unrelieved balance of loss not claimed under s. 380 is carried forward under s. 385. A s. 380 claim must be made within two years of the end of the tax year in which the loss arose – thus Leonard must claim by 5 April 1991.

What about capital allowances? s. 383 gives the taxpayer the option to add capital allowances to the loss. If the taxpayer chooses not to include the capital allowances they are carried forward under s. 385. The taxpayer's right to renounce capital allowances in whole or part gives further flexibility as to the amount of loss available for the claim.

If the taxpayer claiming under s. 380 is married, a further option is given by s. 382. The less claim may be restricted to the *loss-making spouse's* other income or extended to the income of both spouses. This gives a useful opportunity to preserve some income to enable personal reliefs to be obtained. Note that apart from this right to limit the claim to the loss-making spouse's income, it is not possible to make any other partial claim. Thus it is not possible to claim against just some of the available income so as to preserve the benefit of personal allowances.

Norman has run a business for some years as his trading results for recent years have been:

Year ended		
31.12.87	Profit	£10,000
31.12.88	Loss	£24,000
31.12.89	Profit	£ 6,000

He also has investment income of £12,000 per annum. His wife has investment income of £5,000 per annum. s. 380 loss claims are available for 1988/89 and 1989/90. Norman has an amazing range of possible claims:

(i) Make no claim under s. 380 and carry the whole loss forward under s. 385 in 1990/91 and later years.
(ii) Claim under s. 380 for 1988/89 only, against his own and his wife's income of that year, and carry the rest forward under s. 385.
(iii) Claim as in (ii), but against his own income only (s. 382).
(iv) Claim under s. 380 for 1989/90 only against his own and his wife's income of that year, and carry the rest forward under s. 385.
(v) Claim as in (iv), but against his own income only (s. 382 again).
(vi) Claim as in (iv), but for both 1988/89 and 1989/90.
(vii) Claim as in (vi), but restricting the claim to his own income only under s. 382.

We need to develop criteria to guide our choice.

Examination questions sometimes stipulate that relief is to be claimed so as to get the benefit as early as possible. This usually eliminates the need to consider s. 385 claims at least.

If the question requires us to claim so as to maximize the relief (e.g. to minimize loss of personal reliefs) we can apply the following rules, which are arranged in rough order of likely importance:

(i) Try to preserve some income in every tax year. In our example Normal would almost certainly be well advised to claim under s. 380 for both 1988/89 and 1989/90, but against his own income only, which would have the following result:

	£	
Loss	24,000	
s. 380 claim 1988/89	12,000	
	12,000	
s. 380 claim 1989/90	2,000	
	10,000	
s. 385 claim 1990/91	6,000	(income of same trade only)
Balance carried forward	4,000	

In all three years the wife's income of £5,000 remains to absorb personal allowances. There would probably be small tax liabilities in each year but no loss relief would be wasted by offset against income that would not be taxable because of personal allowances.

(ii) Try to equalize income between tax years. This means claiming in the year in which other income is highest, thus minimizing higher rate tax.

(iii) Claim in years when tax rates are highest. Given the choice, we might as well reduce the income of the year when tax rates are highest. Rules (i) and (ii) are likely to have more important effects but if everything else is equal, apply rule (iii).

(iv) Claim so as to get the benefit as early as possible.

There are a number of further points about s. 380 claims. Master thoroughly the material presented so far, then proceed to the following:

(a) Order of offset

The order on which income may be offset by a s. 380 claim is:

(i) Earned income of loss-making spouse
(ii) Investment income of loss-making spouse
(iii) Earned income of other spouse
(iv) Investment income of loss-making spouse

A s. 380 claim must be for all available income – (i) to (iv) – or limited to the loss-making spouse's income – (i) + (ii) only.

(b) Losses not qualifying for relief

In order for s. 380 relief to be available the trade must be conducted on a commercial basis with a view to the realization of profit (s. 384 ICTA 1988). If the trade is farming or market gardening, no relief is normally given if there has also been a loss each of the previous years, unless the taxpayer can show that the business is being conducted with a reasonable expectation of profit (s. 397 ICTA 1988). Any losses excluded from a s. 380 claim under s. 384 or s. 397 may still be carried forward under s. 385.

(c) Charges in loss relief
Loss relief is given against income after deducting charges from that income. This is an important difference compared with the corresponding claim for corporation tax losses, which are offset against income *before* deducting charges.

(d) Successive losses
If there are losses for several years, relief for earlier years is given in priority to losses of later years.

(e) The 'strict' basis of claiming relief under s. 380
In our work so far on s. 380 we have been obtaining the amount of loss available for a given tax year by simply taking the loss shown by the accounts ending in that year. This is the so-called 'concessional' basis usually adopted in practice and in examinations except in these situations:

(i) Opening years
(ii) Closing years
(iii) When the taxpayer elects for the 'strict' basis.

The 'strict' basis requires us to arrive at a loss figure for the year to 5 April by apportioning the profits and losses of the business.

Here is an illustration which shows how the application of the strict basis can help the taxpayer.

Illustration 5.4

Oberon has been trading for many years and his recent results, as adjusted for tax purposes, have been:

Year ended	£
30 June 1986	10,000 profit
1987	6,000 profit
1988	10,000 loss
1989	3,000 profit
1990	9,000 profit

Oberon is single and has no other income. He wishes to claim relief under s. 380 and is wondering if the 'strict' basis of claiming would be beneficial.

Here's how we find out.

(a) Claims on concessional basis
The tax year in which the accounts showing the loss ended vs 1988/89. Claims are therefore possible for 1988/89 and 1989/90, though in 1989/90 there is no income available as this is the year to which the loss would be related.

Oberon's assessments will be:

	£	£
1987/88		10,000
1988/89	6,000	
Less: s. 380 claim	6,000	NIL
1989/90		NIL (loss in basis period)
1990/91	3,000	
Less: s. 385	3,000	NIL
1991/92	9,000	
Less: s. 385 (balance)	1,000	8,000

(b) Claims on strict basis

We claim under s. 380 for any tax year in which there is an apportioned loss, and this actually means 1987/88 for Oberon.

			£
1987/88			
	6.4.87 to 30.6.87	3/12 × profit £6,000	1,500
	1.7.87 to 5.4.88	9/12 × loss £10,000	(7,500)
	Loss available for offset		(6,000)
1988/89			
	6.4.88 to 30.6.88	3/12 × loss £10,000	(2,500)
	1.7.88 to 5.4.89	9/12 × profit £3,000	2,250
	Loss available for offset		(250)

The assessments will be:

	£	£
1987/88	10,000	
Less: s. 380 claim	6,000	4,000
1988/89	6,000	
Less: s. 380 claim	250	5,750
1989/90		NIL
1990/91	3,000	
Less: s. 385	3,000	NIL
1991/92	9,000	
Less: s. 385	750	8,250

The total of the assessments for the five years is £18,000 in both cases, but by electing for the strict basis the taxpayer has managed to spread the loss claims more evenly between 1987/88 and 1988/89, therefore achieving one of our objectives of preserving the benefit of personal reliefs.

You need to understand the strict basis because this is always used for the purpose of a claim under s. 381 ICTA 1988 – see 5 below.

The question of claims under s. 380 and s. 385 for losses in the early years of business is dealt with briefly on page 70.

Losses in early years of a business – s. 381

Losses in the early years of business can be relieved under s. 380 and s. 385, but a further relief gives extra assistance to new businesses, by allowing losses in the first *four* years of a business to be carried *back* on a First In First Out (FIFO) basis for up to *three* years for offset against total income of those years. That could mean that a loss in the first year of a new business, say, could be carried back to give rise to a refund by offsetting it against salary earned and taxed before the business began. The loss available must first be calculated according to the strict rule of s. 380 as explained above.

Illustration 5.5

Pamela began business on 1 January 1987 and made up accounts to 31 December each year. She had previously been employed as an accountant. Her salary and trading results, as adjusted for tax, were as follows:

Year ended		£
5 April 1984	Salary	14,000
5 April 1985	Salary	16,000
5 April 1986	Salary	17,000
5 April 1987	Salary	10,000
31 December 1987	Loss	(30,000)
31 December 1988	Profit	8,000

Pamela wishes to claim under s. 381 ICTA 1988 as this is obviously beneficial because refunds of tax are obtained immediately.

The loss claims available are:

		£	£
1986/87	3/12 × loss £30,000		(7,500)
1987/88	9/12 × loss £30,000	(22,500)	
	3/12 × profit £8,000	2,000	(20,500)

The 1986/87 loss of £7,500 may be carried back and claimed for in 1983/84 in which Pamela had a salary of £14,000. She should therefore obtain a refund of tax on £7,500 at 30 per cent – £2,250.

The loss of £20,500 in 1987/88 can go back to 1984/85. £16,000 will be set against the salary of that year, leading to a refund of all tax paid in that year. The remaining £4,500 will be claimed against 1985/86. Note that the claim is FIFO – we go back three years and come forward, thus maximizing the previous income available for the claim.

Claims under s. 381 ICTA 1988 are subject to broadly the same conditions as those of s. 380 – the claim must be within two years of the end of the year of assessment in which the loss arose, and is subject to the conditions of s. 384 and s. 397 that the trade must have been conducted on a commercial basis with a view of profit. Capital allowances may be included or excluded in the claim at the taxpayer's option and the claim may be limited to the income of the loss-making spouse or extended to cover that of the other spouse.

In the case of Pamela we made our s. 381 claim against her salary before the business began. Note that the claim is actually against *total income* of the eligible years, so if she had had investment income this would also have been available to take the benefit of the claim.

Before turning to terminal losses, it may be useful to consider two more points arising from the Pamela example – the assessments for the business in the opening years and the claims available under s. 380 or s. 385 in respect of the loss, if Pamela chooses to obtain relief under those sections.

The assessments would be:

	Basis	*Assessment*	
		£	£
1986/87	Actual 1.1.87 to 5.4.87 3/12 × loss £30,000		NIL
1987/88	First 12 months' trading 1.1.87 to 31.12.87 loss £30,000		NIL
1988/89	Preceding year Year ended 31.12.87 loss £30,000		NIL
1980/90	Preceding year year ended 31.12.88 less s. 385 (see note below)	8,000 2,000	6,000

Notes: 1989/90 s. 385 claim – The actual loss made was £30,000. £28,000 was relieved under s. 381 (£7,500 + £20,500). The remaining £2,000 may, in this case, be carried forward under s. 385 against the first available profit.

s. 380 claims – as the s. 381 claims were calculated on the strict s. 380 basis, the amounts available if Pamela chose to claim under s. 380 would be the same – Pamela could claim in 1986/87 or 1987/88 for the £7,500 loss, and in 1987/88 or 1988/89 for the £20,500 loss, against any available income.

Terminal losses – s. 388

A 'terminal' loss is one arising in the last twelve months of trading. The loss reliefs we have looked at so far in this chapter are of limited use in such a case. Clearly s. 385 is useless and s. 380 can offer relief for one year only, as relief under s. 380 for the year following the year of the loss is only available if the trade is continuing.

That is where s. 388 comes in. It allows the loss to be carried *back* for up to three years against trading profits of those years. Unlike relief under s. 381 the claim under s. 388 is against the latest available year. Note that any Revenue election to the actual basis of assessment must first be allowed for. The assessments available to offset the terminal loss are the final ones after any Revenue election has been applied.

The rules of s. 388 are quite tricky. First of all, we have to find the loss for *the last twelve months' trading*. This is done on an actual basis by apportioning losses (or profits) in that period. The calculation has to be done in two parts. The last twelve months of trading is split at 5 April and separate calculations made for each period. Do *not* try to short-cut this process. If you do, you will sometimes get the right answer, but more often you won't. (This will become clearer when you study the illustrations which follow shortly.)

What about capital allowances? These may be added to the apportioned losses for the two separate years, if they have not been relieved otherwise.

If capital allowances are included in the claim we include the lower of:

(a) The appropriate proportion of the capital allowances (apportioning on the same basis as profit).
(b) The allowances unrelieved.

Here are the three illustrations showing the calculation of the loss.

Illustration 5.6

Quince, who has traded for many years as a carpenter, ceased trading on 30 June 1988. His adjusted trading results in recent years have been:

Period	£
9 months to 30.6.88	18,000 loss
year ended 30.9.87	10,000 loss
year ended 30.9.86	14,000 profit
year ended 30.9.85	28,000 profit

Capital allowances were:

	£
1988/89	3,000
1987/88	4,000
1986/87	6,000

Quince has no other income outside his business.

Before proceeding to the answer, let us analyse these figures for a moment.

Quince clearly has a loss in his last twelve months' trading. What about his capital allowances? Those for 1988/89 relate to the period 6 April 1988 to 30 June 1988 and must be balancing allowances arising on the sale of assets on cessation, since no writing down allowances are given in the year of cessation. We may therefore include the £3,000 in the s. 388 claim.

To establish the status of the capital allowances for 1987/88, we have to see what profit is assessed in that period. The Revenue will not be making its election to actual under s. 63 for 1986/87 and 1987/88, because the effect would be a considerable reduction in the assessments. On this basis the profits assessed in 1987/88 will be those of the year ended 30 September 1986, which are sufficient to absorb the whole of the £4,000 capital allowances. We therefore *cannot* include them in the terminal loss calculation. It is always necessary to establish this point as in answering a terminal loss question. Note that if we had been able to include these capital allowances in the claim we could have brought in 9/12 × £4,000 or £3,000, since nine months of the year 1987/88 falls within the terminal twelve months.

Let us now proceed to the calculation.

Quince

Calculation of terminal loss, twelve months ended 30 June 1988

		£	£
1988/89			
6.4.88 to 30.6.88			
	3/9 × loss £18,000		6,000
	capital allowances		3,000
1987/88			
1.7.87 to 5.4.88			
	3/12 × loss £10,000	2,500	
	6/9 × loss £18,000	12,000	14,500
	capital allowances 9/12 × £4,000 = £3,000, but already relieved		NIL
			£23,500

Quince may carry £23,500 back against assessments for 1987/88, 1986/87 and 1985/86.

Assessments on Quince will be:

		£	£
1988/89	Actual		
	6.4.88 to 30.6.88		
	(loss in basis period		
	3/9 × £18,000		NIL
1987/88	Year ended 30.9.86	14,000	
	Less: capital allowances	4,000	
		10,000	
	Less: s. 388 claim	10,000	NIL
1986/87	Year ended 30.9.85	28,000	
	Less: capital allowances	6,000	
		22,000	
	Less: s. 388 claim (balance)	13,500	8,500

You can see more clearly now why the £4,000 of capital allowances for 1987/88 cannot be included in the terminal claim.

Illustration 5.7

Let us take the same information as in Illustration 5.6, but this time assume that Quince made a *profit* of £10,000 in the year ended 30 September 1987.

The profits are still on a downward trend, so the Revenue will not exercise their right under s. 63 to revise penultimate and antepenultimate years to actual.

The calculation of the terminal loss will become:

		£	£
1988/89			
6.4.88 to 30.6.88			
	3/9 × loss £18,000		6,000
	capital allowances		3,000
1987/88			
1.7.87 to 5.4.88			
	3/12 × Profit £10,000	2,500	
	6/9 × loss £18,000	12,000	9,500
	Capital allowances already relieved		NIL
			£18,500

We note that if we have a loss and a profit *in the same tax year* in our apportioning, we set them off against one another and include the net amount in the terminal loss claim. That is what you would expect.

But, if the overall result for one of the tax years concerned is a profit, we disregard it in arriving at the total claim as shown in Illustration 5.8.

Illustration 5.8

Information as in Illustration 5.7 except that Quince's loss for the period to 30 June 1988 was £1,500.

The terminal loss is now:

		£	£
1988/89			
6.4.88 to 30.6.88			
	3/9 × loss £1,500		500
	Capital allowances		3,000
1987/88			
1.7.87 to 5.4.88			
	3/12 × profit £10,000	2,500	
	6/9 × loss £1,500	1,000	
	Profit	1,500	IGNORE
	Capital allowances–already relieved		NIL
			3,500

The reason for this apparently arbitrary rule is that the taxpayer would otherwise be unfairly deprived of part of his claim in respect of 1988/89. It is because of this rule that you cannot take a 'short cut' by taking the loss for the last twelve months without making separate calculations for the two tax years involved.

Payments under deduction of tax (charges) in loss claims

If a business makes payments under deduction of tax, referred to as 'charges', it must account for the tax deducted and this is normally achieved by disallowing the amount paid in computing the taxable profit. If the business makes a loss, no tax will be payable and the tax deducted cannot be accounted for in this way. In this situation the Revenue raise an assessment under s. 350 ICTA 1988 for the amount of the payment, thus collecting the tax.

To the extent that the payments assessed under s. 350 are *trade* charges (that is wholly and exclusively for the purpose of the trade) they may be carried forward under s. 387 as if they were losses, alongside any loss being relieved under ss. 385 and 386. Unrelieved trade charges can never be carried back.

In a terminal loss claim, no relief under s. 387 is possible. We may therefore include in the terminal loss claim, to the extent that they are not otherwise relieved:

(a) Charges paid in the final tax year entering into the last twelve months' trading.
(b) The appropriate proportion of the charges paid in the previous tax year entering into the last twelve months' trading.

The full list of the components of the terminal loss claim is thus:

(a) Tax year of cessation
(i) Loss from 6 April to date of cessation
(ii) Capital allowances for that period, if unrelieved
(iii) Any unrelieved trade charges paid (s. 350 assessment)

(b) Tax year before cessation
(i) Loss from beginning of last twelve months to 5 April
(ii) Proportion of capital allowances for the tax year preceding the year of cessation, if unrelieved. (If allowances are partly relieved, the lower of:

- proportion of capital allowances, or
- allowances unrelieved, may be included.)

(iii) Proportion of unrelieved trade charges of that year (s. 350 assessment)

The proportions in (b) (ii) and (iii) are determined according to the number of months in the last twelve months' trading falling into the tax year before cessation.

When making the terminal loss claim against the profits of the three preceding years, the claim is against the profits of those years *after* deducting *trade* charges. If there is other income, trade charges may be deducted from that income, so increasing the profit available for the s. 388 terminal loss claim.

If there are non-trade charges in the years of claim, they are deducted from other income, if any. If this is not possible they are deducted from trading income, *but must also be deducted from the terminal loss being carried to earlier years.*

Summary

If a business makes a loss in the basis period for a particular tax year, the assessment for that tax year is *nil*. It is then necessary to see how that loss can be relieved under the various loss-relieving provisions.

There are four main ways of obtaining relief for a trading loss:

(a) Carrying forward against future profit of the same trade under s. 385
The loss must be used against the first available profit. The claim is against the profits of future years after first deducting capital allowances and charges arising in those years. If the business is subsequently converted to a limited company before relief for the loss has been obtained, the loss *cannot* be transferred to the company. But, under s. 386 the taxpayer may claim for the loss against income derived from the company in salary or dividends, provided at least 80 per cent of the consideration on the transfer is received in the form of shares.

(b) Set off against other income of the year of the loss or the following year under s. 380.
s. 386 offers a range of possible claims, based on the following alternatives:

(i) Claim may be for either one of the two years available or for both
(ii) Claim may include or exclude capital allowances (s. 383)
(iii) For a married claimant, the claim may be confined to the income of the loss-making spouse or extended to include the income of the other spouse. (s. 382)
(iv) The loss available for claim under s. 380 may be taken to be that shown by the accounts ending in the tax year as adjusted for tax purposes (the concessionary basis). In the opening or closing years of the business, or if the taxpayer so requires, the 'strict' basis must be used. In that case the loss available is computed by apportioning losses (and profit) to arrive at the figure for the tax year to 5 April. Relief under s. 380 is only available if the trade has been conducted on a commercial basis.

A claim under s. 380 must be made within two years of the end of the tax year in which the tax arose.

(c) For a loss in the first four years of a new business, carry back on a FIFO basis against the total income of the previous three years (s. 381)
The loss is computed on the 'strict' s. 380 basis, and the other provisions are also as s. 380:

(i) Trade must have been conducted with a view to profit
(ii) Capital allowances may be included or excluded at the taxpayer's option
(iii) Claim may be limited to income of loss-making spouse or extended also to income of other spouse
(iv) Claim must be made within two years of the end of the tax year in which the loss arose.

(d) Terminal loss carried up to three years – s. 388
The rules here are:

(i) Calculate loss for last twelve months' trading in two parts, dividing the twelve month period at 5 April
(ii) Include capital allowances where available, taking the lower of proportionate capital allowances for tax year and capital allowances unrelieved
(iii) Carry loss back (LIFO) against assessments of last three years before year of cessation, remembering to apply the Revenue election under s. 63 where beneficial to the Revenue.

(e) Maximizing income tax loss relief
In choosing the most beneficial way to claim loss relief the following rules should be applied:

(i) Try to preserve some income in each year
(ii) Try to equalize income between tax years
(iii) Claim in years when tax rates are highest
(iv) Claim so as to get the benefit as quickly as possible

(f) Section references in ICTA 1988
It is customary to refer to these loss reliefs by their section references:

s. 380: relief against other income of year of loss or following year
s. 381: relief for loss in early years of business (back three years FIFO)
s. 382: right to restrict s. 380 claim to other income of loss-making spouse
s. 383: right to add capital allowances to a s. 380 loss and claim
s. 384: loss relief under s. 380 only available if the business making the loss is being conducted on a commercial basis with a reasonable expectation of profit.
s. 385: carry-forward of losses into future years
s. 386: carry-forward of losses where business is transferred to a company
s. 388: terminal losses

Progress questions

Attempt the following questions to test your absorption of the material in this chapter. Rework them at intervals for revision. Answers are on page 394.

1 If a business makes a loss, what is the assessment for the tax year in the basis period of which the loss was made?

2 What are the ways in which a trading loss may be relieved?

3 A business which has been running for many years and making up its accounts to 31 December shows a loss in the year ended 31 December 1988. In which two income tax years could a s. 380 claim be made? What date must the claim be made?

4 Are the following statements true or false? Indicate in each case the ICTA 1988 section reference relevant to the point.

	True	*False*	*Section reference*
(a) Trading losses may be carried forward without time limit and offset against the first available profit of future years from the same trade.	✓		S.385
(b) If a business with unrelieved income tax losses is converted into a limited company, those losses may be made available to reduce the future profits of the company for corporation tax purposes.		✓	S385
(c) The advantage of a s. 380 claim compared with a s. 385 claim, is that it is possible to limit the claim so that personal reliefs are not lost.	✓		S.382
(d) A loss in the first four years of a new business may be carried back on a FIFO basis, for up to three years, against total income of those years.	✓		S381
(e) A claim can be made when a loss arises in the last twelve months' trading of a business. Such a loss may be claimed against the taxpayer's total income of the previous three years.	✓		S388

6 Income from land and buildings

Introduction

For the last few chapters we have been concentrating on income tax under Schedule D Cases I and II. It is now time to turn to the other types of income, beginning in this chapter with income from land and buildings. Most such income is taxed under Schedule A, though it is also necessary to consider Schedule D Case VI (for furnished lettings).

Schedule A

Income taxable under Schedule A

Tax is charged under Schedule A on all income derived from land and buildings in the UK, except for the relatively small area covered by Schedule D Case VI, which is dealt with below.

The sources of income from landed property are:

(a) Rents from land and/or unfurnished property
(b) Ground rent (including feuduties and ground annuals in Scotland)
(c) Other miscellaneous receipts such as wayleaves and income from letting sporting rights
(d) Premiums on leases

You may like to have definitions to clarify the meaning of two of these items:

- *Ground rent* – rent paid to a landlord under a lease for the use of land. Ground rent is often encountered as a small annual payment to a freeholder by the lessee of a building, in respect of the occupation of the land on which the building stands.

- *Wayleave* – a payment received in return for granting a right of way or other right over property.

Basis of assessment

Schedule A tax is charged on the basis of rent etc. *due* in the tax year, less allowable expenses. In England and Wales rent is usually due on the so-called 'quarter days'

- 25 March (Lady day)
- 24 June (Midsummer)
- 29 September (Michaelmas)
- 25 December (Christmas)

(It may be easier for you to remember these if you note that for the first three the number of letters in the month is equal to the second digit of the date while for the fourth you are likely to need a mnemonic!)

Illustration 6.1

Robert granted a five year lease of a property as from 25 March 1988 at an annual rent of £4,000, due *in advance* on the normal quarter days.

The first rent falls due on 25 March 1988. Robert is therefore charged to tax under Schedule A in *1987/88* on £1,000, even though only eleven days' ocupation are within that year. The due date is the criterion even if the rent was not in fact paid until after 5 April 1988.

If the rent had been due quarterly in *arrears*, the first due date would have been 24 June 1988 and tax assessments would have begun in 1988/89.

Due date for payment

Schedule A tax is due for payment on 1 January *in the year of assessment*. This gives rise to a practical difficulty because the tax is due before the final amount of net income for the year to 5 April is known. The Revenue overcome this difficulty by raising an estimated assessment for the full estimated amount expected to be due for the year. This is then adjusted, and a further payment made, or refund obtained, when the final result for the year to 5 April is known.

Allowable expenses

The allowability of expenses under Schedule A can be tricky.

The basic rules are that expenses have to relate to the property and to the period of ownership of the property.

Any expenditure representing an improvement to the property will be disallowed as capital. Capital allowances may be available on certain capital expenditure.

Note that the Odeon Theatres case (*Odeon Associated Theatres Ltd* v. *Jones* 1971 – see page 17) relates to Schedule D Case I and does not apply for Schedule A, for which statutory rules exist.

There are restrictions on the allowability of expenditure:

(a) During void periods (e.g. between tenancies)
(b) After acquisition but before occupation by a tenant
(c) When the owner has lived in the property.

These restrictions are dealt with below. Specific expenses normally allowable include:

(a) Repairs and maintenance. Improvements are excluded, as are any costs of repairing dilapidations existing at acquisition
(b) Local authority rates paid by the landlord
(c) Rent payable to a superior landlord
(d) Cost of services provided
(e) Wages of maintenance and other relevant staff
(f) Cost of rent collection (but not rent misappropriated by an agent)
(g) Accountancy and legal costs, preparing accounts and computations
(h) Insurance of property
(i) Interest on a loan or mortgage to finance the purchase. This is allowable *as a charge* (i.e. as a deduction from total income) subject to the following conditions:
   - Property must be let at a commercial rent for more than twenty-six weeks in any period of fifty-two weeks, and when not so let is available for letting, or occupied by the owner or prevented from being available by works of construction or repairs.
   - Interest may only be deducted up to the limit of income from property (any property, not only the property to which it relates), and including income from furnished lettings assessable under Schedule D Case VI.
(j) Capital allowances – Items qualifying can include:
   - Plant used for maintenance
   - Lifts
   - Swimming pools and other amenities (e.g. at a block of flats)
(k) Bad debts – if the landlord has taken all reasonable steps to trace a defaulting tenant, rent due but not paid will not be assessed, nor will rent waived by the landlord to avoid hardship to the tenant.

Treatment of losses

Relief for Schedule A losses is limited in two ways. First of all, Schedule A losses cannot be offset against income outside Schedule A. Secondly, even within Schedule A there are further restrictions which prevent or limit relief for losses on certain types of lease.

We need to consider three different types of lease:

(a) A lease at a 'full rent'* with the landlord responsible for some repairs
(b) A lease at a 'full rent' with the tenant responsible for *all* repairs, internal and external
(c) A lease at less than a 'full rent'

Type (a) properties (landlord's repairing lease) get the most generous treatment – losses on a property of this type may be offset against profits on other type (a) properties of the same year or following years. In other words, the results of all properties in this group are *pooled*.

Type (b) properties (often referred to as 'tenants' repairing leases') are treated individually. If a loss arises it may be relieved against:

(i) The pool profit from type (a) profits of the same year or following years
(ii) profits *from the same type (b) property* in future years

Type (c) properties. These properties are, by definition, almost certain to show a loss. Relief can only be obtained by carrying the loss forward against future profits (if any) from the *same tenancy* of the *same property*. Table 3 summarizes the position.

Table 3

Leases at full rent		*Leases at less than full rent*
Landlord doing some repairs (landlord's repairing lease)	Tenant doing all repairs internal and external (tenants' repairing lease)	
Could be profit or loss	Almost certain profit	Almost certain loss
Loss relief by pooling of properties in same year, any balance of pool loss carried forward into pool for following years	Loss relief by – offset against pool of same year or subsequent years, or by carrying forward against future profits of same *property*	Loss relief by carrying forward against future profits of same tenancy of same property

The 'standard' examination question on this theme has five or six properties let under different types of lease and asks you to work out the net Schedule A assessment and the losses to be carried forward. The opportunities for careless error are considerable!

Try the following illustration for yourself before looking at the answer.

* A 'full' rent is one which, taking one year with another, is sufficient to cover the outgoings.

Illustration 6.2

Sandra owns 6 houses, all of which are let.

Details of the tenancies and of the income and expenditure for 1988/89 are given below.

Property 1	Let on a landlord's repairing lease to J. Smith. Annual rent, payable in advance on the normal quarter days, £2,000, increased to £2,400 as from 25 December 1988. Allowable expenses for year – £1,700
Property 2	Let on a tenant's repairing lease to R. Brown. Annual rent, payable annually on 1 January, £1,800. Allowable expenses for year – £450
Property 3	Let to Sandra's widowed mother at a nominal rent of £200 per annum. Allowable expenses for year – £800. Loss brought forward from earlier years – £3,700.
Property 4	Let for many years on a landlord's repairing lease to A. Robinson. Annual rent, payable in advance on the normal quarter days – £2,800 Allowable expenses, including substantial repairs totalling £3,200–£4,100.
Property 5	Let on a tenant's repairing lease to J. Jones. Annual rent payable in advance on the normal quarter days – £3,600. Jones left the property without notice on 4 August 1988 and cannot be traced. Rent actually received £900. Allowable expenses £1,400.
Property 6	Let on landlord's repairing lease to T. White. Annual rent £2,600 Allowable expenses £1,000.

Our first step is to set up the pool of landlord's repairing lease properties. (Properties 1, 4 and 6). This may then be reduced by the loss on Property 5. The profit on Property 2 must be assessed regardless of the results of the other properties. The loss on Property 3 may only be carried forward against future profits, if they ever arise, from the same tenancy of the same property.

Working that out in figures, we arrive at:

Sandra
Computation of Schedule A income 1988/89

			£	£	£
Landlord's repairing leases					
Property 1	Rent		2,200		
	Less:	expenses	1,700	500	
Property 4	Rent		2,800		
	Less:	expenses	4,100	(1,300)	
Property 6	Rent		2,600		

			£	£	£
	Less:	expenses	1,000	1,600	
				800	
Tenant's repairing leases					
Property 5	Rent		900		
	Less:	expenses	1,400	(500)	300
Property 2	Rent		1,800		
	Less:	expenses	450		1,350
	Schedule A assessment				£1,650
Property 3	Rent		200		
	Less:	expenses	800		
	Loss		(600)		
	Loss brought forward		(3,700)		
	Loss carried forward		(4,300)		

The loss on Property 5 could be carried forward against the following year's Schedule A assessment on that property, but in the absence of clear indications in the question of other relevant factors we should claim so as to get the relief as quickly as possible as above.

Void periods

A 'void period' is a period when there is no tenant in a property. This could be the period between acquisition and obtaining the first tenant, or a period between tenancies.

(a) *Void period between acquisition and obtaining first tenant at full rent* – expenditure during this period is only allowable if it relates to dilapidations occuring after acquisition. Thus general repairs in this period would normally be disallowed. Examples of expenditure which would be allowed are:
   (i) Repairs to fencing damaged in a gale after acquisition
   (ii) Reinstatement costs after a flood occurring after acquisition

(b) *Void periods between tenancies* – expenditure in these periods is only allowed if the void period immediately follows a lease at a full rent *and is followed by a further lease at full rent.* This means, for example, that if the landlord occupied the property for a time and then did some repairs before reletting the property, the costs of the repairs would be liable to be disallowed, since they could obviously be related to his period of occupation.

Premiums on leases

Schedule A taxes rents receivable from property. One obvious way for a landlord to try to reduce his liability to tax is for him to charge a reduced rent, but require the incoming tenant to pay a *premium* on the granting of the lease.

There is provision in Schedule A to charge such premiums to tax, subject to a deduction of 2 per cent of the premium for every complete year of the lease after the first. Thus a lease for more than fifty years would escape the charge.

Illustration 6.3

On 1 January 1988 Thelma granted a twenty-one year lease of a property to A at an annual rent of £12,000 payable monthly in advance and with an initial premium of £40,000. How much will be assessed on Thelma under Schedule A in 1987/88 and 1988/89?

			£	£
1987/88				
	Rent	4 months @ £1,000 per month (due on 1 January, 1 February, 1 March and 1 April!)		4,000
	Premium		40,000	
	less: 2% × (21 − 1) = 40%		16,000	24,000
				£28,000
1988/89				
	Rent			£12,000

There is another interesting feature connected with the payment of premiums. If the person paying the premium is a trader he or she may deduct the *annual equivalent of the amount on which the landlord is liable to pay tax* from profit in each year of the lease. Thus in the illustration above if A was a trader he would be able to deduct £24,000 ÷ 21 or £1,143 from profit in each year of the lease.

Note that the landlord has to pay tax *in full* in the year in which the amount is received, but relief is granted to the tenant in equal instalments over the full term of the lease.

Furnished lettings under Schedule D Case VI

If a property is let furnished, the whole of the income is charged to tax under Schedule D Case VI rather than under Schedule A.

The calculation is much the same as under Schedule A. The taxpayer may claim capital allowances on the furnishings, or may alternatively take a deduction of 10 per cent of the rent receivable less rates.

Losses arising within Schedule D Case VI may only be offset against other Case VI income of the year of loss or following years. To provide a slight concession the taxpayer may elect, within two years of the end of the tax year concerned, to have the rent referable to the use of the *property*, as opposed to the furnishings, assessed under Schedule A. This could be advantageous in two situations:

(a) When there is a loss from furnished lettings under Case VI and a profit from other lettings on landlord's repairing leases under

Table 4

Leases at full rent		*Leases at less than full rent*
Landlord's repairing lease	*Tenant's repairing lease*	
Profits and losses pooled, and balance of loss carried forward into pool	Losses set against pool of landlord's repairing lease or carried forward against future profit of same property	Losses carried forward against future profit from same tenancy of same property

Schedule A. In this case relief is obtained for the Case VI loss which would otherwise have to be carried forward.

(b) When there is a profit from furnished lettings and a loss from lettings at a full rent under Schedule A. Here the election allows the profit to be moved into Schedule A, thus enabling relief for the Schedule A loss to be obtained against it.

The due date for payment of tax under Schedule D Case VI is 1 January in the year of assessment, like Schedule A. Accordingly the Revenue frequently raise an estimated Case VI assessment during the tax year and revise to the final amount when this is known, exactly as explained above for Schedule A.

Summary

Schedule A

Most income from property is taxed under Schedule A. Schedule A taxes rent *due* in the tax year less allowable expenses, and also premiums charged on the granting of a lease subject to a sliding scale of deductions (2 per cent for every complete year of the lease after the first).

If properties show a loss, relief for that loss can only be obtained against other Schedule A income. Within Schedule A, further restrictions are placed on offsetting profits and losses (see Table 4).

Void periods are periods when the property is not occupied. Expenses incurred in void periods between tenancies may only be deducted if the void periods are preceded and followed by lettings at full rent. Expenses incurred during the void period between the acquisition of a property and its first letting may only be deducted if the expenses relate to the period after acquisition – e.g. repairs to damages occurring after acquisition.

Due date for payment of Schedule A tax is 1 January in the year of assessment.

Schedule D Case VI

Furnished lettings are taxed under Schedule D Case VI on broadly the same basis as Schedule A. Capital allowances may be claimed on furniture etc., or alternatively a deduction of 10 per cent of rent less rates may be claimed.

Due date for payment of Schedule D Case VI tax is 1 January in the year of assessment.

Taxpayer may elect to have the part of the Case VI income relating to the use of the premises taxed under Schedule A. This may improve the availability of loss relief.

Progress questions

Attempt these questions to test your absorption of the material in the Chapter. Rework them at intervals as revision. Answers are on page 395.

1 What income is assessed under Schedule A?

2 In what circumstances will repairs expenditure not be allowed as an expense for Schedule A?

3 If properties taxable under Schedule A show a loss, how may that loss be relieved?

4 What relief is available in respect of furnishings when property is let furnished and taxed under Schedule D Case VI?

7 Income from employment – Schedule E

Scope of Schedule E – income chargeable

Schedule E taxes the emoluments of an office or employment. In the vast majority of cases we are looking at employees receiving a salary and taxed under the Pay As You Earn (PAYE) procedure with which most of us are familiar.

Our study of Schedule E needs to concentrate on two aspects – the measurement of the *emoluments assessable* (not always easy because of the vast range of possible benefits that employees may enjoy) and the measurement of *expenses deductible* in arriving at those assessments.

The term 'emoluments' is defined in s. 131 as including 'all salaries, fees, wages, perquisites and profits whatsoever' arising from the employment. Pensions received after the cessation of employment are also taxed under Schedule E.

Basis of assessment

The normal basis of assessment under Schedule E is the amount actually earned in the tax year to 5 April. This will cover basic salary or wage plus commissions, profit-sharing payments, bonuses and, of course, benefits in kind. Some expenses may be deductible, and these are considered below. There are also special rules and arrangements for some benefits in kind enjoyed by employees, which are also covered below. Before moving to these problems, let us look at one point connected with the assessment of income.

Most payments within the scope of Schedule E are regular payments of salaries or wages, and it is no problem to relate them to the tax years – tax is simply levied on the amount actually *paid* in the year. There is sometimes a problem with bonus based on profit of the employer's accounting period and paid some time later. There are basically three ways of handling such payments:

(a) Relate them to the tax year in which they are actually received
(b) Apportion them to tax years
(c) Treat the bonus of the accounting year ending in the tax year as the income of the tax year

Here is an illustration to clarify things:

Illustration 7.1

Jane receives a salary of £18,000 per year and also receives a bonus based on her employer's profits as follows:

Period	*Bonus*	*Date paid*
Year ended 31 December 1987	£6,000	8 June 1988
31 December 1988	£8,000	6 June 1989
31 December 1989	£10,000	18 June 1990

Applying method (a), the amount assessable in 1988/89 will be the amount actually received:

	£
Salary	18,000
Bonus	6,000
	£24,000

Applying method (b), we shall have, for 1988/89:

		£	£
Salary			18,000
Bonus	9/12 × £8,000	6,000	
	3/12 × £10,000	2,500	8,500
			£26,500

Applying method (c) we have:

	£
Salary	18,000
Bonus 1988/89	
Amount relating to year ended 31 December 1988	8,000
	£26,000

It can clearly make a difference which method is adopted. Only method (b), the 'strict' basis, actually relates the bonus *earned* in the tax year to that tax year. Method (b) should be adopted in the examination unless you are instructed otherwise. Per F. Act '90 – this s/b amount PAID i.e. method (c)

Allowable expenses

Introduction

The Schedule E rule regarding the deduction of expenses is very strict. To qualify, expenses must be incurred '*wholly, exclusively and necessarily in the performance of'* the duties (s. 198 ICTA 1988). This may be compared with the more relaxed rule applied for Schedule D Case I and II that expenditure has to be wholly and exclusively for the purpose of the trade, profession or vocation (s. 74 ICTA 1988). The vital differences are first that expenditure must be *necessary* and second that it must be *in the performance* of the duties rather than merely *for the purpose* of the trade etc. The combined effect of these two extra requirements is to disallow for Schedule E several expenses which would be allowable for Schedule D Case I and II, as we shall see.

Before proceeding to specific examples let us first look at the full and precise wording of s. 198. The section actually considers three types of expense:

(a) *Travelling* – travelling costs necessarily incurred in the performance of the duties are allowed
(b) *Other expenses* – other expenses wholly, exclusively and necessarily incurred in the performance of the duties are allowed
(c) *Horses* – the cost of keeping and maintaining a horse necessarily used to enable the employee to perform his or her duties is allowed.

It is pleasing to see that the legislation continues to make provision for horses even though the need for it has almost entirely vanished. No other aspect of the rule affords any pleasure to employees.

The precise application of the rule has been interpreted by a number of legal cases and there are also statutory provisions specifically allowing certain types of expenditure to be deducted.

Statutory deductions

(a) Professional subscriptions
Section 201 allows the deduction of subscriptions to approved professional bodies, learned societies etc. The subscription is only allowed if the activities of the body concerned are relevant to the employment concerned.

(b) Donations to charity – payroll deduction scheme
Section 202 allows the deduction of charitable gifts by an employee, up to £240 per year, made through an approved deduction scheme operated by the employer, who makes payments under the scheme directly to approved charities.

(c) Contributions to approved pension or superannuation schemes
Section 592 (7) allows contributions to approved pension or superannuation schemes to be deducted.

(d) Retirement annuity policies
Section 619 allows premiums paid on retirement annuities to be deducted, subject to the maximum indicated in Chapter 10 below.

(e) Personal pension plans (PPPs)
Section 639 allows contributions to PPPs to be deducted, subject to the maximum indicated in Chapter 10.

Case law

(a) Travelling expenses
Many attempts have been made in the courts to obtain relief for travel between home and work in various special situations. Few have been successful. Illustrative cases:

(i) *Ricketts* v. *Colquhoun* 1925 – a London barrister was also Recorder of Portsmouth. His emoluments for this office were assessed under Schedule E. He claimed deduction for expenses of travel between London and Portsmouth, plus hotel expenses. The deduction was refused because the expenses were not in the performance of the duties, which did not begin until he arrived at the Court in Portsmouth, and were not necessary – he need not live in London but could have lived in Portsmouth.

(ii) *Pook* v. *Owen* 1969 – a doctor carried on a practice at his home and also had Schedule E appointments at a local hospital fifteen miles from his home. He was at times required to be on standby duty. When needed at the hospital, he was telephoned and usually gave instructions to the staff before driving to the hospital. He received a mileage allowance from the hospital which covered a journey of ten miles each way, and which was assessed on him as part of his remuneration. He claimed that the mileage allowance was not assessable and that he was entitled to deduct the excess of his actual car expenses over the hospital allowance. He succeeded on both counts, on the basis that his duties began as soon as he was contacted by the hospital and he gave instructions to the staff.

These cases show the vital point clearly – the doctor was in the performance of his duties before he left home while the barrister was not.

(b) Other expenses

(i) *Brown* v. *Bullock 1961 – club subscriptions* – a West End bank manager joined a club which he visited only to meet bank customers. The bank paid half the subscription, which was assessed as part of the manager's emoluments. The manager claimed deduction for the whole of the subscription paid. It was held that although the expenditure was wholly and exclusively in the performance of the duties, it was not *necessarily* incurred. Not allowed.

(ii) *Elwood* v. *Utitz 1965 – club subscriptions* – the managing director of a Northern Ireland company became a member of two London clubs in order to obtain cheaper accommodation when visiting

London on business. Subscriptions held to be allowable as they saved money for his company.

(iii) *Lupton v. Potts 1969 – examination fees* – fees paid by an articled clerk for sitting the Law Society's examinations held not to be allowable.

(iv) *Humbles* v. *Brooks 1962 – cost of weekend lectures* – expenses of a history teacher in attending weekend lectures to improve his knowledge – not allowable.

(v) *Hillyer* v. *Leeke 1976 – extra wear and tear on clothing* – a computer engineer failed in a claim for cost of clothing (suit, collar and tie) which he was required by his employer to wear at work and which he wore at no other time. It was held that the clothing also provided warmth and decency and was thus not 'exclusively' for a working purpose. The same principle was followed in *Mallalieu* v. *Drummond* 1983, a Schedule D case in which a lady barrister was refused allowance for clothing worn only in Court.

Note: In fact, the Revenue, often in agreement with relevant trade unions, do allow an annual flat rate deduction for the assumed cost of protective clothing, books for lecturers and other similar costs.

Conclusions

In the light of the statutory rules and case law decisions we have just studied, what expenses are likely to be allowable for Schedule E?

(a) Travelling expenses, including capital allowances on cars, falling within the definition in s. 198.
(b) Relevant subscriptions to approved professional bodies
(c) Charitable gifts up to £240 per annum through a payroll scheme
(d) Contributions to approved superannuation schemes
(e) Retirement annuity premiums
(f) Contributions to personal pension plans (PPPs)
(g) Reasonable cost of protective clothing or tools of trade (often in the form of an agreed flat rate allowance)
(h) Proportionate cost of office at home address (proportion of rates, heating, lighting etc.), provided that the provision of such an office is necessary in the performance of the duties
(i) Other expenses within the strict rule in s. 198.

Benefits in kind

The very high rates of tax prevailing in the UK until the 1980s led to the development of a wide range of non-cash benefits for employees – benefits in kind. The most significant and popular of these is the provision of cars. In parallel with the development of such benefits the Revenue here developed legislation to control them, now mainly in ss. 141 to 165 ICTA 1988.

The current position is:

(a) Some benefits remain tax-free to all employees
(b) Some benefits are taxable on all employees
(c) Some benefits are taxable only when enjoyed by directors or 'higher paid' employees

Benefits tax-free to all employees

There are still some important benefits that are tax-free to all employees and a few minor ones as well:

(a) Employer's contribution to approved superannuation or pension scheme

(b) Restaurant or canteen facilities, providing they are available to all employees

(c) Luncheon vouchers up to 15p per day

(d) Relocation costs
A reasonable contribution by an employer to cover removal costs, legal and estate agents' fees, temporary subsistence expenditure and interest on bridging loans may be paid without attracting Schedule E tax. The maximum which an employee may pay for extra housing costs of an employee moved to a higher cost area is now £15,750.

(e) Job-related living accommodation
Although the provision of living accommodation by the employer is usually taxable, it may escape tax if *job-related* – that is, if the accommodation is:

(i) *necessary* for the performance of the duties, or
(ii) provided for the better performance of the duties and it is customary in the trade for accommodation to be provided (e.g. a hotel manager), or
(iii) provided for security purposes when there is a special security risk to the employee.

Exemptions (i) and (ii) above do not apply to directors unless they are full-time working directors owning not more than 5 per cent of the company. Any payment of rates by the employer is also covered by the 'job related' exemption.

(f) Profit-related pay schemes (ss. 169–184)
A profit related pay scheme is set up by the employer and approved by the Profit-Related Pay (PRP) Office. The scheme must define:

(i) The profit period (normally the employing company's financial year)

(ii) The employees to be included. (Controlling directors *must* be excluded, and the employer has the option to include or exclude part-timers, those who have worked for less than three years in the business and up to 20 per cent of all others).

(iii) The method of calculating the distributable profit pool. The Act specifies two methods – Method A and Method B. In Method A the distributable profit is a fixed percentage of the post-tax profit of the employment unit, which may be the whole business or a department of it. The percentage chosen must produce a distributable pool of at least 5 per cent of the standard pay of the employees in the scheme. *In Method B* the distributable pool is arrived at by taking:

$$\text{Profits of } \textit{preceding} \text{ year} \times \frac{\text{Current Year's Profits}}{\text{Preceding Year's Profits}}$$

The rules of the scheme may stipulate that no PRP will be paid if profits fall below a certain level, and it is also permissible to adjust the post-tax profit for non-trade items like interest paid and received, extraordinary items. The scheme may be based on pre-tax profits if desired.

(iv) The basis of distribution to participating employees. All employees included in the Scheme must participate on 'similar' terms, but this does not exclude allowances for length of service, pay levels or other similar factors.

The exemption for exployees on profit-related pay is that 50 per cent of the PRP is exempt from tax, up to a limit of 20 per cent of the employee's total pay, or £3,000, whichever is the less. In calculating total pay for PRP purposes we take gross pay plus the PRP payment and minus superannuation contributions and charitable donations through the payroll up to the statutory limit of £240 per annum.

Illustration 7.2

Jane has a salary of £12,000 per annum. She pays superannuation contributions of £480 and makes charitable donations through a payroll scheme of £240. Her employer runs a PRP scheme for the year ended 31 March 1989 under which she is to receive £2,000:

	£	£
Salary		12,000
Superannuation	480	
Charitable donations	240	720
		11,280
PRP		2,000
		£13,280

Jane will be entitled to relief on the lowest of:

• 20% of total pay £13,280	2,656
• £3,000	3,000
• Actual PRP payment	2,000

The PRP payment qualifies for full relief as it is below both of the limits. Jane will be able to receive 50 per cent of her £2,000 free of tax, and will thus benefit by £250 (£1,000 @ 25 per cent basic rate).

(g) Profit sharing schemes

Quite apart from the PRP scheme described in (d) above, an employer may set up a profit sharing scheme by which a proportion of profit is allocated to independent trustees who buy ordinary shares in the company on behalf of each participating employee. (All full-time directors and employees with at least five years' service must be elegible to participate.)

The value of shares allocated to an employee under such a scheme must be at least £1,250 but not more than the lower of:

- 10 per cent of remuneration excluding pension contributions and benefits in kind
- £5,000.

When shares are allocated to employees there is no charge to tax under Schedule E on the employee and the amount allocated is, of course, an allowable expense to the company.

The shares must be held by the trustees for at least two years before release to the employee, and then by the employee for a further three years, if full Schedule E tax exemption is to be obtained. If the employee sells the shares before the fourth anniversary of the initial allocation to the trustees, the whole of the initial market value of the shares (or the sale proceeds if lower) is charged to tax under Schedule E. If the employee sells the shares in the fifth year (on or after the fourth anniversary but before the fifth anniversary) 75 per cent of the market value (or sale proceeds if lower) is taxed under Schedule E.

Quite independently of the Schedule E position there may be a charge to capital gains tax, in the calculation of which the cost of the shares is taken to be the market value at the time of initial allocation.

(h) Share option schemes in conjunction with a Save as You Earn Scheme (SAYE)

Under these schemes employees enter into a SAYE contract by which a sum between £10 and £100 per month is regularly deducted from salary and used to buy shares under an option previously granted by the company.

For Revenue approval, a scheme must comply with the following conditions:

(i) The scheme must be open to all full-time directors and employees who have at least five years' service, other than one holding more than 25 per cent of the ordinary shares in a close company

(ii) The SAYE contributions must continue for at least five years
(iii) The grant of the share option must be at a price not less that 90 per cent of the market value at the time of the grant
(iv) The time for exercising the option must be fixed at the time it is granted, and must be either five or seven years later
(v) The value of the shares to be acquired must not exceed the amount the employees receives from the SAYE scheme.

At the end of five years, a bonus of fourteen months' contributions are added to the amount in the SAYE scheme, or if the scheme is continued for seven years an additional twenty-eight months' contributions are added instead.

Here is an illustration of the working of a SAYE-based share option scheme.

Illustration 7.3

Jack is an employee of X Ltd, and was granted on 1 January 1986, an option to subscribe for shares in the company at £1 per share, exercisable in seven years. At the same time he began a seven year SAYE scheme with contributions of £100 per month.

On 31 December 1992, at which time the shares are worth £2 each, the scheme matures and its value will be:

	£
Contribution: 84 months at £100 per month	8,400
Bonus: 28 months at £100 per month	2,800
	£11,200

Jack will be able to acquire 11,200 shares at the option price of £1 per share. No Schedule E tax is payable either on the value of the option in 1985/86 or on the increase in value of the shares up to the exercise of the option in 1992/93.

If Jack subsequently sells the shares there may be a capital gains tax liability. The cost of the shares for the purpose of the capital gains tax computation will be the option price of £1 per share.

(i) Share option schemes not linked to SAYE
These are much more ambitious schemes which may be made available to key employees only, unlike the schemes described in (g) and (h) above. An employee may hold options on shares up to a value of the greater of:

- £100,000
- Four times remuneration excluding pension contributions and benefits in kind, for the current or previous year.

The shares must be acquired within ten years of the granting of the option but not earlier than three years after the grant or within three years of exercising another option under the scheme.

Entry to the scheme may be restricted at the employer's discretion and is usually confined to senior executives. To be eligible, employees must be either:

(i) A full-time director (working at least twenty-five hours per week), OR
(ii) an employee working at least twenty hours per week.

Anyone owning more than 10 per cent of the ordinary shares of a close company is excluded.

Here is an illustration.

Illustration 7.4

Jill is the marketing director of Hill Limited. She works full-time in the company and has remuneration, excluding pension contributions and benefits in kind, of £40,000 per annum.

On 1 April 1986 she is granted an option to buy 75,000 ordinary shares in Hill Limited at a price of £2 per share, the market value of the shares at that time.

On 1 April 1990 Jill exercises the option. The shares at that time are worth £3 per share.

The value of the shares over which Jill holds an option is £150,000, within the limit of four times remuneration.

She will accordingly have no Schedule E liability in respect of the increase in value of the shares since the option was granted. If Jill later sells the shares, there may be a capital gains tax liability, in calculating which the cost of the shares will be taken as the £2 option value.

Benefits taxable on all employees

(a) Beneficial living accommodation

If the employer provides living accommodation for any employee, the benefit will be assessed unless the accommodation is *job-related* (see above). The measure of the benefit from the accommodation is taken to be the greater of:

(i) Rent paid by employer, if any
(ii) The annual value of the property for rating purposes

In each case any contribution from the employee is deducted. If the employer pays the rates, that too will be an assessable benefit for all employees.

A further charge may arise if the cost of the property exceeds £75,000.

The value of the additional benefit is calculated by applying the 'official' rate of interest (9.5 per cent from 6 May 1988, previously 10.5 per cent) to the excess of the cost over £75,000. (The 'official' rate varies frequently and will be given in the examination.) If the company has owned the property for the six years preceding its being made available to the employee, the open market value at that time is substituted for the cost.

Illustration 7.5

Keith is an employee of Lewis Enterprises Limited and is provided with a London flat used partly for business purposes and partly for private purposes by his family. For 1988/89 the business use has been agreed at 60 per cent. The cost of the flat when acquired by the company in 1980 was £60,000, and its open market value when Keith first began using it in 1987 was £135,000.

The additional benefit for 1988/89 will be:

Excess of market value over £75,000:		£60,000
Interest		
10.5% × £60,000 × 1/12		525
9.5% × £60,000 × 11/12		5,225
		5,750
Less:	Agreed business use 60%	3,450
	Additional benefit	2,300

If the employer pays bills relating to the property, there will be a further charge for directors and higher-paid employees, as explained in (d) below.

(b) Vouchers exchangeable for cash, goods or services

These are treated as taxable benefits, the measure of the benefit being the cost to the employer of providing it. The only exception is luncheon vouchers up to 15p per day.

(c) Credit tokens

If an employee is provided with a credit token (a company credit card, for example) the employee is taxed on the cost of the cash, goods or services obtained with the token.

Benefits taxable on directors and higher-paid employees only

There is a tendency for companies to provide many of the possible benefits – cars for example – only to directors or higher-paid employees. Stricter rules apply to such employees. A 'higher paid' employee for the purpose of these rules is one whose earnings, *including benefits* but before deducting allowable expenses, are £8,500 or more.

For such directors or employees the employer has to submit a form P11D annually to the Revenue giving details of their benefits. More details about these forms are given below.

Table 5 Car benefits

	Age of car at end of year of assessment	
Cost of car when new	*Under 4 years*	*4 years or more*
Up to £19,250		
1,400 cc or less	£1,050	£700
1,401–2,000 cc	£1,400	£940
Over 2,000 cc	£2,200	£1,450
£19251–£29,000	£2,900	£1,940
Over £29,000	£4,600	£3,060

The benefits taxable only when enjoyed by directors or higher-paid employees are:

(a) Cars

The measure of the benefit derived from the use of a company car is defined in Tables in Schedule 6 ICTA 1988. The rates fixed for 1988/89 by FA 1988 are as shown in Table 5.

The specified scale charges are applied when a car is provided and used for *more than 2,500 miles* per year on business. Journeys from home to work do not count as business use, of course.

If the car is used for 2,500 miles or less per year on business, the scale charges are *increased* by 50 per cent.

If the car is used for 18,000 miles or more per year on business, the scale charge is *reduced* by 50 per cent.

If two or more cars are provided, the scale charge for second and subsequent cars is Table value plus 50 per cent, regardless of the annual business mileage covered in them.

If the car is a '*pool*' car, is no assessable benefit. To qualify, a car must be:

(i) Available for use by, and actually used by, more than one employee;
(ii) Used privately only incidentally to business use;
(iii) Not normally garaged at or near an employee's home.

The scale charges are reduced proportionately if the car is only available for part of the tax year.

If the employee makes a contribution to the cost as a condition of private use, this is deducted in arriving at the taxable benefit.

(b) Car fuel for private motoring

The scale charges for the use of cars cover the car itself plus repairs and other running expenses except fuel. If the employer also provides fuel for private use a further scale charge is treated as a benefit according to Table 6 (s. 158 ICTA 1988).

Table 6

Cylinder capacity of car in cubic centimetres	*Cash Equivalent* £
1,400 or less	480
1,401 to 2,000	600
Over 2,000	900

No fuel charge is made if the employee reimburses the *whole* cost of fuel for private use or, of course, if there is no private use. It is *not* reduced by a partial contribution to the cost of private fuel – it is all or nothing.

Note that there is no distinction, as there is with the car benefit charges, between cars under and over four years old. The fuel charge is *not* increased by 50 per cent if the car is used for 2,500 miles or less per year on business, or if two or more cars are provided. However, it *is* reduced by 50 per cent if business use is 18,000 miles or more per year.

(c) Provision of assets other than cars

If the employer provides assets other than cars, the measure of the benefit derived by the employer is the greater of:

(i) 20 per cent of the market value when first made available
(ii) The cost of hiring or leasing the asset

Any contribution by the employee is deducted. If the asset is subsequently sold to the employee, a further assessable benefit may arise. This is the greater of:

(i) Market value at time of sale, less price paid by the employee
(ii) Original market value when first made available, less the amounts already assessed on the employee and the price paid by the employee

Illustration 7.6

Leonard is a higher paid employee of Hutton Limited. The company provided him with some new furniture which cost £2,000 in 1986/87. As a result there was a taxable benefit of £400 (20 per cent of £2,000) in 1986/87 and 1987/88. The furniture was then sold to Leonard for £500 when the open market value was £800. The benefit arising would be the higher of:

Market value when first made available	£2,000
Assessed 1986/87 and 1987/88	800
	1,200
Price paid	500
	£ 700

Market value at time of sale to Leonard	800
Price paid	500
	£ 300
The assessable benefit on the sale would accordingly be	£ 700

(d) Beneficial loan arrangements (ss. 160–161 and Schedule 7)
If an employer makes loans to employees at no interest, or at a low rate of interest, a benefit arises. The cash equivalent of that benefit is calculated by applying the official rate (fixed by the Treasury and varied from time to time) to the average amount of the loan. The official rate is currently 9.5 per cent as from 6 May 1988. It was previously 10.5 per cent. Any interest actually paid is deducted.

The calculation of the average amount outstanding is made by taking the average of the opening and closing balances at the beginning and end of the tax year. Either the taxpayer or the Revenue may elect to have the calculation made on a day-to-day basis.

If the loan is only outstanding for part of the tax year, the interest charge is scaled down according to the number of *complete income tax months* (ending on 5th) for which the loan is outstanding.

No assessable benefit arises if:

(i) The cash equivalent when calculated does not exceed £200, or
(ii) the loan is for a qualifying purpose (e.g. a loan of up to £30,000 for the purchase of the employee's residence).

(e) Expenses connected with living accommodation
We have seen that the provision of accommodation and the payment of rates for any employees will both give rise to a charge to tax as a benefit unless the accommodation is 'job-related'.

If the employer pays additional expenses these too will be assessed, *on director and higher-paid employees only*. This applies to:

(i) Heating, lighting and cleaning
(ii) Repairs, maintenance and decoration
(iii) The provision of furniture etc. (calculated by taking 20 per cent per annum of the market value at the time the asset was first provided)

If the accommodation is job-related the additional charge is still made as above, but is then limited to 10 per cent of the employee's net emoluments', defined as salary plus other benefits in kind, less allowable expenses but *excluding* the benefit from the expenses in question.

(f) Private medical treatment or insurance
The cost to the employer will be an assessable benefit to directors and higher paid employees.

(g) Scholarships for employees' children
If an employer provides scholarships for employees' children as a result of the fact that they are employees, the value is treated as an assessable

benefit on directors and higher-paid employees. It is possible to escape from these provisions if it can be shown:

(i) That the scholarship is not the result of the employment, and
(ii) that not more than 25 per cent of scholarship payments made by the employer are made by reason of employment. Scholarships to children to lower-paid employees have to be included in the 25 per cent.

(h) Round sum expense allowances
Round sum expense allowances paid to directors or higher-paid employees are taxable as part of remuneration. It is then up to the employee concerned to substantiate expenditure out of the allowance as 'wholly exclusively and necessarily' incurred as explained above.

It is, however, possible to obtain a dispensation from the Inspector of Taxes on the basis that the allowance would be fully covered by an expenses claim.

The P11D Form

At the end of each tax year, an employer is required to submit details of all benefits provided for directors and higher-paid employees and expenses payments made to them otherwise than under a dispensation as explained in (h) above. This enables the Inspector of Taxes to raise any necessary assessments on employees.

By arrangement, it is possible for the employer to submit P11Ds for accounting periods rather than for the tax year.

PAYE procedures

Basic procedure

All but a tiny fraction of the total revenues derived from tax on employments is collected through the PAYE system under which tax is deducted from wages and salaries by the employer at source and remitted monthly to the Collector of Taxes. The deduction allows for the personal reliefs to which the taxpayer is entitled, and can also collect higher rate tax.

For PAYE purposes, the tax year to 5 April is divided into twelve months ending on 5th of each month. The employer deducts tax from employees every time a salary payment is made, and has to remit the tax collected to the Collector of Taxes within fourteen days after the end of the tax month, that is, by the 19th of the month.

To enable the employer to make the necessary calculations, the Revenue provides tax tables and notifies the employees' personal relief entitlements by means of code numbers which vary according to the total reliefs available to each employee. The code number is arrived at by totalling the reliefs available, including adjustments for allowable expenses and benefits in kind, if any, then disregarding the last digit.

A suffix letter is then added to the code number, as follows:

Suffix	*Meaning*
H	Married man (or single person entitled to additional personal allowance for children or widow's bereavement allowance)
L	Single person (or married women entitled to wife's earned income allowance)
V	Married man entitled to age allowance
P	Single person entitled to age allowance
T	Consult tax office before making changes

These suffixes allow the Revenue to instruct employers to adjust codes upwards without individuals notification for each employee affected, as when allowances are increased by Budget changes. For example, all codes suffixed 'H' would be advanced by a standard amount, all codes suffixed 'L' by another amount, and so on.

The use of a code number instead of details of the exact make-up of an employee's tax position provides a measure of confidentiality for the employee.

The tax tables, combined with the employee's code number, enable the employer to calculate the weekly or monthly tax liability to be deducted from pay.

The main tax tables are Table A and Table B. Two forms of Table A are available, one for weekly-paid staff and the other for monthly paid staff. Table A shows, for each week or month, the cumulative total allowances to date for each particular code number. The cumulative allowances to date (called the 'free' pay) are deducted from total pay to date to give taxable pay. The employer then looks this figure up in Table B, which shows the total tax due to date on that income. That figure, *less tax already deducted in previous weeks or months*, is the tax liability for the current week or month.

To illustrate the procedure let us take as an example John, an unmarried man under sixty-five whose salary, paid monthly, is £12,000 per year. If there are no other complications, his code number for 1988/89 will be 260 (total allowances £2,605, ignoring the last digit gives 260).

John's total tax liability for the year is quickly calculated:

	£
Salary	12,000
Single allowance	2,605
Taxable income	9,395
Tax payable	
£9,395 @ 25%	£2,348 (ignoring pence)

One-twelfth of this sum, £195 odd, will be collected each month by deduction from John's salary.

The tax tables enable the employer to calculate the liability as follows:

(a) Month 1 of tax year
The employer looks up code 260 in Table A (monthly) and finds that John has free pay to date of £217. John's gross salary for Month 1 is £1,000, and therefore his taxable pay is £783 (£1,000 less £217). The employer then looks up £783 in Table B to find the tax due on this sum, which is £195.70

(b) Month 2 of tax year
The procedure of Month 1 is followed, with minor modifications. Table A shows free pay to date of £434 for the two months. This is deducted from John's total pay to date, £2,000, to give taxable pay of £1,566.

Table B shows tax due to date on this sum £391.50. John's liability on his May salary is £391.50 less the tax paid in April £195.70, or £195.80.

Procedure in subsequent months is similar to that for Month 2. Each month John's free pay to date will go up by £217. The amount deducted will vary slightly each month, but at the end of the tax year almost exactly the correct tax will have been deducted.

If the taxpayer's allowances change during the year, for example, if John gets married, his code number is changed and the changed allowances are reflected in the tax deduction from the next salary payment.

If the taxpayer is liable to higher rate tax, this too is collected by deduction from salary each month, using a third table provided by the Revenue, Table C.

The Revenue provide a working sheet (P11 (new)), which may be used to make the necessary calculations. Most employers use their own working sheets, however, which are increasingly prepared by computers.

Employees leaving and joining

The PAYE system copes smoothly with changes in employment. When an employees leaves, the employer completes a form P45, a three-part form which gives details of the employee's name, PAYE code number and total pay and tax deducted to date. The employer retains Part 1 of the P45 and hands Parts 2 and 3 to the leaving employee, who passes them to his or her new employer. The new employer can then continue to deduct tax from the point at which the previous employer left off. The new employer retains Part 2 of the Form and sends Part 3 to the Revenue.

If a new employee does not have a Form P45, the employer sends a Form P46 to the Inspector of Taxes, who thereupon sends an income tax return to the new employee to ascertain the reliefs and allowances to which he or she is entitled. When the employee completes the income tax return the Inspector allocates a code number and notifies it to the employer on Form P6 to enable the correct tax deductions to be made. A Notice of Coding (Form P2) is also sent to the employee to enable him or her to check it.

There is a special procedure to handle tax deductions pending the notification of the tax code to the employer in this situation. This is the use of the so-called 'emergency' code which corresponds to that for a single person with no other allowances. This is applied on the 'Week 1/Month 1 basis' – using the tax tables for Week 1 or Month 1 of the tax year repeatedly. This means that no account is taken of pay or tax deducted in earlier periods and avoids excessively generous deductions which might otherwise arise. As soon as the employer is notified of the employee's proper code the deductions will usually revert to the normal basis and as a result the employee may well receive a refund of tax over-deducted.

End of year procedures

During the tax year the employer will have been paying over PAYE tax monthly. At the end of the tax year it is necessary to prepare a summary form P35 which shows the total tax deducted from each employee during the year, which has to be reconciled with the total amount of tax paid over to the Revenue for the year. This has to be submitted by 19 April each year, the due date for the final payment in respect of tax deducted in the last tax month 6th March to 5th April. As well as the summary form P35, the employer also has to submit to the Revenue a Form P14 for each employee, showing details of total pay and tax deducted.

At the end of the year it is also necessary to give each employee a statement of total pay and tax deducted for the year. This is form P60.

Employees with more than one employment

If an employee has more than one employment this could lead to serious under-deduction of tax if each employer was adopting the same code number, effectively giving the allowances twice or more. To avoid this, a special code number will be allocated for the second and subsequent employments. If necessary, the code can require the employer to deduct tax at the higher rate of 40 per cent from the whole of the income. To effect this, the prefix 'D', followed by the required rate, becomes the code number – D40.

Golden handshakes

When an employee leaves employment, he or she may receive a lump sum for redundancy, damages for breach of service contract or as an ex gratia payment on retirement. Such termination payments are colloquially referred to as 'golden handshakes'.

From 1988/89 the first £30,000 of such payments is exempt from tax and the remainder is fully taxable.

If the termination payment is a requirement under the employee's contract of employment, the whole amount is fully taxable.

The Cases of Schedule E

Schedule E is divided into three Cases – I, II and III. The vast majority of Schedule E assessments are under Case I, which deals with the income from employments of those *resident and ordinarily resident in the UK*. (For a definition of these terms take a look forward to page 113 Chapter 8.) There is an important deduction for those absent from the UK (see Table 7).

Case II deals with taxpayers who are not resident in the UK, or if *resident* are not ordinarily resident here. Only income relating to duties within the UK is taxed.

Case III applies to persons not chargeable under Cases I or II but who are resident here. It applies to:

(a) Income earned abroad from a non-resident employer, but only to the extent that those earnings are remitted to the UK.
(b) Overseas earnings of someone resident but not ordinarily resident in the UK (Case II having covered the UK earnings of such a person).

Table 7 summarizes the position:

Table 7

Residential status	*Tax treatment*
Case I Resident and ordinarily resident in UK	All emoluments for UK and overseas duties taxed in full, subject to *100 per cent deduction* if absent from UK for 365 consecutive days (return for up to 63 days or one-sixth of total does not invalidate the deduction)
Case II Not resident, or if resident not ordinarily resident.	All emoluments for UK duties only, taxed in full
Case III Resident, but not under Cases I or II	Emoluments for overseas duties taxed to the extent that they are remitted to the UK

Summary

Basis of Schedule E

Schedule E taxes the emoluments of an office or employment – salaries, wages, fees, commissions, benefits in kind and the like. The basis of assessment is the actual amount earned in the tax year to 5 April.

Allowable expenses

To be allowable, expenses must be 'incurred wholly, exclusively and necessarily in the performance of' the duties (s. 198 ICTA 1988).

There is statutory provision for the deduction of:

(a) Professional subscriptions
(b) Donations to charity up to £240 per year and through a payroll deduction scheme
(c) Pension contributions
(d) Retirement annuity premiums
(e) Contributions to personal pension plans

Case law on Schedule E expenses emphasizes how strictly the rule governing allowability is applied.

Benefits in kind

(a) Benefits free of tax for all employees

(i) Employer's contribution to approved pension scheme
(ii) Restaurant or canteen facilities available to all employees
(iii) Luncheon vouchers up to 15p per day
(iv) Relocation costs (reasonable)
(v) Provision of job-related living accommodation
(vi) Fifty per cent of payments under a profit related pay scheme, up to a limit of 20 per cent of the employee's total pay or £3,000, whichever is the less
(vii) Shares allocated under a profit sharing scheme
(viii) Share option schemes in conjunction with a Save As You Earn scheme (SAYE)
(ix) Share options not linked to SAYE

(b) Benefits taxable on all employees

(i) Beneficial living accommodation (unless job-related)
(ii) Vouchers exchangeable for cash, goods or services
(iii) Credit tokens

(c) Benefits taxable on directors and higher paid employees only

(i) Cars (based on scale rate)
(ii) Fuel for cars (also based on scale rate)
(iii) Provision of other assets
(iv) Beneficial loans
(v) Additional expenses connected with provision of living accommodation
(vi) Private medical insurance
(vii) Scholarships
(viii) Round sum expense allowances

Form P11D

Details of benefits provided for directors and higher-paid employees must be sent to the Inspector of Taxes by completing a Form P11D giving the details for each such director or employee.

PAYE procedures

Most tax under Schedule E is collected by the employer by deduction at source and paid over monthly to the Collector of Taxes. The deductions are calculated using Tables provided by the Collector and information about the total allowances to which each employee is entitled is given in the form of a code number.

When an employee leaves, details of pay and tax deducted to date in the tax year are passed to the next employer by means of a form P45.

At the end of the tax year a summary of all tax collected and remitted (Form P35) must be submitted to the Collector, supported by a form P14 for each employee showing his or her total pay and tax deducted. A copy of form P14 is given to each employee – the employee's copy is called form P60.

Golden handshakes

From 1988/89 the first £30,000 of payments to employees on termination of employment is tax free. The remainder is taxed in full. The £30,000 concession does not apply if the payment is a requirement of the employee's contract of employment.

Progress questions

Attempt these questions to test your absorption of the material in the chapter. Rework them at intervals for revision. Answers are on page 395.

1 What is the basis of assessment under Schedule E?

2 In what three ways may bonuses based on profit and similar receipts be taxed?

3 State the rule (and ICTA 1988 section reference) governing the allowability of expenses for Schedule E.

4 State six items likely to be allowed as expenses or deductions from income under Schedule E.

5 State six benefits normally tax-free to all employees

6 In what circumstances will a car provided for an employee be treated as:

(a) A benefit at scale rate
(b) A benefit at half scale rate
(c) A benefit at one and a half times scale rate
(d) A pool car?

7 Is it possible for an employer to put a tax-free benefit into an employee's hands by providing a loan at no interest? Explain if and when this could happen.

8 Explain the use, in the PAYE system, of the following forms:

(a) P45
(b) P46
(c) P35
(d) P60

8 Miscellaneous income

Introduction

In this chapter we pick up all the types of income not yet dealt with – these are unlikely to be the main subject of a major question but can appear as part of a question.

Schedule C

Schedule C can be dealt with very briefly. A considerable amount of tax is collected very easily under Schedule C. It deals with tax on interest on Government stocks – mainly UK Government Stocks ('gilt edged') but also foreign government stocks if payment of the interest is through a UK paying agent.

When interest on most UK Government stocks is paid, the paying agent deducts basic rate income tax at source and pays the stockholder the net amount. If the stockholder is not liable to the tax he or she can make a repayment claim.

The paying agent is then assessed on the actual amount of interest arising and pays the tax over to the Revenue.

You really need to know no more about Schedule C. Indeed, there is very little more *to* know.

One final point is that there are a few UK Government securities or investments on which the interest is paid gross. Such interest is accordingly outside the scope of Schedule C and is taxed under Schedule D Case III (see below). The only ones you need to remember on which interest is paid gross are $3\frac{1}{2}$ per cent War Loan and National Savings Bank interest.

Schedule D Case III

Introduction

In practice Schedule D Case III deals mainly with interest received gross, including discount on Treasury bills.

In principle, Schedule D Case III also covers debenture interest, patent royalties, income from deeds of covenant and maintenance above the 'small maintenance payments' limits. As these are all paid under deduction of tax, no assessment has to be raised.

Interest received gross

Interest on the following investments is received gross by UK *individuals*

(a) $3\frac{1}{2}$ per cent War Loan and a few other UK Government securities;
(b) National Savings Bank *Ordinary* Accounts (note that the first £70 of such interest is *exempt* from tax).
(c) National Savings Bank *Investment* Accounts
(d) Bank deposits exceedings £50,000 on which more than twenty-eight days' notice of withdrawal must be given.

Basis of assessment

The normal basis of assessment for these items is the income of the *preceding year* (s. 64), with special arrangements for the opening and closing years:

(a) Schedule D Case III basis of assessment in opening years (s. 66)

(i)	First year in which interest received	*actual*
(ii)	Second year in which interest received	*actual*
(iii)	Third and subsequent years	*preceding year*

The taxpayer may elect within six years of the end of the tax year concerned to have the the third year revised to *actual*. Note that unlike Schedule D Case I and II the Schedule D Case III election in the early years relates to one year only.

If the interest first 'arises' on 6 April in the first year, the *second* year is taken on the preceding year basis and the taxpayer's option to actual applies to that year. This is very rare and requires interest to be paid on that date.

(b) Schedule D Case III basis of assessment in closing years (s. 67):
In the year in which the source of income ceases, the assessment is based on *actual*.

Previous assessments remain on the preceding year basis, but with a Revenue option to revise the *penultimate year* to *actual*. Again unlike Schedule D Case I and II the option applies to one year only.

Due date

The due date for payment of tax under Schedule D Case III is 1 January in the year of assessment.

Illustration 8.1

Gordon placed £100,000 in the National Savings Bank special investment account on 1 January 1987. Interest is credited to the account on 31 December each year.

Amounts of interest credited have been:

	£
31 December 1987	6,200
1988	5,800
1989	6,700
1990	6,800
1991	7,100
1992	5,900

On December 1992 Gordon closed the account.

Show the original and find assessments under Schedule D Case III for all the years affected.

Assessments under Schedule D Case III will be:

	Assessments	
	Original £	*Elections*
1987/88 (first year in which interest arose)	Actual 6,200	
1988/89	Actual 5,800	
1989/90	Preceding year 5,800	Taxpayer's election under s. 66 not beneficial
1990/91	Preceding year 6,700	
1991/92	Preceding year 6,800	On cessation, Revenue will increase to actual (£7,100) under s. 67
1992/93 (year of cessation)		Actual 5,900

The amounts stated in the 'original' column will be assessed. The tax due on the 1991/92 assessment (£6,800) will have been paid on 1 January 1992. On cessation on 31 December 1992 the Revenue will raise an additional assessment for tax on the extra £300 due as a result of the change of basis from preceding year to actual.

Bank interest

Until 1984/85 bank interest was paid and assessed under Schedule D Case III. From 1985/86 onwards, however, the position has changed. What happens now is that banks pay the interest net of tax. The recipient grosses the amount up for basic rate income tax and includes that gross equivalent in statutory total income. Basic rate tax on this gross sum is treated as having been paid, but higher rate tax may be due if the taxpayer's income is high enough. Unlike most tax suffered by deduction (e.g. on debenture interest and effectively on UK dividends) *no repayment* of this tax can be obtained by an individual.

The reason why no repayment can be obtained is that the banks account to the Revenue not for full basic rate tax on the gross equivalent but for tax at the so-called 'composite rate' fixed annually by the Revenue. The composite rate is lower than basic rate and is designed to be such that the total tax collected is the same as that which would have been collected if the full basic rate had been charged on the interest, and repayments granted to those taxpayers entitled to them. The composite rate is fixed at a level roughly equivalent to the average rate of tax which would have been borne by the individual taxpayers concerned.

Note that bank interest continues to be paid *gross* to companies, who are liable to corporation tax on it, and to pension funds and registered charities who should be exempt from tax on it.

Building society interest

Building society interest received by individuals is treated in exactly the way described above for bank interest.

Dividends from UK companies

As you will know from your accounting studies, dividends paid by UK companies are paid out of profits which have borne corporation tax. When received by an individual the gross equivalent of the dividend must be included in statutory total income, but the individual's basic rate tax liability is covered by the company's payment of its corporation tax, part of which is imputed to the dividend as a tax credit. It is this tax credit which effectively pays the individual's basic rate tax liability on the dividend. The inclusion of the gross equivalent of the dividend in statutory total income means that higher rate tax may be due on it if the total income is high enough.

The tax on dividends received due under Schedule F is for our purposes always covered by the tax credit imputed to the dividend as described above.

Schedule D Cases IV and V

Introduction – income assessable

Schedule D Cases IV and V deal with tax on income derived from foreign sources. Such income can only be taxed when received by someone 'resident' in the UK. For tax purposes, the term 'resident' has a particular meaning examined in more detail below in relation to individuals. (The factors determining the residential status of companies are considered in Chapter 17.)

The rules of Case IV are really exactly the same as those of Case V, but the income assessable is different.

Case IV: Interest on foreign *securities*, such as debentures in foreign companies or foreign Government securities.
The word 'security' is used here to mean an investment with some underlying security, such as the assets of the company issuing the debentures or the guarantee of a foreign government. For this reason equity shares in foreign companies are assessed under Case V. If interest is paid through a UK paying agent, it is taxed under Schedule C, as explained above.

Case V: Income from foreign *possessions*, including:

- Dividends on foreign shares
- Rents received on foreign properties
- Profits of foreign businesses controlled abroad
- Foreign pensions
  (Salaries and wages derived from abroad are taxed under Schedule E)

Ordinary residence, residence and domicile

These terms are not statutorily defined. The Revenue's normal practice plus case law have led to the following practical definitions:

(a) Ordinary residence
An individual is 'ordinarily resident' in the UK if he or she normally and habitually lives in the UK with some degree of continuity. Thus most of the UK population is 'ordinarily resident' here. A person entering the UK for the first time and intending to remain here permanently will be treated as ordinarily resident from the day of arrival.

(b) Residence
The term 'residence' means, for tax purposes, 'technically resident' – brought within the scope of UK tax by the application of rules to determine precisely when an individual enters the UK Revenue net.

These rules are that an individual becomes resident if he or she:

(i) Spends six months (183 days) or more of the fiscal year to 5 April in the UK.
(ii) Pays 'frequent and substantial' visits to the UK. Revenue practice is to treat visits for three months each year for four consecutive years as frequent and substantial.
(iii) Maintains a place of abode in the UK and visits the UK *at any time* during the fiscal year. (This rule does not apply to a person working full time in a trade, profession, vocation or employment carried on wholly outside the UK (s. 335 ICTA 1988.)

(c) Domicile
A person's domicile may loosely be defined as the country to which he or she intends to return when away from it. The present law is that a person acquires at birth the domicile of his or her father (illegitimate children that of the mother). An adult may subsequently adopt a different *domicile of choice* on transferring wholly to another country and severing all ties with the UK.

The significance of these definitions in determining a person's tax status is considered below. Appeals against the Revenue's determination of an individual's residential status may be made to the Special Commissioners and thence to the Courts (see Chapter 9).

Basis of assessment

The basis of assessment for Schedule D Cases IV and V is exactly as for Schedule D Case III – preceding year basis with the same arrangements in opening and closing years.

The assessment is on the full amount of overseas income arising, subject to two exceptions:

(a) Foreign pensions are entitled to a 10 per cent deduction from the amount arising
(b) Individuals who are either:
    (i) A British subject resident but not *ordinarily resident* in the UK
    (ii) A foreign subject resident but not *domiciled* in the UK, are taxed on overseas income to the extent that it is remitted to the UK

Sundry matters

(a) Unremittable income
If it is impossible for a taxpayer to obtain access to foreign income, perhaps because of exchange control restrictions in the country of origin, no assessment is raised until the income becomes remittable.

(b) Losses from foreign businesses
Case V losses may be relieved in three ways:

(i) By carrying forward against future profits of the same trade
(ii) By offset against other overseas *earned income* of the year of loss or the following year
(iii) By making a terminal loss claim for up to three years against profits of the same overseas trade.

Case V losses can never be relieved against UK-derived income or against overseas investment income.

Schedule D Case VI

Schedule D Case VI taxes any income not within the scope of any other Schedule or Case.

The basis of assessment under Schedule D Case VI is always actual – the actual income of the tax year to 5 April.

We have already met one source of income taxed under Schedule D Case VI in Chapter 6 – income from furnished lettings.

Other examples of Case VI income are:

(a) Post-cessation receipts – if a taxpayer receives income from a trade or profession after it has ceased, these 'post-cessation' receipts are taxed under Schedule D Case VI
(b) Casual commissions and profits from other isolated transactions.
(c) Sub-underwriting commissions
(d) Capital sum received on the sale of the right to receive future earnings

If a loss should arise on any Case VI source that loss can only be offset against other Case VI income of the year of loss or following years. The only escape from this restriction is that a loss on furnished lettings, so far as it relates to the use of the premises rather than to the furnishings, may be transferred into Schedule A and so claimed against profits assessed under Schedule A on landlord's repairing lease properties (see Chapter 6).

Summary

This chapter has dealt with sundry types of income. The most important sections for examination purposes are probably Schedule D Case III and bank interest. Note particularly exactly what income remains assessable under Schedule D Case III and the basis of assessment in opening and closing years.

Progress questions

Attempt these progress questions to test your absorption of the material in the Chapter. Rework them at intervals for revision. Answers are on page 395.

1 What income is assessed under Schedule C?

2 (a) Give three examples of income assessed under Schedule D Case III
(b) Explain (i) the normal basis of assessment under Schedule D Case III; (ii) the special bases in the opening and closing years
(c) What is the due date for tax under Schedule D Case III?

3 What income is taxed under:

(a) Schedule D Case IV:
(b) Schedule D Case V?

4 Explain the meaning given for tax purposes to the following terms:

(a) Residence
(b) Ordinary residence
(c) Domicile

5 When may overseas income of an individual not be taxed on the full amount arising?

6 Give four examples of income taxed under Schedule D Case VI.

9 Sundry matters

The administration of income tax, corporation tax and capital gains tax

So far in this book we have usually referred to the 'Revenue' in general terms without giving a precise definition of the officials concerned and their duties.

Figure 9 shows the hierarchy.

Parliament

The annual Finance Bill embodying the tax proposals for the forthcoming year is presented to Parliament by the Chancellor of the Exchequer in his Budget Speech, usually in March each year.

The Finance Bill is debated in Parliament and emerges, usually in July or August, as the Finance Act.

Parliament thus has the final say as to the content of the legislation.

Chancellor of the Exchequer

The Chancellor of the Exchequer is the link between Parliament and the Treasury. As indicated above, the Chancellor presents the Budget to Parliament and also has control over the permanent civil servants in the Treasury.

Treasury

The Treasury is responsible for the control of Government expenditure and income. Its responsibilities in controlling the assessment and collection of income tax, corporation tax and capital gains tax are discharged through the Board of Inland Revenue.

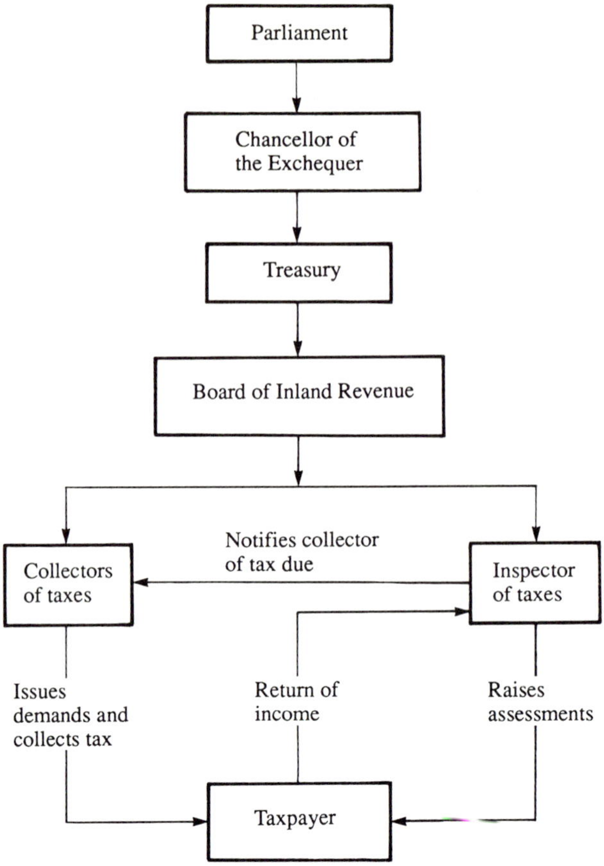

Figure 9 *Tax administration*

Board of Inland Revenue

The Board of Inland Revenue is the 'board of directors' in control of the local inspectors and collectors who have contact with individual taxpayers. The members of the Board of Inland Revenue are the Commissioners of Inland Revenue, who are full-time civil servants.

Inspectors of taxes

The whole country is divided into many tax districts, each under the control of an *inspector of taxes*, whose job it is to assess the tax due from each taxpayer in the district. The inspectors of taxes issue an annual return of income form to taxpayers, on the basis of which assessments are issued. The inspectors of taxes have power to negotiate settlements with taxpayers, who also have extensive rights of appeal which are detailed below. The inspector of taxes concerned in an appeal will usually represent the Revenue at appeal proceedings before the General Commissioners or Special Commissioners (see below).

Collectors of taxes

The inspectors of taxes have nothing to do with the actual collection of tax. There is a parallel organization of *collectors of taxes* who issue demands for the tax and take the necessary steps to secure its payment.

Appeal procedure

If a taxpayer is dissatisfied with an assessment, he has thirty days after issue of the assessment to appeal against it.

The appeal, which must be in writing and state the grounds for the appeal, is lodged with the inspector of taxes. The vast majority of appeals are settled by negotiation between the inspector of taxes and the taxpayer or his or her agent. If they cannot reach an agreement, the taxpayer has a right of appeal as shown in Figure 10.

The taxpayer may choose whether to appeal to the General Commissioners or the Special Commissioners. (Neither of these has anything to do with the Commissioners of Inland Revenue incidentally.)

General commissioners

The general commissioners are unpaid local citizens appointed by the Lord Chancellor. They are not tax experts and the taxpayer would not choose to appear initially before the general commissioners if he wished to argue a complex point of tax law. Their main function is to hear tax appeals.

Special commissioners

The special commissioners are full-time paid civil servants appointed by the Lord Chancellor. They are tax experts and their main function is to hear tax appeals. They are based in London but do go on circuit to provincial centres.

Appeal procedure through the courts

The decision of either general commissioners or special commissioners *on a question of fact* is *final*. On a point of law it is possible for either the taxpayer or the Revenue to appeal to the High Court.

The procedure to initiate an appeal is as follows:

(a) The taxpayer or the Revenue wishing to appeal must *express dissatisfaction* immediately on hearing the commissioners' decision. If this is not done the right of appeal is lost.

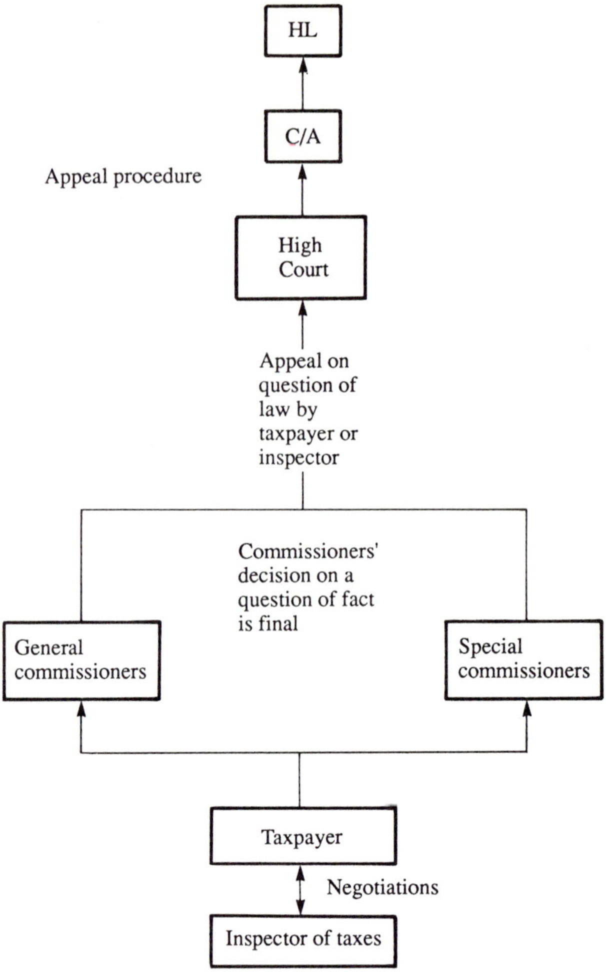

Figure 10

(b) Within thirty days after the commissioners' decision, the taxpayer or Revenue must give written notice to the clerk to the commissioners requesting them to state a case for the High Court (Fee £25).
(c) The case stated by the commissioners must then be sent by the appellant (the person appealing) to the High Court within thirty days of its receipt.
(d) The appeal is then heard in the High Court (Chancery Division) and a decision reached to confirm, increase or reduce the assessment.
(e) Either party may then appeal to the Court of Appeal and then to

the House of Lords, or by the special 'leap-frogging' procedure direct to the House of Lords.

Due dates for payment of income tax, interest on overdue tax and repayment supplements

Normal due dates

Schedule or Case	*Due date*
Schedule A	1 January in year of assessment
Schedule D Cases I and II	In two equal instalments on 1 January in year of assessment and following 1 July
Schedule D Cases III to VI	1 January in year of assessment
Schedule E	Deductions due from employer monthly within fourteen days of end of each month to 5th of month

If an assessment under Schedule A or D is not raised until after these dates, (or within less than thirty days before them) the due date is thirty days after the date of the assessment.

Effect of appeals

If the taxpayer appeals against an assessment, it is usually because he or she considers the amount demanded excessive. Merely appealing does not change the normal due dates shown above. To achieve this, it is necessary to apply for *postponement* of some or all of the tax. The inspector will then consider the application for postponement and agree what is considered reasonable in the circumstances.

When there is an appeal *and* an application for postponement of all or part of the Tax the normal due dates are modified as follows:

(a) For the part of the tax *not* postponed:
Due date is *later* of:
  (i) Thirty days after the Inspector's agreement to the postponement application
  (ii) The normal due date as shown above.

(b) For the part of the tax which *is* postponed:
Due date is *later* of:
  (i) Thirty days after notice of tax due following determination of appeal
  (ii) The normal due date as shown above.

Interest on overdue tax

If tax due is not paid by the dates listed above, interest (currently at 7.25 per cent) may be charged. Such interest is not an allowable deduction for tax purposes. Interest not exceeding £30 is usually waived.

The rate of interest charged varies frequently and rates for examination use will be given in the question.

The interest runs from the 'reckonable' date, which is normally the due date determined as explained above. There is one exception to this rule – if the due date as determined in (a) (i) and (b) (i) above falls later than 1 July following the end of the tax year concerned, the reckonable date is taken as that 1 July. This date of 1 July is referred to as the 'Table' date.

All that must seem unbearably complicated. Here is an illustration to help:

Illustration 9.1

Harriet is in business as a management consultant. For 1988/89 the inspector of taxes issued an assessment on her on 10 November 1988 for £40,000. She appealed against the assessment on 4 December 1988 and for postponement of payment of £15,000 tax, which was agreed by the inspector of taxes on 3 January 1989.

The appeal was determined on 10 August 1989 and the total liability was £28,000.

Payments were made as follows:

£12,500 (first instalment of tax not postponed)	10 February 1989
£12,500 (second instalment of tax not postponed)	6 July 1989
£3,000 in settlement	20 September 1989

Calculate the interest chargeable, assuming a rate of 7.25 per cent throughout.

Applying the rules set out above we have:

	Amount £	*Original due date*	*Due date on postponement*	*Reckonable date*	*Actual payment date*
(i) First instalment	12,500	1 Jan 1989	2 Feb 1989	2 Feb 1989	10 Feb 1989
(ii) Second instalment	12,500	1 July 1989	1 July 1989	1 July 1989	6 July 1989
(iii) Settlement	3,000	1 Jan/1 July 1989	9 Sept 1989	1 July 1989	20 Sept 1989

Interest due will be:

(i)	£12,500 × 7/365 × 7.25%	17.38
(ii)	£12,500 × 5/365 × 7.25%	12.41
(iii)	£3,000 × 81/365 × 7.25%	48.27
		£78.06

Repayment supplements

A repayment supplement is really interest *allowed* by the Revenue on repayments of tax in certain circumstances.

If a repayment of tax is paid more than twelve months after the end of the tax year to which it relates, a tax-free repayment supplement may be due if the tax repayment is £25 or more.

The repayment supplement is calculated at the current rate (7.25 per cent at the time of writing) from the 'relevant time' until the end of the tax month in which the repayment is made.

The 'relevant time' is the *later* of:

(a) The end of the tax year *after* that *for* which the repayment is made.
(b) The end of the tax year in which the tax was originally paid by the taxpayer, *if that payment was more than twelve months after the end of the tax year to which it relates.*

Note that the rate of repayment supplement varies frequently and will be given in the examination if needed.

Illustration 9.2

Ignatius paid tax of £10,000 in respect of 1988/89 in two instalments on 1 January 1989 and 1 July 1989. It was subsequently agreed that the liability should have been only £6,000. A repayment of £4,000 tax was made on:

(a) 10 March 1990
(b) 8 June 1991

Is Ignatius entitled to a repayment supplement?

The tax was paid within twelve months of the end of the tax year to which it relates. Repayment supplement would accordingly begin to run from 6 April 1990. No repayment supplement is therefore due for (a). In (b) however, repayment supplement would run from 6 April 1990 to 5 July 1991:

Repayment supplement due:

£4,000 × 15/12 × 7.25%	£362.50

Note that the repayment supplement period will always begin on 6 April and end at the end of an income tax month. Calculations may therefore be done in months.

Summary

Introduction

Most students regard the contents of this chapter as unnecessary knowledge outside the main stream of tax examination questions. Nevertheless, it is useful to have these matters in your head – you could score heavily and fairly easily if they came up, and in answering other written questions it adds conviction to your answer if you refer to the correct Revenue official, due date etc.

Administration

One important point to grasp here is the distinction between collectors of taxes and H.M. inspectors of taxes. These titles are often confused, yet each title does in fact state the responsibility of the officials concerned.

Appeal procedure

Points to note particularly here are:

(a) The fact that the 'Commissioners of Inland Revenue' who make up the Board of Inland Revenue have nothing at all to do with the 'general commissioners' and 'special commissioners' whose function is to hear appeals by the taxpayer.
(b) The decision of the general commissioners or special commissioners on a question of *fact* is *final*. Either the Revenue or the taxpayer may initiate an appeal through the courts, but only on a question of *law*.

Due dates

As a minimum, be sure you know the normal due dates for all Schedules and Cases.

Progress questions

Attempt these questions to check your absorption of the material in the chapter, and rework tham from time to time for revision. Answers are on pages 395–6.

1 Distinguish between the commissioners of Inland Revenue, the special commissioners and the general commissioners.

2 Explain the procedure of appeal if the taxpayer and the inspector of taxes cannot agree an assessment.

3 What are the normal due dates for payment of tax under:

(a) Schedule D Cases I and II?
(b) Schedule D Case III?

4 How will the normal due dates be affected, if at all, in the following circumstances:

(a) The taxpayer appeals against an assessment but makes no application for postponement?
(b) The taxpayer appeals against an assessment and applies for postponement of part of the tax?

5 What is the meaning of the term 'reckonable date'?

6 Explain the circumstances in which a repayment supplement may be due to a taxpayer.

10 Tax planning for individuals

Introduction

What is tax planning? In a nutshell it means arranging your affairs *within the tax laws* in such a way as to minimize your tax liability.

In a book of this kind we do not need to deal with the complex schemes devised from time to time by 'prospectors digging for wealth in the subterranean passages of the Revenue' as Lord Denning once called them. There are, however, some well-recognized points where it is folly not to take advantage of a concession which is on offer.

Many of the points mentioned below have been dealt with elsewhere in the book. The purpose of this chapter is to bring them all together for convenience of study and reference.

Tax avoidance and tax evasion

Tax *avoidance* means *legally* reducing your tax liability and is another term for tax planning.

Tax *evasion* means trying to do the same thing *illegally*, for example by failing to declare a source of taxable income to the Revenue in your annual return of income.

Retirement annuity policies and personal pension schemes

Introduction

It is normal prudence for an individual to make provision for his or her retirement. Many employees benefit from an employment-based pension scheme, and we have seen in Chapter 7 above that employees' contributions to such schemes are allowable deductions under Schedule E.

What about self-employed individuals, or those in non-pensionable employment? For many years, it has been possible for such people to take out an insurance policy which provides an annuity on retirement, and obtain tax relief on the premiums paid, subject to certain limits.

These arrangements ceased on 30 June 1988, though payments made after that date for policies taken out up to that date continue to qualify for tax relief.

From 1 July 1988 *personal pension* schemes, similar in many ways to the retirement annuity arrangements, are introduced.

Retirement annuity policies

Anyone under seventy-five years of age and either self-employed or in non-pensionable employment can continue to obtain tax relief for premiums paid on policies entered into up to 30 June 1988 to provide an annuity on retirement between the ages of sixty and seventy-five (earlier for some trades or professions) subject to the following conditions:

(a) Limit by reference to net relevant income

The maximum allowable is 17½ per cent of 'net relevant earnings' increased as indicated in (b) below for taxpayers born 1933 or earlier.

'Net relevant earnings' means:

(i) Income taxable under Schedule E, including benefits in kind and less all other allowable expenses
(ii) Adjusted profit of a trade, profession or vocation (Schedule D Cases I or II), less capital allowances and loss relief

Each spouse of a married couple may claim relief in respect of his or her net relevant income.

Up to 5 per cent of the contributions may be used to provide a benefit on death before reaching age seventy-five.

(b) Increased percentage of net relevant income for older taxpayers

The maximum allowable percentage of net relevant income is increased for older taxpayers. The percentages are:

Age of taxpayer at beginning of year	*Percentage*
Up to 50	17½
51 to 55	20
56 to 60	22½
61 or more	27½

(c) Carry forward of unused relief
If the premiums paid in any year are less than the maximum allowable, the shortfall may be carried forward for up to six years and used in later years in which the amount paid exceeds the maximum available in those years.

(d) Carry back of premium
A premium in a tax year may, at the taxpayer's option, be wholly or partly carried back into the immediate preceding tax year or, if there are no net relevant earnings in that year, into the year before that.

(e) Benefits
When the policy matures, the taxpayer receives an annuity which is taxed as earned income. He or she also has the option to receive part of the benefits in the form of a lump sum. The maximum lump sum obtainable is three times the reduced pension produced by the policy after taking out that lump sum, with an overall limit of £150,000.

(f) The policy must be with a UK insurance company

(g) The Revenue must give their approval to the terms of the scheme

Illustration 10.1

Joseph is forty-eight years old and an employee of Q Limited. In 1988/89 his salary was £18,000, benefits in kind totalled £1,400 and allowable expenses were £800. He also runs a small business which in 1988/89 had adjusted profits of £2,900. Capital allowances were £900.

Joseph paid £4,000 premium on an approved retirement annuity contract in 1988/89. His net relevant income and retirement annuity premiums in previous years have been:

	Net relevant income	*Retirement annuity premiums paid*
	£	£
1982/83	14,000	1,000 (first premium)
1983/84	16,000	2,000
1984/85	18,000	3,000
1985/86	18,000	3,000
1986/87	19,000	5,000
1987/88	20,000	4,000

Premium allowable in 1988/89 is:

$17\frac{1}{2}\% \times ((£18{,}000 + £1{,}400 - £800 + (£2{,}900 - £900)) =$	£3,605
Brought forward from earlier years per working below	275
Total allowable	£3,880

No relief can be obtained for the remaining £120 of the £4,000 premiums paid.

	Net relevant income	*17½% thereof*	*Premium paid*	*Balance*
	£	£	£	£
1982/83	14,000	2,450	1,000	1,450
1983/84	16,000	2,700	2,000	2,150
1984/85	18,000	3,150	3,000	2,300
1985/86	18,000	3,150	3,000	2,450
1986/87	19,000	3,325	5,000	775
1987/88	20,000	3,500	4,000	275

The unused relief for the years 1982/83 to 1985/86 is mainly used in 1986/87 and 1987/88, leaving £275 to be carried forward to 1988/89.

Personal pension schemes

As from 1 July, no new retirement annuity policies of the type described above can be taken out. However, a new scheme introduced as from that date retains the principle and many of the details of the old scheme just described.

Differences in the new scheme are:

(a) The age range within which the annuity may normally commence is increased to 50–75 (from 60–75)
(b) When the policy matures, the lump sum option is limited to 25 per cent of the total value of the benefits under the scheme, up to a maximum of £150,000. (This means a small reduction in the proportion of the benefit available as a lump sum.)
(c) Employers may contribute to schemes for their employees
(d) The Department of Health and Social Security (DHSS) will make a contribution to the scheme
(e) The contributions to the scheme will be paid net of income tax at basic rate
(f) Personal pension schemes may be offered by banks, building societies and unit trusts as well as by insurance companies.

Deeds of covenant

A deed of covenant is a legally binding agreement in which one person (the covenantor) agrees to transfer some of his or her income each year to a beneficiary. Until 14 March 1988, the use of covenants was a popular tax avoidance device, because their effect, if some basic conditions were met, was to transfer the income for tax purposes from the covenantor to the beneficiary. Thus if, for example, a parent wanted to contribute to the support of a son or daughter over eighteen at universi-

Table 8

Covenant	*Tax treatment*
To a registered charity	Provided the covenant is irrevocable and for a period which can exceed *three years*, the first £5,000 of the payment is deductible by the payer in calculating basic rate tax liability. The payer deducts tax at basic rate in making the payment and the charity, being exempt from income tax, can obtain a refund of the tax deducted.
To an individual and entered into on or after 15 March 1988	No tax effect. The payer will get no relief and the beneficiary will not be able to claim a refund. No tax will be deducted from the payments.
To an individual and entered into before 15 March 1988	Provided the covenant is irrevocable, for a period which can exceed *six* years, and *not* in favour of the taxpayers' infant (under 18) unmarried child, the payment is deductible by the payer in calculating basic rate tax liability and is treated as the income of the payee. The payer deducts tax at basic rate in making the payment and the payee will obtain a refund to the extent that the tax deducted exceeds his or her tax liability.

ty, a deed of covenant would transfer some of the parent's income to the child.

As from 15 March 1988, however, a different system has been introduced by FA 1988. It will no longer be possible for *new* covenants entered into on or after that date to operate as a transfer of income for tax purposes, except when the beneficiary is a registered charity. Covenants entered into before that date will continue to attract tax relief.

The income tax position of deeds of covenant is shown in Table 8.

Opening years of a new business

The income tax rules for the opening years of a business offer plenty of opportunity for tax planning. For example, the choice of accounting date, and of the period of the first accounts, can make a big difference to tax liabilities, since the result of the first twelve months' trading will form the basis of three years' assessments.

We may have two objectives in choosing the first accounting period and accounting dates:

Make up accounts so that the result for the first twelve months is as low as possible

Illustration 10.2

A new business commences on 1 January 1988. Trade builds up slowly and the results in the early years are:

	£
Year ended 31 December 1988	3,000
9 months ended 30 September 1989	18,000
3 months ended 31 December 1989	6,000

Calculate the assessments for the first years of business if the first accounts are made up for:

(i) 12 months to 31 December 1988
(ii) 21 months to 30 September 1989

Ignore taxpayer's option s. 62 ICTA 1988. Work out your own answer before studying the rest of the illustration – it will give you useful revision of the opening year rules.

(i) Accounts for 12 months to 31 December 1988

		£
1987/88	Actual 1.1.88 to 5.4.88 3/12 × £3,000	750
1988/89	1st 12 months 1.1.88 to 31.12.88	3,000
1989/90	Preceding year	3,000
1990/91	Preceding year	24,000
		£30,750

(ii) Accounts for 21 months to 30 September 1989

		£
1987/88	Actual 1.1.88 to 5.4.88 3/12 × £21,000	3,000
1988/89	1st 12 months 1.1.88 to 31.12.88	
	12/21 × £21,000	12,000
1989/90	As 1988/89	12,000
1990/91	Year to 30.9.89	
	12/21 × £21,000	12,000
		£39,000

There is a considerable tax advantage in this case in making up first accounts for a twelve month period.

Make up accounts to a date early in the tax year rather than later, to get the maximum deferral of the due date

This is perhaps a subsidiary objective, to be pursued if there is no other dramatic benefit to be derived. If everything else is equal, an accounting date of 30 April implies a due date twenty months later, whereas an accounting date of 31 March leads to one only nine months later.

Finally, bear in mind that non-tax considerations may dictate a preferred accounting date. If a business is heavily dependent on bank finance, and the cyclical nature of the business causes the overdraft to fluctuate widely, it may be intelligent to choose an accounting date at which the overdraft is relatively low. Other businesses may choose a date when stocks are cyclically low.

Selection of date of cessation of business

The rules governing the Revenue's rights on cessation of a business were explained in Chapter 3. A tax planning point is that it can make a considerable difference when a business does in fact cease. A taxpayer may have plans to cease trading at 31 March, but may be in a position to continue until 30 April if necessary. The choice of that date may be critical, because it will affect the tax year of cessation and hence the two years to which the Revenue's option may apply. Since the profits of some period must escape taxation on cessation if the business has traded long enough to get onto the preceding year basis of assessment, the taxpayer's choice of termination date may have a big influence on the benefit to the Revenue of their option.

Illustration 10.3

G has been in business for several years and has recently been experiencing a very successful period of trading. A limited company, in the same trade, has made a very attractive cash offer for the business, which G has decided to accept.

The sale is to take place some time during the spring of 1987 and the following information relating to G's recent profits, as agreed for tax purposes, is available:

	£
Year ended 31 December 1983	8,000
Year ended 31 December 1984	24,000
Year ended 31 December 1985	36,000
Year ended 31 December 1986	48,000

G estimates that the profits for the next few months will be:

	£
Three months to 31 March 1987	6,000
One month to 30 April 1987	1,000

You are required to

(a) Advise G as to whether he should dispose of the business at 31 March 1987 or 30 April 1987. Your advice should be supported by computations of the income assessable under Schedule D Cases I for all of the tax years concerned under each alternative;

Again work out your own answer before proceeding – incidentally this illustration is part of Q5 from the May 1987 CIMA Business Taxation paper.

(a) Cessation at 31 March 1987
Assessments:

			Revenue option	
				£
1986/87	Actual 6.4.86 to 31.3.87			
		£		
	9/12 × £48,000	36,000		
	1.1.87 to 31.3.87	6,000		
		42,000		
1985/86	Year ended 31.12.84	24,000	Actual	
			9/12 × £36,000	27,000
			3/12 × £48,000	12,000
				£39,000
1984/85	Year ended 31.12.83	8,000	Actual	
			9/12 × £24,000	18,000
			3/12 × £36,000	9,000
				£27,000

(b) Cessation at 30 April 1987

			Revenue option	
		£		£
1987/88	Actual 6.4.87 to 30.4.87	1,000		
1986/87	Year ended 31.12.85	36,000	Actual	
			9/12 × £48,000	36,000
			1.1.87 to 5.4.87	6,000
				42,000
1985/86	Year ended 31.12.84	24,000	Actual	
			9/12 × £36,000	27,000
			3/12 × £48,000	12,000
				39,000
1984/85	Year ended 31.12.83	8,000		

Final assessments for all years will be:

	Cessation 31.3.87	*Cessation 30.4.87*
	£	£
1987/88		1,000
1986/87	42,000	42,000
1985/86	39,000	39,000
1984/85	27,000	8,000
	£108,000	£90,000

By continuing to trade for another month G earns an extra £1,000 profit and still effects a reduction of £18,000 in the total tax assessments of the four years affected.

Loss relief strategy

Optimum strategy for income tax losses has been explained in Chapter 5, but is repeated here to provide convenient coverage of all tax planning points.

The final objective must be to obtain the greatest possible reduction in tax liability or tax refund. That means trying not to use loss relief to eliminate income which would in any case be covered by personal reliefs. Under s. 380 this can frequently be arranged by not extending the claim to the loss-making spouse's income. The size of the loss may be manipulated to some extent by either not extending the claim to include capital allowance, or including capital allowances in the loss claim after first having renounced part of them.

We may set up the following objectives and methods of achieving them.

Objectives		*Methods*	
1	Preserve some income in each year so as not to lose benefit of personal reliefs	(a)	Do not extend s. 380 claim to spouse's income
2	Equalize income between tax years to minimize higher rate tax	(b)	If advantageous exclude capital allowances from claim, or renounce capital allowances in part before including them
3	Claim under s. 381 of possible, are highest to maximize benefit	(c)	Claim under s. 380 for only one of the two years for which a claim is possible
4	Claim so as to get relief as quickly as possible	(d)	Claim under s. 381 of possible, to involve more years in the claim

Maximizing capital allowances

As we have seen from the previous section, intelligent handling of the taxpayer's right to renounce capital allowances can be beneficial when a loss has been made.

One other basic point should also be mentioned – it may be useful to remounce capital allowances when profits are below personal allowance level, or would be reduced below that level if capital allowances were claimed in full.

Consider too the de-pooling election for short life assets (look back to Chapter 4 if you've forgotten how this works).

Business Expansion Scheme

The Business Expansion Scheme was introduced to encourage investment in smaller companies. In a nutshell it is the right to deduct from income any capital sums invested in UK companies carrying on a qualifying trade, up to a limit of £40,000 per year. Each investment must have a minimum value of £500 to qualify. This is obviously a considerable attraction to a taxpayer with an income of, say £150,000 per year, a substantial part of which would be taxed at 40 per cent.

Obviously such an attractive scheme must have restrictions built into it, not least restrictions on the taxpayer's right to retain the relief if the shares are sold after acquisition.

Here are brief details of the conditions:

(a) The relief is only available to individuals (not companies etc.), who are resident and ordinarily resident in the UK and not 'connected' with the company issuing the shares within the period beginning two years before the issue and ending five years after it. 'Connected' for this purpose means being:

  (i) an employee of the company
  (ii) a partner of the company
  (iii) a director of the company (unless no remuneration is received)

The restriction extends to bar the relief if close relatives and other associates occupy such positions.

(b) Not more than 30 per cent of the share capital may be acquired.
(c) The shares must be acquired from the company issuing them and not from another holder.
(d) The shares must be unquoted equity shares carrying no preferential rights.
(e) For issues after 15 March 1988 the maximum raised by a company making an issue under the Business Expansion Scheme is generally £500,000.
(f) The company must be resident in the UK, carrying on a qualifying trade (see (g) below) and not a subsidiary of another company.
(g) Relief will only be available if the company issuing the shares is carrying on a 'qualifying trade' on a commercial basis. The following trades or operations do not qualify:

  (i) dealing in commodities, shares, securities, land or futures,
  (ii) dealing in goods otherwise than in the course of wholesaling or retailing
  (iii) banking, insurance, moneylending, hire purchase financing,
  (iv) leasing, or receiving royalties or licence fees
  (v) providing legal or accounting services
  (vi) farming
  (vii) property development. Note: The Finance Act 1988 does, however, extend relief to a company providing residential accommodation under assured tenancies.

(h) If the shares are sold or given away within five years of acquisition, or other conditions are broken, the relief is withdrawn by means of a Schedule D Case VI assessment for the tax year in which relief was obtained. If the shares are given away, the whole of the relief is taken back. If they are sold, the relief is reduced by the consideration received on disposal.

The calculation of any capital gains tax due on the disposal is also affected. This aspect is illustrated in Chapter 22.

Illustration 10.4

Saskia had an income for tax purposes of £80,000 in 1988/89. During 1988/89 she invested £20,000 in shares of Rembrandt Limited, a company which qualified for her to obtain relief under the Business Expansion Scheme. Three years later she sold the shares for £18,000.

Show how her tax position will be affected by these transactions.

(a) *1988/89* – In 1988/89 Saskia's statutory total income will be reduced by £20,000, thus reducing her tax liability by £20,000 at 40 per cent, or £8,000.
(b) *Year of sale* – In the year of sale, a Schedule D Case VI assessment for 1988/89 will be raised on Saskia in the sum of £18,000. She will thus have to pay back the benefit obtained earlier. If the shares had been sold for £28,000 the maximum which could be clawed back would, of course, be tax on the £20,000 on which relief was originally obtained, or £8,000.

Summary

This is an important chapter. You should expect that questions not directed solely at tax planning will have tax planning aspects to be commented upon. One of the important tasks of accountants in an organization is to advise on the tax consequences of different courses of action and to ensure that tax liabilities are minimized where possible in planning and executing transactions.

Tax planning for companies is dealt with in Chapter 18 and capital gains tax planning in Chapter 24.

Progress questions

Attempt these questions to test your absorption of the material in the chapter. Rework the questions at intervals for revision. Answers are on page 396.

1 Is tax avoidance legal?

2 Are the following statements true or false?

		True	False
(a)	17½ per cent of the premiums paid under a retirement annuity or a personal pension scheme may be deductible for tax purposes by an individual aged fifty or under		✓
(b)	If retirement annuity premium or personal pension scheme in excess of the percentage limit is paid in any tax year, the excess may be carried forward and relieved in the next tax year.		
(c)	The taxpayer may elect to relate premiums paid in one tax year back to the previous tax year.		

3 What is 'net relevant income'?

4 List six differences between personal pension schemes and the old retirement annuity arrangements.

5 What deeds of covenant remain tax deductible for 1988/89 and later years?

6 What two major objectives, from a tax point of view, should an individual have in choosing his or her first accounting period and accounting date when starting a new business?

7 Why may the choice of cessation date affect the tax liability of a trader?

8 List your objectives in maximizing loss reliefs and explain briefly the methods by which they may be achieved. Quote relevant ICTA 1988 section references.

9 How can the de-pooling election available for most short life plant and machinery be beneficial?

10 What are the main conditions to be satisfied for an investment to qualify for the Business Expansion Scheme?

11 List five trades or activities which do not qualify for the Business Expansion Scheme.

Part Two Corporation Tax

11 Corporation tax – basic principles

Introduction and definitions

We now turn to one of the most important sections of the CIMA syllabus, corporation tax. Much of the work you have done on income tax carries over into corporation tax. For example, the adjustment of profit and capital allowances are very similar, and corporation tax loss reliefs have much in common with these for income tax.

Corporation tax is chargeable on companies resident in the UK or trading in the UK through a branch or agency. It is also chargeable on the taxable income of unincorporated associations like clubs, but we shall concentrate entirely in this book on the liability of companies to corporation tax.

Corporation tax was introduced in 1965 and in setting it up the opportunity was taken to discard many of the old-established rules of income tax to try to achieve simplicity, at least in the basic structure. The first and most important difference with income tax is that the preceding year basis of assessment is not used, and 5 April has little significance. The structure of the Schedules and Cases is retained, however, it is quite correct, for example, to refer to a Schedule D Case I assessment to corporation tax.

Here is a summary of the basic rules of corporation tax:

- The rate of corporation tax is fixed for the year ended 31 March. We refer to the year to 31 March as the *financial* year, identifying it by naming the calendar year in which it *begins*. Thus 'the financial year 1987' means the year ended 31 March 1988. Rates of corporation tax in recent years have been:

Financial year	*Full rate (%)*	*Small companies rate (%)*
1983	50	30
1984	45	30
1985	40	30

	Full rate (%)	*Small companies rate* (%)
1986	35	29
1987	35	27
1988	35	25

The full rate applies to companies with a profit over £500,000 and the small companies rate to those with *profits* below £100,000. Between these two levels of profit there is a marginal arrangement explained in the next chapter.

- The period for which a company makes up its accounts is called its 'period of account'. This will normally be one year but need not necessarily be, of course.
- Companies pay corporation tax on the basis of the adjusted profits of their *accounting periods*. Most of the time the accounting period is the same as the company's period of account, but there can be differences. For example, one of the rules of the game is that an accounting period cannot exceed twelve months in length, so if a company makes up its accounts for a period of more than twelve months, that *period of account* has to be split into two *accounting periods*. The first twelve months of the period of account constitutes one accounting period and the remainder constitutes another. The corporation tax liability must be calculated separately for each accounting period. You can see that this rule is considerably simpler than the corresponding income tax rules using the preceding year basis. As a result, for corporation tax the following income tax problems disappear:

    (i) Overlapping basic periods in opening years. Instead, we have a straightforward sequence of accounting periods, usually coinciding with the company's periods of account.
    (ii) Gaps between basic periods in closing years
    (iii) Difficult rules for change of accounting date
    (iv) Special arrangements for capital allowances in the opening years. In fact, in a corporation tax computation we deduct capital allowances *in arriving at* the adjusted profit, instead of deducting them *from* the adjusted profit as we do for income tax

- Accounting periods are normally the same as periods of account – most companies usually make up their accounts for twelve month periods. The following special rules define more precisely when an accounting period of a company is treated as beginning or ending:

    (i) An accounting period *begins* whenever a company not previously within the charge to corporation tax comes within it. An example would be a company not resident in the UK acquiring a source of income within the UK.
    (ii) An accounting period *ends*:
    – 12 months after its beginning
    – at the company's accounting date

  - when the company begins or ceases to trade
  - when the company begins or ceases to be resident in the UK
  - when the company ceases to be within the charge to corporation tax
  - on the company passing a resolution that it should be wound up, or on the presentation of a winding up petition followed by a winding up order.
- Companies pay corporation tax on their chargeable capital gains as well as on their income.
- The normal due date for payment of corporation tax for most companies is nine months after the end of the accounting period. Transitional arrangements are currently in force to ensure that all companies standardise to this interval by 1990. Thus a company making up accounts regularly to 30 April each year would be liable to pay its corporation tax on 1 February nine months later. If it gives a later due date, 30 days after the raising of the assessment is the alternative.

Corporation tax computations

A corporation tax computation is rather like the personal computation of an individual, as briefly explained in Chapter 1. We have to bring together the company's taxable income from all sources to arrive at the total income. Chargeable capital gains are added, and charges, such as debenture interest paid, are deducted. That gives us the amount chargeable to corporation tax.

Here is an example of the layout of a corporation tax computation, using illustrative figures:

X Limited – Corporation tax computation for accounting period of twelve months ended on 31 March 1988

	Reference to tutorial notes	£
Schedule D Case I	1	656,000
Schedule A	2	28,000
Schedule D Case III – bank interest	3	9,000
Building society interest received (grossed up)	4	1,000
Debenture interest received	5	2,000
Chargeable gains	6	4,000
		700,000
Less: Interest paid	7	40,000
Amount chargeable to corporation tax		660,000
Corporation tax at 35%		231,000
Less: Income tax relating to building society interest; £1,000 @ 25%		250
		£230,750

Tutorial notes

1 A separate working will deal with the adjustments necessary to obtain this figure from a given profit and loss amount. Capital allowances will be calculated and deducted in arriving at the adjusted profit. Any income not assessable under Schedule D Case I will be deducted and shown separately in the main computation as shown above.

2 The net income under Schedule A will be computed exactly as for income tax.

3 Bank interest received by a company continues to be received gross. The composite rate scheme described in Chapter 8 applies to individuals only. The amount included will be the interest actually *received* in the accounting period.

4 Building society interest received by companies is subject to corporation tax but is paid net of income tax. In a corporation tax computation the building society interest is first grossed up for income tax (net amount times, for 1988/89, 100/75), and that gross equivalent is included in the company's income.

5 Debenture interest received from other UK companies will be received under deduction of tax. Include the gross equivalent here. The treatment of the income tax deducted from it is explained in Chapter 12. Once again it is the gross equivalent of the amount actually *received* in the accounting period that must be included in the computation. (Note that when adjusting the profit and loss amount to get at the Schedule D Case I the amount eliminated from the profit and loss amount could have been the accrued amount. Thus the figure deducted in adjusting the profit is not necessarily the same as the figure brought into the computation.)

6 Chargeable gains – chargeable gains by companies are first computed according to the rules of capital gains tax, then charged to corporation tax at 35 per cent or 25 per cent depending on the profit level.

7 Interest paid – The deduction here is the gross amount of the interest actually *paid* in the year. Once again there may be a difference between the *accrued* interest disallowed in adjusting the profit and loss amount and the interest *paid* deducted as a charge at the end of the computation.

Allowable and disallowable expenditure for Schedule D Cases I and II

The rules for allowing and disallowing expenditure in a company's Schedule D Case I/II computation are broadly as for income tax. Before proceeding further, take a look back to Chapter 2 to revise the income tax rules. There are minor differences for corporation tax which are:

(a) There can be no disallowance of expenses as being private expenditure of the proprietor. If directors of the company enjoy benefits of this kind the full amount is allowable in the company's computation and the individual is subject to tax on the benefits derived under the Schedule E rules explained in Chapter 7.
(b) Capital allowances are calculated and deducted in the computation (see below).
(c) Appropriations of profit like dividends, transfers to reserve etc. are obviously disallowed. (It is normal to begin the computation with the profit before tax and before these appropriations, so it is unlikely that an actual adjustment for these items will be required.)
(d) Companies (other than close companies, see Chapter 16) are allowed to make charitable donations on a basis not available to individual taxpayers. They may donate up to 3 per cent of the *dividends paid* in any given accounting period. The payment is made under deduction of basic rate income tax which will be accounted for by the company as explained in Chapter 13. As payment is made under deduction of tax the item in the profit and loss account will be disallowed, and then the gross amount deducted as a charge at the end of the computation.
(e) Pre-trading expenditure – s. 401

A company incurring expenditure in the three years before it commences to trade may obtain relief for that expenditure as if it had been incurred on the day the trade is first carried (s. 401).

Relief is obviously dependent upon the expenditure being of an allowable nature.

This contrasts with the income tax position. For income tax purposes such pre-trading expenditure is treated as if it were a loss sustained in the year of assessment in which the business commenced.

Capital allowances

Capital allowances for corporation tax are calculated almost exactly as for income tax and as described in Chapter 4. Points of difference are:

(a) There are no problems in opening and closing years, or on change of accounting date, because in corporation tax there is never an overlap or gap between profit basis periods.
(b) The simplification in (a) allows capital allowances to be deducted *in arriving at* the adjusted profit rather than being deducted from the adjusted profit.
(c) There can be no private use of assets by a company. Capital allowances on assets with private use by directors will therefore be taken in full. The director may then have a liability under Schedule E as explained in Chapter 7. Note that for both income tax and

corporation tax private use *by employees* does not restrict capital allowances but may lead to a liability under Schedule E.

(d) Writing down allowances in corporation tax are apportioned according to the length of the accounting period. (This happens also in income tax, but far less frequently, being confined to the first assessment on a new business.) Note one further point. For corporation tax the 4 per cent writing down allowance on industrial buildings is apportioned according to the length of the basis period whereas for income tax it is not.

Income chargeable to corporation tax

As we have seen, income chargeable to corporation tax is broadly the same as income chargeable to income tax. We bring in income under the Schedules and Cases, except for Schedule F dealing with dividends from other UK companies (see (a) below). We also bring in the gross equivalent of debenture interest received and building society interest received.

Points of difference are:

(a) *Dividends received from other UK companies* – these are *exempt* from corporation tax, because paid out of profits which have already borne corporation tax in the hands of the company paying the dividend.

(b) *Bank interest* – bank interest is taxable whether received by an individual or by a company. The difference is that a company receives such interest gross and it is taxable under Schedule D Case III.

Treatment of capital gains

As explained above, any capital gains made by companies are taxed along with income at 35 per cent or 25 per cent, depending on the company's level of profit.

Charges

In the context of corporation tax the term 'charge' means a payment that a company is required to make out of its *total* income in the nature of interest or other annual payments such as patent royalties.

As we saw in above a company may make uncovenanted donations to charities under deduction of tax and these are treated as charges.

For our purposes it is reasonable to say that all charges paid by a company are paid under deduction of tax. Examples of charges on a company are:

(a) Loan interest or debenture interest paid
(b) Patent royalties

(c) Payments under deed of covenant
(d) Charitable donations paid under deduction of tax

In adjusting a company's profit for corporation tax purposes all these items are always *added back* in arriving at the company's Schedule D Case I income, and then the gross equivalent of the amount *paid* in the accounting period is deducted as a charge as the last item in the computation.

Working 1 (*for solution to example on page 146*)
Computation of Schedule D Case I Trading Income, accounting period ended 31 March 1989.

	£	£
	+	–
Net profit per accounts	98,000	
General expenses		
Entertainment (since 15.3.88 all disallowable)	7,000	
Legal expenses – re new office	500	
Cost of successful tax appeal	500	
Architect's fees	1,100	
Depreciation	30,000	
Capital allowances		28,000
Dividends from other UK companies		15,000
Profit on sale of shares		7,250
Building society interest		750
Rent received less outgoings		9,000
Bank interest receivable		4,000
	137,100	64,000
	64,000	
Trading income Schedule D Case I	£ 73,100	

Pantagruel Limited
Corporation tax computation, accounting period ended 31 March 1989

	£	£
Schedule D Case I (per working 1)		73,100
Schedule A		9,000
Building society interest (£750 × 100/75)		1,000
Schedule B Case III bank interest		4,000
		87,100
Chargeable capital gain		7,250
Amount chargeable to corporation tax		£94,350
Corporation tax at 25% – due 1 January 1990		23,587
Less: income tax relating to building society interest £750 × 25/75		250
		£23,337

A basic example

Pantagruel Limited was formed in 1970 and makes its accounts to 31 March each year. Its profit and loss account for the year ended 31 March 1989 was as follows:

	£	£
Sales		690,000
Cost of sales		480,000
Gross profit		210,000
Expenses		
Salaries and wages	69,000	
General expenses (see Note 1)	48,000	
Depreciation	31,000	
		148,000
Trading profit		62,000
Dividends from other UK companies (amount received)		15,000
Profit on sale of shares (see Note 3)		7,250
Rents received less outgoings (all allowable)		9,000
Building society interest received (net)		750
Bank interest received		4,000
Net profit		£ 98,000

Notes

1 General expenses consisted of:

		£	£
Entertainment expenses:	UK Customers	3,000	
	Overseas customers	4,000	7,000
Legal expenses:	Debt collection	1,000	
	Staff service contracts	800	
	Negotiation of short lease for new offices	500	2,300
Cost of successful tax appeal			
Architect's fees for designing a new office which was not proceeded with			1,100
Sundry allowable items			37,600
			£48,000

2 Capital allowances for the year amounted to £28,000.

3 Shares purchased in 1985 for £12,500 were sold in September 1988 for £19,750. Take the gain for tax purposes to be £7,250 ignoring indexation.

Summary

The purpose of this chapter is to provide an elementary introduction to corporation tax. Examination questions will usually also involve matters dealt with in the next two chapters.

Definitions

Financial year Accounting period Period of account	Be sure you understand the meaning of each of these terms.

The accounting period

The events marking the beginning or end of an accounting period need to be known in readiness for a possible non-computational question on the subject.

An accounting period ends:

- 12 months after its beginning
- At an accounting date
- Commencement or cessation of trade
- Commencement or cessation of UK residence
- Company ceasing to be within the charge to corporation tax (a period *begins* when a company first comes within the charge to corporation tax)
- At winding up

Due date for payment

Nine months after the end of the accounting period or thirty days after the raising of the assessment, whichever is later.

Corporation tax computations

Study the form of the corporation tax computation. There is a specimen format above and an illustration above.

Generally speaking, the adjustment of profit for Schedule D Case I and capital allowance computation follows the same lines whether they are for income tax or for corporation tax.

Charges

Note the meaning of the term charge and the examples given. The vital point is that charges *accrued* in the profit and loss account must be added back in computing the company's Schedule D Case I trading income. The amount *paid* in the accounting period is then deducted as the last item in the computation.

Progress questions

Attempt the following questions to test your absorption of the material in this chapter. Rework them from time to time for revision. Answer are on page 397.

1 Match the following terms with their correct definitions:

Term	*Definition*
(a) Financial year	(a) Period for which a company makes up its accounts
(b) Accounting period	(b) Period for which the rate of corporation tax is fixed.
(c) Period of account	(c) Period for which corporation tax is charged.

2 What is the standard due date for payment of corporation tax?

3 List four differences between the adjustment of a company's profit or loss for Schedule D Case I and the corresponding adjustment for a sole trader.

4 List four differences between capital allowances for companies and capital allowances for individuals.

5 Are capital gains by companies subjected to capital gains tax or corporation tax? At what rate?

6 What are charges? Give three examples and explain how they are treated in a corporation tax computation.

12 Advance corporation tax and income tax

Advance corporation tax – introduction

A company pays its dividend out of profits which have borne corporation tax. Individual shareholders receiving the dividend are then taxed on the gross equivalent of the amount received. That could lead to a very heavy tax burden:

Illustration 12.1

	£
Company profit	100,000
Corporation tax @ 25%	25,000
	75,000
Dividend	75,000
	—

The total tax payable could be:

	£
Paid by company as above £100,000 @ 25%	25,000
Paid by individual shareholder £75,000 × 100/75 @ 25%	25,000
	£ 50,000

Half of the profit has disappeared in tax, and the individual shareholders may still have higher rate tax to pay.

That inequitable result is not what actually happens, as you may know from your accountancy studies.

What actually happens is that the individual shareholder's basic rate income tax liabilities are deemed to be discharged out of the company's corporation tax payment.

From the Revenue's point of view, the system is likely to be more satisfactory if they receive a payment on account of the company's eventual corporation tax liability at the time the dividend is paid. When a company pays a dividend it is required to pay *advance corporation tax* (ACT) to the Revenue at a rate linked to the basic rate of income tax. That ACT may then be deducted from the company's eventual corporation tax liability for the year, subject to limitations, and is taken as discharging the individual shareholders' basic income tax liabilities.

Thus continuing the illustration above, and assuming that the dividend of £75,000 was actually paid in the year, we should have:

On payment of £75,000 dividend: company would pay to the Revenue:
25/75 × £75,000 = £25,000 as ACT

By taking 25/75, we arrive at 25 per cent (basic income tax rate) on the gross equivalent of £100,000.

In this example the company would have no more corporation tax to pay, as the whole of the available profit for the year was distributed and the small companies rate of corporation tax is the same as the basic income tax rate.

Accounting for ACT

The system for accounting for ACT is fairly simple – the financial year to 31 March is divided into four return periods for the quarters to 30 June, 30 September, 31 December and 31 March and a company has to pay over its ACT on all distributions made in each quarter within 14 days after the end of the quarter. If the company's accounting period does not end on one of these four dates, the quarter in which the accounting date falls is divided into two return periods.

Details of the distributions made are notified to the Revenue on a form CT 61.

Dividends received

We noted in Chapter 11 that if a company receives a dividend from another UK company, that dividend is not subject to corporation tax because it is paid out of profit that has already been taxed in the hands of the paying company. There is a further point – the paying company will have paid advance corporation tax at the time the dividend was paid. That means that the receiving company is entitled to credit against its own ACT payment for ACT already paid.

Dividends received by one UK company from another are required by SSAP 8 to be included in the profit and loss account at the amount received plus the tax credit, the tax being shown as part of the tax charge for the year. The figure of dividends received plus tax credit is referred to as *franked* investment income, the word 'franked' being used here in the sense of 'passed' or 'approved' as having already been taxed. (The term 'franked payments' is used for the total of dividends etc. paid plus the associated tax credit.)

Distributions

So far we have spoken only of dividends received and paid, and these constitute the bulk of the distributions made by a company. However there are certain other distributions on which ACT also has to be paid. These 'qualifying distributions' include:

(a) Dividends, including capital dividends
(b) Interest in excess of a normal commercial rate
(c) Transfers of assets to members at below their market value (or acceptance of assets from members at *above* their market value)
(d) Bonus issue of shares followed by a repayment of share capital
(e) A repayment of share capital followed by a bonus issue.

There are other even more obscure ones. As you can see, these are all attempts to place value in the hands of members and as such must attract an ACT liability.

Illustration 12.2

In the year ended 31 March 1989, Actinia Limited had the following transactions:

1988		£
6 May	Received dividend	750
10 July	Received dividend	375
14 Aug	Paid dividend	75,000
10 Oct	Received dividend	1,200
1989		
20 Feb	Paid dividend	150,000

To sort out the ACT payments to be made it is first necessary to allocate the transactions to the return periods.

1 April to 30 June 1988

In the first return period to 30 June there is the receipt of a dividend, to which a tax credit of £250 (25/75 × £750) is related. No refund of this credit can be obtained, however, since it is only possible to use these credits to reduce ACT. A refund during the year is only possible when ACT has already been paid in an earlier return period within the accounting period.

1 July to 30 September 1988

In the second return period we have a dividend received and a dividend paid. The tax credit on the dividend received, and the tax credit on the dividend received in the first return period, may be used to reduce the ACT due on the dividend paid.

1 October to 31 December 1988
Here a dividend is received, and a refund may be obtained for the tax credit of £400, because of the ACT payment made for the previous quarter.

1 January to 31 March 1989
A dividend is paid, there are no other relevant transactions, and the result is a simple payment of the £50,000 ACT involved.

The easiest way to present the answer is to use columns, as shown below. Note that you must calculate from the 'grossed up' amounts of franked payments and franked investment income. Do not try to cut corners by working with the amounts actually paid and received – this can lead to errors in more complicated examples.

Return period	*Franked payments*	*Franked investment income*	*ACT Paid*	*ACT Refund*	*Due date*
	£	£	£	£	
3 months ended					
30 June 1988		1,000			
30 Sept 1988	100,000	500	24,625		14 Oct 88
31 Dec 1988		1,600		400	14 Jan 89
31 Mar 1989	200,000		50,000		14 Apr 89
	300,000	3,100	74,625	400	

The net ACT paid of £74,625 will be offset against the corporation tax liability for the year ended 31 March 1989, subject to the limitations explained below.

Offset of ACT

ACT paid is exactly what its name implies – a payment on account of the corporation tax liability of the accounting period in which the relevant distributions were made. In the normal course of events all the ACT can be deducted from the total corporation tax liability. The balance of corporation tax remaining to be paid after deduction of ACT is referred to as *mainstream* corporation tax (MCT). There is a limit to the amount that can be offset – the maximum is the income tax rate of 25 per cent (1988/89) applied to the company's profit chargeable to corporation tax.

If full offset cannot be obtained, the ACT may be carried *back* for up to six years (LIFO) and offset in earlier years in which the ACT did not use up the maximum available for offset. If a claim to carry ACT back is made, the ACT relating to the year concerned is offset first, and only the balance of tax available (up to the maximum) is used to relieve the ACT carried back. It is also possible for a holding company to surrender the benefit of ACT to a 51 per cent subsidiary – see Chapter 15. Both of these claims must be made within two years of the end of the accounting period to which the ACT relates. If no claim is made for either of these, the surplus ACT is carried forward without time limit into future years.

To summarize, the order of offset, disregarding the surrender to subsidiaries, is:

(a) Against the corporation tax liability of the current accounting period, up to a limit found by applying the income tax rate to the profit chargeable to corporation tax.
(b) Backwards (LIFO) against any corporation tax liability of the previous six years, subject to the same limit as (a).
(c) Forwards without time limit against future corporation tax liabilities, again subject to the limit in (a). The right to carry forward surplus ACT may be lost if within a three year period there is a change in the ownership of the company combined with a change in the nature of its trade, or there is a major decline in the company's activities and a change in ownership after which its trade revives (s. 245).

One final point – the limit is now found by applying the basic income tax rate to *profit* – income plus capital gains. This has only been the case as from accounting periods beginning on or after 17 March 1987. Before that the limit was found by applying the basic income tax rate to income only, excluding capital gains.

Illustration 12.3

Overact Limited was formed on 1 April 1985 and makes up its accounts to 31 March each year. Results and dividends paid since formation have been:

	Year ended 31 March			
	1986	*1987*	*1988*	*1989*
	£	£	£	£
Trading income	500,000	600,000	700,000	800,000
Chargeable gains	—	—	40,000	70,000
Dividends received		71,000	73,000	75,000
Dividends paid	336,000	461,500	730,000	660,000
Corporation tax rates	40%	35%	35%	35%
ACT rates	3/7	29/71	27/73	25/75

None of the dividends were paid or received between 1 April and 5 April.

Discussion

For the year ended 31 March 1988 the ACT paid will have been 27/73 × £657,000 = £243,000. This exceeds the limit (27 per cent × £740,000 = £199,800) by £43,200. Relief may be sought by carrying this back into earlier years. Let us see what is available. We go first to the year ended 31 March 1987. The limit is 29 per cent of £600,000 or £174,000. The dividends paid in that period total £461,500 less dividends received £71,000, giving ACT paid of £159,500. Some of the 1988 excess can be used, and the remainder carried back into 1986, where the maximum offset is £150,000 (30% of £500,000), and only £144,000 is used. The balance of ACT still unrelieved is carried forward into 1989.

1988 ACT Relief Memorandum

	£
ACT paid in 1988	243,000
Relieved in 1988	199,800
	43,200
Carried back to 1987	14,500
	28,700
Carried back to 1986	6,000
Carried forward	22,700
Relieved in 1989	22,500
Carried forward into 1990	200

(see more detailed computation on page 156.)

Surplus of franked investment income

We have seen that if a company's franked payments for an accounting period exceed its franked investment income, ACT is paid and offset against the corporation tax liability.

What if franked investment income (FII) exceeds franked payments? This is fairly unlikely for a trading company, but could happen if, for example, a company with some dividend income paid no dividend of its own for some reason. In this situation no ACT will have been paid for the period, and there will be unrelieved tax credit attaching to the surplus FII.

The surplus FII is carried forward for relief in future periods against the franked payments of those periods. Note that it is the *FII* that is carried forward, not the value of the tax credit itself. The FII carried forward is treated as if it were received in the year in which offset is possible, and relief may therefore not be at the rate in force in the year in which the surplus arose. This point emphasizes the importance of working with the 'gross' amounts (franked payments and FII) rather than with tax or net figures when calculating ACT payable or repayable.

Changes in the rate of ACT

When the rate of ACT changes, two problems can arise:

(a) The maximum set-off of ACT for the accounting period will have to be computed

This is done by apportioning the income between the two parts of the accounting period *as if they were separate accounting periods* and applying the appropriate percentage to each part.

Here are the full calculations. It is realistic to compute each year separately, then see what scope exist for surplus ACT to be carried back.

	1986		*1987*		*1988*		*1989*	
	£	£	£	£	£	£	£	£
Trading income		500,000		600,000		700,000		800,000
Capital gains						40,000		70,000
		500,000		600,000		740,000		870,000
Corporation tax @ 40%		200,000						
@ 35%				210,000		259,000		304,500
ACT paid	144,000		159,500		243,000		195,000	
ACT brought forward							22,700	
							217,700	
Maximum offset								
30% × £500,000	150,000							
29% × £600,000			174,000					
27% × £740,000					199,800			
25% × £870,000							217,500	
ACT offset		144,000		159,000		199,800		217,500
Unused	6,000		14,500					
Excess					43,200		200	
Mainstream Corporation tax		£56,000		£50,500		£59,200		£87,000
Refund on carry-back of 1988 ACT	6,000		14,500					

The underlined phrase means that there could be a restriction on the offset of FII, which operates fully only within the same accounting period.

Of course, this problem does not arise if the company's accounting date is 31 March.

Illustration 12.4

Straddle Limited makes up its accounts for the year ended 30 September each year. In the year ended 30 September 1988 it had trading income of £500,000 and paid dividends as follows:

10 November 1987	73,000
14 August 1988	375,000

The rates of ACT were

1987/88	27/73
1988/89	25/75

The rate of corporation tax was 35 per cent throughout.

The corporation tax computation for the accounting period ended 30 September 1988 will be:

	£	£
Trading income		500,000
Corporation tax @ 35%		175,000
Less: ACT		
£73,000 × 27/73	27,000	
£375,000 × 25/75	125,000	
	152,000	
Limited to:		
27% × 6/12 × £500,000	67,500	
25% × 6/12 × £500,000	62,500	
	130,000	130,000
Mainstream corporation tax		£ 45,000

The unrelieved ACT of £22,000 (£152,000 minus £130,000) will be relieved as explained above. Let us now continue the illustration by inserting some franked investment income.

Suppose both the dividends were paid on or before 5 April 1988 but that the company had received a dividend of £30,000 in August 1988. The effect would be that the benefit of the tax credit on the dividend could not be obtained against the dividends, because we have to treat the year ended 30 September as consisting, for quarterly accounting purposes only, of two separate accounting periods, one up to 5 April and the other onwards from 6 April.

The corporation tax computation will become:

	£	£
Trading income		500,000
Corporation tax @ 35%		175,000
less: ACT		
£73,000 × 27/73	27,000	
£375,000 × 27/73	138,699	
	165,699	
Maximum offset – as before	130,000	130,000
Surplus ACT	35,699	
Mainstream corporation tax		£ 45,000

The surplus ACT will be available for relief.

The dividend of £30,000 was received in the separate accounting period 6 April 1988 to 30 September 1988. It cannot be 'carried back' to the accounting period 1 October 1987 to 5 April 1988 in which the dividends were paid. The surplus FII of £40,000 (£30,000 + 25/75 × £30,000) will be carried forward for relief in subsequent accounting periods.

Note that the limitation is purely for quarterly accounting purposes. The offset of ACT against the total corporation tax liability is still available – it is only that it may not be possible to obtain full credit for tax attributable to FII.

(b) Special arrangements have to be made for distributions between 1 and 5 April inclusive

The rate of ACT is fixed for the financial year ending 31 March, whereas the income tax rate to which it is linked is fixed for the year ending 5 April.

If the rate of ACT changes we therefore have to cope with distributions made between these two dates.

During these five days, the 'old' rate of ACT continues to apply. A separate ACT return (CT61) has to be made for the period, and the ACT is payable fourteen days after 5 April, that is on 19 April. Note that this only happens when the rate of ACT changes.

Income tax

Most annual payments made by a company are paid under deduction of income tax – debenture interest for example. The company deducts income tax at source and pays it over to the Revenue using the same form CT61 and the same quarterly accounting periods as for ACT.

If the company receives interest etc. which has been taxed at source, it is entitled to credit for tax, since companies are liable to corporation tax on their profits, not income tax. That credit is given in three possible ways:

(a) By offset against tax to be paid over on interest paid through the quarterly return periods

(b) by deduction from mainstream corporation tax
(c) If (a) and/or (b) do not give relief, by refund.

Items covered by these arrangements include those shown on Table 9.

Table 9

Annual payments	*Unfranked investment income (UFII)*
Debenture interest paid	Debenture interest received
Loan interest paid (if under deduction of tax)	Loan interest received (if under deduction of tax)
Patent royalties paid	Patent royalties received
Payments under deeds of covenant	Building society interest

The gross equivalent of the interest etc. received is included in the company's corporation tax computation, and charges paid are, of course, deducted from the total profit, as explained in Chapter 11.

Changes in the rate of income tax

Changes in the rate of income tax during an accounting period do not give rise to the problems encountered with ACT. Illustration 12.5 clarifies the point.

Illustration 12.5

Alba Construction, a non-close UK company formed in 1970, makes up its accounts to 30 June each year. Its trading profit for the year ended 30 June 1988 showed a tax adjusted trading profit of £502,000. The following transactions took place during the year:

1987		
1 July	Received bank deposit account interest	£ 730
10 July	Received dividend from UK company	£14,600
31 July	Paid debenture interest	£10,950 (net)
1 Oct	Paid interim dividend of	£18,250
10 Oct	Paid final dividend of £29,200. This dividend was declared at the annual general meeting on 30 August 1987 and related to the accounting year ended 30 June 1987.	
7 Nov	Received debenture interest of	£16,060 net
1988		
31 Jan	Paid debenture interest	£10,950 (net)
1 May	Paid preference dividend	£ 7,500
7 June	Received debenture interest	£16,500 (net)

The company has no surplus franked investment income brought forward from previous accounting periods.

You are required:

(a) To show the entries to be made in the quarterly returns for ACT and income tax (CT61), stating clearly the amounts payable to or refundable by the Inland Revenue
(b) To compute the company's corporation tax liability for the year ended 30 June 1983
(c) To state the due dates for payment of all amounts.

Discussion

The first thing to do is to divide the transactions up into the appropriate quarterly return periods. Transactions relating to ACT and transactions relating to income tax must be dealt with entirely separately throughout.

Note that you have to deal with the quarterly returns and with the corporation tax computation. That means that the transaction on 1 July 1987 is not a complete red herring. Bank deposit interest is received *gross* by companies, and so is outside the income tax accounting system. Nevertheless it is taxable income to be included in the company's corporation tax computation.

The transaction on 10 October 1987 could confuse. The dividend is stated to be 'related to' the year ended 30 June, 1987, but this is irrelevant. The criterion is the date of payment, not the date of declaration and certainly not the year to which the dividend relates.

Alba Construction Ltd

Corporation tax computation, period ended 30 June 1988

	£	£
Schedule D Case I		502,000
Case III – bank interest		730
Debenture interest received		44,000
		546,730
Less: Charges – debenture interest paid		30,000
		£516,730
Corporation tax @ 35%		180,855
Less: Advance corporation tax – per CT61		14,650
		166,205
Less: Income tax		
Surplus from CT61		3,340
Corporation tax due 1 April 1989		£162,865
(or 30 days after date of assessment if later.)		

Tutorial notes

1 Note the difference between the two sections of the CT61 – the ACT returns show the 'gross' figures of franked payments and franked

Alba Construction Ltd

ACT returns – CT61

	Franked payments £	Franked investment income £	ACT Paid £	ACT Refunded £	Due date
3 months ended					
10 Sept 1987		20,000			
31 Dec 1987	25,000				
	40,000		12,150 (£45,000 @ 27%)		14 Jan 1988
31 Mar 1988	no return required				
30 June 1988	10,000		2,500		14 July 1988
	75,000	20,000	14,650		

Income tax returns – CT61

	Rate (%)	Tax suffered £	Tax payable £	Income tax Paid £	Income tax Refunded £	Due date
3 months ended						
30 Sept 1987	27		4,050	4,050		14 Oct 1987
31 Dec 1987	27	5,940			4,050	14 Jan 1988
31 Mar 1988	27		4,050	2,160		14 Apr 1988
30 June 1988	25	5,500			2,160	
		11,440	8,100	6,210	6,210	
		8,100				
Deductible from MCT liability		3,340				

investment income, whereas the income tax returns show the tax suffered and paid. The effect of the change in the rate of income tax from 27 per cent to 25 per cent for the fourth quarter simply alters the arithmetical total without introducing any further complications.

2 The income tax return illustrates the point that refunds can only be obtained through the quarterly accounting procedure to the extent that income tax has been paid in the accounting period. Thus the refund for the quarter ended 31 December 1987 is limited to the tax already paid. The benefit of the remainder of the £5,940 suffered is offset in the quarter ended 31 March 1988 to produce the reduced payment of £2,160 (£8,100 minus £5,940).

3 Note the trap on the Schedule D Case III bank interest. The figure given is £730 to 'invite' you to gross the amount up to £1,000 for income tax at 27 per cent. This would be wrong, of course, because companies receive bank interest gross, without deduction of tax.

4 The ACT offset is well below the limit for the year, which would be:

	£
£516,730 × 9/12 × 27%	104,638
£516,730 × 3/12 × 25%	32,296
	£136,934

Summary

Introduction

When a company pays a dividend or makes any other distribution, it must pay over a sum on account of its corporation tax liability. This ACT is treated as covering the basic rate income tax liability of the shareholders. A company receiving a dividend is exempt from corporation tax on it and may offset the tax credit on it against ACT payable.

Accounting for ACT

ACT is paid over to the Revenue quarterly. The year is divided into four return periods to 31 March, 30 June, 30 September and 31 December. If the company's accounting period does not end on one of these four dates, the period in which the accounting date falls is divided into two return periods. Details of distributions are sent to the Revenue on form CT61.

Distributions

Many different ways in which a company may seek to pass a benefit to members are treated as distributions.
The term 'distribution' includes:

(a) Dividends, including capital dividends
(b) Interest in excess of a normal commercial rate
(c) Transfer of assets to members at below the market value, or acceptance of assets from members at more than their market value
(d) Bonus issue of shares followed by a repayment of share capital
(e) Repayment of share capital followed by a bonus issue

Offset of ACT

Once paid, ACT may be offset in several different ways:

(a) Against the corporation tax liability for the year in which the distributions were made, up to a limit calculated by applying the basic rate of income tax to the company's profit chargeable to corporation tax
(b) By carrying back (LIFO) against the corporation tax liabilities of the six previous years, subject to the same limit
(c) By carrying forward without time limit against future corporation tax liabilities (same limit)
(d) By surrender to a 51 per cent subsidiary

Surplus of FII

If a company's FII exceeds its dividends paid, the surplus may be carried forward and offset as if it were a distribution in future periods.

Changes in the rate of ACT

If the rate of ACT changes, and the company's accounting date is not 31 March, it will be necessary to compute the maximum available ACT offset by splitting the accounting period into two and apportioning profit on a time basis between them. There may also be restrictions on the extent to which tax credits on FII are deductible in computing the amount of ACT payable caused by the fact that the two parts of the accounting period are regarded as separate accounting periods for the purpose of quarterly accounting.

If distributions are made on any of the five days 1 to 5 April, the 'old' rate of ACT continues to apply to them and a separate return must be made for the five day period.

Income tax

Accounting for income tax suffered and deducted is initially similar to the procedures for ACT and tax credit on dividends. Any excess of income tax suffered at the end of the accounting period may be deducted from the corporation tax liability for that period and if that is insufficient to give relief, a refund may be obtained.

Progress questions

Attempt these questions to test your absorption of the material in the chapter. Rework them at intervals for revision. Answers are on page 397.

1 What is advance corporation tax (ACT)?

2 How is a company's liability to ACT ascertained, and how is it accounted for to the Revenue?

3 What difference does it make to a company's ACT liability if the company has received dividends from other UK companies?

4 What other payments besides dividends may give rise to the need to pay ACT?

5 How is ACT paid offset?

6 What happens if franked investment income exceeds franked payments?

7 What happens if the rate of ACT changes?

8 Give three examples of:

(a) payments
(b) income

taken into account in calculating a company's income tax payable or refundable in the quarterly return periods.

13 Corporation tax – more advanced points

Period of account exceeding one year

As we saw in Chapter 11, an accounting period for corporation tax cannot exceed twelve months. If a company makes up its accounts for a period of account exceeding this, we must divide it into two accounting periods. This presents no great problem, but we must have rules for the apportionment of the different types of income and expense.

These rules are:

(a) *Schedule D Cases I and II* – adjusted trading income for the *period of account before* capital allowances is apportioned on a time basis. Capital allowances are then calculated separately for the two accounting periods and deducted.

Illustration 13.1

Q Limited made up its accounts for the fifteen months ended 30th June 1989. Its profit for the period, after adjustment for corporation tax purposes excluding capital allowances, was £75,000. The pool balance of plant and machinery at 1 April 1988 was £20,000. During the period further expenditure on plant was incurred as follows:

6 September 1988	£8,000
4 April 1989	£16,000

The computation will be:

	Accounting periods	
	12 months to 31.3.89	*3 months to 30.6.89*
	£	£
Trading income before capital allowances	60,000	15,000
Capital allowances per computation below	7,000	2,313
	£53,000	£12,687

Capital allowances
Accounting period of 12 months ended 31 March 1989

	£
Pool balance brought forward	20,000
Additions	8,000
	28,000
WDA 25%	7,000
	21,000
Accounting period of 3 months ended 30 June 1989	
Additions	16,000
	37,000
WDA 25% × 3/12	2,313
	34,687

(b) All other income is allocated to periods according to the date it arises or the date it is due.
(c) Capital gains are allocated to the accounting period in which the disposal took place, with a separate computation for each period.
(d) Charges (interest etc. paid) and dividends paid are allocated to the accounting period in which they are *paid*.

Accounting periods straddling 31 March

If an accounting period straddles 31 March, this causes a problem *if the rate of corporation tax changes*. The rate is fixed for the financial year to 31 March, and this means that income and capital gains for the accounting period must be charged to tax at the different rates. Note that the mere changing of rate at 31 March does *not* require the application of the apportionment rules explained in the previous paragraph, because we are still dealing with a single accounting period.

Remember that if the rate of corporation tax does not change, there is no special problem.

Illustration 13.2

Here is an illustration in which it is assumed that the corporation tax rates are:

Financial year	1987	35%
	1988	40%

R Limited made up its accounts for the year to 30 September 1988 with the following results as adjusted for corporatioin tax:

	£
Schedule D Case I	480,000
Schedule A	40,000

	£
Schedule D Case III	10,000
Capital gains (indexation ignored)	30,000
Debenture interest paid	(40,000)

The computation of the corporation tax liability will be:

	£
Schedule D Case I	480,000
Schedule A	40,000
Schedule D Case III	10,000
Capital gains	30,000
	560,000
Less:	
Charges: debenture interest paid	40,000
	520,000
Corporation tax liability	
Financial year 1987 £520,000 × 6/12 @ 35%	91,000
1988 £520,000 × 6/12 @ 40%	104,000
	£195,000

No apportionment of the income or changes was necessary. The result is that all elements making up the £520,000 are taxed at the weighted average rate for the accounting period.

Group income and charges

Fuller details of corporation tax problems of groups of companies are given in Chapter 15. It is necessary to pick up just one point now, because it is relevant when considering small companies (see section on small companies below).

A group of companies may elect to pay dividends between group companies without accounting for advance corporation tax (ACT). Such an election does not save tax, since ACT may be offset against corporation tax liabilities, but it does improve group cash flow. Dividends received 'gross' in this way are referred to as 'group income'. The election may be made when companies are linked by group shareholdings of more than 50 per cent.

A similar election may be made in respect of group charges. These also may be paid gross, without accounting for income tax, when passing between companies linked by group shareholdings of more than 50 per cent.

Small companies

Introduction

The basic rate of corporation tax is reduced for companies coming within the statutory definition of 'small'.

The rules are:

(a) If the company's 'profit' is under £100,000, the small companies rate of 25 per cent applies to both income and capital gains.
(b) If the company's 'profit' is over £500,000, the full rate of 35 per cent applies to both income and capital gains.
(c) If the company's 'profit' is between £100,000 and £500,000, a special calculation is required – see below.

The term 'profit' in these rules means the amount chargeable to corporation tax (income, plus capital gains, minus charges) *plus* franked investment income (the gross equivalent of dividends from other UK companies.) Franked investment income received from other companies in the same group is excluded. This does not mean to say that the franked investment income is to suffer corporation tax, merely that its existence can influence the rate of tax suffered on the amount chargeable to corporation tax.

In s. 13 ICTA 1988, the amount chargeable to corporation tax is described as 'basic profit', as opposed to 'profit', which is basic profit plus franked investment income. This terminology is used in the remainder of this chapter.

For accounting periods of less than one year the figures of £100,000 and £500,000 are proportionately reduced.

If a company is a member of a group of companies, the £100,000 and £500,000 are divided by the number of companies in the group carrying on a business, and every company in the group receives the same limits. Thus a company with one subsidiary would have limits of £50,000 and £250,000 as would its subsidiary. Such other group companies are referred to in the tax legislation as 'associated companies' and a shareholding of more than 50 per cent is the most important criterion determining whether companies are associated. Two companies which are both 50 per cent subsidiaries of a third are also treated as associated.

Small companies relief

If a company's profit exceeds £500,000 or is less than £100,000, no special problem arises. If the profit lies between these limits we have to make a calculation which effects a smooth transition from the 25 per cent rate to the 35 per cent rate – the small companies marginal relief calculation.

The basic profit is first taxed at 35 per cent, and the tax charge is then reduced by the result of the following calculation:

$$\frac{1}{40}\ (£500{,}000 - \text{profit})\ \frac{\text{Basic profit}}{\text{profit}}$$

The fraction of 1/40 varies according to the corporation tax rates and is the one for the financial year 1988. It will be given to you in the examination if you need to use it. The fractions applicable in recent years have been:

Financial year	*fraction*
1988 (Year to 31 March 1989)	1/40
1987	1/50
1986	3/200
1985	1/40
1984	3/80

The upper and lower limits (£500,000 and £100,000) were the same in all these years.

Illustration 13.3

Smallish Limited, which has no associated companies, makes up its accounts to 31 March. Its accounts for the year ended 31 March 1989 showed the following, as adjusted for corporation tax:

	£
Schedule D Case I	300,000
Schedule D Case III	50,000
Capital gains (indexation ignored)	60,000
	410,000
Less:	
Charges	60,000
Basic profit	350,000
Dividends from other UK companies (37,500 × 100/75)	50,000
Profit	£400,000

Corporation tax payable:

	£
£350,000 @ 35%	122,500
less:	
Small companies marginal relief	
$\frac{1}{40}\ (£500{,}000 - £400{,}000)\ \frac{£350{,}000}{£400{,}000}$	2,188
	£120,312

The effect of the marginal calculation is actually to tax profits in the marginal band at 37½ per cent. This is less easily seen if we have franked investment income, but if we assume that Smallish Limited had no franked investment income the calculation would be:

		£
	£350,000 @ 35%	122,500
Less:		
	Small companies marginal relief	
	$\frac{1}{40}$ (£500,000 – £350,000)	3,750
		£118,750
This is equal to:		
	£100,000 @ 25%	25,000
	£250,000 @ $37\frac{1}{2}$%	93,750
		£118,750

The method of calculation in the examination must follow the 'formula' method first shown – the fact that the marginal rate is $37\frac{1}{2}$ per cent is mentioned only as a tax planning point, because tax planning should ensure, say, that in groups of companies the smallest possible amount is taxed at that rate, or in a single company that all legal steps are taken to keep the profit below £100,000.

For example, let us compare the tax payable on profits of £50,000 and £150,000 in two consecutive years compared with two years at £100,000 per year:

		£	£
(a)	Year 1 £50,000 @ 25%		12,500
	Year 2 £150,000 @ 35%	52,500	
	Less:		
	marginal relief		
	$\frac{1}{40}$ (£500,000 – £150,000)	8,750	43,750
			£56,250
(b)	Year 1 £100,000 @ 25%		25,000
	Year 2 £100,000 @ 25%		25,000
			£50,000

The tax saving of £6,250 could, for example, make it worth while to take a capital gain in the first year rather than in the second if the increased profits of the second year could be forecast in time:

	Year 1	*Year 2*
	£	£
Trading income (forecast)	50,000	100,000

Taking a capital gain of £50,000 in Year 1 would lead to (b) above, while taking it in Year 2 would lead to (a) above.

Small companies relief, accounting dates other than 31 March

If a company's accounting period straddles 31 March and the rates of tax change, the small companies marginal relief calculation has to proceed along the same lines as indicated above.

Illustration 13.4

Tiger Limited makes up accounts to 31 December each year. Its accounts for the year ended 31 December 1988 showed the following results after adjustment for corporation tax purposes.

	£
Schedule D Case I	200,000
Capital gains (indexation ignored)	80,000
	280,000
Less:	
Charges	40,000
Basic profit	240,000
Dividends from other UK companies (£15,000 × 100/75)	20,000
Profit	£260,000

The rates of corporation tax for the two financial years concerned were:

	Financial Year	
	1987	*1988*
Full rate	35%	35%
Small companies rate	27%	25%
Small companies marginal relief fraction	1/50	1/40

It is first necessary to apportion the basic profit and profit between the two periods 1 January 1988 – 31 March 1988 and 1 April 1988 – 31 December 1988:

	Financial Year	
	1987	*1988*
	£	£
Basic profit	600,000	180,000
Profit	65,000	195,000
Small company limits –		
upper – £500,000	125,000	375,000
lower – £100,000	25,000	75,000

The corporation tax payable will be:

	£	£
£240,000 @ 35%*		84,000
Less:		
Small companies marginal relief		
Financial year 1987		
$\frac{1}{50}$ (£125,000 − £65,000) $\frac{£60,000}{£65,000}$	1,108	
Financial year 1988		
$\frac{1}{40}$ (£375,000 − £195,000) $\frac{£180,000}{£195,000}$	4,154	5,262
Corporation tax payable 1 October 1989		£78,738

Summary

Period of account exceeding one year

An accounting period cannot exceed twelve months. Whenever the period of account exceeds that length it is necessary to split it into two accounting periods. The first twelve months of the period of account constitutes one accounting period and the remainder of the period of account forms another accounting period.

Income, capital allowances, capital gains and charges must then be apportioned between the two periods as explained above. This is *not* a simple time-based apportionment except for trading income before deducting capital allowances.

Accounting period straddling 31 March

31 March is the date at which the rate of corporation tax may change, since it marks the end of one financial year and the commencement of the next.

If a company's accounting period straddles this date, it is necessary to make a simple time-based apportionment of all the company's income, chargeable gains and charges, so as to tax for the accounting period at the weighted average rate for the period.

Group income and charges

When companies are members of the same group and linked by a shareholding of more than 50 per cent, or are under common control, dividends and interests may be paid between them without accounting for ACT or income tax.

* If the full rate had also changed at 31 March 1988, it would have been necessary to charge £60,000 at the 1987 rate and £180,000 at the 1988 rate.

Small companies

There are two rates of corporation tax – 35 per cent for companies with profits over £500,000 and 25 per cent for companies with profits up to £100,000. Between £100,000 and £500,000 there is a marginal calculation which effects a smooth transition between the two rates.

If the small companies marginal relief calculation has to be done for a period which straddles 31 March *and* rates of corporation tax change, it is necessary to apportion basic profit and profit on a time basis and make separate calculations of marginal relief for each part of the year.

Apportionments

Several of the matters covered in this chapter have required apportionment. Remember that it is *only* when two *accounting periods* are involved that the more complex apportionment procedure explained on page 165 is necessary. When there is one accounting period which simply straddles 31 March, only a time-apportionment is necessary, as explained above.

Progress questions

Attempt these questions to test your absorption of the material in the chapter, and rework them at intervals for revision. Answers are on page 397.

1 Are the following statements true or false?

	True	*False*
(a) If a company makes up its accounts for more than twelve months, it is necessary to divide its period of account into two accounting periods, one for the first twelve months and the other for the remainder.		
(b) If a company's period of account is split into two accounting periods, income, capital gains and charges are split between them on a time basis.		
(c) If a company's accounting period straddles 31 March, it is always necessary to calculate the corporation tax liability separately for the two parts of the accounting period, after having split income, capital gains and charges on a time basis.		

2 What is group income?

3 Define the terms 'basic profit' and 'profit' as they are used in connection with small companies relief.

4 Why is it important to keep a company's profit out of the marginal area £100,000 to £500,000 if possible?

14 Corporation tax relief for losses

Introduction

Corporation tax reliefs for losses achieve broadly the same effect as those for income tax, but the detailed rules are different, not least because the complications caused for income tax losses by the preceding year basis of assessment do not exist for corporation tax.

The main loss reliefs available are:

(a) Carry forward of loss to offset against future trading income derived from the same trade (s. 393 (1) and ss. 343–344).
(b) Offset against other income and chargeable gains of the same accounting period (s. 393 (2)).
(c) Once any possible claim under (b) above has been made in full, offset against other income and chargeable gains of earlier accounting periods equal in length to the accounting period of the loss (s. 393 (2) and (3)).
(d) Carry forward of unrelieved trade charges (s. 393 (9)).
(e) Terminal loss relief (s. 394).
(f) Group loss reliefs (ss. 402–403).

Each of these reliefs is considered in detail below, though a detailed explanation of group loss reliefs is deferred until Chapter 15, where all group tax matters are dealt with together.

Note that it is customary to refer to these reliefs by quoting the ICTA 1988 section (and sub-section!) reference.

Carrying forward a trading loss under s. 393 (1)

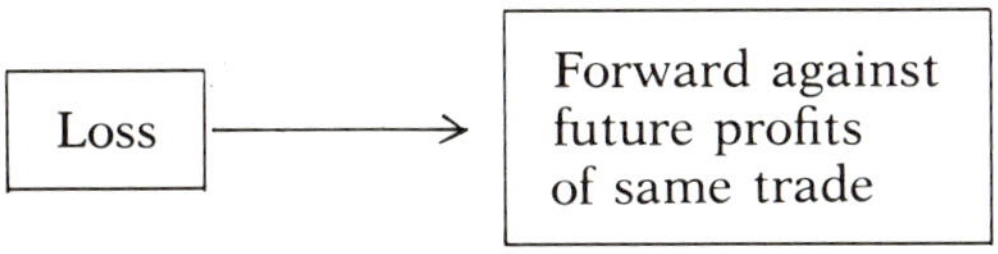

A trading loss in one accounting period may be carried forward without time limit to offset profit of the same trade in future periods. Although there is no limit on the time within which the loss may be offset, a claim to establish the loss must be made within six years of the end of the accounting period in which the loss was made. Relief under s. 393 (1) is given against trading profits *before* deducting charges (see page 178), and must be made against the first available profit.

Relief may be lost if there is, within the same period of three years, both a change in ownership of the company, and a change in the nature of the trade. For this purpose a change in ownership occurs if one or more persons acquire more than 50 per cent of the company's ordinary share capital (ss. 768–769). The reason for this restriction is to limit dealings in 'tax loss' companies – one company attempting to obtain loss relief by buying the shares in another company with unrelieved tax losses.

Carrying forward a trading loss after a company reconstruction (ss. 343–344)

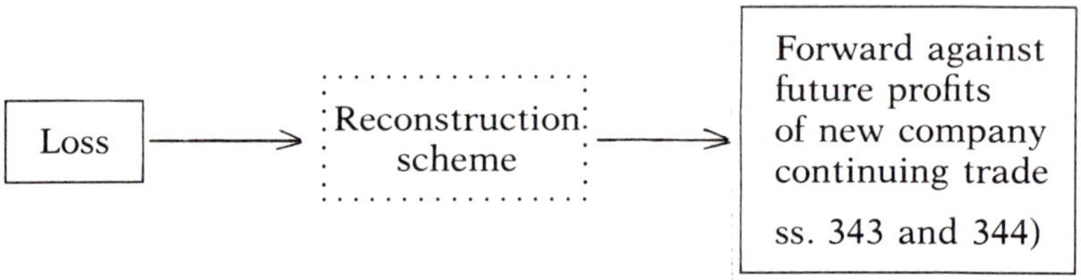

If a company participates in a reconstruction scheme, the right to carry forward any trading losses it may have may be transferred to a new company formed in the course of the reconstruction to continue the trade, provided at least 75 per cent of the ordinary share capital of both companies has belonged to the same shareholders at some time during the period beginning one year before the reconstruction and ending two years after it.

The relief may be restricted or lost if the 'old' company is insolvent at the time of the reconstruction and the 'new' company does not take over all its liabilities.

Offset of trading losses against other income (s. 393 (2) and 393 (3))

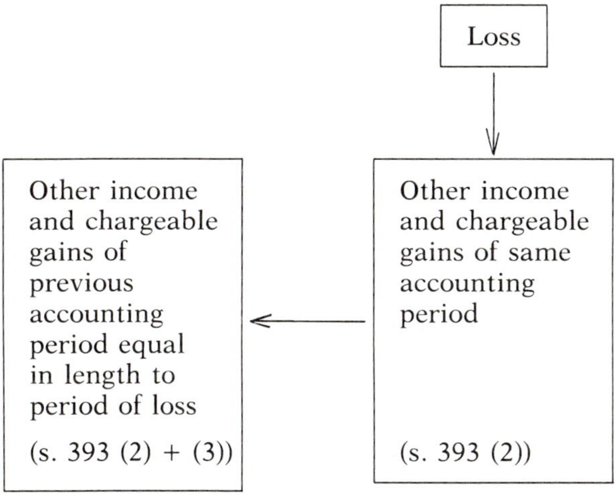

(a) Offset in same accounting period

A company may claim, within two years of the end of an accounting period, to set any trading loss arising against other income plus chargeable gains of that period. The claim is against other income etc. *before* deducting charges. That could leave no income against which the charges can be relieved. Any such unrelieved trade charges are carried forward under s. 393 (9) alongside trading losses (see page 178).

Illustration 14.1

Crepus Ltd incurred an adjusted trading loss in the year ended 31 December 1987 of £8,000. In that year the company had rental income of £3,000 and made a capital gain of £4,000 (after indexation). The company also paid £2,000 debenture interest (gross) in the year.

Compute the company's corporation tax position for the accounting period ended 31 December 1987:

(i) If the company makes a claim under s. 393 (2)
(ii) If the company makes no such claim.

(i) Claim under s. 393 (2)

Corporation tax computation, year ended 31 December 1987

Schedule A rental income	£3,000
Capital gain	£4,000
	£7,000
Less s. 393 (2) claim (part)	£7,000
	Nil

The loss claim eliminates the other income from which the debenture interest would have been deducted as a charge. We should accordingly carry forward into 1988 and subsequent years:

Under s. 393 (1) – balance of £8,000 loss	£1,000
Under s. 393 (9) – unrelieved charge	£2,000
	£3,000

(ii) No claim under s. 393 (2)

Crepus Ltd
Corporation tax computation, year ended 31 December, 1987

Schedule A rental income	£3,000
Capital gain	£4,000
	£7,000
Less: charge	£2,000
amount chargeable to corporation tax	£5,000
Loss carried forward under s. 393 (1)	£8,000

(b) Offset in earlier accounting period
If some unrelieved loss remains after a claim under s. 393 (2), the company may carry that balance *back* for a period equal in length to the period of loss, and set it off against the total income plus capital gains of that earlier period (s. 393 (2) and (3)). Once again the offset is against income etc. before deducting charges.

If not all the accounting periods involved are one year long, we may get some slight complication, but the solution is to apply the stated rule exactly, and here are some examples.

(i) *Loss is in nine month period, previous periods all of twelve months* – after making all possible claims against other income of the nine month period under s. 393 (2), the balance may be carried back against 9/12 of the income and chargeable gains of the previous twelve-month period.
(ii) *Loss is in a one year period, previous period is of nine months* – after once again making all claims in the year of the loss, any balance will be carried back, first against the income and chargeable gains of the nine month period and then, assuming the period before that to be one year, against 3/12 of the income and chargeable gains of that year.

Charges in corporation tax loss relief – (s. 393 (9))

As we saw in Chapter 11, there are certain payments made by companies which are not allowable as deductions in computing Schedule D Case I profits, but which are allowed to be deducted from total income. These 'charges' present a special problem in loss relief.

Charges most frequently encountered in corporation tax computations are:

(a) Debenture interest paid
(b) Loan interest paid
(c) Patent royalties paid
(d) Payments under deed of covenant

Notice that the amount deducted is always the amount actually *paid* in the accounting period.

When considering loss relief, we need to distinguish between 'trade' charges and 'non-trade' charges. 'Trade' charges are those paid for the purpose of the business being carried on (as would almost certainly be the case for items (a) to (c) above). 'Non-trade' charges are those not paid out wholly and exclusively for the purpose of the business, as would be the case with covenanted payments to charities, for example.

Charges of both types are deductible from total profits chargeable to corporation tax, but because losses are deducted from profit before *deducting* charges, we may be left with charges paid in a year which have no profit available from which they may be deducted. s. 393 (9) allows *trade* charges in this situation to be carried forward as if they were a trading loss. Relief for non-trade charges is lost if they cannot be offset within the year in which they are paid. To minimize the effect of the restriction of relief to trade charges only, non-trade charges may be deducted in priority to trade charges when there is insufficient to cover both, thus maximizing the amount that can be carried forward.

Before proceeding to look at any more forms of corporation tax loss relief, it will be helpful to have some illustrations of the workings of those we have considered so far, as they frequently come together in a question.

The range of loss reliefs available, even within s. 393, means that it will be useful if we can develop a standard approach, and this is done in answering the questions which follow. Let us see how and why the standard approach adopted has been arrived at.

A basic corporation tax computation may look something like this:

	£
Trading income	X
Other chargeable income	X
	X
Chargeable capital gains	X
	X
Less charges	X
Amount chargeable to corporation tax	£X

Loss reliefs under s. 393 (1) or s. 393 (9) are deductible from *trading income*, while loss reliefs under s. 393 (2) and s. 393 (3) are deductible from the *taxable profit before deducting charges*.

In answering a question requiring us to deal with several years, we

Illustration 14.2

S Limited commenced trading on 1 January 1985 and its results for the first four years of trading have been:

	Years ended 31 December			
	1985	*1986*	*1987*	*1988*
	£	£	£	£
Trading profit (loss) after capital allowances	60,000	7,000	(61,000)	28,000
Bank interest received	2,000	3,500	2,500	3,000
Capital gains (assume fully taxable in all years)	1,500		4,500	
Debenture interest paid (gross)	4,000	4,000	4,000	4,000

Compute the mainstream corporation tax payable for each year, claiming all losses and reliefs as early as possible. Assume corporation tax at 25 per cent throughout.

Discussion

The main point of this illustration is to show the method of setting up the working for the inclusion of loss relief.

We first set up the tabulation including all the figures *except* the loss of £61,000. This is shown below. Then we add the available loss reliefs in order:

(i) s. 393 (2)
(ii) s. 393 (2) + (3)
(iii) s. 393 (1)
(iv) s. 393 (9) arising from (i) and (ii)

We keep a memorandum loss calculation going, showing the progressive use of the available loss.

S Limited

	1985	*1986*	*1987*	*1988*
	£	£	£	£
Trading income	60,000	7,000		28,000
↕ *Space to insert loss claims under s. 393 (1) and (9)*				
Schedule D Case 111	2,000	3,500	2,500	3,000
Capital gains	1,500		4,500	
↕ *Space to insert loss claims under s. 393 (2) and (3)*				
Less:				
Charges	4,000	4,000	4,000	4,000

(This is the initial stage. The loss reliefs are then added to produce the final answer shown below. In answering a question you would, of course, add the loss claims to your initial figures above!) The completed answer appears on page 182.)

Illustration 14.2

	1985	*1986*	*1987*	*1988*
	£	£	£	£
Trading income	60,000	7,000		28,000
Less:				
loss claim				
s. 393 (9) 1986				(4,000)
s. 393 (9) 1987				(4,000)
s. 393 (1)				(20,000)
				Nil
Schedule D Case 111	2,000	3,500	2,500	3,000
Capital gains	1,500		4,500	
	63,500	10,500	7,000	
Less:				
Loss claim s. 393 (2)			(7,000)	
s. 393 (2) + (3)		10,500	Nil	
		Nil		
Less:				
Charges	(4,000)	(4,000)	(4,000)	(4,000)
	59,500	(4,000)	(4,000)	(1,000)
		Carried forward under s. 393 (9) into 1988	Carried forward under s. 393 (9) into 1988	Carried forward under s. 393 (9) into 1989

may not know precisely what losses are available for relief in various ways. For example, any relief under s. 393 (1) may be dependent on exactly how much of the loss can be relieved under s. 393 (2) and/or s. 393 (3).

We accordingly set up a format in which the incomes for the years involved are entered in columnar style, with space left to insert the loss reliefs when they are known.

We therefore need a format for each year like that illustrated below:

	£
Trading income	X
→ *Leave six lines to insert loss relief under s. 393 (1) and s. 393 (9)*	
Other income	X
	X
Chargeable capital gains	X
	X
→ *Leave six lines to insert loss reliefs under s. 393 (2) and s. 393 (3)*	
Less:	
Charges	X
Amount chargeable to corporation tax	X
	X

An illustration begins on page 180.

Loss relief memorandum

	£
Loss for year ended 31 December, 1987	61,000
(i) s. 393 (2) claim in same year	(7,000)
	54,000
(ii) s. 393 (2) + (3) claim in previous year	(10,500)
	43,500
Add:	
s. 393 (9) losses arising (£4,000 + £4,000)	8,000
	51,500
(iii) s. 393 (1) and (9) claim in 1988	(28,000)
Unrelieved loss carried forward	23,500
Add:	
s. 393 (9) claim for 1988	1,000
Balance of unrelieved loss carried forward into 1989	24,500

Effect of loss relief on advance corporation tax

The impact of loss relief can have an important effect on a company's ability to offset advance corporation tax (ACT). You will recall from Chapter 12 that ACT paid can be relieved in three main ways:

(i) Deducted from the corporation tax liability for the year in which the distribution was made
(ii) Carried *back* (LIFO) for up to six years
(iii) Carried *forward* into future accounting periods.

(Surplus ACT may also be surrendered to subsidiaries, and this point is dealt with in Chapter 15.)

In all cases, the maximum offset available in any one accounting period is currently limited to 25 per cent of the profits chargeable to corporation tax. (For earlier years the percentage was different as explained in Chapter 12.)

So how does this affect loss claims?

The point is that a loss claim can reduce the profit chargeable to corporation tax and hence reduce the amount of ACT that can be offset in a year. Thus ACT which was initially relieved becomes unrelieved, and has to be carried back to an earlier year within the six year limit or, of course, carried forward.

Illustration 14.3

T Limited was formed on 1 April 1985 and makes up accounts to 31 March each year. Results as adjusted for corporation tax have been:

	Year ended 31 March		
	1987	*1988*	*1989*
	£	£	£
Trading profit (loss)	16,000	18,000	(20,000)
Chargeable gain (ignore indexation)			1,000
Dividends paid (net)		7,300	nil
Dividends received (net)		3,650	nil

In the year ended 31 March, 1988, the corporation tax payable would have been:

		£
£18,000 @ 27%		4,860
Less:		
ACT		
Dividends paid £7,300 × 100/73	10,000	
Dividends received £3,650 × 100/73	5,000	
	5,000	
ACT @ 27% (Maximum offset £4,360)		1,350
Corporation tax payable.		£3,510

If relief for the loss in the year ended 31 March 1989 is claimed under s. 393 (2) and (3) we shall have:

	Years ended 31 March		
	1987	1988	1989
	£	£	£
Trading profit	16,000	18,000	
Chargeable gain			1,000
Less:			
Loss claims			
s. 393 (2)			(1,000)
s. 393 (2) + (3)		(18,000)	
	16,000	nil	nil

The loss claim in the year ended 31 March 1988 has eliminated the income of that year and as a result the ACT cannot now be offset. It will be carried back into the previous year with the following result:

Corporation tax payable for year ended 31 March 1987

	£	£
Corporation tax originally paid		4,640
£16,000 @ 29%		
Corporation tax now due		
£16,000 @ 29%	4,640	
less ACT carried back	1,350	3,290
Refund obtainable		£1,350

Terminal loss claim – s. 394

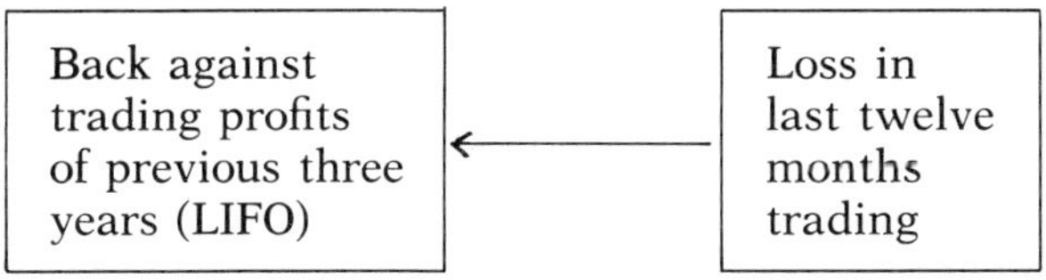

A loss in the final year of a company's trading may not be able to be relieved fully under the provisions of s. 393, which allow it to be set against other income of the year concerned and then back for one year.

Once all possible claims under s. 393 have been made, s. 394 allows a loss in the last twelve months' trading to be carried back for *up to three years* (LIFO) against *trading income only*. The claim must be made within six years of the date of cessation.

The calculation of the terminal loss available is somewhat similar to that for an income tax terminal loss under s. 388.

If the last accounting period is less than twelve months, it will be necessary to include the appropriate proportion of the previous accounting period in the twelve months. If the calculation for either period results in a profit, it is *ignored*.

There are two points of detail concerning charges:

(a) The terminal loss available for relief may be increased by any unrelieved *trade* charges paid in the final accounting period plus, if necessary, the appropriate fraction of those paid in the previous period. Non-trade charges cannot be included.
(b) The terminal loss is carried back against trading income, but sufficient of that income must be retained to cover *trade* charges of the years of the claim. However, if there is other income an interesting point arises. The terminal loss claim is against trading income only. Any non-trade income is thus available to cover trade *and* non-trade charges. This point is picked up in the illustration below.

As a question on terminal loss claims will probably involve claims under s. 393 (2) + (3), the basic format of the answer can be broadly the same as that suggested above. An illustration begins on page 188. Study this before the discussion below.

Discussion

We have a claim under s. 393 (1) and 393 (2) and (3) in respect of the loss in the year ended 31 March, 1986, and we may also claim under the same sections for the loss in the last accounting period. All these claims must be dealt with before making the terminal loss claim.

As the last accounting period is only nine months long, it is theoretically necessary to include 3/12 of the result for the year ended 31 March 1988, though as this is a profit it is *ignored* in the calculation of the amount available for the terminal loss claim.

The terminal loss, once calculated, may be carried back and offset (LIFO) against the trading profits as far back as 31 December, 1984 (three years before the beginning of the last twelve months' trading). We may thus include in the claim, if necessary, the following trading profits:

Year ended 31 March 1988	9/12
Year ended 31 March 1987	The whole year
Year ended 31 March 1986	The whole year
Year ended 31 March 1985	3/12

The answer adopts the format introduced above.

Loss relief memorandum

	£	£
1 Loss for year ended 31 March 1986		3,600
Claims		
s. 393 (2)		(500)
		3,100
s. 393 (2) + (3)		(3,100)
		Nil

		£	£
2 Loss for 9 months ended 31 December 1988			7,000
Claims			
s. 393 (2)			(375)
			6,625
s. 393 (2) + (3)			(1,950)
Balance unrelieved under s. 393			£4,675

	Schedule D I	*Schedule D III*	
3 Terminal loss			
per working			5,035
Claims:			
year ended 31.3.88			
	£	£	
Income	2,100	500	
Less:			
s. 393 (2) + (3)	1,575	375	
	525	125	
Charges: non-trade (*see* Tutorial note 4 (a))		(100)	
trade	335	(25)	
Available for s. 394	190		190
			4,845
Year ended 31 March 1987			
Trading income	2,500		
Less:			
s. 393 (9)	360		
Available for 394	2,140		(2,140)
			2,705

Note: In year ended 31.3.87 the whole of the charges for that year may be set off against the Schedule D Case III income.

Year ended 31 March 1986			
No s. 394 claim – no trading income			
			2,705
Year ended 31 March 1985			
Trading income		5,000	
Less:			
s. 393 (2) + (3)		3,100	
		1,900	
Available for s. 394	3/12 × £1,900		(457)
Balance unrelieved			2,230

Illustration 14.4

D Ltd ceased trading on 31 December, 1988. It made up its accounts annually to 31 March – the results for the last five accounting periods were as follows:

			Accounting periods ended		
	31 March 1985	*31 March 1986*	*31 March 1987*	*31 March 1988*	*31 December 1988*
	£	£	£	£	£
Adjusted trading profits (losses)	5,000	(£3,600)	2,500	2,100	(7,000)
Interest received (gross sum)	500	500	500	500	375
Charges paid (gross sums)					
Trade	(360)	(360)	(360)	(360)	(360)
Non-trade	(100)	(100)	(100)	(100)	(100)

You are required to calculate the sum on which corporation tax is payable for each accounting period, showing clearly the treatment and amount of the loss reliefs claimed, assuming that all loss relief is claimed at the earliest opportunity.

A discussion and workings appear on pages 186–7. Study these in conjunction with the final answer below.

Answer

	12 months ended				*9 months ended*
	31 March 1985	*31 March 1986*	*31 March 1987*	*31 March 1988*	*31 December 1988*
	£	£	£	£	£
Trading profit	5,000		2,500	2,100	
s. 393 (9)			(360)		
s. 394	(475)		(2,140)	(190)	
	4,525		–	1,910	
Interest received	500	500	500	500	375
Less:					
Loss claims					
s. 393 (2)		(500)		(1,950)	(375)
s. 393 (2) + (3)	(3,100)				
	1,925	–	500	460	
Charges Trade	(360)	(360)	(360)	(360)	
Non-trade	(100)	(100)	(100)	(100)	
	£1,465	(460)	40	Nil	Nil
		£360 trade charges c/fwd under s. 393 (9) No relief for non-trade charges.			

Working
Calculation of terminal loss nine months ended 31 December, 1988

	£
Unrelieved loss per loss relief memorandum 2	4,675
Unrelieved trade charges	360
3 months ended 31 March 1988 – profit	Nil
	£5,035

Tutorial notes to answer

1 This is a complicated question which will repay careful study. You may well needed to spend an hour or more on it before you understand it fully.

2 Note the procedure. We first set up our columnar format. All s. 393 (2) and s. 393 (2) + (3) claims must first be dealt with, including those claims in respect of the terminal nine month accounting period. This gives rise to a s. 393 (9) claim for the £360 unrelieved trade charges of the year ended 31 March, 1986, which are claimed against the trading profit of the following year as shown.

3 *Calculating the terminal loss* – the terminal loss is composed exclusively of the balance of the loss unrelieved from the nine months to 31 December 1988, plus the *trade* charges of that period. Non-trade charges may only be relieved to the extent that there is sufficient income, *in the period in which they are paid*, to relieve them. (For the period ended 31 March 1988, 3/12 of which theoretically enters the last twelve months' trading, there is a profit and all trade charges are relieved.)

4 Calculating the relief for the terminal loss:

(a) *Year ended 31 March 1988* – here it is necessary to deal separately with the Schedule D Case I profit and the Schedule D Case III interest, because only 9/12 of the year is available to be relieved by the terminal loss. 9/12 of the interest is eliminated by the s. 393 (2) + (3) claim, leaving £125 to cover charges. Notice how the non-trade charges are deducted *first* from the £125 so as to get maximum relief. The remaining £25 of the non-trading income is used next in order to leave the minimum amount of trade charge (£335) to be deducted from the balance of trading income potentially available for the s. 394 claim.

(b) *Year ended 31 March 1987* – the s. 393 (9) claim is dealt with first, and the balance of the trading profit £2,140 may be relieved by the terminal loss claim. All the charges may be offset against the Schedule D Case III income, leaving £40 chargeable to corporation tax.

(c) *Year ended 31 March, 1986* – there is no trading income available for a terminal loss claim here. (Note the effect of the s. 393 (2) claim – it leaves the charges with no income against which they may be offset, but only the trade charges may be carried forward under s. 393 (9).)

(d) *Year ended 31 March 1985* – only 3/12 of the trading income of this year is available to be relieved by the terminal loss claim. The trading income is already reduced by £3,100 from the s. 393 (2) + (3) claim. Sufficient income remains to cover both trade and non-trade charges.

Relief against surplus franked investment income – s. 242

Although franked investment income is completely exempt from corporation tax, there is one way in which its existence is relevant in claiming relief for losses.

If in the same accounting period a company has unrelieved trading losses *and* a surplus of franked investment income (i.e. franked investment income exceeded franked payments), the position would be, if there were no special provision, that the unrelieved loss could be carried forward under s. 393 (1) for relief against trading profits of future years, while the surplus of franked investment income would be carried forward for relief against the franked payments of future periods.

Section 242 introduces an interesting additional possible loss claim in this situation. It allows a company to offset the loss against surplus franked investment income (FII). The effect is that the company is able to obtain an immediate *refund* of the tax credit attaching to the surplus FII. A claim under s. 242 must be made within two years of the end of the accounting period in which the trading loss was made, or within six years if the claim is in respect of unrelieved charges (see (d) below).

Illustration 14.5

Spintext Limited makes up its accounts to 31 March each year. Its recent results have been:

	Year ended 31 March		
	1987	*1988*	*1989*
	£	£	£
Trading profit/loss	30,000	(50,000)	20,000
Franked investment income	12,000	20,000	20,000
Franked payments	(12,000)	(12,000)	(30,000)

Assume a 25 per cent income tax rate throughout

Let us look at the two situations in the year ended 31 March, 1988. In this period the company has:

(a) Surplus FII of £8,000
(b) A loss of £50,000, £30,000 of which may be relieved by a claim under s. 393 (2) + (3) against the profit of the preceding year, leaving £20,000 to carry forward under s. 393 (1).

Section 242 allows the company to offset £8,000 of the loss against the surplus FII thus liberating a repayment of the tax credit attaching to this income of £2,000.

In order to obtain this refund, however, the company has had to give up two claims – the right to carry forward the surplus FII and £8,000 of the £20,000 trading loss. s. 242 (5) allows the company to *reinstate* the loss claim in a later year in which the company makes a profit *and* has franked payments exceeding the surplus FII brought forward sufficient to cover the loss to be reinstated.

The following computations show first the result if the company makes no s. 242 claim, then the effect of the s. 242 claim.

No s. 242 claim

	Year ended 31 March		
	1987	*1988*	*1989*
	£	£	£
Trading profits	30,000		20,000
Less:			
s. 393 (1)			(20,000)
			Nil
Less:			
s. 393 (2) + (3)	(30,000)		
	Nil	Nil	Nil

The claim under s. 393 (2) + (3) would mean the refunding of all corporation tax paid for 1987.

ACT,	12,000	20,000	20,000
FII brought forward			8,000
			28,000
Franked payments	(12,000)	(12,000)	(30,000)
	Nil	8,000	2,000
ACT payable	Nil	Nil	£ 500
			(£2,000 @ 25%)

With s. 242 claim

	Year ended 31 March		
	1987	*1988*	*1989*
	£	£	£
Trading profit	30,000		20,000
Less:			
s. 393 (1)			
£12,000 + £8,000 reinstated			(20,000)
			Nil
Less:			
s. 393 (2) + (3)	(30,000)		
	Nil	Nil	Nil

The corporation tax paid for the year ended 31 March, 1987 would again be refunded as a result of the s. 393 (2) + (3) claim.

ACT			
FII	12,000	20,000	20,000
Franked payments	(12,000)	(12,000)	(30,000)
	Nil	8,000	10,000
Refund of tax credits			
£8,000 @ 25%		£2,000	
ACT payable			
£10,000 @ 25%			£2,500

The s. 242 claim has replaced a net payment of £500 in the year ended 31 March 1989 with a refund of £2,000 in the year ended 31 March 1988, followed by a payment of £2,500 in the following year. No overall difference, except that the company's cash flow is improved, something which could be important in a period in which a trading loss was made.

Illustration 14.5 showed the elementary aspects of a s. 242 claim. Some further points to note are:

(a) All possible claims under s. 393 (2) and 393 (2) + (3) must be made before a s. 242 claim may be made.
(b) If a s. 242 claim is made, the reinstatement shown in the illustration is automatic – no claim is necessary.
(c) A s. 242 claim may be made for the current year and, if necessary, for the previous period of equal length, as for claims under s. 393 (2) + (3).
(d) Unrelieved charges which would otherwise be carried forward under s. 393 (9) may also be set against surplus FII, but for the current year only (no carry back).
(e) After a s. 242 claim, the company's right to offset ACT paid against corporation tax is restricted. In the Spintext illustration above, for example, the payment of £2,500 ACT for the year ended 31 March 1989 would not all be able to be offset against the company's corporation tax liability for that year. £2,000 of the ACT would simply be the return of the refund obtained in the previous year, and only £500 would be offsettable in the normal way.
(f) The amount of tax payable with and without a s. 242 claim were exactly the same in the Spintext illustration. The amounts may differ, however, if tax rates change.

Capital losses

Companies pay corporation tax on their chargeable gains. If a loss arises on the disposal of a chargeable asset, the loss may be set against chargeable gains of the same accounting period, or carried forward without time limit against chargeable gains of future periods. No other methods of relief are available, though in the case of a group of companies transfers of chargeable assets within the group before disposal to third parties may enable relief to be extended to all gains made by group companies (see Chapter 15).

Group loss relief

If a company in a group makes a trading loss the benefit of that loss may, subject to conditions, be surrendered to another group company. Details are in Chapter 15.

Summary

Methods of loss relief for companies

Companies may obtain relief for trading losses in five main ways:

		ICTA 1988 section
(a)	Carrying forward against future trading income of the same trade	393 (1) and 343–344
(b)	Set against other income and chargeable gains of:	
	(i) accounting period of loss	393 (2)
	(ii) previous period equal in length to accounting period of loss	393(2) + (3)
	Losses claimed under s. 393 (2) or 393 (2) + (3) are set against income and chargeable gains *before* deducting charges. Any *trade* charges becoming unrelieved because of this are carried forward to be offset against *trading income only* of subsequent years.	393 (9)
(c)	Carrying back for up to three years a loss in the last twelve months' trading.	394
(d)	Surrender to another group company (see Chapter 15)	ss. 402–413
(e)	Against surplus FII	s. 242

Carry forward under s. 393 (1)

Relief may be lost if the ownership and the nature of the trade both change within three years.

Carry forward after a reconstruction (ss. 343–344)

A loss may be carried forward through a company reconstruction if at least 75 per cent of the ordinary share capital of both companies have belonged to the same shareholders during a period beginning one year before the reconstruction and ending two years after it.

Offset against other income s. 393 (2) and s. 393 (2) + (3)

Claim must first be made against the period of loss, then extended back to the previous period of equal length. The taxpayer may claim for the same period only, and carry the remainder forward under s. 393 (1). Claim is against the capital gains *before* deducting charges.

Loss reliefs and ACT

Loss relief claims can reduce the amount of ACT which may be deducted in the year of the claim. Be on the alert for ACT consequences in questions on losses – look out for loss questions in which details of dividends paid are given!

Terminal loss claims – s. 394

Terminal loss claims under s. 394 may only be made after all possible relief under s. 393 has been obtained. Relief is for trading losses of the last twelve months' trading plus unrelieved *trade* charges of the same period. The offset is against trading profits of the previous three years, but sufficient profit must be retained in each year of claim to cover *trade* charges not covered by non-trading income.

Relief against surplus FII – s. 242

Trading losses or unrelieved charges may be used to obtain a refund of tax credits on surplus FII. When such a claim is made, the loss relief may be reinstated in a later year in which there is both sufficient profit to absorb the loss and a surplus of franked payments over FII.

Progress questions

Attempt these questions to test your absorption of the material in the chapter. Rework them at intervals for revision. Answers are on page 398. Quote ICTA 1988 section references as much as possible in your answers.

1 Section 393 (1) gives the right to carry forward losses against trading income of future years. In what circumstances might the right to relief be lost?

2 State how loss relief under s. 393 (2) and s. 393 (2) + (3) would be available in the following situations:

(a) Loss in an accounting period of six months immediately following an accounting period of twelve months.

(b) Loss in an accounting period of twelve months immediately following a period of nine months.
(c) Loss in a *period of account* of fifteen months immediately following one of twelve months.

3 Distinguish between trade charges and non-trade charges and explain how their treatment in loss claims may differ.

4 Set up a proforma loss claim layout, indicating clearly exactly where the different loss claims may appear.

5 How may loss claims affect the offset of ACT?

6 (a) What elements may form part of a terminal loss claim?
(b) For what period may a terminal loss claim be carried back?
(c) Against what income may a terminal loss claim be set?
(d) Why is sufficient trading profit retained to cover trade charges when making a terminal loss claim?
(e) Can non-trade charges ever be relieved in years covered by a terminal loss claim?

7 What are the time limits for making claims for losses under:

(a) s. 393 (1)
(b) s. 393 (2) + (3)
(c) s. 394
(d) s. 242?

8 How do loss claims under s. 242 work?

15 Corporation tax – groups of companies

Introduction

This chapter is concerned with the special corporation tax problems relating to groups of companies. We need to deal with four matters:

(a) Group loss relief
(b) Consortium relief
(c) Surrender of ACT
(d) Transfer of assets within a group (see also Chapter 23)

One other matter has already been covered – the meaning of the term 'group income'. Refer back to page 167 for an explanation of this.

Group loss relief (ss. 402–413)

If one company in a group makes a loss while others are making profits, it is possible, subject to conditions, to transfer the benefit of the loss where it can most advantageously be relieved.

The conditions are:

(a) All companies concerned must be resident in the U.K.
(b) All companies concerned must be members of a group and linked by shareholdings of at least 75 per cent. This means that fellow subsidiaries may surrender losses to each other, provided both the subsidiaries are at least 75 per cent owned by the holding company.

Illustration 15.1

H Ltd owns 80 per cent of A Ltd, 80 per cent of B Ltd and 70 per cent of C Ltd. A Ltd also owns 80 per cent of D Ltd (see Figure 11). Companies H Ltd, A Ltd, and B Ltd, may interchange losses among themselves, but

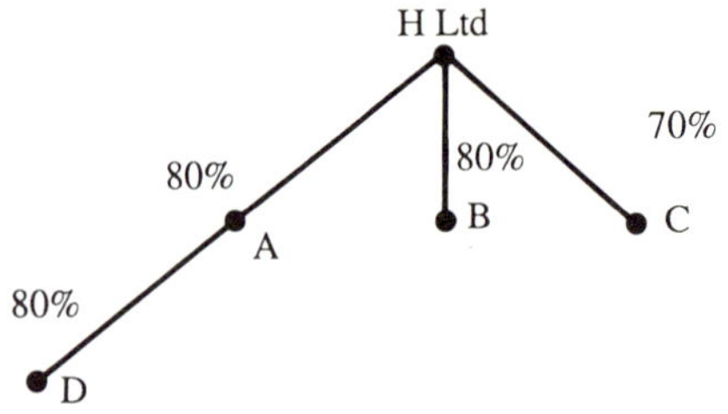

Figure 11

C Ltd and D Ltd must both be excluded. D Ltd is excluded from full participation in group loss exchange as it is only 64 per cent (80 per cent × 80 per cent) owned by H Ltd. It may exchange losses with its parent company, A Ltd.

(c) Only losses of the current accounting period may be surrendered, and they may be offset against the claiming company's profits for the same period.
(d) The surrendering company need *not* first claim all internal loss reliefs available to it.
(e) The claiming company must first claim its own losses in the current period and any losses brought forward from earlier periods. Losses being brought back from future periods must not be allowed for before group relief, however.
(f) The claim must be made within two years of the end of the surrendering company's accounting period showing the loss. The claim is made by the claiming company but the formal consent of the surrendering company is also required.
(g) Any reasonable payment made by the claiming company is disregarded for all tax purposes.
(h) As well as trading losses, the following may also be surrendered:
    (i) Excess charges, including non-trading charges
    (ii) Excess management expenses of investment companies.

Note that capital losses cannot be surrendered.

If the accounting periods of the surrendering company and the claiming company are not the same, relief is given by apportioning the loss over the claiming company's accounting periods.

Illustration 15.2

Loser Limited makes up its accounts to 31 December each year, and in the accounting period ended 31 December 1987 showed a loss of £40,000. Its holding company, Taker Limited, owns 90 per cent of the ordinary share capital of Loser Ltd and makes up its accounts to 30 June. In the years ended 30 June 1987 and 30 June 1988 its profits were £30,000 and £80,000 respectively. Show what claims for group loss

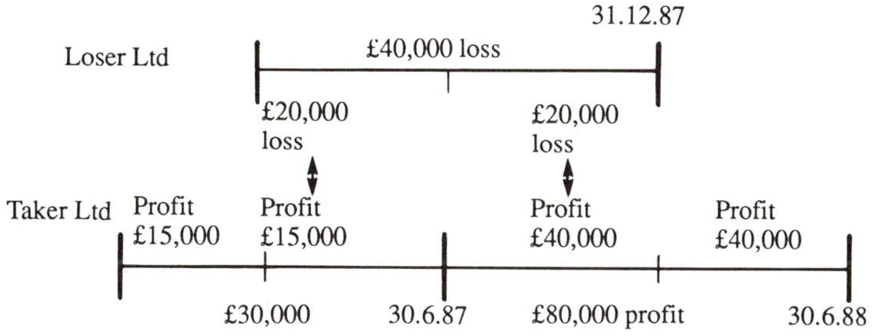

Figure 12

relief are available to Taker Ltd in respect of the £40,000 loss by Loser Ltd (see Figure 12).

The £20,000 loss for the first six months of 1987 may be offset against 6/12 of Taker's profit for the year ended 30 June 1987. Thus only £15,000 of the £20,000 can be relieved.

The £20,000 loss in the second six months may be offset against 6/12 of Taker's profit for the year ended 30 June 1988, and may thus be fully relieved.

The total of group loss relief available is £35,000. The unrelieved balance of £5,000 must be relieved within Loser Ltd., perhaps by being carried forward under s. 393 (1).

A further illustration appears on page 201, with answer below and on page 200.

Discussion

It is necessary to remember small companies relief – the limits are halved as there are two companies in the group. It would be nice if we could reduce the high profits to P Limited for the year ended 31 March, 1988, but unfortunately group loss relief may only be claimed for the year to 31 March 1989, the year in which Q Limited's loss occurred. As both P Limited and Q Limited are 'small' for the year ended 31 March, 1989, it makes little difference whether Q Limited surrenders the loss to P Limited or first claims all available loss claims of its own. The answer which follows is based on full claims by Q Limited under s. 393 (2) and s. 393 (2) + (3) before the surrender.

It is sensible to work out the position of the loss-making company first, to see what loss is available for surrender.

Remember that capital gains and losses may only be relieved within the company making them, in the year they are incurred or by carrying forward to future years.

Answer

Q Limited

	Year ended	
	31 March 1988	*31 March 1989*
	£	£
Trading income	12,000	
Loan interest received	1,200	1,200

	Year ended 31 March 1988	Year ended 31 March 1989
	£	£
Capital gains	2,400	3,600
	15,600	4,800
Less:		
s. 393 (2)		(4,800)
s. 393 (2) + (3)	(15,600)	
	Nil	Nil
Corporation tax payable	Nil	Nil

P Limited

		Year ended 31 March 1988	Year ended 31 March 1989
		£	£
Trading income		136,000	45,000
Loan interest received		4,800	4,800
Capital gains (The £1,600 loss in the year ended 31 March 1989 must be carried forward)		1,800	
		142,600	49,800
Less: charges		(5,000)	4,000
		137,600	45,800
Less: s. 402 group relief (see page 202)			3,600
		£137,600	£42,200
Corporation tax payable			
£137,600 @ 35%		48,160	
Less: small companies marginal relief			
$\frac{1}{50}$ (£250,000 − £137,600)		(2,248)	
£42,200 @ 25%			10,500
Less: Advance corporation tax			
Dividend paid: £2,100 × 100/75	2,800		
Dividends received £360 × 100/75	(480)		
	£2,320		
£2,320 @ 25%			(580)
			9,970
Less:			
Income tax £4,800 − £4,000 @ 25%			(200)
Mainstream corporation tax payable		£45,912	£9,770

Tutorial notes appear on page 202.

The following information relates to P Ltd and its wholly owned subsidiary Q Ltd for the years ended 31 March 1988 and 31 March 1989.

	P Ltd		*Q Ltd*	
	Year ended 31.3.88	*Year ended 31.3.89*	*Year ended 31.3.88*	*Year ended 31.3.89*
	£	£	£	£
Adjusted trading profits (losses)	136,000	45,000	12,000	(24,000)
Capital gains (losses)	1,800	(1,600)	2,400	3,600
Loan interest received (gross sum)	4,800	4,800	1,200	1,200
Dividends received from UK companies	–	360	–	–
Dividends paid	–	(2,100)	–	–
Loan interest paid (gross sum)	(5,000)	(4,000)	–	–

You are required to calculate the mainstream corporation tax payable by both P Ltd and Q Ltd for both the years ended 31 March 1988 and 1989, assuming that all claims available are made as early as possible.

Amount available for group loss relief claim:

	£
Q Limited's loss, year ended 31 March 1989	24,000
Relief under s. 393 (2)	(4,800)
s. 393 (2) + (3)	(15,600)
Available for surrender to P Limited.	£3,600

Tutorial notes

1 Note that group loss relief is deducted from P Ltd's profit *after* deducting charges.

2 You must always be alert in a question like this to check whether you have to calculate the amount *chargeable* to corporation tax or the corporation tax payable. If, as here, you have to calculate the corporation tax payable, you must be sure to include the deductions for ACT and income tax suffered on interest received.

3 If Q Limited had had any charges paid in the year ended 31 March 1989 these too could have been surrendered to P Limited.

Consortium relief

The group relief provisions described above can also apply to a *consortium* consisting of several companies jointly controlling at least 75 per cent of the ordinary share capital of another, with each consortium member holding at least 5 per cent.

X Ltd is 100 per cent owned by A Ltd, B Ltd, C Ltd, and D Ltd, but is a subsidiary of none of them (see Figure 13). In this situation, any trading loss by X Ltd may be surrendered to the four owning companies in proportion to their holdings. Also, a loss by an owning company may be surrendered to X Ltd, but for offset only against the proportion of X Ltd's profit attributable to the loss-making company.

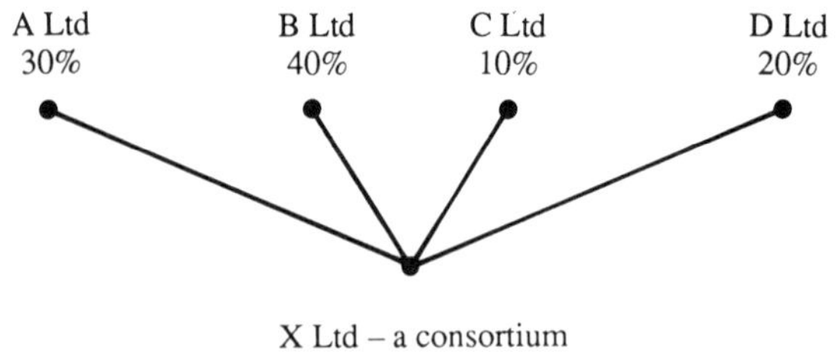

Figure 13

The conditions to be met for consortium relief to be available are broadly the same as those outlined above for group relief, except that the owned company must claim relief for its loss against its own other income for the current period under s. 393 (2) before the surrender.

Surrender of ACT to subsidiaries (s. 240)

A company paying a dividend or other qualifying distribution has to pay ACT quarterly to the Inland Revenue. ACT so paid may then be deducted from the company's corporation tax liability for the period in which the dividends were paid. If relief cannot be obtained in this way, unrelieved ACT may then be carried back and offset in any accounting period beginning within the previous six years (LIFO). In all years the offset is limited to a percentage, equal to the income tax rate in force for the year concerned, of the profit chargeable to corporation tax (income plus capital gains less charges). Before 17 March, 1987, the percentage is applied to *income* less charges only.

For groups of companies a further possibility exists. A holding company may surrender all or part of its ACT relating to *dividends* (not ACT relating to other distributions) to a 51 per cent subsidiary. Note that it is not possible for a subsidiary to surrender its ACT paid to its holding company or to another subsidiary, nor is the relief available to consortia.

Detailed provisions governing the surrender of ACT in this way are:

(a) The surrendering company must submit a claim within six years of the end of the accounting period in which the dividend was paid. The consent of the subsidiary is also required.
(b) A claim is only possible if the subsidiary has been a subsidiary throughout the holding company's accounting period in which the dividend was paid.
(c) All or part of the ACT paid may be surrendered, and it may be surrendered to one or more subsidiaries so as to obtain the maximum benefit.
(d) There is no need for the holding company to relieve the ACT paid against its own corporation tax liability before the surrender.
(e) The subsidiary receiving the surrendered ACT may relieve it as if it had paid a dividend of its own on the date the holding company paid the dividend to which the ACT relates. However, relief is limited to offset in the subsidiary's current accounting period or carry-forward to subsequent periods – there is no six year carry-back.
(f) For relief to be available to the subsidiary, it must have been a subsidiary throughout *its own* accounting period in which the dividend is paid.
(g) If the subsidiary has ACT of its own to offset, as well as ACT surrendered to it by the holding company, the surrendered ACT is offset against its corporation tax liability in priority to its own.

(This has the advantage that the subsidiary's own ACT may then be available to be carried back for up to six years.)

(h) Any payment between the companies (up to an amount equal to the ACT surrendered) is ignored for all corporation tax purposes.

Illustration 15.3

S Ltd is a wholly-owned subsidiary of H Ltd. Both companies make up their accounts to 31 March each year. For the year ended 31 March 1989 the companies' profits and dividends paid were as follows:

	H Ltd	*S Ltd*
	£	£
Trading income	54,000	40,000
Capital gains		4,000
Charges paid	8,000	
Dividends – amounts paid	75,000	–

As both companies have profits below £50,000, they qualify for the small company rate of 25 per cent.

H Limited will have paid £25,000 of ACT in respect of its dividend. Its maximum offset is 25 per cent of £46,000 or £11,500.

(a) No claim under s. 240

If H Ltd does not surrender ACT the position will be:

	H Ltd	*S Ltd*
	£	£
Trading income	54,000	40,000
Capital gains		4,000
		44,000
Less:		
charges paid	(8,000)	–
Amount chargeable to corporation tax	£46,000	£44,000
Corporation tax payable @ 25%	11,500	11,000
Less:		
ACT (maximum offset)	(11,500)	
	£ Nil	£11,000

£11,000 of corporation tax will be payable by S Ltd. H Ltd may be able to obtain repayments by carrying the surplus ACT of £13,500 back for up to six years.

(b) Claim made under s. 240

H Ltd could claim to surrender all or part of the ACT paid to S Ltd. One possibility (shown below) would be for H Ltd to surrender £11,000 ACT to S Ltd. That would leave £2,500 with H Ltd which could be carried *back* up to six years or *forward* without time limit.

Another possibility would be to surrender the whole of the £13,500 surplus ACT to S Ltd. In that case the £2,500 which S Ltd cannot use in the current year would be carried *forward* for use by S Ltd in later years.

Effect of surrender of £11,000 ACT

	H Ltd	*S Ltd*
	£	£
Amount chargeable to corporation tax	£46,000	£44,000
Corporation tax at 25%	11,500	11,000
Less:		
ACT (maximum offset)	11,500	
ACT surrendered from H Limited		11,000
	£ Nil	£ Nil

A very worthwhile result, especially if H's ability to obtain relief by carrying ACT back was restricted.

See Chapter 18 for examples in which it may pay to withdraw the election.

Transfer of assets within a group

When assets are transferred from one group company to another, they are deemed to be transferred at a price which gives neither profit nor loss, provided the companies concerned are linked by shareholdings of 75 per cent or more. The 75 per cent rules are slightly different from those of group loss relief (see above). For asset transfers a 75 per cent subsidiary of a 75 per cent subsidiary *does* count as part of the group (see Figure 14).

As the group loss relief provisions do not apply to capital losses, the ability to transfer assets within a group without attracting tax is useful, because it means that all group sales and purchases can, if necessary, be funnelled through one group company, thus maximizing the offset of profits and losses.

Further details of the calculations of the 'no gain no loss' price are given in Chapter 23.

Summary

It is reasonable that companies in a group should have concessions enabling them to interchange tax reliefs, because if they were organized as a single company with branches, such interchange would obviously be automatic.

Group loss relief	Group asset transfers
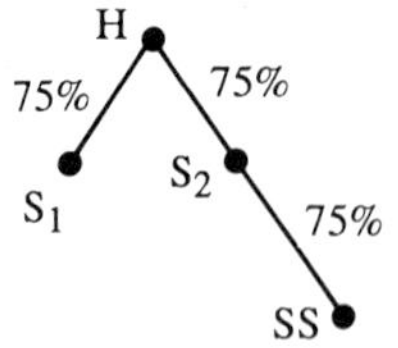	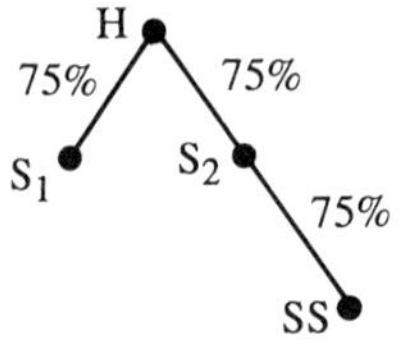
H, S_1 and S_2 may surrender trading losses, and so may S_2 and SS, but H and SS may not	All companies may transfer assets on a 'no gain or loss' basis

Figure 14

Table 10

Relief	*Required shareholding link*
Group loss relief (trading losses, excess charges, excess management expenses of investment companies)	At least 75 per cent of all companies owned directly or indirectly by the holding company
Surrender of ACT	More than 50 per cent
Asset transfers	Link – at least 75 per cent shareholding

Note the different definitions of 'group' for these purposes shown on Table 10.

Relief corresponding to group loss relief may also be obtained by consortia, as described on page 202.

Progress questions

Attempt these questions to test your absorption of the material in the chapter. Rework them at intervals for revision. Answers on page 399.

1 (a) What shareholding link between companies is necessary for group loss relief to be claimed? 75%

(b) What happens in a group loss relief claim if the accounting periods of the two companies are not the same?

2 Are the following statements true or false?

	True	*False*
(a) In a claim for group loss relief any loss surrendered in excess of the available profit of the claiming company is carried forward for relief against future profits of the claiming company under s. 393 (1)		✓
(b) The surrendering company must make all available loss claims of its own before a group loss claim can be made.		✓
(c) The claiming company must first make all available loss claims of its own (other than losses carried back under s. 393 (2) + (3)) before a group loss claim can be made.		✓

3 When may consortium relief be claimed? total 75% holdings

4 (a) When may it be advantageous for a holding company to surrender ACT to its subsidiary?

(b) What shareholding link is necessary for ACT to be surrendered? ≤51%

(c) Can all ACT be surrendered by a holding company to its subsidiary? Yes – subject to rest.

(d) When the subsidiary has received the surrendered ACT, it may obtain relief:

	Yes	*No*
(i) By offset against its own corporation tax liability for its accounting period in which the holding company's dividend was paid	✓	
(ii) By carrying back into its earlier accounting periods for up to six years		✓
(iii) By carrying forward against its corporation tax liabilities of later years	✓	

(e) If a subsidiary receiving the benefit of surrendered ACT also has ACT of its own to offset, which takes priority, the subsidiary's own ACT or the surrendered ACT? How does the order of priority benefit the company?

surrender. → leaves own ACT to be c/d back

5 (a) What shareholding link is necessary for group companies to make asset transfers on a 'no gain no loss' basis?

(b) How does this rule differ from the rule for group loss relief?

(c) What are the advantages to a group of companies to make transfers of assets on this basis?

16 Corporation tax – close companies

Introduction and definition

An individual taxpayer pays income tax on his or her income, initially at 25 per cent (1988/89) but rising once the higher rate tax threshold is crossed to 40 per cent. Companies on the other hand pay corporation tax at the same basic rate of 25 per cent up to a much higher level, and even when the small companies rate maximum is exceeded the full rate of corporation tax is only 35 per cent.

It would thus appear advantageous to an individual to run his or her business through a company and to retain as much profit as possible in the company, withdrawing money from it by way of loans or other devices, thus reducing or eliminating higher rate income tax liability.

To limit the scope for taking advantage of this easy route to tax avoidance, the corporation tax legislation places restrictions on companies under the control of a small number of people and thus capable of being manipulated for the benefit of the members.

Such companies are called 'close' companies, the strict definition of which is a UK resident company controlled by:

(a) Five or fewer participators plus their associates or
(b) its directors plus associates, regardless of their number.

To understand this definition fully we need to add further definitions of 'control', 'participator', 'associate' and 'director'.

(a) Control

Control is usually determined, both in practice and in examination questions, by ownership of more than 50 per cent of the company's *total* share capital or voting power. Note that the preference share capital, if any, is *included* here.

Other determinants of control are:

(i) Ability to exercise control over the company's affairs
(ii) Entitlement to more than 50 per cent of the income of the company if distributed.
(iii) Entitlement to more than 50 per cent of the assets (e.g. in the event of a winding up of the company).

(b) Participator
The shareholders of a company are usually the most important participators for the purpose of determining close company status.
Other participators are:

(i) Loan creditors excluding banks making loans in the normal course of their business
(ii) Any persons entitled to secure for themselves the benefit of any income or assets of the company.

(c) Associate
In determining the shareholding of any participator, it is necessary to include, along with that participator's own shareholding, those of any 'associate' he or she may have.
Associates are:

(i) Close relatives – this includes spouse, brothers and sisters, lineal ancestors or descendants. More distant relatives like uncles or cousins are not included
(ii) Business partners
(iii) Trustees of settlement by participator or any relative as defined in (i) above

Figure 15 summarizes the position.

Illustration 16.1
Mr A and Mr B are both married, and they and their spouses all hold shares in X Ltd. Mr A and Mr B are also in partnership in AB and Co.
Thus shareholdings in X are:

	Number of shares
Mr A	14,000
Mrs A	16,000
Mr B	10,000
Mrs B	8,000

Figure 16 shows the extent to which they will be treated as associated for close company purposes.
Mr A has associates Mrs A and Mr B. Their combined shareholding is:

	Number of shares
Mr A	14,000
Mrs A	16,000
Mr B	10,000
	40,000

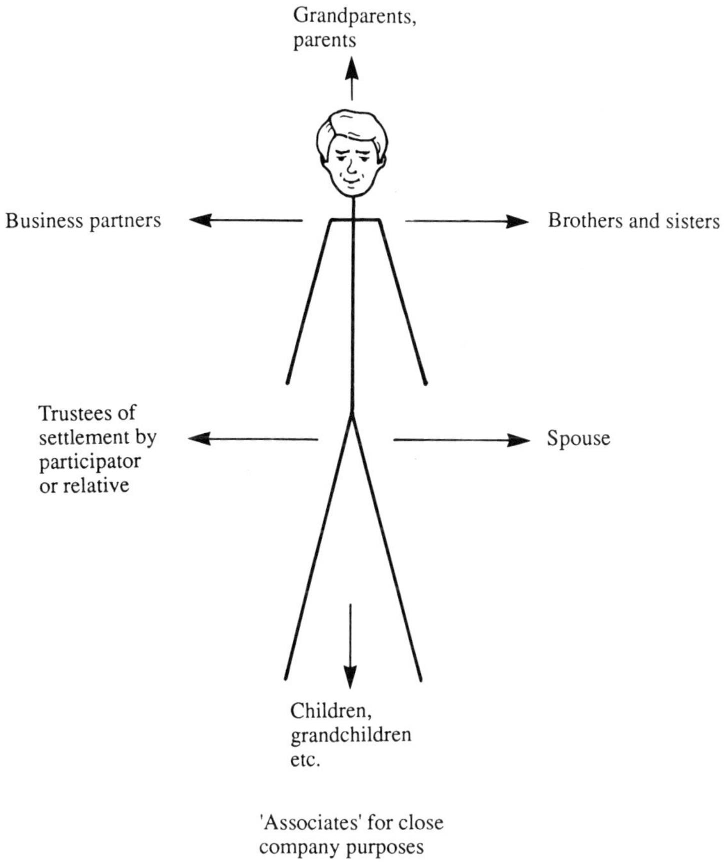

Note that associates of associates are not included

Figure 15

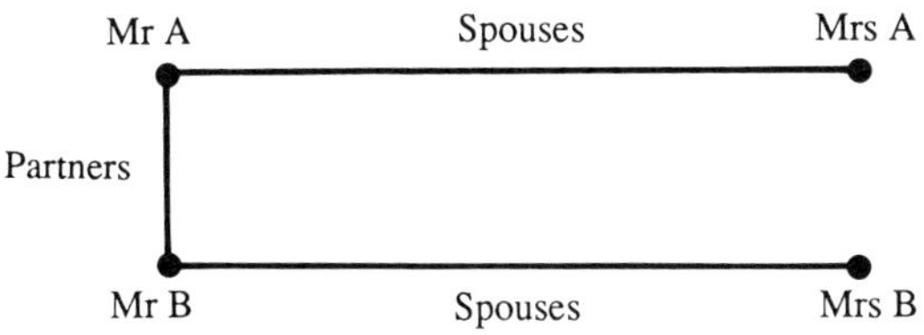

Figure 16

We may also consider Mr B and his associates:

	Number of shares
Mr B	10,000
Mrs B	8,000
Mr A	16,000
	34,000

In determining whether X Ltd was a close company we should take the larger of these two groupings. Mr A and his associates would be treated as one participator holding 40,000 shares, and Mrs B would count as a second independent participator with 8,000 shares.

(d) Director
The term 'director' will obviously normally mean those persons legally appointed as the directors of the company. For close company purposes the following persons are also included:

(i) Any person having the position of a director regardless of the name of their position
(ii) Any person in a position to issue instructions to the directors
(iii) Any manager of the company holding 20 per cent or more of the ordinary share capital. Associates of the manager are included in building up the 20 per cent. Note that this definition refers to ordinary share capital, not total share capital.

Before moving to the practical application of these definitions we need to consider two exceptions:

(i) *Quoted companies* – a quoted company cannot be close if 35 per cent or more of its voting power (ordinary share capital) is beneficially held by members of the public and there has been at least one dealing in the preceding twelve months. This exception does not apply if the 'principal members' of the company hold more than 85 per cent of the voting power. A principal member is one with 51 per cent or more of the voting power *and* is one of the five largest shareholders. A principal member can also count as a member of the public, but directors of the company and their associates, or companies under their control, cannot.
(ii) *Companies controlled by non-close companies* – a company controlled by one or more non-close companies, or a company which can only be brought within the definition of 'close' by including a non-close company as one of its five participators, will *not* be a close company.

Determining close company status

Determining close company status means applying the rules explained above to practical situations. Here is an illustration:

Illustration 16.2

Proximus Ltd is an unquoted company with share capital of 10,000 £1 ordinary shares which are held as follows:

	Number of shares
A	850
B (A's wife)	400
C (A's father)	400
D (A's uncle)	550
E (B's brother)	650
F (D's son)	700
G (E's sister)	300
H (unrelated)	450
I (unrelated)	400
J (unrelated)	400
K (unrelated)	400
L (unrelated)	300
Centauri Limited (ordinary share capital owned equally by D,H,I,J,K, and L above)	1,200
Sundry other unrelated persons, not one of whom owns more than 200 shares	3,000
	10,000

Discussion
We have to study these holdings to find the shares held by the five largest participators and their associates.

It is clearly convenient to begin with A, the largest shareholder apart from Centauri Limited, and consider his associates. (The holdings of A and his associates B and C total a higher figure than those of B and her associates A and E.)

D is not an associate of A since he is an associate of an associate. The answer is therefore:

		Shares	*Shares*
1	A	850	
	A's associates B – wife	400	
	C – father	400	1,650
2	D	550	
	D's associate F – son	700	1,250
3	Centauri Limited		1,200
4	E	650	
	E's associate G – sister	300	950
5	H		450
			5,500

Proximus Ltd is therefore close as more than 50 per cent of its £10,000 share capital is held by five or fewer participators as shown. In fact it is controlled by the first four participators listed, since they collectively hold 5,050 shares.

Consequences of being a close company

A close company is subject to restrictions in three main areas:

- Loans to participators
- Benefits enjoyed by participators
- Amount of profit to be distributed, and apportionment of income

(a) Loans to participators
If a close company makes a loan to a participator or an associate of a participator, it has to pay the Revenue an amount equal to advance corporation tax at the current rate, which the Revenue refund when the loan is repaid. The payment is kept entirely separate from any actual ACT the company may pay, and can only be recouped, as stated, on the repayment of the loan.

A close company has to give notice to the Revenue on the making of any such loan.

If the loan is waived, the company loses the right to recoup the ACT, and the gross equivalent of the amount waived is treated as the income of the participator concerned.

These rules do not apply to:

(i) Loans made in the normal course of the company's business
(ii) Loans not exceeding £15,000 to a participator who is a full-time working director of the company who does not, with associates, hold more than 5 per cent of the company's ordinary share capital

(b) Benefits enjoyed by participators
If a benefit is provided for a participator (or associate of a participator) who is not a director or higher paid employee, that benefit has to be treated as a distribution. In other words, it will be disallowed in computing the company's adjusted profit for corporation tax purposes. (Benefits provided for directors and higher paid employees do not have to be included because this will already be assessed on the recipients under the Schedule E rules explained on page 97.)

(c) Amount of profit to be distributed
(i) *Distributable income and relevant income* – as explained above the members of a company might well be content to see profits retained and built up in the company rather than distributed to them. There are provisions which may enable the Revenue to apportion some of the income of a close company among the members as if it had been distributed as a dividend. In determining the amount which may be apportioned, it is first necessary to see what the company's *distributable income* for the period is. Distributable income means the aggregate of:

- Profits chargeable to corporation tax, less corporation tax thereon (this includes chargeable gains)
- Dividends received by the company (amount received, *not* the gross equivalent)
- Any group income of the company

Fortunately, not all of the distributable income has to be distributed to avoid the risk of an apportionment. The maximum amount which may be apportioned is the company's *relevant income*.

The maximum relevant income is calculated as explained in (ii) below, but the result may be further reduced by demonstrating that the requirements of the company's business for funds limits the amount which can be prudently distributed.

(ii) *Calculating maximum relevant income* (see Table 11)

Table 11

Type of income	*Maximum extent to which apportionable*
(i) Trading income (Schedule D Cases I and II)	Not apportionable at all
(ii) Estate income (income from property (Schedule A or Schedule D Case VI)	50 per cent of total after deducting variable abatement (see below)
(iii) Investment income (interest etc. receivable *including* dividends from other UK companies)	100 per cent of total after deducting abatement (see below)
(iv) Chargeable gains.	Not apportionable at all.

Although trading income is not apportionable, it is necessary to include it initially in the calculation of the maximum which can be apportioned, because it enters into the calculation of the abatement deductible from the estate income.

(iii) *Abatements*

- *Abatement from estate income:*
  - Small total of estate plus trading income. If estate income plus trading income after corporation tax does not exceed £25,000, the *whole* of the estate income is abated.
  - Large total of estate plus trading income. If estate income plus trading income after corporation tax exceeds £75,000, there will be *no* abatement.
  - Medium total of estate plus trading income. If estate income plus trading income after corporation tax lies between £25,000 and

£75,000, we abate the *estate income* by the amount resulting from the following formula, which is best considered in two stages:

$$\text{Stage I} \quad £75{,}000 \times \frac{E}{E + T} = X$$

$$\text{State II} \quad \frac{X - E}{2} = \text{Abatement}$$

(E = estate income, T = trading income)

The limits of 25,000 and £75,000 are reduced proportionately for accounting periods of less than one year, or if there are several companies in a group.

- *Abatement from investment income*: after the complications of the abatement from estate income, this one is relatively simple. The abatement is the lower of:

  (i) £3,000
  (ii) 10% of E + T.

Study Illustration 16.3 carefully, especially the tutorial notes following it:

Illustration 16.3

Propinque Ltd is a close company, and its profit for the year ended 31 March, 1989, was:

	£
Trading income	70,000
Schedule A income	30,000
Debenture interest received	60,000
Franked investment income (gross)	20,000
Chargeable gains	40,000
	220,000
Trade charges paid	40,000
	180,000

Take corporation tax at 35 per cent, ignoring small companies relief, and income tax at 25 per cent.

	Reference to Tutorial notes	*Trading income* £	*Estate income* £	*Investment income* £
As given above		70,000	30,000	60,000
Less: charges	1			40,000
				20,000
Loss: corporation tax at 35%	2	24,500	10,500	7,000
		45,000	19,500	13,000
Dividends (amount received)	3			15,000
				28,000

	Reference to Tutorial notes	*Trading income* £	*Estate income* £	*Investment income* £
Less: abatements				
Estate income				
$75{,}000 \times \frac{£19{,}500}{£65{,}000} = £22{,}500$				
$\frac{£22{,}500 - £19{,}500}{2}$			1,500	
Investment income:				
Lower of: £3,000				
10% of £65,000				3,000
			18,000	25,000
50% of estate income				9,000
Maximum relevant income				34,000

Tutorial notes

1 The charges may be deducted from whichever type of income the taxpayer prefers. It is normally most beneficial to take it against investment income, since 100 per cent of it is included in relevant income. This would not be the case if investment income was so small that it would be eliminated by the abatement – in that case it would be better to deduct the charges from the estate income.

2 In this illustration a corporation tax rate of 35 per cent is to be assumed. In fact it would be necessary to calculate the marginal small companies relief and then allocate the tax appropriately.

3 These are about the only occasions in the whole of UK taxation in which figures net of tax enter a calculation!

4 It is not necessary to include capital gains in the calculation as no part of them can be apportionable. The trading income is only included because the post-tax amount enters into the calculation of the abatement on the estate income.

When we have calculated the maximum relevant income, this is not automatically the amount to be apportioned, or the amount which the company would have to distribute to avoid an apportionment. First of all, we may deduct any distributions already made by the company *for* the accounting period in question. This will cover distributions declared for the period and actually paid during the period or within a 'reasonable' time thereafter. The Revenue will normally regard a period of up to eighteen months after the end of the accounting period as reasonable.

Also, for trading companies or members of a trading group, no apportionment is made if the amount by which distributions made fall short of relevant income is less than £1,000.

Finally, and perhaps must important, a company may seek to establish that the requirements of the business would make it imprudent to pay out a dividend of the size required by the rules we have been examining.

The onus is on the Revenue to show that the company is able to make a distribution as above.

Reasonable arguments which the taxpayer may put forward are:

(a) The business is in a high-risk trade
(b) The business has only recently commenced and is in the process of being established
(c) The liquidity position would make the payout difficult
(d) Resources are needed for planned fixed asset purchases
(e) The legally distributable profit is below the figure produced by the maximum relevant income calculation
(f) Losses of a later period are likely to arise and be carried back into the year under review

Apportionment of income

As you may have realized from reading the above section, it is fairly unusual for a trading company to have problems with the distributions, since neither trading profits nor capital gains are apportionable, and relatively few trading companies enjoy substantial estate income or investment income (except in examination questions on close companies).

Suppose, however, that we have a trading company with insufficient distributions. What happens next?

We may take the position of Propinque Ltd in Illustration 16.3. Let us assume some further information:

(a) Shareholders in Propinque Ltd are:

	Number of £1 shares
A	40,000
B	30,000
C	20,000
D	7,000
E	2,000
F	1,000
	100,000

(b) A, B and C are directors of the company receiving directors' remuneration of £30,000 per annum each.
(c) No dividend has yet been paid for the year ended 31 March, 1989.

The company has two main alternatives:

(i) To pay a dividend of £33,000 for the year within 18 months of 31 March, 1989. This will reduce the excess relevant income to £1,000, the level at which the Revenue cease to apportion.

In this case the company will have to pay ACT on the dividend at the going rate at the time of payment, (say 25/75 × £33,000 = £11,000) and this will be offset against its corporation tax liability in the usual way. The members will receive the dividend and will have to include the gross equivalent in their statutory total income. In the case of the three directors at any rate, they will have to pay higher rate tax on the gross equivalent of the amount received since their income is already well above the higher rate tax threshold. The tax paid by the company already covers basic rate tax, so the amount actually payable by (say) A will be:

	£	
Dividend received 40% of £33,000	13,200	
Grossed up for 25%	4,400	
	17,600	
Tax liability:		
Higher rate tax rate	40%	
Less: basic rate tax already covered:	25%	
	15% × £17,600	£2,640

(ii) To do nothing and wait for the Revenue to apportion the income

What happens now is that the Revenue will treat the company *as if* it had made a distribution of £34,000 (not £33,000) on the last day of the accounting period (31 March 1989).

'Notional' ACT of £11,333 (25/75 × £34,000) will arise but the company will not normally have to pay it since it will be relieved against the corporation tax liability for the period, or carried back for up to six years.

The deemed distribution plus the notional ACT is then apportioned among the members as if they had received a dividend. The result for shareholders of Propinque Ltd will be:

	Shareholding (%)	*Apportionment* £
A	40	18,133
B	30	13,600
C	20	9,067
D	7	3,173
E	2	907
F	1	453
	100	£45,334

The grossed up amounts apportioned to E and F are below the £1,000 limit and also less than 5 per cent of the total to be apportioned. No assessments will accordingly be raised on them, but A, B, C and D will be assessed and required to pay tax as if they had received a dividend on the last day of the accounting period concerned.

A's position will be:

			£
Gross equivalent apportioned as above			18,133
Tax liability:			
Higher rate tax			
less: Basic rate tax already covered by the company's notional ACT	25%		
	15%x	18,133	£2,720

If the shareholders decline to pay the tax, as they usually do, the amount may be collected from the company.

Clearance

A trading company may make application to the Revenue for clearance from the risk of an apportionment, sending all possible supporting information concerning the requirements of the business. The inspector then has three months to decide whether to make an apportionment. If within the three months the inspector requests further information he then has a further three months from the receipt of the information to make a decision. If no apportionment is made within the time limit the Revenue's right to do so is lost unless:

(a) The company failed to disclose all material facts
(b) The company goes into liquidation or ceases to trade within twelve months after the end of the accounting period concerned.

Summary

Introduction and definitions

The close company rules mainly exist to prevent a company within the control of a small number of people from manipulating its affairs so as to reduce the liability to income tax of those people.

To understand the rules, it is necessary to understand these definitions:

(a) Control
(b) Participator
(c) Associate
(d) Director

Consequences of being close

The consequences of a company being close are that limits are placed on the following ways in which the company may seek to place money or value in the hands of participators:

(a) Loans to participators
(b) Benefits to participators

Also, the participators in a close company may suffer the apportionment of part of the profits of the company among them, with consequent higher rate income tax liability. If the participators fail to pay that higher rate tax, as they usually will, the company may be called upon to pay it.

Progress questions

Attempt these questions to test your absorption of the material in the chapter. Rework them at intervals for revision. Answers are on page 400.

1 Why does the Revenue consider it necessary to place restrictions on close companies?

2 (a) What is a close company?
  (b) Support your explanation with definitions of the following terms:
    (i) Control
    (ii) Participator
    (iii) Associate
    (iv) Director
  (c) Are associates of associates included in determining close company status?

3 In what three main areas are restrictions placed upon close companies?

4 (a) If a close company makes a loan to a participator, what must it also do?
  (b) If such a loan is not repaid, what happens?
  (c) Are there any exceptions to the treatment explained in (a) and (b) above?

5 What happens if a close company provides benefits for participators other than directors and higher paid employees?

6 (a) What is meant by:
    (i) distributable income?
    (ii) relevant income?
  (b) Explain how maximum relevant income is calculated, including details of any abatements.
  (c) What arguments may a company put forward to reduce its relevant income by claiming that the requirements of the business do not allow a given level of distribution?

17 Corporation tax – overseas aspects

Introduction

Overseas income gives rise to some of the most complex problems in taxation. For the purpose of the Business Taxation syllabus, however, we need to look at the more basic aspects. The syllabus specifically mentions four areas, and these are dealt with in this chapter as indicated:

(a) Taxation of international businesses; position of companies trading internationally
(b) Overseas subsidiaries
(c) Double tax relief
(d) Controlled foreign companies (CFCs)

Taxation of international businesses; position of companies trading internationally

Introduction

The fundamental problem for international businesses is determining the extent to which their activities are liable to UK corporation tax.

A company resident in the UK will generally be liable to UK corporation tax on the whole of its worldwide profits. A company not resident in the UK will be liable on its UK profits only if it carries on a trade in the UK through a UK branch or agency.

We may thus have three situations:

(a) Full liability to UK tax	–	UK resident
(b) Partial liability to UK tax	–	non-resident company with branch or agency in UK

(c) No liability to UK tax – non-resident and with no branch or agency in the UK (though possibly supplying goods from overseas directly to UK customers).

We now need to ask what constitutes residence and what constitutes a UK branch or agency.

Determining residence

An important amendment to the rules determining a company's residential status was made by s. 66 FA 1988. As from 15 March 1988, a company incorporated in the UK is automatically regarded as resident there.

UK companies which had already changed their residence before that date are allowed to retain that foreign residence, but will permanently lose it if they again become resident in the UK. If a company's 'management and control' is exercised from the UK, it will be held to have UK residence. Thus a company which has migrated overseas could lose its overseas status if control should revert to the UK. Companies registered abroad will be deemed to be UK-resident if their management and control is in the UK.

Determining the existence of UK branch or agency

Merely trading with persons in the UK is not sufficient to establish the existence of a branch or agency. The essential point is that there should be actual trading operations carried on in the UK (*Firestone Tyre and Rubber Co. Ltd* v. *Llewellin* 1956).

Overseas subsidiaries or branches

An overseas subsidiary set up by a UK company, *and controlled from abroad* may be able to escape UK tax on its profits, but the UK holding company would be liable to tax under Schedule D Case V on dividends received.

Losses made by the subsidiary would not be available for a group loss relief claim, as one of the conditions of a claim under s. 402 for group loss relief is that the companies concerned must be resident in the UK. It might therefore be more advantageous, if losses are expected in the early years of operation, to begin overseas with a branch rather than a subsidiary, then to transfer to an overseas subsidiary once profits began.

When the UK parent has trading transactions with an overseas subsidiary, the opportunity might be taken to effect the transactions at a price which effectively transfers profit which would have been chargeable to UK tax to an overseas destination. s. 770 gives the Revenue power to substitute the 'arm's length' price for the actual price. s. 772 gives the Revenue wide powers to require details of transactions it might wish to challenge.

Double tax relief (DTR)

Introduction

A company resident in the UK will generally be liable to UK corporation tax on its income from all sources worldwide. It may also be liable to overseas tax to the extent that its overseas activities fall within the tax net of other countries. Also, dividends and interest paid by overseas companies to UK shareholders may have suffered withholding tax in the country of origin and then be taxable again in the UK under Schedule D Case IV or V.

DTR, as its name implies, exists to reduce the heavy tax burden so arising. In essence, its effect is to ensure that the taxpayer finally suffers tax at no more than the higher of the two tax rates involved.

DTR is given according to the terms of double tax agreements which the UK has entered into with most countries in the world. Obviously you will not need to know the detailed requirements of individual agreements for the examination. We are going to look at the principles followed in most agreements. Claims for DTR must be made within six years of the end of the accounting period concerned.

Relief available

(a) Relief by deducting foreign tax suffered from UK tax
This is by far the commonest form of relief. It will be given under a double tax agreement or, if no such agreement exists, unilaterally. Relief in respect of foreign profits is explained in illustration 17.1.

Illustration 17.1

Mondial Limited is a UK resident company which receives overseas income from two overseas countries as shown below:

	Tax rate (%)	*Income* £
UK income	35	600,000
Utopian income	20	40,000
Erewhonian income	50	30,000

The whole of the world income will be liable to UK corporation tax, but DTR will then be deducted.

	£	
Schedule D Case I		600,000
Schedule D Case V		
Utopia	40,000	
Erewhon	30,000	70,000
		670,000
Corporation tax @ 35%		234,500
less: DTR		
Utopia £40,000 @ 20%	8,000	
Erewhon £30,000 @ 35%	10,500	18,500
		216,000

No relief can be obtained for the Erewhonian tax paid in excess of the UK rate.

Mondial Limited has thus suffered tax as follows:

UK tax as above	216,000
Utopian tax £40,000 @ 20%	8,000
Erewhonian tax £30,000 @ 50%	15,000
	239,000

This is equivalent to tax at the higher of the two rates involved on each source of income.

UK income @ 35%	210,000
Utopian income @ 35% (higher of 35% and 20%)	14,000
Erewhonian income @ 50% (higher of 50% and 35%	15,000
	£239,000

In making the DTR computation, charges may be deducted so as to maximise the relief available. By deducting them as far as possible from the UK income or capital gains, the corporation tax attributable to overseas income is greater and thus the amount of DTR available is also potentially greater.

If the UK company has paid ACT, this is deducted from corporation tax *after* taking DTR. This too increases the amount of DTR potentially available.

Relief in respect of foreign dividends received is examined in Illustration 17.2. In many countries, dividends paid abroad are subject to a 'withholding tax', often at 15 per cent. For UK tax purposes, the amount to be included in income is the gross equivalent. The overseas withholding tax is then deducted from the UK liability.

Illustration 17.2

Global Limited has UK profits of £50,000 and also received a dividend of £850 from an overseas investment. A withholding tax at 15 per cent was deducted from the dividend in the country of origin.

Global Limited's UK tax liability will be:

	£
Schedule D Case I	50,000
Schedule D Case V	
£850 × 100/85	1,000
	£51,000
Corporation tax @ 25%	12,750
Less: DTR for withholding tax suffered	150
	£12,600

Relief for 'underlying' tax is examined in illustration 17.3. If a company receives a dividend from an overseas company in which it holds at least 10 per cent of the voting power, relief is also given for the tax on the profits out of which the dividend was paid. This tax is referred to as the *underlying tax*.

Illustration 17.3

Intercosmic Limited owns 20 per cent of Monde SARL, a French company. In the year ended 31 March, 1989, the company's UK profits were £800,000. It also received a dividend of £190,000 from Monde SARL, whose profit and loss account (translated into £ sterling) was as follows:

Monde SARL
Profit and loss account for the year ended 31 March 1989

	£
Profit	4,000,000
Less: Taxation at (say) 25% (amount eventually paid)	1,000,000
	3,000,000
Less: Dividend	950,000
	£2,050,000

A withholding tax at 5 per cent was deducted in France from the dividend received by Intercosmic.

To calculate the final UK corporation tax liability, it is necessary to compute the equivalent of the amount received in the UK grossed up for both withholding tax and underlying tax. The precise method of calculation in practice was established in *Bowater Paper Corporation Ltd* v. *Murgatroyd* (1969) and requires the use of the tax *actually paid* for the year (here £1,000,000) and the profit available for distribution as shown in the accounts (here £3,000,000).

The underlying tax rate is:

$$\frac{£1{,}000{,}000}{£1{,}000{,}000 + £3{,}000{,}000} = 25\%$$

In this straightforward example the result of the calculation is to arrive at the exact rate taken in the accounts, but this could vary in a more complex practical example.

The amount to include in Intercosmic's tax computation as Schedule D Case V income is thus:

Dividend received £		*Gross up for withholding tax 5%*			*Gross up for underlying tax 25%*
190,000	×	100/95	=£200,000	× $\frac{100}{75}$	= £266,667

The UK corporation tax liability of Intercosmic will be:

	£	£
Schedule D Case I		800,000
Schedule D Case V		266,667
		£1,066,667
Corporation tax @ 35%		373,333
less: Double tax relief Withholding tax	10,000	
Underlying tax £266,667 @ 25%	66,667	76,667
UK corporation tax payable		£ 296,666

(b) Relief by deduction from foreign source

It is almost always better for the taxpayer to claim reliefs described above in which foreign tax suffered is deducted from UK tax. There are a few instances in which it will be preferable to claim instead to deduct the foreign tax from the foreign income and bring the net sum into charge to UK tax. This could be beneficial if, for example, the UK company has a loss:

Illustration 17.4

Galacton Ltd carries on business in the UK and also has foreign income. Results for the year ended 31 December, 1988, were:

	£
UK business (Schedule D Case I) loss	(100,000)
Foreign income (Schedule D Case V)	10,000
(foreign tax suffered £3,000)	

A claim under s. 393 (2) will relieve part of the loss against the Case V income and UK corporation tax will thus be nil. The computations below show the effect of claiming credit relief (as in (a) above) and relief by deduction of the tax from foreign income.

	Credit relief £	*Deduction as expense* £
Foreign income	10,000	7,000
s. 393 (2) claim	10,000	7,000
	Nil	Nil

Although the result is in each case a nil UK tax liability, with foreign tax deducted as an expense the loss available for other reliefs is £93,000 rather than £90,000.

Controlled foreign companies (ss. 747–756)

A controlled foreign company (CFC) is a company which is:

(a) Resident outside the UK
(b) Controlled by persons resident in the UK
(c) Subject to a lower level of tax in the country of residence than it would suffer by way of UK corporation tax if it were a UK company. This condition will be deemed to be satisfied if the tax in the overseas country is less than 50 per cent of the UK tax that would be payable on its profits.

Unless the CFC falls within one of four exemptions, the Revenue may direct that its profits (excluding chargeable gains) are to be apportioned among its members and subjected to UK income tax (for individual members) or corporation tax (for company members) in their hands.

The exemptions are:

(a) The direction may be made if the CFC pursues an 'acceptable' distribution policy – that is, if dividends paid to UK residents exceed 50 per cent of available profits if a trading company, or 90 per cent of available profits if not a trading company
(b) No direction may be made if the company's activities are 'exempt'. To qualify as exempt, the company must show that it is managed in and from the country of residence and that its business does not involve dealing in goods to or from the UK or to or from connected persons
(c) No direction may be made if the CFC is a quoted company in which not less than 35 per cent of the shares were held by the public throughout the accounting period. Also, the voting power held by the company's principal members must not exceed 85 per cent.
(d) No direction is to be made if the profits excluding capital gains do not exceed £20,000 per annum.
(e) No direction will be made if the Revenue are satisfied that the main purpose of the CFC's existence, and of its transactions, was not a reduction in UK tax liability of any person.

Summary

International companies

Companies trading internationally are taxed according to their country of residence. Section 66 FA 1988 establishes that as from 15 March 1988 a company registered in the UK has and must retain UK residential status.

A company resident in the UK will be liable to UK corporation tax on its world income. A company not resident in the UK will be liable only on profits derived from the operation of a UK branch or agency.

Overseas subsidiaries or branches

Losses made by overseas subsidiaries are not available for a group loss claim, though losses by an overseas branch would be included automatically in computing overall profit.

If transactions between a UK holding company and an overseas subsidiary take place at transfer prices not on an arm's length basis, the Revenue have the right under s. 770 to substitute the arm's length price.

Double tax relief

If a UK company has income derived from overseas, it may be liable to both UK tax and foreign tax on the same income. Double tax relief (DTR) exists to reduce the total tax suffered down to the higher of the two tax rates being charged. DTR is usually given by means of a deduction of foreign tax suffered from the UK tax liability.

Controlled foreign companies (CFCs)

A CFC is defined in s. 747 as a company resident outside the UK but controlled by persons resident in the UK and subject to a lower rate of tax overseas than the UK corporation tax that would have been chargeable had the income arisen in the UK.

The Revenue have extensive powers, subject to exceptions, to direct that the income of CFC's should be apportioned among its members and so brought into charge to UK income tax or corporation tax.

Progress questions

Attempt these questions to test your absorption of the material in the chapter. Rework them at intervals for revision. Answers on page 400.

1 What must a non-resident have in order to bring itself within the UK tax net?

2 Is it possible for a UK company to change its residence? Give reasons.

3 What is the normal result of most double tax relief claims?

4 How are: (a) charges, (b) ACT paid treated when there is a DTR claim?

5 What is (a) withholding tax, (b) underlying tax?

6 (a) What is a controlled foreign company?
   (b) What power does the Revenue have in relation to controlled foreign companies?
   (c) When may the company be outside the power given to the Revenue over controlled foreign companies?

18 Tax planning for companies

Introduction

The basic concepts of income tax planning were covered in Chapter 10, where we saw among other things the clear distinction that must be drawn between tax *avoidance* – legally reducing tax liabilities – and tax *evasion* – trying to do the same thing illegally. We now turn to a brief review of the possibilities for companies in reducing their corporation tax liabilities.

Loss relief strategy

The huge range of alternative reliefs available for income tax losses is somewhat reduced for corporation tax. The main alternatives are:

(a) Claim under s. 393 (2), then carrying the remainder of the loss forward under s. 393 (1)
(b) As (a) but with a claim against the previous period as well as the current period (s. 393 (2) + (3))
(c) Claim under s. 393 (1) only
(d) Surrender of loss to '75 per cent' companies in the same group
(e) Relief against surplus FII

Factors to consider in deciding how best to claim are:

(a) Tax rates in the periods affected
(b) Effect on ACT
(c) Effect on charges (which may become unrelieved and have to be carried forward under s. 393 (9))
(d) Speed with which relief or refund is obtained
(e) Effect on small companies relief calculation

In general we shall want to claim in the year in which tax rates are highest, not forgetting that profits between £100,000 and £500,000 are taxed at an effective rate of about 37.5 per cent in the small companies relief calculation.

A loss claim under s. 393 (2) or s. 393 (2) + (3) may lead to ACT problems – ACT which had previously been relieved ceasing to be so as the loss claim eliminates the profit concerned. However, the ACT should be relievable in earlier years by carrying it back.

Similarly, charges paid may become unrelieved. Then *trade charges only* may be carried forward under s. 393 (9).

It may be possible to manipulate the amount of the loss by exercising the right to renounce all or part of capital allowances, or by timing capital expenditure, or even revenue expenditure, suitably. Remember too that in a group relief claim the surrendering company does not need to claim all internal loss reliefs available to it. The fact that trading losses are offsettable against other income *and chargeable gains* may introduce further flexibility as the timing of realisation of capital gains is often easily controlled.

Small companies relief

Small companies relief is helpful to companies with profits up to £100,000, but in the marginal band between £100,000 and £500,000 is less so, since the rate here is 37½ per cent. It was shown on page 170. that a useful tax saving may be made by equalizing profits of two years so as to keep a company out of the marginal band.

ACT and income tax management

Timing of dividends

A fundamental point here is that a company may obtain a small cash flow advantage by paying a dividend at the beginning of a new quarterly return period rather than at the end of one. For example, a dividend paid on 30 June would require the payment of the related ACT fourteen days later on 14 July. By deferring payment of the dividend by one day, settlement of the ACT liability would be deferred until 14 October.

Another point is that payment of dividends late in the *accounting* period shortens the waiting time for the offset against corporation tax.

Similar considerations apply to payments of loan interest and the income tax to be accounted for on it.

Group income

51 per cent subsidiaries may pay dividends to their holding company, or to fellow 51 per cent subsidiaries, without accounting for ACT provided the joint election under s. 257 has been made. This is normally a

good idea as it improves group cash flow. However, there are situations in which it will be beneficial *not* to treat such dividends as group income, and the companies concerned may give notice to the Revenue that they do not wish the election to apply to certain dividends.

The situations in which it will be beneficial for the group income election not to apply are:

(a) If the subsidiary has franked investment income it can only obtain relief for it by making a *franked* payment. All or most of this will pass to other group companies. They in turn can pay a dividend, using the benefit of the tax credit on the franked investment income to reduce their own ACT payments.

(b) If the subsidiary has not used all available ACT set-offs of earlier years, the only way to use this is to make a franked payment of its own, since surrendered ACT cannot be carried back. The holding company can surrender ACT to the subsidiary, to be set off by the subsidiary in priority to its own ACT, which can then be carried back. The receipt of the franked payment also reduces the holding company's ACT. (You may have to read that through twice before you grasp it!)

Groups of companies

Group income

This has already been discussed above.

Group loss relief

If one company in a group has trading losses, the possibility of surrendering them to other 75 per cent group companies must obviously be considered. A surrender which would have the effect of reducing the profit of a subsidiary in the marginal small companies band would save tax at 37½ per cent. Remember that in a group the small company limits would be reduced. If there is no company in this situation, a surrender to a 'large' company would be preferable to a surrender to a 'small' company. As capital losses cannot be transferred between group companies, it is essential to maximise relief for such losses by channelling all group sales of chargeable assets through one company in the group. (Although capital losses cannot be transferred, capital assets themselves may be transferred between group companies at a 'no gain, no loss' price.)

Maximizing capital allowances

Judicious timing of capital expenditure and the use of the right to renounce capital allowances are useful devices to adjust the company's profit so as to make the best use of loss relief and the small companies reduced rate.

Another important consideration is the use of the 'de-pooling' election for short life plant and machinery. (See page 41.)

Company takeovers

When one company takes over another it may be important to preserve the availability of loss relief and the carrying forward of unrelieved ACT.

Factors to consider are:

(a) Relief under s. 393 (1) may be lost if, within the same period of three years, there is both a change in ownership of a company (more than 50 per cent of ordinary share capital transferred), and a change in the nature of its trade. It is therefore necessary to continue the existing trade beyond the three year limit (ss. 768–769).
(b) Relief under s. 393 (1) may also be lost if there is a change of ownership after the company's trade has reduced to a small or negligible level. There is no three year time limit on this one (ss. 768–769).
(c) The right to carry forward unrelieved ACT may be lost in the situations described in (a) and (b) above (s. 245).
(d) If there is a company reconstruction involving the transfer of the business to a new company, the right to carry forward the losses of the old company into the new company is only available if at least 75 per cent of the ordinary share capital of both companies has belonged to the same shareholders at some time during the period beginning one year before the reconstruction and ending two years after it.

Integration of tax planning into the budgeting process

Awareness and consideration of tax aspects should be automatic for all those concerned with budgeting.

Capital expenditure

The procedure for authorizing capital expenditure should ensure that tax effects have been allowed for in discounted cash flow or other appraisal techniques. These effects include:

(a) Capital allowances on expenditure, including balancing adjustments on disposal
(b) Corporation tax on cash flow generated
(c) Availability of relief for losses, if these are expected in the early years of a project

(d) Planning industrial buildings so that where possible the whole structure qualifies for industrial buildings allowance (i.e. non-industrial portion does not exceed 25 per cent)
(e) Choosing tax-allowable expenditure rather than non-allowable where possible, e.g. movable partitions rather than fixed ones
(f) Timing effects – the tax benefit of expenditure will be felt one year earlier if, say, capital expenditure is incurred in December rather than January by a company with a 31 December accounting date. In general, the cash flow effects of tax will occur in the year following the related expenditure or profit, bearing in mind the normal due date of nine months after the end of the accounting period.

Cash budgets

It is an obvious but necessary point that cash budgets and cash flow forecasts must include taxation payments or refunds.

Summary

Tax planning is an essential consideration in many aspects of the management of a business. This chapter summarizes some important points in relation to:

(a) Loss relief
(b) Use of small companies relief
(c) ACT and income tax management
(d) Groups of companies
(e) Company takeovers
(f) Integration of tax planning into the budgeting process

Progress questions

Attempt these questions to test your absorption of the material in the chapter. Rework them at intervals for revision. Answers are on page 401.

1 What factors need to be considered in optimising company claims for relief for trading losses?

2 Give three examples of ways in which a company may legally increase or reduce its profit or loss for tax purposes in a given accounting period.

3 Why is it important that companies stay out of the marginal small companies relief band if possible?

4 What factors need to be considered by a company in managing its ACT/income tax position?

5 In what circumstances may it pay for a group of companies to give notice that a group income election is not to apply to certain distributions?

6 How may the benefit of capital allowances be maximised?

7 State three tax factors to consider in connection with company takeovers.

8 State six tax planning factors to consider in relation to budgeting.

Part Three Capital Gains Tax

19 Capital gains tax – basic principles

Introduction

Capital gains tax (CGT) was introduced in 1965 to tax gains arising on disposals of assets in circumstances that would not normally attract income tax. The most important type of transaction caught by CGT is the sale of listed stocks and shares. A large number of assets are exempt from CGT, many of them as a matter of convenience in collecting the tax.

CGT as such is levied only on individuals and is charged at the individual's marginal rate of tax (25 per cent or 40 per cent). If companies make gains, they are calculated broadly according to the rules of CGT, but then subjected to corporation tax at 25 per cent, or 35 per cent depending on whether they are 'small' companies or not. The application of corporation tax to chargeable gains was illustrated in Chapters 11, 13 and 14 above.

The Finance Act 1988 introduced a major change into CGT by 're-basing' the tax. For 1988/89 onwards, gains on the disposal of assets held on 31 March 1982 are generally to be based on the market value of the assets at that date. In other words, gains accruing before that date are to be ignored.

In some circumstances, however, gains or losses arising before 1982 may be relevant. This point is pursued further in Chapter 20 below.

The liability to CGT for an individual is calculated by reference to the year to 5 April. The gains and losses on all chargeable transactions are calculated, and tax is then payable on the net chargeable gains, less the annual exemption of £5,000 (1988/89). The due date for payment is 1 December following the year of assessment, or thirty days after the issue of the assessment if later.

The governing legislation for CGT is the Capital Gains Tax Act 1979 (CGTA 1979) as amended by subsequent Finance Acts.

Chargeable and exempt assets

Exempt assets

The principle is that all assets are chargeable unless exempted, but the list of exemptions is fairly long.

The following are all exempt:

(a) An individual's principal private residence – this is obviously an important exemption. It will normally be fully available, but there are cases in which it is restricted – see below. If an individual has more than one residence he or she must elect, within two years of commencing ownership of the second one which is to be treated as exempt.
(b) A second residence provided for a dependent relative. One other residence provided *rent free* for a dependent relative may also be exempt, *provided it was so occupied on or before 5 April 1988.*
(c) Private motor vehicles.
(d) Chattels (tangible movable property) sold for less than £3,000. This exemption takes out of the charge to CGT most of the assets an individual owns. If a chattel is sold for slightly more than £3,000, the tax charge is limited – see below for more details.
(e) Chattels which are wasting assets (i.e. those with a life of less than fifty years) – these are fully exempt from CGT unless they are trading assets on which capital allowances are available. Examples could be boats, caravans, animals.
(f) UK Government stocks (exempt for sales after 1 July 1986).
(g) Qualifying corporate bonds (also exempt for sales after 1 July 1986) – a 'qualifying corporate bond' is one which was *issued* after 13 March 1984 or, if issued before that date, was acquired by the taxpayer after that date. The exemption applies to all listed securities expressed in sterling, and thus covers, for example, UK company debentures satisfying the conditions.
(h) Betting winnings.
(i) Currency for private use – this exemption covers incidental gains or losses arising on, for example, foreign currency obtained for holiday purposes. It does not cover purchases and sales which are currency speculations.
(j) Surpluses on the maturation of life assurance policies.
(k) Decorations for valour (unless acquired by purchase).

Exempt disposals

In addition to these exempt *assets* there are also some exempt *disposals:*

(a) Disposal on death – no chargeable gain or allowable loss arises when assets pass to others on death. A separate tax, inheritance tax, may be levied on the capital value of the estate, however.
(b) Gifts to a non-profit making body of land, buildings, works of art

and the like, provided the gift is for the public benefit and public access is allowed.

(c) Sale of works of art and the like to approved UK national or local institutions (art galleries or museums for example).
(d) Gifts of any type of asset for charitable purposes to an approved charity.
(e) Transfers to the Inland Revenue in settlement of inheritance tax liabilities.

Allowable deductions

In principle, the calculation of the gain or loss on a disposal is simply proceeds of sale less cost or value at 31 March 1982, subject to the indexation adjustment explained below. However, there are some other possible deductions:

(a) Incidental costs of acquisition (commissions, brokerage, for example)
(b) Further expenditure on improving the asset
(c) Legal expenses in defending title to the asset
(d) Incidental costs of disposal

Indexation

A tax on capital gains would be unfair if based on the simple comparison of cost and sale proceeds. Some allowance for the effect of inflation over the period of ownership is needed.

This is done by allowing the cost to be 'indexed up' according to the movements in the retail price index during the period of ownership (or from 31 March 1982 to date of sale for assets purchased before that date).

Illustration 19.1

An asset which cost £10,000 in February 1987 was sold in April 1988 for £20,000.

Retail price indices were:

February 1987	100.4
April 1988	105.8

The calculation of the chargeable gain will be:

	£	£
Proceeds of sale		20,000
Cost	10,000	
Indexation		

	£	£
£10,000 × $\left[\frac{105.8 - 100.4}{100.4}\right]$		
= £10,000 × 0.054	540	10,540
Chargeable gain		£ 9,460

In making the calculation, the result of the boxed calculation is rounded to three places of decimals – 0.0537848 thus becomes 0.054.

The indexation adjustment can reduce a gain, as here, and can also convert a gain into an allowable loss.

You may also see the indexation factor given in the form of a percentage – for example in the above case the equivalent percentage would be 5.4 per cent. (A percentage to one place of decimals gives the same degree of accuracy as three places of decimals.) Percentage indexation factors are given in the remainder of this book.

CIMA have announced that indexation factors will be given in the examination, and you will not, therefore, have to do calculations with the RPI indices themselves. In the remainder of our coverage of CGT the factors only are shown in calculations, and there is a complete Table of them beginning on page 404. You should familiarize yourself with the use of the table by confirming with the table factors given in illustrations.

The principal private residence exemption

An individual's principal private residence is exempt, together with land up to one acre (or such additional area necessary for the enjoyment of the property as a residence). Restrictions may arise if the taxpayer is not resident in the property for the whole period of ownership, but there are fairly generous rules which allow certain periods of absence to be disregarded:

(a) Absence for up to three years for any reason
(b) Absence for any length of time while the individual is employed abroad
(c) Absence for up to four years while working elsewhere in the UK
(d) Absence for any period while required to live in job-related accommodation elsewhere, provided the taxpayer intends to occupy the house as his main residence at some time in the future
(e) The last two years of ownership (this exemption is intended to allow time for selling a house after having moved to another)

Exemptions (a), (b), and (c) are only available if the taxpayer has lived in the property at some time before *and* after the period of absence, but the requirement for occupation after the absence is waived if the employee is prevented from doing so because his employment requires him or her to work elsewhere.

There is a further relief for owner-occupiers who let their property. If a charge to CGT arises on such property the gain is reduced by the lower of:

(a) The amount exempt because of owner occupation
(b) £20,000

The chattels exemption

As we saw in 2 (e) above, chattels sold for less than £3,000 are completely exempt from CGT. If the proceeds of sale slightly exceed £3,000 the chargeable gain is limited to five-thirds of the excess.

If a loss arises on the sale of a chattel which had cost more that £3,000 and is sold for less than £3,000, the allowable loss is cost less £3,000, not the full difference between cost and sale proceeds.

Illustration 19.2

Chippendale bought an antique table for £2,000 in February 1987 and sold it in April 1988 for £3,600. (Indexation factor 5.4 per cent.) The gain on the disposal will be:

	£	£
Proceeds		3,600
Cost		2,000
		1,600
Indexation		
£2,000 × 5.4%		108
		£1,492
Limited to:		
5/3 × (£3,600 − £3,000)		£1,000

The chargeable gain will be £1,000

Illustration 19.3

Sheraton bought an antique chair for £3,500 in February 1987 and sold it in April 1988 for £2,500.

The allowable loss on the disposal will be:

	£	£
Proceeds (deemed to be £3,000)		3,000
Cost		3,500
Loss		500
Indexation		
£3,500 × 5.4%		232
Allowable loss		£ 732

If a chattel consists of a set of items, the £3,000 chattels exemption will not be available if the set is sold piecemeal *to the same person* or to someone connected with him or her. In this situation the sales are treated as forming a single transaction and the £3,000 limit, if relevant, will be applied to the total proceeds.

Persons chargeable to CGT

Individuals domiciled and resident or ordinarily resident, in the UK are liable to CGT on the disposal of any chargeable asset anywhere in the world. Those resident here but not *domiciled* in the UK are liable only on UK assets, or on gains arising on foreign assets only if remitted to the UK. Someone not resident in the UK is only liable to CGT if carrying on a business through a UK branch or agency, and then only on disposals of the assets of that branch or agency.

There are several groups of *exempt* persons including:

(a) Registered charities
(b) Approved pension schemes
(c) Friendly societies
(d) Local authorities.

As stated on page 141, companies are subject to corporation tax on their chargeable gains.

Disposal

The main way in which a charge to CGT arises is on the sale of an asset. Other events which can give rise to a charge to capital gains tax, or an allowable loss, are:

(a) The sale of part of an asset (see page 249).
(b) Gift of the asset – in this case the donor is charged on the difference between cost and the market value at the time of the gift, subject to an election explained on page 270.
(c) Receipt of a capital sum connected with an asset, as when an insurance policy provides compensation for loss or damage.
(d) Complete loss in value of an asset, as when a company goes into liquidation leaving nothing for the shareholders, thus rendering the shares valueless.

Treatment of losses

In principle, losses are calculated in the same way as gains. Loss relief is granted by allowing losses to be carried forward, without time limit, against future chargeable gains.

In the year in which an individual uses loss relief *brought forward*, it is only required to be used to the extent necessary to reduce gains to the level of the annual exemption for that year.

Summary

Introduction

Capital gains tax was introduced in 1965 but as from 1988/89 applies only to gains arising after 31 March 1982.

Individuals pay capital gains tax on 25 per cent or 40 per cent, depending on their marginal income tax rate. It is due for payment on 1 December following the year of assessment, or thirty days after the issue of the assessment if later.

Companies pay corporation tax on their gains, at 25 per cent or 35 per cent depending on whether they are 'small' companies or not. (In the marginal small companies band the rate will be different, as explained in Chapter 13.) The due date for companies is the normal corporation tax due date, as the tax simply forms part of the total corporation tax liability.

Exempt assets

There are many exempt assets:

(a) Principal private residence
(b) Second residence occupied rent-free by dependent relative (provided the occupation began on or before 5 April 1988)
(c) Private motor vehicles
(d) Chattels sold for less than £3,000
(e) Wasting chattels (unless trading assets on which capital allowances are available)
(f) UK Government stocks
(g) Qualifying corporate bonds
(h) Betting winnings
(i) Currency for private use
(j) Surpluses on life assurance policies
(k) Decorations for valour

Exempt disposals

There are also exempt *disposals:*

(a) Disposals on death
(b) Gifts to non-profit making bodies for the public benefit
(c) Sale of works of art etc. to National or local institutions
(d) Gifts to charity
(e) Transfers to Inland Revenue in payment of inheritance tax.

Indexation

Allowance is made for inflation by indexing the cost upwards to allow for the movement in the Retail Price Index (RPI) between acquisition and disposal.

Principal private residence

Exemption may be partly lost if the individual is not in residence for the whole period of ownership.

Persons chargeable

Individuals resident or ordinarily resident in the UK are the main persons chargeable to CGT. Companies pay corporation tax on their chargeable gains.

Those exempt from CGT include:

(a) Registered charities
(b) Approved pension schemes
(c) Friendly societies
(d) Local authorities.

Disposal

The following events may constitute a disposal for CGT purposes:

(a) Sale
(b) Gift
(c) Receipt of compensation for loss or damage
(d) Destruction or other complete loss in value of an asset.

Losses

Losses are set off against gains of the same year to 5 April. Any unrelieved balance is carried forward for relief in future years. When losses are brought forward, they need only be used to the extent necessary to reduce the chargeable gains of that year to the level of the annual exemption (£5,000 in 1988/89).

Progress questions

Attempt these questions to test your absorption of the material in the chapter. Rework them at intervals for revision: Answers are on page 401.

1 From what date does CGT operate for 1988/89 and subsequent years?

2 Fill in the blanks in the sentence below:

For individuals, CGT is charged for years to ... and is due for payment.... The first £ ... (1988/89) of gains each year is exempt. To adjust for the impact of inflation on CGT, the ... of an asset disposed of is ... according to movements in the ... between the date of purchase (or ... if later) and the date of sale.

3 Name ten assets exempt from CGT

4 Name four types of disposal exempt from CGT

5 What periods of absence may be disregarded in computing the exemption available on the sale of a principal private residence?

6 Explain how the £3,000 chattels exemption works in relation to:

(a) Disposals at a profit
(b) Disposals at a loss

7 (a) Who is chargeable to CGT?
(b) Name three persons or bodies exempt from CGT

8 Give four examples of events which are regarded for CGT purposes as disposals of an asset.

9 How are capital losses relieved?

20 Capital gains tax – computations

Introduction

The basic form of a CGT computation was explained in Chapter 19. We now turn to some special computations and deal with:

(a) Assets held at 31 March 1982
(b) Part disposals
(c) Enhancement expenditure
(d) Wasting assets other than leases
(e) Leases

Quoted and unquoted shares and securities present special problems and a consideration of these is deferred until Chapter 21.

Assets held at 31 March 1982 (the 1988/89 starting point for CGT)

When an asset held at 31 March 1982 is sold, the 'cost' is taken to be the market value at that date, and the indexation adjustment is applied to that value.

The only provised is that if a smaller gain *or smaller loss* would arise if the original cost were to be used as the basis, then that original cost basis is used. In that case indexation is applied *from 31 March 1982 only* to the higher of cost and 31 March 1982 market value.

If the '31 March 1982 market value' basis produces a gain and the 'original cost' basis produce a loss, or vice versa, the disposal is to be treated as giving rise to a 'no gain no loss' result.

The taxpayer has the option, under s. 96 FA 1988, to elect for the use of the 31 March 1982 market value for all assets. That election must be made within two years of the end of the accounting period (companies) or year of assessment (individuals) in which the first relevant disposal is made.

It is to be expected that most taxpayers will gain by making the election. The advantages of doing so will be:

(a) Considerable saving of time and expense in computing gains or losses based on cost of assets held on 31 March 1982.
(b) Saving of tax, as it is much more likely that a smaller gain will arise by general application of the 31 March 1982 market value basis.

A taxpayer should not make the election only if it is clear that there will be an overall reduction in gains if the right to use the original cost is retained.

Part disposals

When there is a part disposal of an asset (other than shares – see Chapter 21) it is necessary to apportion the cost (or 31 March 1982 market value) between the part sold and the part retained.

This is done by reference to sale proceeds and *market value at date of sale*:

Cost of part sold is:

$$\text{Allowable costs} \times \frac{\text{Sale proceeds}}{\text{Sale proceeds} + \text{Market value (as at date of disposal) of part retained}}$$

The sale proceeds used in the calculation are taken *before* deducting costs of sale.

Illustration 20.1

A Ltd bought a plot of land in April 1983 for £26,000. In May 1988 part of it was sold for £40,000. The market value of the remainder at the date of sale was agreed to be £60,000.

The computation will be:

	£
Proceeds of sale	40,000
Cost £26,000 $\times \dfrac{£40,000}{£40,000 + £60,000}$	10,400
Chargeable gain (subject to indexation)	£29,600

Note: This computation shows the standard treatment for part disposals. In fact, as this is a part disposal of land, the Revenue will accept, in accordance with their Statement of Practice D1, any 'fair and reasonable' method of allocating cost to the part disposed of. This variation applies only to land and buildings.

Small part disposals

If the partial disposal represents no more than 5 per cent of the value of the whole at the time of sale (20 per cent for land and buildings if sale proceeds do not exceed £20,000) the taxpayer may elect to deduct the proceeds from the cost of the asset when calculating the gain or loss on the subsequent disposal of the whole.

Illustration 20.2

Ernest purchased a plot of land for £18,000 in May 1984. In May 1987 he sold part of it for £10,000 when the value of the remainder was agreed to be worth £50,000. In May 1988 he sold the remainder of the plot for £70,000.

Indexation factors:

May 1984 to May 1987	14.5%
May 1984 to May 1988	19.4%
May 1987 to May 1988	4.2%

Ernest may simply pay CGT in May 1987 on the basis of the normal part disposal rules (or any 'fair and reasonable' method as the asset is land).

Alternatively, he may claim to 'roll over' the transaction by deducting the proceeds from the cost for the purpose of the subsequent disposal in May 1988. If this is done, the gain in May 1988 will be:

	£	£	£
Proceeds			70,000
Cost £18,000 − £10,000		8,000	
Indexation:			
£18,000 × 19.4%	3,492		
Less:			
Referable to rolled over proceeds			
£10,000 × 4.2%	420	3,072	11,072
Chargeable gain			£58,928

Enhancement expenditure

If capital expenditure on improving an asset is incurred, that is an allowable addition to the original cost (or 31 March 1982 valuation). The only complication is that indexation will run from the date of each item of expenditure and must therefore be computed separately for each one.

Illustration 20.3

G Ltd bought a house in 1980 for £30,000. Extensions were carried out in March 1985 at a cost of £10,000 and further capital work in April 1987 cost £20,000. The house was sold in May 1988 for £180,000.

The market value at 31 March 1982 was £40,000.

Indexation factors:

March 1982 to May 1988	33.7%
March 1985 to May 1988	15.5%
April 1987 to May 1988	4.3%

	£	£	£
Proceeds of sale			180,000
Less: Market value 31 March 1982	40,000		
Indexation £40,000 × 33.7%	13,480	53,480	
Cost March 1985	10,000		
Indexation £10,000 × 15.5%	1,550	11,550	
Cost April 1987	20,000		
Indexation £20,000 × 4.3%	860	20,860	85,890
Chargeable gain			£94,110

Wasting assets other than leases

A wasting asset is one with an expected life of less than fifty years. The CGT treatment of wasting assets depends upon their nature:

(a) Wasting chattels – these are exempt from CGT altogether
(b) Wasting assets which are plant and machinery on which capital allowances could have been claimed. Gains are fully chargeable to CGT, but there is no relief for losses, which will have been covered by the capital allowances.
(c) Other wasting assets (apart from leases which are dealt with below)

There are few wasting assets apart from the categories already mentioned. Possible examples are copyrights or trade marks. For CGT purposes, such assets are deemed to waste away over their predictable life on a straight line basis.

Illustration 20.4

In May 1983 Cecily Ltd purchased a copyright with a predictable life of twenty years. The cost was £4,000. In May 1988 it was sold for £8,000.

The gain on the disposal will be:

	£	£
Proceeds		8,000
Less: Cost £4,000 × 15/20	3,000	
Indexation £3,000 × 25.5%	765	3,765
Chargeable gain		£4,235

Leases

Introduction

The disposal of a short lease requires a special calculation because they are assumed not to waste away on a straight line basis, but slowly at first then accelerating according to a table in Schedule 3 Capital Gains Tax Act 1979, reproduced as Table 12.

Table 12

Years	*Percentage*	*Years*	*Percentage*
50 (or more)	100	25	81.100
49	99.657	24	79.622
48	99.289	23	78.055
47	98.902	22	76.399
46	98.490	21	74.635
45	98.059	20	72.770
44	97.595	19	70.791
43	97.107	18	68.697
42	96.593	17	66.470
41	96.041	16	64.116
40	95.457	15	61.617
39	94.842	14	58.971
38	94.189	13	56.167
37	93.497	12	53.191
36	92.761	11	50.038
35	91.981	10	46.695
34	91.156	9	43.154
33	90.280	8	39.399
32	89.354	7	35.414
31	88.371	6	31.195
30	87.330	5	26.722
29	86.226	4	21.983
28	85.053	3	16.959
27	83.816	2	11.629
26	82.496	1	5.983
		0	0

Any necessary figures will be given to you in the examination.

If you study Table 12 you can see that the value of the lease reduces very little between years fifty and forty-nine (by 0.343 per cent to be exact), but the rate steadily increases so that between years 1 and 0 the reduction is 5.983 per cent.

Illustration 20.5

Chasuble Limited acquired a forty year lease in May 1983 for £50,000. It was sold in May 1988 for £60,000. (Indexation factor 25.5 per cent.)

Discussion
The calculation of the gain must take into account the fact that at the time of sale the length of the lease is only thirty-five years, and part of the cost must be attributed to the five year period of ownership before the sale.

The cost of the 35 year lease sold is taken to be:

$$\text{Original cost} \times \frac{\text{Percentage applicable to remaining life on disposal}}{\text{Percentage applicable to remaining life on acquisition}}$$

The computation is therefore:

		£
Proceeds		60,000
Less:		
Cost £50,000 × $\frac{91.981}{95.457}$	48,179	
Indexation £48,179 × 25.5%	12,286	60,465
Allowable loss		465

Note that no Schedule A charge arises here. The whole leasehold interest is being assigned, whereas the Schedule A charge on premiums only arises when a lease is granted out of another or out of a freehold interest.

In Illustration 20.5 the life of the lease was an exact number of years at both relevant dates. If this is not the case, the percentage is determined by linear interpolation between two figures. Thus the percentage for a lease with thirty-five years and four months to run would be:

$$91.981 + \frac{4}{12}(92.761 - 91.981) = 92.241$$

Disposal of a sublease out of a short lease

If a sublease is granted out of a short lease we have to identify the percentage referable to the part sold. Thus if in the previous illustration Chasuble Limited has granted a five year lease in May 1988 for a premium of £10,000 the position would have been:

	£	£
Proceeds		10,000
Less:		
Cost £50,000 × $\frac{91.981 - 87.330}{95.457}$	2,436	
Indexation £2,436 × 25.5%	622	2,858
Chargeable gain		7,142

The use of the percentages for thirty-five years and thirty years in arriving at the numerator of the fraction correctly identifies, according to the rules, the proportion of cost attributable to the five years disposed of.

That is not the end of the computation, however. Chasuble Limited will have a Schedule A liability on the premium received of £10,000 − 2(5 − 1)% = £9,200. (If you have forgotten your Schedule A, take a look back at page 83.) The amount of the premium under Schedule A (£9,200) is assessed in full, then deducted from any gain chargeable to CGT. If, as here, the Schedule A assessment exceeds the chargeable gain, the gain is reduced to nil but no loss can be created.

Disposal of a long lease out of a freehold or another long lease

In this case there is no Schedule A assessment because the Schedule A premium rules apply only to short leases. We have a normal part disposal situation.

Illustration 20.6

Prism Ltd acquired a freehold property in January 1983 for £100,000 and in April 1988 granted a ninety-nine year lease for £160,000. At that time the reversionary interest (the value of the right to the return of the property at the end of the lease) was worth £40,000. Indexation factor 28.6%.

The computation will be:

	£	£
Proceeds		160,000
Less:		
Cost $£100{,}000 \times \dfrac{£160{,}000}{£160{,}000 + £40{,}000}$	80,000	
Indexation £80,000 × 28.6%	22,880	102,880
Chargeable gain		£ 57,120

Disposal of a short sublease out of a long lease

Provided the original lease is still a long lease at the time of the grant of the sublease, the Schedule 3 Table percentages do not have to be used.

As the lease granted is a short lease, there will be a Schedule A assessment.

In this case, however, the amount assessed under Schedule A is deducted from the consideration as shown in Illustration 20.7.

Illustration 20.7

Facts as in Illustration 20.6 except that Prism Ltd granted a forty-one year lease for £75,000 and the value of the reversionary interest was agreed to be £125,000.

Computation

		£
(a) Amount assessable under Schedule A		
Premium		75,000
Less: £75,000 × 2(41 − 1)%		60,000
		£15,000

	£	£
(b) CGT computation		
Proceeds		75,000
Less: Schedule A assessment		15,000
		60,000
Less: Cost		
$£100{,}000 \times \dfrac{£75{,}000 - £15{,}000}{£75{,}000 + £125{,}000}$	30,000	
Indexation £30,000 × 28.6%	8,580	38,580
Chargeable gain		£21,420

Notice how the £15,000 Schedule A assessment is deducted from the proceeds and also from the *numerator only* in apportioning cost.

Summary

Assets held at 31 March 1982

Gains and losses on assets held at 31 March 1982 are generally calculated using the market value at that date, unless the use of original cost produces a smaller gain or a smaller loss.

Part disposals

When part of an asset is disposed of, the cost attributable to the part sold is calculated by using the formula:

$$\text{Cost of part sold} = \text{Total cost} \times \frac{\text{Proceeds of sale}}{\text{Proceeds of sale plus market value of remainder}}$$

In the case of land or buildings another 'fair and reasonable' method may be agreed instead.

Small part disposals

The taxpayer may elect to have disposal proceeds not exceeding 5 per cent of the total value at the time of sale (20 per cent for land and buildings up to £20,000 proceeds) deducted from cost, thus deferring a chargeable gain until the remainder of the asset is sold.

Enhancement expenditure

If capital expenditure is incurred at several times, the calculation of the gain is exactly as normal except that indexation must be applied separately to each element of the cost as from the date it was incurred (or 31 March 1982 if later).

Wasting assets

Wasting assets may be divided into four groups as shown in Table 13.

Table 13

	Type of wasting asset	*CGT treatment*
1	Wasting chattels	Exempt
2	Wasting assets which are plant and machinery on which capital allowances can be claimed	Gains fully chargeable (no relief for losses!)
3	Short leases	Cost assumed to lose value according to a table in Schedule 3 CGTA 1979
4	Other wasting assets (e.g. copyrights, trade marks)	Cost assumed to depreciate on a straight line basis

Relationship between Schedule A tax on premiums and CGT on disposals of leases

(a) *Disposal of sublease out of a short lease* – the assessment under Schedule A on the premium is calculated and payable in the normal way. The Schedule A assessment is then deducted from the CGT chargeable gain but cannot create a CGT loss.

(b) *Disposal of a sublease out of a long lease* – the assessment under Schedule A is deducted from the proceeds and in arriving at the numerator of the part disposal fraction.

Progress questions

Attempt these questions to test your absorption of the material in the chapter. Rework them at intervals for revision. Answers are on page 401.

1 (a) How are gains and losses on assets held at 31 March 1982 calculated?

(b) What option does the taxpayer have?

2 (a) When part of an asset is disposed of, what fraction of the original cost is normally deducted from the proceeds?
(b) Explain any exceptions to the normal procedure in (a).

3 Explain the CGT treatment of wasting assets other than short leases.

4 How is the appropriate fraction of cost arrived at when a short lease is disposed of?

5 When the premium on the granting of a sublease is subject to both Schedule A income tax and CGT, which tax takes priority?

21 Capital gains tax – shares and securities

Introduction

One of the most important areas of capital gains tax is the impact of the tax on shares and securities. Most aspects apply to all shares and securities, but it is sometimes necessary to distinguish between quoted shares and securities and unquoted shares and securities. Incidentally, the term 'quoted' shares is taken to *exclude* shares dealt in on the USM (Unlisted Securities Market). The Business Taxation examination will deal with transactions in shares and securities by companies, and the examples in this Chapter follow that.

Securities exempt from CGT

Certain securities are completely exempt from CGT:

(a) Gilt edged stocks (British Government stocks)
(b) National Savings Certificates, Premium Bonds and other non-marketable savings media
(c) Corporate bonds (loan stock and debentures) issued after 13 March 1984 by a company quoted on a recognized stock exchange or on the USM

Pooling

Basic principles of pooling

When a holding of shares has been acquired by several separate purchases, they are treated as making up a single 'pool' of shares out of which disposals are taken as they occur.

That sounds simple, but a complication arises because of the need to index the costs of acquisition as from 31 March 1982. To allow for this, we have to 'index' the pool every time there is a transaction.

Illustration 21.1

Hermia Ltd acquired shares in Lysander Ltd as follows:

May 1985	1,000 shares for £2,000
August 1986	3,000 shares for £8,000
October 1987	4,000 shares for £12,000
In may 1988	4,000 shares were sold for £15,000.

Indexation factors:

May 1985 to August 1986	2.7%
August 1986 to October 1987	5.2%
October 1987 to May 1988	3.2%

We set up a working with three columns:

Number of shares	*Unindexed pool value* £	*Indexed pool value* £

Each time shares enter or leave the pool, the pool balance is indexed to allow the shares concerned to enter or leave the pool consistently.

The computation will be:

	Number of shares	*Unindexed pool value* £	*Indexed pool value* £
May 1985	1,000	2,000	2,000
August 1986:			
Indexation			
£2,000 × 2.7%			54
			2,054
Shares acquired	3,000	8,000	8,000
	4,000	10,000	10,054
October 1987			
Indexation			
£10,054 × 5.2%			523
			10,577
Shares acquired	4,000	12,000	12,000
	8,000	22,000	22,577
May 1988			
Indexation			
£22,577 × 3.2%			723
			23,300

	Number of shares	*Unindexed pool value* £	*Indexed pool value* £
Shares sold	4,000	11,000	11,650
Balance carried forward	4,000	11,000	11,650

The CGT computation will be:

	£
Proceeds	15,000
Less:	
Indexed cost	11,650
Chargeable gain	£ 3,350

Note that the effect of indexing the pool by stages is exactly the same as indexing in one step from the acquisition of each holding to the date of sale.

This system was introduced as from 31 March *1985* (5 April for individuals). Any acquisitions before that date, including holdings on 31 March 1982 entering the pool at their market value, on that date, are first 'indexed up' from 31 March 1982 or later date of purchase to 31 March 1985. The indexed pool so created is then indexed up to date as shown in Illustration 21.1.

Valuation at 31 March 1982

In setting up the pool it is necessary to value shares as at 31 March 1982. For unquoted shares a professional valuation may be necessary – certainly a value must be negotiated with the Revenue. For quoted shares, the Stock Exchange price on 31 March 1982 obviously provides a basis for valuation. In this situation we do not, however, take the mid point between the buying and selling prices listed. Instead, two possible bases of valuation are laid down in s. 150 CGTA 1979:

(a) '¼ up' from the lower of the two prices
(b) The mid point between the highest and lowest prices at which bargains were recorded on the day.

The lower of (a) and (b) is taken to be the value.

Illustration 21.2

On 31 March 1982 shares of Transcosmic Corporation Limited are priced at 139p–143p. This means that they could be sold at 139p or bought at 143p. The 'spread' of 4p represents the profit margin of the dealer. In practice it is found that deals typically take place with a smaller spread than than nominally given in the Stock Exchange Daily Official List. Valuation (a) would therefore be:

139p + ¼ × 4p or 140p

If the bargains recorded for the day were: 138, 139, 141, 144, valuation (b) would be (138 + 144) /2 or 141p. The 31 March 1982 value would thus be taken as 140p.

Identification rules

In general, shares are pooled as described on page 258. There are minor exceptions:

(a) Acquisitions and disposals on the same day are matched together and are not pooled. Thus, if a taxpayer wishes to realize a gain by selling shares and then buying them back, the sale must be on one day and the purchase on the next, hence the colloquial name of 'bed and breakfast' for such transactions. (See page 284.)
(b) Acquisitions within the nine days before the disposal are matched on a FIFO basis.

No indexation is allowed in these cases.

Bonus issues

A bonus issue is the allocation of additional shares to existing shareholders without cost. The additional shares are strictly speaking treated as increasing all previous acquisitions in the pool, but as no indexation is required (because no cost is incurred) it is sufficient to simply add the shares to the 'shares' column with no further adjustment.

When a bonus issue is made on shares acquired before 31 March 1982, it is necessary to be careful in setting up the pool in the first place, which will be done by multiplying the *number of shares held at that date* by the price on that date.

It is easy to make a mistake – multiplying the number of shares as increased by the bonus issue by the price on 31 March 1982. This would only be correct if the question told you that the given 31 March 1982 price had been *adjusted for the subsequent bonus issue.*

Rights issues

(a) Rights issue shares entering the pool
In a rights issue extra shares are acquired as in a bonus issue, but of course some cash is also paid. It is therefore necessary to apply indexation to that cash, and to 'index up' the pool balance as at the date of purchase as with any acquisition of shares other than a bonus issue.

(b) Sale of rights
When there is a rights issue the holder may sell the rights instead of taking them up. This is possible because rights issues to existing shareholders are usually priced below the current market value of the shares,

so that the right to buy at that price has a value which can be realized by sale of the rights.

The disposal of the rights actually represents a part disposal of the original shares held, and thus a part disposal calculation is necessary. The formula used is similar to that shown on page 249 for any part-disposal:

$$\frac{\text{Proceeds of sale of rights}}{\text{Proceeds of sale of rights + Market value of shares on first dealing day after the issue}} \times \text{Cost}$$

As also explained on page 250, the proceeds of sale may instead be *deducted from the cost of the shares* if the amount received does not exceed 5 per cent of the total value at the time of sale (i.e. proceeds of sale of rights plus ex rights price of shares).

Illustration 21.3

R Ltd holds 1,000 shares in Q Ltd which had cost £1,000 in June 1984. In April 1988 there was a rights issue of 1 new share for every 10 held at 90p per share. R Ltd did not take up the rights issue but sold the rights for £110. The market value of the shares on the first dealing day after the rights issue (the ex-rights price) was 189p.

	£	£
Proceeds		110
Less: Cost		
$\left(\frac{\text{Proceeds of sale of rights}}{\text{Proceeds of sale of rights + Market value of shares ex rights}} \times \text{Cost}\right)$		
$\frac{£110}{£110 + £1{,}890} \times £1{,}000$	55	
Gain		
Indexation		
£55 × 18.6%	10	65
Chargeable gain		£ 45

In this case the proceeds of sale amounted to more than 5 per cent of £2,000 (£110 plus £1,890). If the proceeds had instead been only £90, it would have been possible to deduct that amount from the £1,000 cost of the shares in any subsequent disposal. There would thus be no immediate liability but the gain on the subsequent disposal would be greater. (Indexation on the subsequent sale would be based on cost less the rolled over £90, or £910.)

When rights are sold, the pool cost of the main holding of shares must still be reduced. The pool balance will be indexed up to the date of sale, then the indexed cost (£65 in the illustration above) deducted. If the proceeds do not exceed 5 per cent of value the consideration (£90 in the second part of the illustration) would be deducted.

Takeovers and mergers

When there is a takeover or merger, shareholders may receive cash, shares or loan stock in exchange for their original holdings. If they receive cash, they have obviously disposed of their shares and a normal CGT computation is made. If, however, they receive shares and/or loan stock, the cost of the original shares is deemed to be the cost of the new shares or stock and there is no disposal until their sale. Indexation continues to date from the date of acquisition of the original holding (or 31 March 1982 if later, of course).

If two or more different securities are received on the takeover (say a mixture of ordinary shares and loan stock), it is necessary to apportion the cost of the original holding between them. For quoted securities this is done in proportion to the market value on the first dealing day following the takeover, using market values determined as explained on page 260 (¼ up or mid point between highest and lowest recorded bargains). For unquoted securities the procedure is entirely different, being based on the open market value at the date of *the first disposal* of the new securities.

Illustration 21.4

S Ltd owned 10,000 shares of £1 each in Trend Limited, a quoted company, which had been acquired in 1980 for £20,000. The market value of the shares at 31 March 1982 was £30,000 and S Ltd has elected under s. 96 FA 1988 for the use of market value for all disposals.

In April 1988 Trend Limited was taken over by Vend Limited and as a result S Ltd received, for every £1 share in Trend:

1 £1 share in Vend
£2 10% loan stock.

On the first dealing day after the takeover, the market values of the Vend Ltd securities were:

Ordinary shares	£4
Loan stock	80p

In December 1988 S Ltd sold the ordinary shares for £50,000. The value of the loan stock at this time was 90p.

Required:

(a) Compute the effect of the takeover on S Ltd
(b) Compute the gain on the December 1988 disposal
(c) Compute the gain on the December 1988 disposal if the shares had all been unquoted, assuming that their agreed market values were as stated.

Assume indexation March 1982 to December 1988 to be 38.0 per cent

Answer

(a) The takeover in April 1988 does not count as a disposal. For the purpose of subsequent disposals the 31 March 1982 value will be apportioned as follows:

			£
10,000 shares:	$\frac{£4}{£4 + £1.60} \times £30,000$	=	21,429
£20,000 Loan stock	$\frac{£1.60}{£4 + £1.60} \times £30,000$	=	8,571
			£30,000

		£
(b)	Proceeds of sale	50,000
	Market value 31 March 1982 per (a)	21,429
		28,571
	Indexation £21,429 × 38.0%	8,143
	Chargeable gain	£20,428

(c)	Proceeds of sale	50,000
	Market value 31 March 1982	
	$\frac{£50,000}{£50,000 + £18,000} \times £30,000$	22,059
		27,941
	Indexation £22,059 × 38.0%	8,382
	Chargeable gain	£19,559

Summary

CGT rules for quoted and unquoted securities

Quoted and unquoted securities form one of the most important types of asset chargeable to CGT. The rules are basically the same for both, though there are differences.

Securities exempt from CGT

(a) All UK Government securities
(b) National Savings Certificates, Premium Bonds and other non-marketable savings media
(c) Corporate bonds (company loan stocks and debentures issued after 31 March 1984 and quoted on a recognized stock-exchange or on the USM).

Pooling

When a holding of shares has been acquired in several parcels, a 'pool' is created and every time shares enter or leave the pool it is necessary to index the pool up from the last date it was indexed.

Exceptions to the pooling rules are:

(a) Purchases and sales on the same day are matched together and not pooled
(b) Purchases within the nine days before a disposal are matched with that disposal and not pooled

Valuation at 31 March 1982 for quoted shares is by taking the lower of:

(a) '¼ up'
(b) Mid point between highest and lowest recorded bargains

Valuation for unquoted shares is based on a professional valuation and/or negotiation with the Revenue.

Shares acquired through bonus issues are added to the 'shares' column in the pooling calculation with no other adjustment.

Shares acquired by way of a rights issue are also added to the pool but the fact that a price is paid means that the pool must be indexed up to permit the cost of the rights issue shares to be added.

Takeovers and mergers

Shares acquired as a result of a takeover or merger are deemed to have been acquired at the cost of the original shares. No gain or loss arises on the takeover or merger except to the extent that cash is received.

Progress questions

Attempt the following questions to test your absorption of the material in the chapter. Rework them at intervals for revision. Answers are on page 402.

1 Briefly list the shares or securities exempt from CGT.

2 When a holding of quoted or unquoted shares has been built up from several acquisitions a 'pool' is created. What events require the pool to be indexed up?

3 Explain how the market value at 31 March 1982 is arrived at for quoted and unquoted shares.

4 What exceptions are there to the general rule that all acquisitions of shares are pooled?

5 How are: (a) bonus issues, (b) rights issues dealt with for CGT purposes?

6 On a takeover or merger, how is the cost of the original holding allocated when necessary between two or more different securities received in exchange for: (a) Quoted securities, (b) Unquoted securities?

22 Capital gains tax – reliefs

Introduction

In this chapter we deal with sundry reliefs not yet discussed:

(a) Retirement relief
(b) Gift relief
(c) Rollover relief and hold-over relief
(d) Relief on the transfer of a business to a limited company
(e) Relief for losses on business loans
(f) Relief for losses on shares in unquoted companies

Retirement relief – sale of business by an individual

When a person retires from a trading business and sells that business or its assets a substantial concession is available. The first £125,000 of the gain plus half the gain between £125,000 and £500,000 is exempt from CGT, provided certain conditions as satisfied.

The conditions are:

(a) The taxpayer is retiring at age sixty or above, or is retiring below that age because of ill-health
(b) The taxpayer has owned the business for at least ten years. If this condition is not met, the available relief is scaled down. If the taxpayer has owned the business for less than one year there is no relief. From one year upwards, relief is granted at the rate of 10 per cent for each year of ownership (pro rata for parts of a year). If the taxpayer making the disposal had inherited the business from his or her spouse, or had received it by gift from the spouse, the qualifying period may be extended by the spouse's previous period of ownership.

(c) The assets for which relief is claimed must be *chargeable business assets*.

Chargeable business assets include:

(i) Goodwill
(ii) Land and buildings
(iii) Plant and machinery (but not private cars and not individual items of plant bought for less than £3,000)

The following assets must be excluded:

(i) Investments
(ii) Current assets (stock, debts, cash, less liabilities).

The gains on the disposal of the chargeable business assets are calculated and indexed in the normal way. The resultant gains are then reduced by the retirement relief available. It may well be, of course, that there remains some CGT liability in respect of the disposal of chargeable assets which are not business assets, such as investments.

Retirement relief – sale of shares in a family trading company by a full-time working director of the company

Retirement relief is also extended to cover sales of shares by directors of 'family' companies. The conditions include *some resembling* those for sales by individuals, but some further conditions are added. These are:

(a) The company must be a 'family' company, that is either:
  (i) a trading company in which the disposer holds not less than *25 per cent* of the voting rights, or
  (ii) a trading company in which the disposer holds not less than *5 per cent* of the voting rights *and* his or her family holds more than *50 per cent* of the voting rights
  (For (ii), the 50 per cent is based on shareholdings of the disposer, his or her spouse, plus their brothers, sisters, and lineal ancestors and descendants.)
(b) The disposer is a *full-time working director* of the company – that is, one who devotes substantially the whole of his or her time to the company in a managerial or technical capacity.

These rules effectively prevent relief being available to someone who merely holds an investment in a company without active participation.

Relief is granted by deduction from the gain arising on the *shares* disposed of, but the calculation must bring in the assets of the company at their value at the time of sale. In an examination question these details are usually given in the form of a balance sheet, sometimes with the addition of current market values which must be substituted for the book values in the balance sheet.

Illustration 22.1

Morgan commenced business with a chain of greengrocer's shops in January 1985 and retired in April 1988 aged sixty-one. He sold the business for £1,300,000 made up as follows:

	Cost	*Proceeds of sale*
	£	£
Goodwill	nil	300,000
Freehold property (all acquired January 1985)	560,000	850,000
Quoted investment (acquired June 1985)	100,000	150,000

Indexation factors are: January 1985 to April 1988: 12.2%
June 1985 to April 1988: 10.9%

The chargeable gain will be:

	£	£
Goodwill		
Proceeds	300,000	
Less: Cost	nil	
	300,000	
Indexation (no cost to index)	nil	300,000

Freehold property		
proceeds	850,000	
Less: Cost	560,000	
	290,000	
Indexation		
£560,000 × 12.2%	68,320	221,680
Gain on chargeable business assets		521,680
Less:		
Retirement relief		
Fully exempt: 3.25/10 = 32.5% × £125,000	40,625	
Half exempt: ½ × 32.5% × £375,000	60,938	101,563
		420,117
Quoted investment		
Proceeds	150,000	
Less: Cost	100,000	
	50,000	
Indexation		
£100,000 × 10.9%	10,900	39,100
		£459,217

Illustration 22.2

Ogwen is a full-time working director of Snowdon Limited and holds 30 per cent of the issued ordinary share capital. He has been associated with the company since 1960. In April 1988 he retired, aged sixty-four. He sold his shares for £800,000. Their market value at 31 March 1982 was agreed to be £400,000.

The balance sheet of Snowdon Limited at the date of sale showed:

	£
Goodwill	300,000
Land and buildings	800,000
Plant and machinery	
Costing over £3,000 per item	600,000
Costing under £3,000 per item	500,000
Motor vehicles	100,000
Net Current assets (including quoted investments £100,000)	300,000
	£2,600,000

It is agreed that the market value of the goodwill at the time of the sale was £700,000. Indexation factor March 1982–April 1988: 33.2%.

The answer is on page 272.

Relief for gifts

The gift of an asset constitutes a disposal deemed to be at market value but relief may be available on gifts from one individual to another.

The relief is given by treating the asset as being transferred at a 'no gain no loss' value. On the subsequent sale of the asset by the donee, the amount of the gain arising on the gift has to be deducted from the cost of the asset, thus increasing the gain on the sale.

The benefit of the relief is, of course, that no CGT has to be paid until the donee sells the asset.

Both parties must jointly claim the relief.

Illustration 22.3

Gordon bought 10,000 shares in Bennett Limited for £18,000 in August 1985. In April 1988 he gave them to his daughter, Kate. Their market value at that time was £30,000. Kate sold them in February 1989 for £32,000.

(Indexation: August 1985 to April 1988 10.8%, April 1988 to February 1989 4.0% (assumed).)

	£
Market value at time of gift	30,000
Cost	18,000
	12,000

	£
Indexation	
£18,000 × 10.8%	1,944
Chargeable gain	£10,056

Provided Gordon and Kate so claim, the gain of £10,056 will be 'held over' until Kate sells the shares.

On the sale by Kate we shall have:

	£	£
Proceeds of sale		32,000
Market value at time of gift	30,000	
less: Held over gain	10,056	20,056
		11,944
Indexation		
£20,056 × 4.0%		803
Chargeable gain		£11,141

Note that the indexation adjustment on the sale is made on the value at the time of the gift *as reduced by the held over gain.*

Gift relief is also available for transfers from individuals to trustees, from trustees to individuals or between trustees.

If the transfer is made at an undervalue instead of by gift, the relief is still available. However, if the price paid, though below full market value, is above the original cost of the asset, CGT will be payable at the time of the gift to the extent that a gain is realized by the donor.

See page 277 for a modification to the computation if the held-over gain is attributable to an asset acquired before 31 March 1982 and transferred by gift before 6 April 1988.

Interrelation between gift relief and retirement relief

If a business, or shares in a family trading company, are disposed of by gift on retirement the holding over arrangements of gift relief can apply to any balance of the gain after deduction of retirement relief.

Roll-over relief and hold-over relief

Roll-over relief

When a sole trader or company sells a business asset there may be a capital gains tax charge. If the asset is replaced by another business asset, it is possible to defer the charge to tax until the replacing asset is sold – and when the replacing asset is sold, the same relief is available. It is possible for an individual to continue the sequence until the business is finally sold and not replaced, when the retirement relief explained on page 271 could be available. For a company, with con-

Discussion and answer

It is first necessary to pick up from the balance sheet the totals of chargeable assets and chargeable business asset:

	Chargeable assets	*Chargeable business assets*
	£	£
Goodwill	700,000	700,000
Land and buildings	800,000	800,000
Plant and machinery		
Costing over £3,000 per item	600,000	600,000
Costing under £3,000 per item	–	–
Motor vehicles	–	–
Net current assets	100,000	–
	£2,200,000	£2,100,000

This means that 21/22 of the gain on the disposal of the shares qualifies for retirement relief.

Chargeable gain:		£
Proceeds of sale		800,000
Market value at 31 March 1982		400,000
		400,000
Indexation		
£400,000 × 33.2%		132,800
less: Retirement relief		267,200
$£267,200 \times \frac{£2,100,000}{£2,200,000} = £255,055$		
Relief available		
First	125,000	
Half × remaining £130,055:	65,028	190,028
Chargeable gain 1988/89		£ 67,172

tinuous existence, the deferral can be for an indefinite time, provided the conditions are fulfilled.

So what are the conditions?

(a) Both the asset disposed of and the replacement asset must belong to the following groups of asset (not necessarily the same group):
   (i) Land and buildings
   (ii) *Fixed* plant and machinery (e.g. not vehicles apart from those in (iv) and (v) below
   (iii) Goodwill
   (iv) Ships, aircraft or hovercraft
   (v) Satellites, space stations and spacecraft (including launch vehicles)
   (vi) Milk quotas and potato quotas
(b) The replacement must be made within the period beginning one year before the disposal and ending three years after it.
(c) To get full relief the whole of the proceeds of sale must be reinvested. If only part of the proceeds is reinvested, there will be some CGT to pay immediately if there is a chargeable gain.

The relief is given by deducting the gain from the cost of the replacing asset for CGT purposes, thus increasing the gain on its disposal.

Illustration 22.4

In April 1988, Aragon sold the building from which she conducted her business for £120,000. She had originally bought it for £40,000 in 1979. Its market value at 31 March 1982 was £60,000. In January 1989 she bought a replacement building for £180,000. This building was sold in January 1990 for £200,000. Aragon claimed roll-over relief on the 1988 sale.

Assume indexation factors to be: March 1982 to April 1988 33.2 per cent, January 1989 to January 1990 3.6 per cent (assumed).

The calculation of the chargeable gains arising will be:

1 Sale in April 1988

	£
Proceeds	120,000
Market value at 31 March 1982	60,000
	60,000
Indexation	
£60,000 × 33.2%	19,920
Chargeable gain to be rolled over	£ 40,080

2 Sale in January 1990

	£	£
Proceeds of sale		20,000
Cost	180,000	
Less: Rolled over gain	40,080	139,920
		60,080
Indexation		
= £139,920 × 3.6%		5,037
Chargeable gain		£ 55,043

The gain of £55,043 on the second sale would be available for roll-over relief against a subsequent purchase of a qualifying asset within the time limit of three years from January 1990 that is, by January 1993.

Note that the indexation is applied to the cost as reduced by the rolled over gain.

Hold-over relief

If the replacing asset is a depreciating asset (defined as a wasting asset or one which will become a wasting asset within ten years – i.e. an asset with a life of less than sixty years), roll-over relief is not available but a modified form popularly referred to as 'hold-over' relief may be claimed. If conditions (a) to (c) on page 273 are met, payment of the tax is deferred to the earliest of the following three dates:

(i) Date of disposal of the replacement asset
(ii) Date the replacement asset ceases to be used for the purpose of the trade
(iii) Ten years after the date of acquisition of the replacement asset.

However, if within the applicable time period a non-depreciating asset is purchased, rollover relief may be claimed on it by deducting the held-over gain from its cost.

Continuing Illustration 22.4, if the replacement asset had been a depreciating asset, fixed plant for example, tax on the gain of £40,080 on the first sale would have been deferred until the plant was sold or scrapped, or until ten years after the acquisition of the replacement plant.

Restricted relief when only part of the sale proceeds is reinvested

In Illustration 22.4 the whole of the sale proceeds of the building was reinvested into the second. If this is not the case, there may be a capital gains tax liability on any part of the gain not reinvested.

Illustration 22.5

Again continuing Illustration 22.4, we had a gain of £40,080 on the first sale.

Let us assume that the replacing building cost £100,000 – less than the proceeds of the first sale.

Our computation would become:

	£
Sale in April 1988	
Proceeds	120,000
Market value 31 March 1982	60,000
	60,000
Indexation	19,920
Gain	40,080
Proceeds not reinvested	
£120,000 – £100,000	20,000
Available to be rolled over	£ 20,080

Aragon would have to pay CGT on £20,000 immediately

See page 277 for a modification to the computation if roll-over relief or hold-over relief is attributable to an asset acquired before 31 March 1982 and disposed of before 6 April 1988.

Transfer of business to a limited company

If an *individual or partnership* transfers a business as a going concern to a company, that would normally lead to a CGT liability on any profit arising. However, to the extent that the consideration is in shares or loan stock, no gain arises until the shares or loan stock are sold.

Illustration 22.6

Parr sold her business in April 1988 to a company, Parr (1988) Limited on the following terms:

	Agreed value £
10,000 Ordinary £1 shares	130,000
£10,000 Loan stock	120,000
Cash	100,000
	£350,000

At the date of sale her business balance sheet showed:

	Balance sheet £	*Original cost* £
Goodwill	20,000	nil
Land and buildings (acquired June 1982)	200,000	100,000
Net current assets	130,000	
	£350,000	

Indexation factor: June 1982 to April 1988: 29.2%

The gains arising on the sale will be:

	£	£
Goodwill		
Proceeds	20,000	
Cost	nil	
	20,000	
Indexation – nil – no cost	–	20,000
Land and buildings		
Proceeds	200,000	
Cost	100,000	
	100,000	
Indexation		
£100,000 × 29.2%	29,200	70,800
		£90,800

The gain of £90,800 must be divided proportionately – the part attributable to the shares and loan stock is rolled over and there is an immediate liability on the part attributable to cash:

Roll over: $\frac{£130,000 + £120,000}{£350,000} \times £90,800$ 64,857

Immediate $\frac{£100,000}{£350,000} \times £90,800$ £25,943

£90,800

The £64,857 rolled over will be allocated proportionately to the shares and loan stock and deducted from their cost when calculating the profit or loss on their subsequent disposal. See page 277 for a modification to the computation if the rolled over gain is attributable to an asset acquired before 31 March 1982 and transferred to the company before 6 April 1988.

Relief for losses on business loans

Losses incurred on business loans would not normally qualify for income tax or corporation tax relief under Schedule D Cases I or II, because they were not made in connection with the trade. However, such losses may qualify as allowable for *CGT*-purposes, provided the loan was made for business purposes to a borrower resident in the UK. Loans by one spouse to the other, or between associated companies or companies in the same group, cannot qualify.

Relief for losses on shares in unquoted company (ss. 573–576 ICTA 1988)

Relief for individuals

An individual who has *subscribed* for shares in an unquoted company, and who subsequently makes a loss on their disposal, will have an allowable CGT loss. However, he may, as an alternative, claim relief for the loss against income as if it were a trading loss. Conditions:

(a) The shares must have been subscribed for – that is, issued by the company and not bought from another shareholder
(b) The company must be a UK resident trading company which has either operated as such for a continuous period of six years or operated as such for a shorter continuous period without ever being an investment company
(c) The disposal must have been at arm's length for full consideration, or a distribution on winding up, or a deemed disposal on the basis that the shares have become of negligible value
(d) The claim must be made within two years after the end of the tax year for which relief is claimed.

The relief when available is given in a similar way to an income tax loss claim under s. 380, but it takes precedence over any relief for trading losses under s. 380 or s. 381 (losses in early years). As under s. 380, relief may be claimed for the year of loss or if any balance of loss remains, the following year.

Relief for investment companies

Section s. 573 ICTA 1988 extends similar relief to that described above to *investment* companies. Relief is only available subject to broadly the same conditions, and the additional conditions that the investment company must not control or be controlled by the trading company or under common control with it, and must not be a member of the same group as the trading company.

Deferred charges on gains before 31 March 1982

There is one special situation which can affect roll-over relief, hold over relief and relief for gifts. It arises from the re-basing of CGT to 31 March 1982.

Suppose a taxpayer sells a chargeable asset in 1989 which he bought in 1984. So far, no problem. The CGT result is simply computed by taking the difference between proceeds and indexed cost. But – suppose further that the cost of the 1984 asset is reduced by rollover relief on another asset bought in 1976 and disposed of in 1984. What happens is that the disposal in 1989 gives rise to a CGT liability in part at least attributable to the rolled-over gain which accrued between 1976 and 1984. That is unfair, because the Finance Act 1988 has re-based CGT to 31 March 1982, and gains before that date are now generally not chargeable.

In the interests of simplicity, Schedule 9, FA 1988 provides for an arbitrary solution to the problem. In the situation just described, the rolled-over gain is halved. The same solution is applied when a gain is held over following replacement by a depreciating asset, when an asset is acquired by gift, or when a gain is rolled over on the conversion of a business to a company.

Illustration 22.7

Alpha Ltd bought a building in 1976 for £10,000. It was sold in April 1984 for £50,000, and immediately replaced by another building which cost £80,000. The replacement building was sold in December 1988 for £150,000. The value of the building on 31 March 1982 was £20,000. Rollover relief was claimed on the April 1984 sale. Take indexation for April 1984 to December 1988 as 25.0 per cent.

The computations will be:

	£	£
Sale in April 1984		
Proceeds		50,000
less: Cost	10,000	
Indexation (based on 31 March 1982 value)		
£20,000 × 11.6%	2,320	12,320
Rolled over gain		£ 37,680
Sale in December 1988		
Proceeds		150,000
less: Cost	80,000	
less: rolled over gain ½ × £37,680	18,840	
	61,160	
Indexation £61,160 × 25.0%	15,290	76,450
Chargeable gain		£ 73,550

If it had not been for the provisions of Schedule 9 FA 1988 the result would have been:

Proceeds		150,000
Cost	80,000	
less rolled over gain	37,680	
	42,320	
Indexation £42,320 × 25.0%	10,580	52,900
Chargeable gain		£ 97,100

In order for this halving of the rolled over or held over gain to apply, all three of the following conditions must be present:

(a) A disposal on or after 6 April 1988
(b) The acquisition of the asset disposed of after 31 March 1982
(c) A deduction from the cost of the asset in (b) attributable to an asset acquired before 31 March 1982.

Illustration 22.7 has these three characteristics. Study it until you understand what the problem is – there is no logic in the arbitrary solution which was chosen for the sake of simplicity.

Summary

Retirement relief

Retirement relief is available to an individual who retires from a business, or sells shares in a family business on retirement, at age sixty or above (or below that age because of ill-health).

The maximum relief is exemption for the first £125,000 of gains, plus half of any gains from £125,000 to £500,000. To qualify for this maximum the business must have been owned for at least ten years before retirement. Between one year and ten years of ownership, relief is given pro rata at the rate of 10 per cent per year. If the business has been owned for less than one year, no retirement relief is available.

Gift relief

On the gift of an asset the donor and donee may jointly claim to have the gain arising on the gift rolled over until the donee sells the asset concerned. The relief may also apply to a sale at an undervalue, though in that case there may be a partial charge to CGT if the consideration exceeds the original cost.

Roll-over relief and hold-over relief

If an individual or company sells a qualifying business asset, and uses the proceeds to buy another qualifying business asset, it is possible to elect to have any gain arising on the sale 'rolled over' so that no CGT is payable until the replacing asset is sold. The process may be repeated over and over again, so that an individual may, for example, dispose of one business and buy another several times before finally retiring and qualifying for retirement relief on the accumulated gains.

If the replacing asset is a depreciating asset, payment of the CGT is deferred until the sale or scrapping of the asset, or ten years after the acquisition of the replacing of the asset, whichever is the earlier.

Transfer of a business to a limited company

If an individual or partnership transfers a business as a going concern to a company, there will be no immediate CGT liability to the extent that the consideration is in the form of shares or loan stock.

Relief for losses on business loans

A loss incurred because of the non-repayment of a business loan may qualify as a CGT loss if the borrower was a UK resident.

Relief for losses on shares in unquoted companies

An individual who has subscribed for shares in an unquoted company and subsequently makes a loss on their disposal at arm's length may claim relief for the CGT loss arising but may also claim for it as an income tax loss.

There are similar provisions for *investment* companies to claim such a loss for corporation tax purposes.

Progress questions

Attempt these questions to test your absorption of the material in the chapter. Rework them at intervals for revision. Answers are on page 402.

1 When a person retires, how much of any gain arising from the disposal of his or her business may be exempt from CGT?

2 What conditions must be satisfied to obtain the relief in 1 above

(a) On disposal of an unincorporated business?
(b) On disposal of shares in a family trading company?

3 Distinguish between 'chargeable assets' and 'chargeable business assets'.

4 Are the following statements true or false?	*True*	*False*
(a) On a disposal by gift there can be no CGT		
(b) Any CGT arising on the gift of an asset is automatically deferred until the donee sells the asset.		
(c) If retirement relief is claimed, gift relief cannot also be claimed on the same disposal.		
(d) Roll-over relief could apply to someone who sold a sweet shop and used the proceeds to buy a space station.		
(e) For roll-over relief to be obtained, the replacement asset must be bought within the period beginning one year before the disposal and ending three years after it.		

	True	*False*
(f) If the whole proceeds of sale of an asset are not reinvested in a replacement asset, there will be a CGT liability on the proportion of the gain relating to the proceeds not reinvested.	✓	
(g) Hold-over relief is available instead of roll-over relief whenever the replacing asset is a depreciating asset.	✓	
(h) Relief for losses on business loans is not available for CGT but relief may be obtained against income tax by a claim similar to that under s. 380.		✓
(i) A shareholder in an unquoted company who makes a loss on the sale of his shares may obtain relief either in CGT or in income tax.		

23 Capital gains tax – group aspects

Introduction

We have already seen in our study of corporation tax that *trading* losses may be exchanged by group companies between whom there is a 75 per cent shareholding link, or who are 75 per cent subsidiaries of a holding company. That relief does *not* extend to capital losses. However, there is a relief available. For CGT purposes, transfer of chargeable assets between such companies are treated as being at a price which gives rise to neither profit or loss (i.e. normally cost plus indexation).

Intra-group transactions

As indicated above, the transfer of a chargeable asset from one 75 per cent group company to another does not give to a chargeable gain. How may this be used to obtain a form of 'capital loss relief'? By nominating one group company as the one through which all external sales of chargeable assets pass. Any group company wishing to dispose of a chargeable asset outside the group first transfers it to the nominated company, which then effects the sale to the third party. In this way all group capital gains and losses arise in one company, thus achieving a free offset of chargeable gains and losses.

To prevent abuse of the relief, there are rules applied to companies leaving a group. If a 75 per cent group company leaves a group, and within the previous six years has acquired an asset from another group company, it is deemed to have disposed of that asset at market value *as at the date of the intra-group transfer*. This effectively withdraws the benefit obtained at the time of the transfer.

Another way in which the rule could be abused is if a holding company acquired a subsidiary which owned an asset with a current value much in excess of its original cost (say a freehold building), then transferred the asset out to another group company on a no gain no loss basis. So far all is well. But what if the holding company then sold the shares in the subsidiary? These are now worth much less, as an important asset has been stripped out of it, so the holding company makes a useful loss on the sale which can be offset against other gains. A very interesting device, but unfortunately, the loss relief on the sale of the shares will be wholly or partly disallowed whenever there is a 'depreciatory transaction' which has materially reduced the value of the shares. (In this case, of course, the sale of the asset to the other group company was a depreciatory transaction.)

Group roll-over relief

For roll-over relief purposes, all 75 per cent group companies are counted as one. Chargeable gains on a disposal by one group company may thus be rolled over against the cost of a replacing asset acquired by another group company.

Summary

The most important CGT point for examination purposes in relation to groups is obtaining the maximum offset between gains and losses. This is simply achieved by taking advantage of the ability to transfer assets among 75 per cent group companies to ensure that all sales of chargeable assets outside the groups pass through one group company within which gains and losses are offset.

Another useful group point is maximizing roll-over relief by ensuring that claims are made when one company in the group disposes of qualifying assets while others are acquiring replacement assets.

Progress questions

Attempt these questions to test your absorption of the material in the chapter. Rework them at intervals for revision. Answers are on page 402.

1 (a) What shareholding link is necessary in order for group companies to transfer assets chargeable to CGT on a 'no gain no loss' basis?

(b) What restrictions are placed on such transfers to prevent abuse?

2 Is roll-over relief available when one company in a group disposes of a chargeable asset and another replaces it?

24 Capital gains tax – planning

Introduction

Several of the CGT planning points explained below have already been dealt with in earlier chapters. The purpose of this chapter is to bring them all together for convenience.

CGT planning for individuals

Using the annual exemption

An individual is entitled to an annual exemption of £5,000 (1988/89). As it cannot be carried forward, it makes sense to try to use it each year. It will obviously be possible to sell shares showing a suitable gain before 5 April each year, but suppose the taxpayer wishes to retain the shares? He or she sells them to realize the gain, then buys them back the following day. (The buy-back could not be on the same day, as the identification rules would relate the purchase and the sale together, thus negating the purpose.) The sale is typically made at the end of dealing on one day and the purchase at the beginning of dealing on the next, hence the colloquial name for the transaction – 'bed and breakfast'.

Maximizing loss relief

All gains and losses on disposals within each tax year are offset, and CGT is payable on the excess of gains over losses, subject to the annual exemption. But – losses *brought forward* are only offset to the extent necessary to reduce gains to the amount of the annual exemption. It follows that losses brought forward are more valuable than losses arising within the year. That suggests a possible strategy – if a taxpayer has made no disposals in a particular tax year as 5 April approaches, and cannot use the strategy above because he or she has insufficient gains, a sale to realize a loss will create the chance of benefit in future years, since as stated that loss will only be offset against gains to the extent necessary to reduce them to the amount of the annual exemption.

Illustration 24.1

In mid-March 1989, Patrick had as yet made no disposals of chargeable assets in 1988/89. He therefore sold stocks before 5 April 1989 to realize losses totalling £8,000.

In 1989/90 he realized gains totalling £6,000. Ignoring indexation and assuming that the 1988/89 exemption of £5,000 continues unchanged, the result will be:

1989/90	£
Gains	6,000
less: annual exemption	5,000
	1,000
less: loss brought forward	1,000
	nil

£7,000 of the 1988/89 loss remains to be carried forward

If Patrick had deferred his 1988/89 sales until 1989/90, the effect would have been:

1989/90	£
Gains	6,000
Losses	(8,000)
Losses carried forward	£ 2,000

By taking the losses in 1988/89, Patrick has increased his losses carried forward into 1990/91 and beyond from £2,000 to £7,000.

Using husband and wife election

Husband and wife are, for 1988/89, treated as a single unit for CGT purposes, with one £5,000 exemption. If separate assessment is claimed, the exemption will be shared between them in proportion to their net gains. Such an election makes no difference to the CGT payable, it merely makes the wife legally liable for her own CGT.

Another election may be more useful – either spouse may elect, before 6 July following the tax year, for his or her losses not to be offset against the other spouse's gains but instead to be carried forward against the electing spouse's gains in future years. Such an election could operate to prevent the annual £5,000 exemption from being wasted.

Retirement relief

A taxpayer will obviously obtain the benefit of retirement relief when possible by deferring retirement until at least age sixty.

Roll-over relief

Sales and purchases of chargeable assets will obviously be made in such a way as to attract roll-over relief where possible.

Gift relief

The deferral of liability when gifts are made should be used.

Death exemption

The fact that assets passing on death do not attract CGT means that an older taxpayer needing to realize some cash should, from a CGT point of view, sell assets with a smaller element of gain in them rather than a large element which will escape tax altogether when it passes on death.

CGT planning for companies

Timing of disposals

As explained on page 170 a company may plan its CGT disposals in such a way as to minimize the extent to which the company is taxed in the £100,000 to £500,000 profit area in which a marginal rate of about 37½ per cent is suffered. This may be easier than manipulating the trading profit, since the CGT gain or loss falls into the accounting period in which the disposal takes place, and the timing of the disposal is entirely within the company's control.

Groups of companies

(a) Maximizing loss relief
As CGT losses cannot be transferred among group companies, it is important to ensure that group transactions in chargeable assets are passed through one designated company in the group.

(b) Maximizing roll-over relief
Groups of companies must be alert to ensure that all claims for roll-over relief are made, bearing in mind that a gain on a disposal by one group company may be rolled over against an acquisition by another.

CGT on incorporation

A new company is often formed by taking over an unincorporated business. If the consideration is shares or loan stock, any CGT liability of the seller may be deferred until the sale of the shares or loan stock, but only if the business is transferred as a going concern, with *all* the assets (other than cash) being transferred. It makes sense to plan such a transaction so as to take advantage of this relief.

Summary

Individuals

Basic CGT planning for individuals means:

(a) Using the annual exemption where possible, perhaps by making use of 'bed and breakfast' transactions
(b) When strategy (a) is not available, realizing losses because losses brought forward are more valuable than losses relieved in the year (see page 285)
(c) Using the husband and wife election for separate treatment of losses
(d) Ensuring that retirement relief is obtained and maximized
(e) Ensuring that roll-over relief, hold-over relief and gift relief are obtained where possible.
(f) For older taxpayers, leaving assets with large gains on them to pass on death rather than being sold during a lifetime

Companies

Companies should consider the following basic tax planning points:

(a) Timing of disposals to minimize the extent to which the company is taxed in the £100,000 to £500,000 marginal band
(b) Ensuring that maximum relief for group losses is obtained by channelling sales through one group company
(c) Maximizing roll-over relief and hold-over relief (including the matching of disposals by one group company, with acquisitions by another)
(d) Obtaining deferral of liability on incorporation when an existing business is taken over

Progress questions

Attempt these questions to test your absorption of the material in the chapter. Rework them at intervals for revision. Answers are on page 402.

1 Explain three ways in which an individual may seek to maximize the annual CGT exemption.

2 Explain three ways in which a company may seek to reduce its CGT liability.

Part Four Value Added Tax

25 Value added tax

Introduction

Value added tax (VAT) is an entirely different tax from the ones we have studied so far. It is not a tax on profits or gains, and is not even eventually borne by most businesses to a material extent. Nevertheless, it is important to businesses, because its charge and collection enter into many, even most, business transactions. The charge and collection of VAT are handled by the Commissioners of Customs and Excise, and are governed by the Value Added Tax Act 1983 (VATA 1983) as amended by subsequent Finance Acts.

Ultimately, VAT mainly falls on the final consumer of goods or services. However, all those involved in the chain of transactions between the manufacturer and the retailer are first charged VAT and then pass it on to the next person in the chain. It is at present levied at 15 per cent, though there is a second rate of VAT, the 'zero' rate, for certain items as we shall see.

Illustration 25.1

A manufacturer M Limited, produces refrigerators. These are sold first to a wholesaler, W Limited, who sells in turn to a retailer, R Limited. Finally, R Limited sells to the ultimate consumer, C. The prices at which these transactions take place, excluding VAT) are as follows:

M sells to W for £100
W sells to R for £160
R sells to C for £300

The VAT finally due from C is £300 @ 15 per cent or £45. This is collected by R who pays it over to the Customs and Excise along with the VAT due on other sales. But – R Limited first deducts all the VAT suffered on its 'inputs' – its purchases. This will include the VAT charged by W Limited on the supply of the refrigerator, and VAT suffered on items such as stationery, telephone and other overhead costs of goods and services. The overall effect on M Limited, W Limited and R Limited is that most of the VAT paid by them on their inputs (purchases) is deducted when accounting for VAT on their outputs (sales).

Considering only the VAT relating to the sale and purchase of one refrigerator, the accounting will be as follows:

Company	*Input tax*	*Output tax*	*VAT paid*
	£	£	£
M Ltd – Sale to W		15	15 paid by M
W Ltd.			
Purchase from M	15		
Sale to R		24	9 paid by W
R Ltd			
Purchase from M	24		
Sale to C		45	21 paid by R
Total suffered by C			45

The overall effect on M Ltd, W Ltd and R Ltd is nil. Each has collected VAT on making a sale and paid this over to Customs and Excise, first deducting any VAT paid on purchases and other inputs. C, the ultimate consumer, pays £45 and has no-one to pass it on to. He or she thus bears the tax which has been collected by Customs and Excise in the three stages shown.

This is a vast over-simplification of the process. Each registered trader has to submit a return, usually quarterly, to Customs and Excise showing VAT collected on sales (outputs) and VAT suffered on purchases of goods and services (inputs). The difference must be paid to Customs and Excise within one month of the end of the quarterly period.

Transactions liable to VAT

Most business transactions are within the scope of VAT, which has to be accounted for whenever there is a *taxable supply*. A taxable supply means the supply of goods or services in the UK in the course of business, other than supplies which are exempt for one reason or another.

Exemption and zero rating

Introduction

It is essential to understand the difference between exemption and zero rating.

A supply of goods or services in the UK in the course of business must be one of three things:

(a) Standard rated – within the scope of VAT and taxable at 15 per cent
(b) Zero rated – within the scope of VAT and taxable at 0 per cent
(c) Exempt – outside the scope of VAT

At first sight there appears to be no practical difference between zero rating and exemption, but there is. If a trade or business is concerned with transactions that are zero rated (the supply of most types of food, for example), no VAT is charged on sales but the supplier may obtain a *refund* of VAT suffered on input costs to the business – some purchases plus costs like stationery, telephone and the like. This is because the sale is inside the VAT system.

If, on the other hand, the transaction is *exempt*, again no VAT is charged on sales but now the business will be unable to obtain any credit for its input tax – VAT suffered on purchases and overhead costs – because its trade is outside the scope of VAT.

Examples of zero-rated transactions

Subject to minor exceptions, the following are zero rated:

(a) Sale of most types of food
(b) Printed matter including books, newspapers etc.
(c) Fuel and power (not petrol or diesel)
(d) Construction of buildings
(e) Caravans and houseboats used for permanent residences
(f) Children's clothing and footwear
(g) Transport (by bus, ships, aircraft, but not taxi fares and the like)
(h) Exports
(i) Supplies to charities
(j) Drugs and medicines supplied on prescription

Examples of exempt transactions

(a) Land
(b) Buildings sold, leased or hired (excluding hotel charges and holiday lettings)
(c) Insurance
(d) Postal services
(e) Finance, e.g. banking operations
(f) Betting, gaming and lotteries
(g) Education (if non-profit making)
(h) Health – services provided by doctors, dentists etc.
(i) Undertakers' services (e.g. burial or cremation, but excluding headstones etc.)

Partially exempt trades

A business could conduct several activities, some within the charge to VAT as standard rated or zero rated, and some in the 'exempt' categories listed above.

Such businesses are *partially* exempt. This means that their right to offset input tax is restricted.

To calculate the proportion of input tax which is deductible, a method which is 'practical, accurate and fair' must be agreed. The standard method is to divide input tax into three as shown in Table 14.

Table 14

Input tax category	*VAT treatment*
(a) Input tax on items wholly used in making taxable supplies (whether standard rated or zero rated)	Reclaimable in full
(b) Input tax on items wholly used in making exempt supplies or for any other activity	Not reclaimable at all
(c) Other input tax (partly for items used in making taxable supplies)	Reclaimable pro rate to the extent to which the items relate to taxable supplies

The pro rata calculation could be based on the ratio that the input tax directly attributable to taxable supplies bears to total input tax, but disregarding input tax attributable to:

(i) Goods supplied on in the same state
(ii) Capital items
(iii) Cars
(iv) Entertainment expenses } see page 299

There is an important exception to the need to restrict the right to reclaim input tax. A business may be treated as fully taxable (i.e. with no restriction on the right to reclaim input tax) if the *exempt input tax* is less than:

(i) £100 per month on average; or
(ii) both £250 per month on average and 50 per cent of all input tax; or
(iii) Both £500 per month on average and 25 per cent of all input tax

Registration

Introduction

If you are in business making taxable supplies, you are liable to register for VAT as soon as your turnover exceeds £7,500 for one quarter (three months ending March, June, September or December) or £22,100 for the last four quarters.

An application for registration must be made within thirty days of the end of the relevant quarter and will normally take effect as from the end of the month in which the thirtieth day falls, though an earlier registration date may be agreed.

You are also liable to register if it is clear that your turnover for the ensuing year will exceed £22,100. In that case registration is required within thirty days of the beginning of that year unless an earlier date is agreed.

Until a trader is registered, no VAT may be charged or recovered. For this reason, a person about to commence trade may seek to apply for advance registration.

Voluntary registration

Some traders will wish to remain unregistered as long as possible. If supplies normally taxable at 15 per cent are made to the general public as consumers, there will be a competitive edge available because no VAT needs to be charged to customers until registration, though of course, VAT on purchases cannot be recovered.

However, it is open to a trader to register voluntarily, even though turnover is below the limits.

This may be beneficial in the following situations:

(a) When sales are predominantly to businesses registered for VAT. In this situation the customers will want to reclaim VAT on their purchases, and this implies registration by the supplier, who will then in turn also be able to reclaim VAT in his inputs
(b) When the trader wishes to conceal the small size of the business from customers
(c) When sales are of zero rated items and the trader wishes to reclaim input VAT

Deregistration

A trader may apply for cancellation of registration if it becomes clear that turnover in the forthcoming year is not likely to exceed £21,100 (£1,000 less than the registration limit).

Group registration

A group of companies (as defined in the Companies Act 1985) may register each company separately for VAT, but there is the option for *group* registration, in which only one representative company registers.

The advantages of group registration are:

(a) No VAT is charged on intra-group transactions
(b) Only one VAT return is necessary each quarter to cover the whole group

Divisional registration

A company with several divisions will normally prepare a single VAT return for the whole company, but it has the option to register each division separately. If the option for separate registration is exercised, it is *not* necessary for VAT to be accounted for on transfers between divisions.

Avoidance by disaggregation

The attempt could be made to avoid VAT by dividing a business into small parts, each part being too small to require registration because it is below the £22,100 limit.

If the Customs and Excise are satisfied that such an attempt is being made with intent to avoid registration, they may direct that the businesses are to be deemed to be carrying on the business together, and they will be registered for VAT as from the date of the direction.

Consequences of registration

Consequences of registration are:

(a) The business becomes a registered person entitled to charge VAT on sales and to reclaim VAT on inputs
(b) A VAT number is allocated. This VAT number must be quoted on all invoices and credit notes
(c) Appropriate quarterly tax return periods are allocated – to equalize the work involved in processing quarterly returns, one of three groups of return periods may be allocated:
   (i) Quarters ending March, June, September and December
   (ii) Quarters ending February, May, August and November
   (iii) Quarters ending January, April, July and October

   Quarters coinciding with the business accounting year are normally given.
(d) Satisfactory tax invoices and credit notes must normally be prepared to provide evidence of VAT charged
(e) Adequate records must be kept of all taxable goods and services received or supplied, and exempt supplies made

VAT invoices

The central document in the VAT system is the tax invoice. This is your evidence that you have charged VAT and the customer's evidence that he or she has incurred it.

A tax invoice must normally be issued within thirty days of the 'tax point', and must show:

(a) An identifying serial number
(b) Supplier's name, address and VAT number
(c) Time of supply
(d) Customer's name and address
(e) Type of supply (sale, hire purchase, hire etc.)
(f) Description of the goods or services supplied and the quantity supplied
(g) For each item, the charge excluding VAT and the applicable rate of VAT
(h) Total charge made excluding VAT
(i) Rate of any cash discount
(j) Total VAT payable.

The rate of cash discount is important, because VAT is calculated on the value *net of the cash discount, whether the customer takes the discount or not.*

Retailers may issue a less detailed sales invoice if the charge is £50 or less (including VAT). This simplified form gives:

(a) Supplier's name, address and VAT number
(b) Time of supply
(c) Description of goods or services
(d) Charge made, including VAT
(e) Rate of VAT

A customer who is a registered person may still ask for a full tax invoice.

Credit notes

When a credit note is issued to a customer who can reclaim all the tax on the original supply as input tax, it is not actually necessary to adjust the original VAT charge, *provided both sides agree*. If there is no such agreement, a credit note adjusting the original VAT charge should be issued.

Such a credit note must show:

(a) An identifying serial number and date of issue
(b) Supplier's name and address and VAT number
(c) Customer's name and address
(d) Reason for the credit
(e) Description of the goods or services concerned
(f) Quantity and amount credited for each description
(g) Total amount credited, excluding VAT
(h) Rate and amount of VAT credited

The number and date of the original tax invoice should also be shown on the credit note if possible.

Tax point

The concept of the tax point is another important feature of the VAT system. It is necessary to define exactly when a transaction is deemed to take place so that the correct rate of VAT is charged and the transaction is accounted for in the correct quarterly period.

The rules for determining the tax point are:

(a) Goods

For goods, the basic tax point is usually the date the goods are sent to the customer or he takes them away. This includes supplies under hire purchase, credit sale or conditional sale agreements.

If the goods are not sent or taken, perhaps because they are installed on site, the basic tax point is the date the goods are made available for the customer to use.

The *basic* tax point may be modified to an *actual* tax point according to the invoicing and payment arrangements:

(i) If a tax invoice is issued, or payment is received, *before* the basic tax point, the tax point is the date the invoice is issued or the date payment is received, whichever happens first

(ii) If a tax invoice is issued within fourteen days *after* the tax point, that invoice date may become the actual tax point, subject to any earlier date established as in (a) above. The period of fourteen days may be extended by arrangement with Customs and Excise. It is important to realize that the tax invoice must be sent to or handed to the customer. Merely preparing the invoice does not count as 'issuing' it.

(b) Services

For services, the basic tax point is the date when the service is performed. The basic tax point for services may be modified as indicated in (a) above for goods.

If services are provided on a continuous basis, there is a tax point every time an invoice is issued or payment is received, whichever happens first.

(c) Goods on sale or return or on approval

As no sale takes place until the goods are adopted by the customer, the tax point will be the earlier of the date of adoption or the expiry of the time limit for adoption. If no date for adoption is set, the expiry of twelve months from the date of sending will be the tax point.

(d) Supplies for personal or non-business use

VAT must be accounted for, on the cost of the goods, the tax point being the time when the goods are taken or set aside.

If goods are taken temporarily but remain part of the business stock, there is a tax point on the last day of each tax period that the goods are used. The VAT charge will be based on the cost to the business (e.g. depreciation of the item) during the period of non-business use.

VAT records

Registered persons are required to keep adequate records and to retain them for six years. Records must show details of all taxable goods and services received or supplied, and all exempt supplies made.

Business records include:

(a) Orders and delivery notes
(b) Relevant business correspondence
(c) Purchases and sales books
(d) Cash books and other account books
(e) Purchase invoices and sales invoices
(f) Records of daily takings such as till rolls
(g) Annual accounts, including trading and profit and loss accounts
(h) Import and export documents
(i) Bank statements and paying-in slips
(j) VAT account
(k) Credit or debit notes issued or received

Records may be computerized or maintained by a computer bureau provided it is possible for them to be made available to the Customs and Excise when required.

VAT returns

The basic quarterly return – Form VAT 100

A VAT return must be submitted within thirty days of the end of each return period, showing:

(a) Total VAT due – output tax charged on sales or other income, including sales of business assets, gifts or loans of goods and sales to staff
(b) Total VAT deductible on inputs – purchases and other expenses
(c) Under – and over – declarations from previous returns

Input tax not recoverable

In arriving at VAT on inputs, both capital and revenue expenditure will be included, but there are some important items on which input tax is *not* recoverable:

(i) Purchases not for the business
(ii) All business entertainment – including overseas customers
(iii) Motor cars

Refunds

It is important to realize that the VAT returns may show refunds due to the trader. For example, a trader in zero-rated goods will be regularly reclaiming VAT on inputs. In that situation the trader may elect for one-month tax periods so that repayments are received more quickly.

Cash accounting scheme

If the annual value of taxable supplies excluding VAT does not exceed £250,000, it is possible to elect for the cash accounting scheme. VAT is then accounted for on cash actually received and paid rather than on tax invoices issued and received.

A business electing for this scheme must make application to Customs and Excise, and once approval is given must remain in the scheme for a minimum of two years.

The cash accounting scheme has two main advantages for the trader:

(a) Payment of VAT is deferred until cash has actually been received from customers
(b) Automatic relief is given for bad debts (see below)

A trader in the cash accounting scheme still has to issue tax invoices and comply with all the other rules of VAT.

Annual accounting scheme

A business with a turnover not exceeding £250,000, and which has been registered for at least a year, may apply for annual accounting for VAT. If the application is approved, the business will submit one annual VAT return within two months of the end of the year. Payments are made on account, based on the previous year's VAT liability. The agreed annual amount is payable in ten instalments beginning in the fourth month of the year. The first nine instalments are 10 per cent of the agreed annual amount and the tenth, which is due with the annual return two months after the year end, will be the balancing figure to make up the actual amount for the current year.

Sundry matters

Bad debts

In general, no relief is given for bad debts (except when the cash accounting system described above is adopted). However, relief may be given if:

(a) The debtor is formally insolvent
(b) Title to the goods passed to the purchaser
(c) The claim to the liquidator is for the debt excluding VAT.

Self supply

(a) Stationery
If goods made in the business are used in that business, no VAT is normally due because there has been no supply. However, if the trade conducted is exempt or partly exempt, VAT on the self supply of stationery must be accounted for if the self supply exceeds £22,100. This is because an exempt operation would be unable to reclaim VAT on bought-out stationery and might therefore seek to produce its own.

VAT is due on the open market value, or full cost of production plus 10 per cent, whichever the supplier chooses.

(b) Motor cars
Self-supply of motor cars by manufacturers and dealers must be treated in a special way, because VAT on motor cars is not recoverable when the purchaser is the final consumer. A car dealer *can* recover VAT on cars sold on in the course of trade, but must be required to account for tax on cars used in the business for demonstration purposes and the like, since in that situation the dealer is the final consumer.

Transfer of business as a going concern

If a business is sold as a going concern, it does not count as a taxable supply and no VAT is accounted for provided all the following conditions are satisfied:

(a) The effect of the transfer must be to put the new owner in possession of a business which can be operated as such. A sale of capital assets is not in itself a transfer of a business as a going concern, but if the effect is to put the purchaser in possession of a business, that is a transfer of a going concern, even if the assets are transferred on different dates.
(b) The business, or part business, must be a going concern at the time of the transfer. It can still be a going concern even though it is unprofitable, or is trading under the control of a liquidator or administrative receiver, or a trustee in bankruptcy, or an administrator appointed under the Insolvency Act 1986.
(c) The assets you are transferring must be intended for use by the new owner in carrying on the same kind of business. If the new owner uses the assets to carry on a completely different kind of business you must charge VAT in the normal way.
(d) The new owner must be registered for VAT or, at the time of the transfer, become liable to be registered, or be accepted for voluntary registration. If the taxable turnover of the business (or part business) which is being transferred exceeded the current registration limit immediately before the transfer, the new owner will normally become liable to be registered when the business is transferred.
(e) There must be no significant break in the normal trading pattern

before or immediately after the transfer. A short period of closure which does not significantly disrupt the existing trading pattern, e.g. for redecoration, will not prevent a business from being transferred as a going concern.

(f) If you are transferring only part of your business, that part must be able to operate alone. It does not matter whether it will, in fact, be operated separately from any other businesses the new owner carries on.

Special schemes for retailers

There are a number of special VAT schemes available to retailers. Details are outside the scope of the current syllabus.

Compliance and penalty provisions

The Customs and Excise have wide powers to enforce compliance with the VAT regulations. Extensive new penalty provisions were introduced by the Finance Act 1985 and some of them have come into force in the years up to 1988. These changes reflect the recommendations of the Keith Report.

Visits by VAT officers

Once a business is registered for VAT, it will be visited from time to time by a Customs and Excise officer to confirm that the regulations are being complied with. The officer has a statutory right to enter premises at any reasonable time and to inspect goods and records to confirm that VAT returns are complete and accurate.

A visit should be expected within eighteen months of registration. After that, the interval between visits will depend on the size and complexity of the business. Those who send in late, inaccurate or seemingly inconsistent VAT returns may be visited more frequently.

Default surcharge

As from 1 October 1986, a trader who is late with two VAT returns within one year is sent a *surcharge liability notice*. That means that if within one year from the issue of the notice a third return is received late, a surcharge of 5 per cent of the tax paid late, or £30 if greater, will be made. Every time a surcharge is made, a further notice is issued for another twelve month period. A fourth late return attracts a surcharge of 10 per cent and so on up to a maximum of 30 per cent for the eighth and subsequent occasions of surcharge.

Repayment supplement

If the Customs and Excise do not make repayments due to a trader within a reasonable time, a repayment supplement of 5 per cent of the tax due to the trader, or £30 if greater, may be payable.

The supplement becomes payable if instructions for the repayment have not been issued within thirty days of the receipt of the return (or thirty days from the end of the period concerned if later).

To qualify for the supplement the trader must be up to date with all returns and payments, the return on which the supplement is due must be lodged within two months of the end of the period and the trader's entitlement to input tax must not have been overstated by more than £250, or 5 per cent of the refund due, whichever is greater.

Serious misdeclaration (to be introduced in 1989)

Section 14 Finance Act 1985 as amended by s. 16 Finance Act 1988, creates three civil offences and prescribes penalties for them.

The three offences constituting 'serious misdeclaration' are:

(a) Making a return understating the VAT liability
(b) Claiming a refund to which the claimant is not entitled
(c) Failing to notify Customs and Excise within thirty days that an assessment received from them understates his or her liability.

The penalty is 30 per cent of the tax which would have been lost if the inaccuracy had not been discovered, but only if that amount equals or exceeds:

(a) 30 per cent of the true amount of the tax
(b) £10,000, or 5 per cent of the true amount of the tax, whichever is greater

Persistent misdeclaration (s. 14A FA 1985 inserted by s. 17 FA 1988) (to be introduced in 1989)

If a VAT return understates the liability by at least £100 or 1% of the true tax for the period, and within two years another return also understates the liability by an amount over the limits, the Customs and Excise may issue a 'penalty liability notice' which will have effect for two years from its date of issue. If within that period of two years a third VAT return understates the liability in the same way there will be a penalty of 15 per cent of the tax lost by the inaccuracy in that third VAT period.

Section 14A refers to an error of at least £100 or 1 per cent of the true tax as a 'material' error. It also provides that an inaccuracy will not be regarded as material even if it exceeds the limits if:

(a) the person concerned can satisfy the Customs and Excise (or a VAT Tribunal on appeal) that there was a reasonable excuse for the inaccuracy, or;

(b) the person made full and voluntary disclosure to the Customs and Excise of the inaccuracy.

Late registration and unauthorized issue of VAT invoices s. 15 FA 1985 as amended by s. 18 FA 1988 (to be introduced in 1989)

The Finance Act 1985 specified penalties for late registration and for unauthorized issue of VAT invoices.

After amendment by s. 17 FA 1988 these penalties are, as from 16 March 1988:

(a) Late registration	*Penalty*
(i) If the late registration is not more than nine months after the date on which registration should have been effected	10% of tax
(ii) If registration is between nine and eighteen months late	20% of tax
(iii) If registration is more than eighteen months late	30% of tax

In each case the penalty is the specified percentage of the tax for the period commencing when the person should have registered and ending on the date of registration or the date Customs and Excise became fully aware of the failure to register.

(b) Unauthorized issue of VAT invoices
For unauthorized issue of VAT invoices the penalty is 30 per cent of the amount shown on the invoice as tax or the amount which is to be taken as representing tax.

For both (a) and (b) there is a fixed penalty of £50 if there is no loss of tax (e.g. where input tax exceeds output tax).

It is open to the person to establish 'reasonable excuse' for the failure to register or the unauthorized issue of the invoice, but neither shortage of funds nor reliance on some other person (an accountant, for example) can constitute reasonable excuse (s. 33 (2) FA 1985).

Other offences

(a) Criminal offences
Offences involving fraudulent evasion, using false documents or providing false information are punishable by imprisonment for up to seven years and unlimited fines on conviction by indictment in the Crown Court, or imprisonment for up to twelve months and fines of up to three times the tax understated on summary conviction in the Magistrates' Court.

(b) Civil offences
(i) *Civil fraud* – the offence of civil fraud applies where a trader evades VAT and his or her conduct involves dishonesty. It carries a pen-

alty of 100 per cent of the tax evaded, which may be reduced to 50 per cent by the Customs and Excise or, on appeal, by the VAT Tribunal depending on the degree of co-operation shown during the investigation.

(ii) *Breaches of regulatory provisions* – there is a wide range of possible breaches of the VAT provisions. Offences carry varying penalties. For example, failure to retain records for six years carries a penalty of £500 and there are daily default fines for offences like failure to notify cessation of taxable supplies, failure to keep proper records and failure to furnish information or produce documents.

The daily default fines may be levied only when Customs and Excise have issued a written warning.

Daily default penalties, from 16 March 1988 are as shown in Table 15.

Table 15

Number of previous failures within two years	*Prescribed daily rate higher of (1) and (2)* (1)	(2)
None	£5	1/6% of tax due
1	£10	1/3% of tax due
2	£15	1/2% of tax due

Appeal procedure

If a trader cannot settle his or her VAT liability by negotiation with Customs and Excise, an appeal may be made to the local regional VAT Tribunal, after having given notice to Customs and Excise.

The Tribunal's decision on a question of fact is final, but either the trader or the Customs and Excise may appeal on a point of law to the High Court and thence to the Court of Appeal and the House of Lords.

A VAT Tribunal will only consider an appeal against an assessment if a VAT return has been made for the period concerned, and the VAT paid, unless the appeal relates to goods not accounted for or input tax.

Summary

Introduction

VAT is administered by H M Customs and Excise as a tax on many goods and services. It is ultimately borne by the final consumer in most cases, but is collected by manufacturers, wholesalers and retailers as the goods pass through the distribution chain to the consumer.

Rates of VAT

VAT is currently charged in the UK at two rates – 15 per cent and 0 per cent.

Exemption and zero rating

Some types of business are exempt from VAT. This means that no VAT is charged on sales but the input tax suffered cannot be recovered.

If a trade or transaction is zero rated, this too means that no VAT is charged on sales, but now the input tax suffered by the business can be recovered, because the business is within the scope of VAT.

Registration

A business making taxable supplies above the limit is liable to register for VAT within thirty days. It is also possible to register voluntarily. On registration a VAT number is allocated and the business has to submit quarterly returns of VAT charged and suffered, paying over or receiving a refund of the balance.

VAT invoices and credit notes

A registered trader must issue a VAT invoice or credit note giving full details of every chargeable transaction. This provides evidence that VAT has been charged and enables the customer to reclaim the VAT if he or she is entitled to.

Tax point

It is necessary to define exactly when a transaction is deemed to take place to fix the tax rate applicable and the period for which the VAT must be accounted for.

The basic tax point for goods is the date the goods are sent to the customer. An earlier date, the actual tax point, is established by prior invoicing or payment. A later date may be adopted if an invoice is issued within fourteen days after the supply.

For services, the basic tax point is the date the service is performed.

VAT records

A registered person must retain adequate records of transactions for six years.

VAT returns

VAT returns are normally submitted quarterly, with a cheque for the VAT due, within thirty days of the end of the quarter. An alternative annual scheme also exists for businesses with a turnover not exceeding £250,000.

Bad debts

No relief is given for bad debts unless:

(a) The cash accounting system for businesses with a turnover not exceeding £250,000 is adopted; or
(b) The debtor is formally insolvent, title to the goods passed to the purchaser and the claim to the liquidator is for the debt excluding VAT

Self supply

It may be necessary to charge VAT on goods transferred for use in the business. This applies particularly to stationery (for exempt or partially exempt businesses) and to motor cars.

Transfer of business as a going concern

No VAT should arise on the transfer of a business as a going concern.

Compliance and penalty provisions

VAT offices will visit registered businesses periodically to confirm compliance with regulations.

A default surcharge of 5 per cent, rising to 30 per cent, may be charged if a trader is persistently late in submitting VAT returns.

Imprisonment, fines and penalties may be imposed for a variety of offences in connection with VAT.

Appeal procedure

A trader may appeal to the local VAT Tribunal in the event of disagreement with Customs and Excise. On a question of law, either the trader of Customs and Excise may appeal to the High Court and thence to the Court of Appeal and the House of Lords.

Progress questions

Attempt these questions to test your absorption of the material in the chapter. Rework them at intervals for revision. Answers are on page 403.

1 What transactions are liable to VAT?

2 Distinguish between exemption and zero rating for VAT purposes.

3 Give four examples of transactions normally:

(a) zero-rated;
(b) exempt from VAT.

4 What happens if a business is partially exempt from VAT?

5 Why is it important for a business to register for VAT?

6 It may be advantageous for a trader below the turnover limit to register for VAT voluntarily. When may this be a good idea?

7 What are the consequences of registration?

8 What information must appear on a VAT invoice?

9 (a) What is the meaning of the term 'tax point' in VAT?
(b) Explain how the tax point may be arrived at for:
 (i) goods
 (ii) services

10 How long must business records be retained for VAT purposes?

11 What information has to be shown on the quarterly VAT return – Form VAT 100?

12 (a) When may the cash accounting scheme be adopted, and what advantages does it have for a business?
(b) How does it work?

13 (a) When may the annual accounting scheme be adopted, and what are its advantages?
(b) How does it work?

14 How may a trader obtain relief for bad debts incurred?

15 Why is it required that VAT is accounted for on the self-supply of:

(a) Stationery?
(b) Motor cars?

16 Is VAT normally charged on the transfer of a business as a going concern?

17 Explain what is meant by a default surcharge.

18 What offences constitute 'serious misdeclaration'?

19 Is it possible to appeal against a VAT assessment? If so, what is the procedure?

Part Five Practice Questions

Introduction

It is scarcely possible to prepare for any examination without adequate practice at answering questions on an unseen basis – that is, without looking at the answers first.

The purpose of this part of the book is to provide that practice. Many of the questions used are from past examinations and their source is indicated both for your guidance and to acknowledge the kind permission of the professional bodies concerned to use their questions. Where necessary, questions have been up-dated to reflect changes in legislation since they were originally set.

In a three-hour examination, you have 180 minutes to earn 100 marks. The number of marks awarded for a question thus gives a guide to the time you have to spend on it.

To begin with, your objective is to finish the question almost regardless of time, but as the examination approaches you should gradually work towards speeding up your answering to achieve examination time (1.8 minutes per mark) or better.

The Business Taxation examination contains a considerable proportion of non-computational work, much of it advice on the tax consequences of transactions to reflect the 15 per cent weighting given in the syllabus to tax planning.

For example, in the May 1988 examination the approximate breakdown was:

	Computational	*Non-computational*	*Total*
Q. 1	15	10	25
Q. 2	15	5	20
Q. 3	14	6	20
Q. 4	–	20	20
Q. 5	15	5	20
Q. 6	–	15	15
Q. 7	15	–	15
Q. 8	5	10	15
	79	71	150

This almost equal balance emphasizes that you must also practise your skills at writing reports (Questions 4 and 6 above both required the writing of a report or memorandum) as well as the more obvious computational skills.

In answering such questions remember the stages you should go through:

read
think
plan
write

- *Read* the question and take on board its exact requirements.
- *Think* about the sources for your answer and the points you want to make.
- *Plan* the answer. Arrange your points in some kind of logical order, perhaps by jotting down paragraph topics in one or two words, then numbering them to indicate the order in which you plan to deal with them.
- *Write*, following the plan but deviating where necessary as further points come to you.

Remember to answer all parts of a question.

The practice questions are mainly allocated to a particular chapter and deal with the subject matter of that chapter. At the end is a set of revision questions which have been selected because they deal with two or more taxes or because they are especially suitable for pre-examination revision.

Questions

1 Income tax – basic principles
1 Schedules and Cases
2 Collection of tax

2 Income tax Schedule D Cases I and II – adjustment of profit
3 Badges of trade
4 Adjustment of profit
5 Rules for allowability of expenditure
(See also Question 15 for Chapter 5)

3 Income tax – Schedule D Case I and II – basis of assessment
6 Opening years of business – basic
7 Closing years of business – basic
(See also Questions 8 and 9 for Chapter 4 which deal with assessments and capital allowances in opening and closing years, and also with tax planning aspects)

4 Capital allowances
8 Opening years
9 Opening and closing years
10 De-pooling election
11 Industrial buildings allowance

5 Income tax – relief for trading losses
12 Section 380 relief – basic
13 Relief under s. 380 and s. 385
14 Loss in early years – s. 381
15 Terminal loss, including adjustment of profit or loss

6 Income from land and buildings
16 Explanation of Schedule A tax
17 Computation

7 Schedule E
18 Schedule E expenses
19 Schedule E benefits
20 Schedule E benefits – P11D

8 Miscellaneous income
21 Basis of assessment, Schedule D Cases III, IV and V

9 Sundry matters
22 Diagrams showing hierarchy of administration of taxation and procedure on appeal
23 Postponement, interest on overdue tax

10 Tax planning for individuals
24 Personal pension schemes
25 Opening and closing years; loss relief

11 Corporation tax – basic principles
26 Corporation tax computation

12 Advance corporation tax and income tax
27 Quarterly returns
28 Quarterly returns and computation

13 Corporation tax – more advanced points
29 Fifteen month accounting period
30 Computation, marginal small company

14 Corporation tax – relief for losses
31 Computation s. 393 (2) and s. 393 (2) + (3)
32 Terminal loss

15 Corporation tax – groups of companies
33 Group loss relief and surrender of ACT

16 Corporation tax – close companies
34 Maximum relevant income computation

17 Corporation tax – overseas aspects
35 Controlled foreign companies

18 Tax planning for companies
36 Tax differences between sole trader and limited company

19 Capital gains tax – basic principles
(Covered by progress questions)

20 Capital gains tax – computations
37 Part disposals
38 Leases

21 Capital gains tax – shares and securities
39 Pooling
40 Takeover

1 Income tax – basic principles

Question 1 Schedules and Cases

Draw up a table summarizing the income assessed under each Schedule and Case, the normal basis of assessment and the normal due date for payment. *(12 marks)*

Question 2 Collection of tax

(a) State three sources of income enjoyed by individuals and normally received after deduction of tax at source or in 'net' form.
(b) Explain how tax is collected on income received under deduction of tax.
(c) Explain how tax is collected on income received without deduction of tax at source. *(12 marks)*

2 Income tax Schedule D Cases I and II – adjustment of profit

Question 3 Badges of trade

What factors are generally taken to be relevant in determining whether an activity constitutes a trade? Briefly explain the meaning of each of them. *(15 marks)*

Question 4 Adjustment of profit

Pertwee has been running a clog-making factory for many years and prepares accounts to 30 June each year. His summarized profit and loss account for the year ended 30 June 1989 is set out below:

	£		£
Wages and national insurance	45,689	Gross profit	83,145
Rent and rates	7,391	Profit on sale of van	341
Lighting, heating and power	3,642	Interest on deposit account	760
Motor expenses	1,320		
Bad and doubtful debts	1,055		
Depreciation of machinery	2,500		
Sundry trade expenses (below)	6,928		
Net profit	15,721		
	£84,246		£84,246

Notes

(a) The charge for bad and doubtful debts is arrived at as follows:

	£
Provision for doubtful debts (2 per cent of debtors)	1,278
Less: provision already made at 1st July 1988	1,031
	247
Trade debts written off	608
Loan to former employee written off	200
	£1,055

(b) The analysis of sundry trade expenses is:

	£	£
Stationery, postage and telephone		2,410
Repairs and maintenance of buildings		1,371
Subscriptions: local charity	100	
political party	250	
		350
Entertaining: UK customers	1,110	
overseas customers	516	
		1,626
Legal fees: renewal of 7 year lease	222	
collecting bad debts	148	
		370
Cost of new lathe including installation charge £85		801
		£6,928

You are required to compute the adjusted trading profit for the year ended 30th June 1989, stating the Schedule and Case under which it will be assessed, and the year of assessment.

Ignore capital allowances. (*16 marks*)

SCCA

Question 5 Rules for allowability of expenditure

(a) What is the general rule governing the allowability of expenditure for income tax Schedule D Cases I and II?

(b) State with reasons whether the following items are allowable expenses. Cite statutory or case law authorities where relevant.

- (i) National Insurance contributions
- (ii) Repairs expenditure
- (iii) Renewal of short lease
- (iv) Salary to proprietor's spouse
- (v) Fines imposed for breaking the law
- (vi) Entertainment expenses:
  - Foreign customers
  - Foreign suppliers
  - Staff
- (vii) Costs of obtaining a patent or trade mark
- (viii) Redundancy payments
- (ix) Costs of obtaining loan finance
- (x) Value Added Tax (*20 marks*)

3 Income tax Schedule D Cases I and II – basis of assessment

Question 6 Opening years of business – basic

F commenced trading on 1 June 1985 and decided to have a permanent accounting date of 30 April.

His adjusted trading results were as follows:

	£
Period ended 30 April 1986	22,000
Year ended 30 April 1987	21,000
Year ended 30 April 1988	30,000

You are required to calculate the net Schedule D Case I assessments to be made on F for the first four income tax years, showing clearly any alternative assessments for which F can elect. (*12 marks*)

CIMA (part of question)

Question 7 Closing years of business – basic

Grace has been in business for some years, making up accounts to 31 December, but decided to cease her business on 30 September 1988. Her profits in recent years, as adjusted for income tax, have been:

	£
Year ended 31 December 1984	6,000
Year ended 31 December 1985	12,000

	£
Year ended 31 December 1986	10,000
Year ended 31 December 1987	16,000
9 months ended 30 September 1988	9,000

You are required to show the original and final assessments for all tax years involved. (*10 marks*)

4 Capital allowances

Question 8 Opening years

Harold, a married man, commenced business on 1 January 1988, making up accounts for calendar years. His profits, as adjusted for tax purposes, amounted to £6,000 in the year ended 31 December 1988 and are expected to increase substantially.

Neither he nor his wife has any other income. During 1988 he purchased the following assets for use in the business:

1 January 1988	Car	£8,800
1 May 1988	Plant	£8,000

(a) Calculate the assessments and capital allowance for the first three years of the business
(b) Explain any options available to Harold. (*12 marks*)

Question 9 Opening and closing years

Mr S commenced trading on 1 February 1983 and ceased trading on 30 April 1988. He makes up accounts annually at 30 September and his profits, as agreed for tax purposes, were:

		£
Period ended 30 September	1983	4,000
Years ended 30 September	1984	18,000
	1985	36,000
	1986	16,000
	1987	1,200
Period ended 30 April	1988	350

The following assets were purchased for use in the business:

		£
1 May 1983	Motor car (private use 20%)	4,000
1 March 1984	Equipment	2,000

These assets were sold on 29 March 1988 realising:

	£
Motor car	400
Equipment	300

You are required to

(a) Show all the assessments under Schedule D I raised on Mr S during the lifetime of his business, assuming maximum capital allowances are claimed. *(14 marks)*

(b) State what advice you would have given him had he approached you early in 1988 and demonstrate the effect of this advice. *(6 marks)*

Note: FYA available at 1 March 1984 was 100 per cent.

(Total: 20 marks)
CIMA

Question 10 De-pooling election

The Finance Act 1985 introduced a system of de-pooling certain assets for capital allowance purposes. Describe briefly the purpose of de-pooling and explain the practicalities involved in calculating the allowances granted on the sale of the asset within the prescribed period.

Illustrate your explanation by distinguishing in the treatment between pooling and de-pooling provisions of an asset purchased in the year ended 30th June, 1987 for £10,000 and sold in the year ending 30th June, 1989 for £2,000. *(6 marks)*
CIMA

Question 11 Industrial buildings allowance

J incurred the following capital expenditure on 1 January, 1985, in the financial year ended 30 June, 1985:

	£
Industrial building	250,000
Attached office accommodation	50,000
Land	100,000
	£400,000

The building was sold on 31 March, 1990 to C for £500,000 – the sale proceeds being allocated: industrial building £350,000; office accommodation £25,000; land £125,000.

You are required to calculate the industrial buildings allowances available to both J and C for all years involved (assuming J claimed the full initial allowance available of 50 per cent on purchase). *(8 marks)*

5 Income tax – relief for trading losses

Question 12 Section 380 relief – basic

Angus has been in business for many years. His results in recent years, as adjusted for income tax purposes, have been:

Year ended 31 December	*Profit/(Loss)*
	£
1984	30,000
1985	10,000
1986	40,000
1987	(30,000)
1988	20,000

His wife is employed and had a salary of £3,000 per year in each of the above years. Angus has no other income.

You are required:

(a) To explain, *without computation*, the alternative ways in which Angus could claim relief for his loss, indicating which you would recommend, with reasons
(b) To compute the assessments on the assumption that Angus claims relief on the basis you recommend in (a)
(c) To state the latest dates by which Angus must claim his loss reliefs

(*10 marks*)

Question 13 Relief under s. 380 and s. 385

Alfred Smith has been in business for a number of years and his recent results, as adjusted for tax purposes, have been:

Year ended		£
30 June 1987	Profit	20,000
30 June 1988	Loss	34,000

He has investment income of £8,000 in both years. His wife also runs a business and her adjusted profits have been:

	£
1988/89	6,500
1989/90	7,500

Write a letter to Alfred advising him of the most beneficial way of claiming relief for the loss. (*12 marks*)

Question 14 Loss in early years – s. 381

X, for many years an employee of DEF Limited, decides to start business on his own on 1 July 1987.

His salary with DEF Limited has been:

1984/85	14,000
1985/86	14,500
1986/87	15,000
3 months to 30 June 1987	4,000

In his first year's trading to 30 June 1988 he incurred a loss of £42,000.

He has no other income but his wife has earnings of £5,000 per annum throughout the whole period.

Advise X as to the most advantageous method of claiming loss relief.

(*14 marks*)
CIMA

Question 15 Terminal loss

AY, a sole trader, has traded since 1968. His recent tax-adjusted profits were as follows:

	£
Year ended 30 June 1984	18,000
Year ended 30 June 1985	24,000
Year ended 30 June 1986	15,300
Year ended 30 June 1987	12,600

Due to the general downturn in trade AY decided on a permanent cessation of trading on 30 June 1988. His accounts for the year ended 30 June 1988 showed the following results:

	£	£
Gross trading profit		16,750
Less: Salaries and wages	35,240	
Rent and rates	4,625	
Heat, light and power	3,220	
Depreciation	1,850	
Telephone and other tax allowable expenses	2,662	
Miscellaneous expenses	787	
		48,384
Net trading loss		£31,634

Additional information:

(i) Analysis of miscellaneous expenses:

	£
Staff outing expenses	250
Patent royalties (gross sum)	400
Sundry allowable expenses	137
	£787

The patent royalties are always paid on 31 May.

(ii) The royalties paid in previous years were as follows:

	£
1984	2,500
1985	1,750
1986	900
1987	700

(iii) All private expenses had been adjusted and charged to AY personally.

(iv) The written-down values for capital allowances, at 5 April 1985 were:

plant pool	£16,400
motor car	£6,500

(There have been no acquisitions or disposals since 30 June 1981.)

(v) Private use of motor car has been agreed at 40%.

(vi) The plant and motor car were disposed of on 30 June 1988 for £6,000 and £2,000 respectively.

(vii) AY has no income other than profits arising from his business.

You are required to compute the final net assessments arising to income tax, for the income tax years 1985/86 to 1988/89 inclusive, showing the measurement and relief of the terminal loss.

(20 marks)
CIMA

6 Income from land and buildings

Question 16 Explanation of Schedule A tax

Frederick Jones is considering the purchase of several houses which he intends to convert into flats and let unfurnished at a full rent. He is however unfamiliar with the income tax system regarding the taxing of the rental income he will receive and seeks your advice.

You are required to write a letter to Frederick Jones explaining:

(a) The basis of assessing the rental income and the due date for payment.

(b) Briefly the nature of any expenses which may be deducted.

(c) The treatment of any losses (where the expenditure on a property exceeds the income).

(Equal marks are awarded to (a), (b), and (c) above). *(20 marks)*
ACCA

Question 17 Computation

Fred Stone is the Managing Director of a Textile Printing Company and has invested some of his earnings in the following properties in the United Kingdom which he lets.

Shop 1 A butcher's shop on a tenant's repairing lease. The annual rental is £1,650 expiring on 29 September 1987 and the lease was renewed on that date at £2,350 per annum for 7 years.

Shop 2 A shop selling textiles also on a tenant's repairing lease. The annual rental is £1,500 under a 7 year lease expiring on 25 March 1989.

The quarter's rent due on 25 March 1988 was not paid until 30 April 1988.

Shop 3 A shop selling light fittings. This was let to a relative of Mr Stone at an annual rental of £100 when a commercial rent would have been £1,200. Mr Stone's relative is responsible for all outgoings, with the exception of insurance.

Shop 4 This shop had been let on a tenant's repairing lease at an annual rental of £3,500 until 24 June 1987, when the tenant, who had been selling clothing, informed Mr Stone that he could not afford to pay the rent and vacated the premises forthwith. Mr Stone agreed through his agent to re-let the premises to a new tenant from 25 March 1988, who would be selling pottery imported from Scandinavia. The new rental was £4,000 per annum for 10 years and Mr Stone also received a premium of £1,000 from the incoming tenant on 25 March 1988.

House 1 A furnished house let on weekly tenancies. During 1987/88 the property was let for 37 weeks. The all-inclusive weekly rental was £105. An election has been made for the rent in respect of the property (agreed with the Inland Revenue at £95 per week) to be assessed under Schedule A instead of Schedule D, Case VI.

House 2 A furnished house also let on weekly tenancies. During 1987/88 the property was let for 43 weeks. The all-inclusive weekly rental was £120. An election has been made for the rent in respect of the property (agreed with the Inland Revenue at £105 per week) to be assessed under Schedule A instead of Schedule D, Case VI.

With the exception of the houses the rents are due in advance on the normal English quarter days, 25 March, 24 June, 29 September and 25 December. Details of expenditure in the year ended 5 April 1988 were:

	Shop 1	*Shop 2*	*Shop 3*	*Shop 4*	*House 1*	*House 2*
	£	£	£	£	£	£
Insurance	97	123	95	210	135	117
Ground Rent	20	10	–	100	5	6
Repairs & Decorating	–	–	–	1,527 (note 1)	1,296 (note 2)	1,935 (note 3)
Accountancy	25	25	25	25	35	35
Newspaper Advertising	–	–	–	–	117	134
Gardeners' Wages	–	–	–	–	120	132
Rates	–	–	–	–	95	112

Mr Stone employs agents to collect the rents of shops 1, 2 and 4. He pays them 10 per cent when they collect the rent (not applicable to the premium).

The expenditure on the houses has been agreed with the Inland Revenue as that being applicable to the rent of the property (as opposed to the rent of the furniture). In addition, all necessary apportionments to the expenditure on a time basis have already been made in arriving at the figures shown.

Notes on Repairs

1 Included in the figure of £1,527 is £725 which was spent on decorating the premises in July and August 1987.

2 This figure of £1,296 includes £1,050 spent on dry-rot remedial treatment. The dry-rot was present in the house when Mr Stone purchased it in November 1986.

3 Included in the figure of £1,935 is an amount of £1,428 spent on re-tiling the house roof. The old tiles were re-used whenever possible to comply with local planning regulations.

You are required to:

(a) Calculate the Schedule A assessment for 1987/88, and *(18 marks)*

(b) state the procedure which the Inland Revenue will adopt when making the 1988/89 Schedule A assessment. *(1 mark)*

(19 marks)

ACCA

7 Schedule E

Question 18 Schedule E expenses

Expenses deductible from Schedule E income are often the subject of argument between an individual and the Inspector of Taxes.

State the rules under which such expenses may be allowable and discuss briefly five decided cases in your answer. *(20 marks)*

ACCA

Question 19 Schedule E benefits

You have been consulted by one of the directors of your company, who has no shareholding in the company, concerning the taxability of emoluments and benefits received. The following information is provided for the tax year 1988/89

(a) Salary £14,000.

(b) Bonus of £3,600, based on company profits for the year ended 31st December, 1988 and paid in March 1989. (It is unlikely that there will be a bonus for the financial year 1989.)

(c) An expenses allowance of £2,500 which for 1988/89 was expended as follows:

	£
Business travelling	1,800
Entertainment:	
Overseas customers	400
Overseas suppliers	100
United Kingdom customers	200

(d) Benefits for the year:
  (i) Free accommodation in a company flat. This is a condition of his employment and is necessary for him to carry out his duties.
  The company spent during the year £3,380 on redecorations, cleaning and employment of a part-time gardener. Other expenses (eg light, heat) were paid personally by the director.
  (ii) The company purchased hi-fi equipment for the director's personal use at a cost of £800.
  (iii) Medical insurance £300.
  (iv) He was given new suits of clothing which cost the company £400.

You are required to calculate the amount chargeable under Schedule E for 1988/89 and to write brief explanatory notes for your director's guidance. (*18 marks*)
CIMA

Question 20 Schedule E benefits – P11D

You have been asked to assist in the completion of forms P11D in respect of the directors of your company for the year 1988/89.

The following benefits are enjoyed by various directors:

(a) The use of a private house, owned by the company, valued at £80,000. The annual value of the house is £2,000 and the director concerned pays rent to the company of £1,500 p.a. plus all running costs.
(b) A video system, which had been provided during 1985/86 for the use of a director and which had cost the company £1,500, was taken over by the director on 6 April 1988 for a payment of £400. The present market value of the system is £600.
(c) A director has a loan of £20,000 at 5% interest to enable him to purchase his sole residence.
(d) A dishwasher was purchased by the company for £280 and given to a director. The retail price was £350.
(e) Medical Health Insurance premiums were paid for a director and his family, under a group scheme at a cost to the company of £1,200. Had the director paid for this as an individual the cost would have been £1,600.

You are required to show how each of the above benefits would be quantified for inclusion in the forms P11D.

Note: For the purposes of this question you may assume a commercial rate of interest to be 12% p.a. (*15 marks*)
CIMA

Question 21 Basis of assessment, Schedule D Cases III, IV and V

Explain how assessments in the opening and closing years are dealt with for income tax under Schedule D Cases III, IV and V. (*6 marks*)

9 Sundry matters

22 Diagrams showing hierarchy of administration of taxation and procedure on appeal

Draw diagrams explaining:

(a) The hierarchy of the administration and control of taxation
(b) The procedure for appeal against an income tax assessment

(*14 marks*)

Question 23 Postponement, interest on overdue tax

In relation to tax assessed under Schedule D Case I

(a) What action should a taxpayer take when he receives an assessment which he believes to be incorrect? What are the consequences if no action is taken? (*4 marks*)
(b) Following an application for postponement of income tax how is the due and payable date of the tax assessed and not postponed arrived at? (*2 marks*)
(c) How is the reckonable date for the purposes of interest on overdue tax determined for income tax which has been postponed but is later agreed to be payable? (*4 marks*)
(d) If the income tax finally determined as payable is in excess of the income tax originally assessed how is the reckonable date for the excess tax determined? (*2 marks*)

(*12 marks*)
CACA

10 Tax planning for individuals

Question 24 Personal pension schemes

Explain the rules governing new personal pension schemes introduced as from 1 July 1988. (*12 marks*)

Question 25 Opening and closing years's loss relief

Explain how an individual may maximize the income tax benefits available from:

(a) Schedule D Case I and II rules in opening and closing years
(b) Relief for losses under Schedule D Cases I and II (*14 marks*)

11 Corporation tax – basic principles

Question 26 Corporation tax computation

Cortex Limited is a manufacturing company formed in 1968 and has always made up its accounts to 31 March each year. The company's profit for the year ended 31 March 1989 was £532,600.

In arriving at this figure the following items of income and expenditure have been included:

	£
(a) Income	
Interest on Government securities (received gross)	500
Building society interest (amount received)	1,500
Rent receivable less related expenses	4,000
(b) Expenditure	
Depreciation	20,000
Specific provision for doubtful debts (including £1,000 relating to a debt due from a member of staff)	3,000
Legal expenses	
Cost of defending an employee against a criminal charge	1,200
Acquisition of new 5 year lease of premises	500
Entertaining: UK customers	10,000
Foreign customers	5,000
Staff Christmas party	2,000
Interest on debentures – accrued amount (gross)	10,000

The gross equivalent of the amount paid in the year was £8,000.

Capital allowances for the year amounted to £14,000.

You are required to calculate the amount chargeable to corporation tax for the year ended 31 March 1989. *(18 marks)*

12 Advance corporation tax and income tax

Question 27 Quarterly returns

D Ltd has been trading since 1970 and during its accounting year ended 31st December, 1988 it made the following payments and had the following receipts:

	Interest paid and received net		
Date	*Paid (gross sum)* £	*Received (gross sum)* £	*Building society interest received* £
21 February		5,000	
31 March	6,000		
30 April		2,500	2,100
6 May	1,000		
31 October	600		630
5 November		2,500	
31 December		1,200	

You are required to:

(a) Show the quarterly returns to be made by D Ltd for the accounting year ended 31st December, 1988, in respect of the above interest receipts and payments, indicating the date by which such returns should be made; *(9 marks)*

(b) Advise the management of D Ltd of the effect which the transactions referred to would have on the amount of Mainstream Corporation Tax payable, indicating the date on which the adjusted MCT is due and payable. *(5 marks)*

(Total: 14 marks)

CIMA

Question 28 Quarterly returns and computation

H Ltd, a company with no associates, which had commenced trading in 1968, has the following financial results for the year ended 31st March, 1989:

	£	
Income:		
Adjusted trading profit	520,000	
Debenture interest received on 30th June, 1988	5,000	(gross sum)
Chargeable gains	12,000	
Dividends received from UK companies on 30th November, 1988	4,200	
Outgoings:		
Debenture interest paid:		
on 30th September, 1988	3,000	(gross sum)
on 31st March, 1989	3,000	(gross sum)
Dividends paid during the year:		
final for year ended 31st March, 1988 on 1st May, 1988	1,875	
interim for year ended 31st March, 1988 on 31st December, 1988	2,625	

At 1st April, 1988, there were unrelieved capital losses brought forward of £15,000.

There was no surplus FII brought forward.

You are required to compute the amounts of income tax and corporation tax payable or repayable for the year ended 31st March, 1988 stating in all cases the dates of payment and repayment. *(18 marks)*

CIMA

13 Corporation tax – more advanced points

Question 29 Fifteen month accounting period

Andrell Ltd was incorporated on 1 April 1970 and has always prepared accounts to the 31 March each year. The company have now decided to change their accounting date to the 30 June and the accounts for the 15 months to the 30 June 1988 are as follows:

		£
Gross trading profits		177,310
Add:	£	
Bank deposit interest received (*Note 1*)	3,450	
Rents receivable (*Note 2*)	1,000	
Profit on sale of plant (*Note 3*)	6,000	10,450
		187,760
Deduct:		
Wages and salaries	43,000	
Light and heat	23,000	
Legal and professional charges (*Note 4*)	1,860	
Depreciation	3,000	
Bad debts (*Note 5*)	4,600	
Debenture interest (*gross*) (*Note 6*)	11,250	
Rent and rates	10,000	96,710
		£91,050

Andrell Ltd is a non close company with no associates and the following information is given in relation to the above accounts.

Note 1: The bank deposit interest was received on the following dates:

	£
30 June 1987	1,200
31 December 1987	1,850
30 June 1988	400

Note 2: On the 1 June 1988 the company negotiated to rent out part of its storage facilities, the annual rent of £1,000 being payable in advance on the 10 June. Due to an industrial dispute however, the first payment was not received by Andrell Ltd until the 10 July 1988.

Note 3: An extract from the asset disposal account relating to the sale of plant showed:

	£
Cost (purchased 1 March 1987)	12,000
Less: accumulated depreciation	2,500
	9,500
Sale proceeds (sold 12 February 1988)	15,500
Profit on sale	6,000

Note 4: The legal and professional charges were made up of:

	£
Accountancy charge re annual audit	1,500
Accountancy charge for negotiating successful tax appeal	150
Legal charge for negotiating successful appeal against rates	210
	1,860

Note 5: Bad debts comprise:

	£
Increase in specific reserve	1,800
Increase in general reserve	2,000
Bad debts written off	1,200
	5,000
Less: Bad debts recovered	400
	4,600

Note 6: The debenture interest paid relates to an issue of £50,000 of 15% debentures, the interest on which is payable half yearly on the 30 June and 31 December. All interest was paid on the due date.

The company had a pool balance brought forward for plant and machinery of £276,000 and the only capital additions during the period of account were:

	£
1 June 1981 purchased new plant	3,000
1 May 1982 purchased 12 saloon motor cars for use by the company salesmen, each car costing £8,000	96,000

The company paid a final dividend of £480 (net) on the 30 June 1988 and had no balances or losses brought forward other than those shown.

You are required to compute the advance corporation tax and mainstream corporation tax payable and show the due dates for payment. You are to assume that all allowances and reliefs are claimed as soon as possible. Ignore indexation of the capital gain. (*20 marks*)

ACCA

Question 30 Computation, marginal small company

Stonyhurst Limited is a trading company, resident in the United Kingdom, which makes up its annual accounts to 31 March. It has no associated companies. The company's profit and loss account for the year ended 31 March 1988 was as follows:

Notes		£	£
	Gross trading profit		372,100
1	*Add:* Surplus on sale of house	17,150	
	Debenture interest (gross)	3,250	
	Dividends received from UK companies (gross)	4,600	
	Building society interest received (Net)	700	
2	Bank deposit interest	360	26,060
			398,160
	Deduct: Lighting & heating	1,290	
	Repairs & renewals	1,600	
3	Depreciation	34,650	
	Wages & salaries	24,450	
	Directors' remuneration	35,480	

		£	£
4	Subscriptions & donations	1,350	
	Postage stationery & telephone	525	
5	Loan interest payable	17,500	
6	Professional expenses	6,820	
7	Miscellaneous expenses	1,815	125,480
Net profit			272,680

Notes

1 The asset disposal account of the house sold during the year was:

	£		£
Cost (April 1983)	17,850	Accumulated depreciation	4,000
Profit and loss account	17,150	Sale proceeds (September 1987)	31,000
	35,000		35,000

Ignore indexation

2 The bank deposit account was opened 17 August 1987 and interest of £300 was credited to the account on 31 December 1987. £60 interest had accrued on the account at 31 March 1988.

3 *Depreciation*
Profits/losses on the disposals of plant and equipment/cars have been included in arriving at this figure.

4 *Subscriptions and donations*

	£
Golf club subscription for sales director	150
National Trust	50
Political party	300
Local charities	75
Works social club	750
Trade association	25
	1,350

5 *Loan interest*
There was an accrued liability at 31 March 1988 for loan interest of £1,500. There was no opening accrual.

6 *Professional expenses*

	£
Audit and accountancy	3,000
Costs of successful tax appeal	500
Legal fees re collection of bad debts	180
Costs of defending action by a former director for wrongful dismissal	300
Legal costs on acquisition of a new seven-year lease on a warehouse	500
Architect's fees for designing a new warehouse which was not proceeded with	2,340
	6,820

7 *Miscellaneous expenses*	£
Entertaining – foreign suppliers	70
– UK suppliers	340
– UK customers	180
Round-sum expense allowances to company salesmen	1,225
	1,815

You are also given the following information.

1 The company paid a dividend of £18,900 to its shareholders on 13 March 1988.

2 The written down values of capital assets at 1 April 1987 were:

	£
Plant and machinery (main pool)	72,125
Car Pool	10,438
Expensive car (i.e. costing over £8,000) No. 1	8;598
Expensive car (i.e. costing over £8,000) No. 2	10,520

The following items were purchased and sold during the year ended 31 March 1988:

Purchases		£
11 August 1987	Car for salesman	6,500
23 October 1987	Moveable office partitioning	3,518
7 March 1988	Plant and machinery	42,500
28 March 1988	Plant and machinery	17,192

Notes

(i) The private usage of the salesman's car is one-quarter

(ii) The company's offices do not qualify for Industrial Buildings Allowances

Sales		£
19 April 1987	Plant and machinery	150
29 July 1987	Expensive car No. 2	7,500
11 August 1987	Car (purchased on 13 August 1982 for £4,500)	2,150

3 The Industrial Buildings Allowance for the year ended 31 March 1988 is £4,106.

You are required to compute the mainstream corporation tax payable for the year ended 31 March 1988. *(25 marks)*

ACCA

14 Corporation tax – relief for losses

Question 31 Computation s. 393 (2) and s. 393 (2) + (3)

J Clark Electrical Ltd, a non-close UK resident company, was incorporated in 1950. It has one associated company, Sparks Ltd., in which it holds 60% of the ordinary share capital.

The recent financial results of J Clark Electrical Ltd (as adjusted for taxation purposes) have been:

	Year ended 30 June		*Period*	
	1986	*1987*	*1 July 1982 to 31 December 1987*	*Year ended 31 December 1988*
	£	£	£	£
Trading profit	135,000	650,000	60,000	–
Trading loss	–	–	–	430,000
Bank interest	4,150	7,000	5,000	8,400
Debenture interest received (net)	1,500	–	–	–
Chargeable gains	6,000	–	3,350	–
Capital loss		2,600	–	–
Dividends received from UK companies (not from Sparks Ltd)	2,100	3,500	7,000	3,500
Dividends paid	–	14,000	21,000	210,000

The company has no balances brought forward from previous years. Chargeable gains are shown at the chargeable amounts.

You are required to compute the mainstream corporation tax for each accounting period claiming all losses and reliefs as early as possible. Assume tax rates of 35% (CT) and 25% (IT and small companies CT rate) throughout. *(20 marks)*

ACCA

Question 32 Terminal loss

Burlington Limited, which has been a trading company for many years, permanently ceased to trade on 31 March 1988. It had always made accounts up to 30 September. The following information is made available to you.

	Year ended 30 September				*Period ended 31 March*
	1984	*1985*	*1986*	*1987*	*1988*
	£	£	£	£	£
Trading profit/(loss) adjusted for tax	28,000	10,000	6,000	(15,000)	(20,000)
Unfranked investment income (gross)	5,000	5,000	5,000	5,000	2,500
Loan interest paid (gross)	7,500	7,500	7,500	7,500	3,750

You are required to calculate the income chargeable to corporation tax for all chargeable accounting periods after making any claims for loss relief as early as possible. *(20 marks)*

15 Corporation tax – groups of companies

Question 33 Group loss relief and surrender of ACT

The following diagram represents the relationships, in terms of ordinary share capital held, between the companies shown:

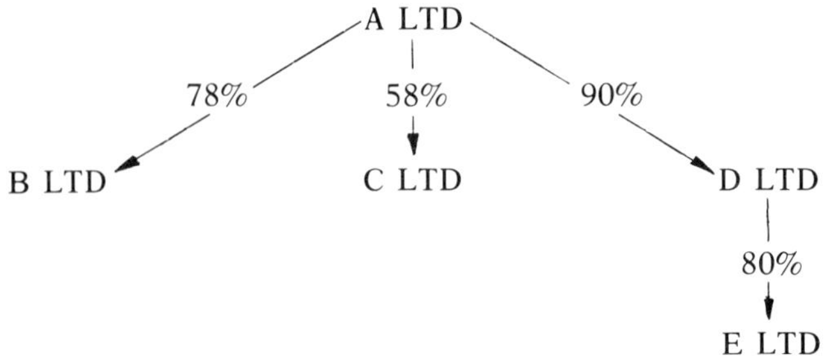

The following information relates to the year ended 31 March 1989.

	Schedule D I	*Schedule D III*	*Loan interest paid (gross)*
	£	£	£
A Ltd profit	46,000	–	3,000
B Ltd loss	24,000	3,000	1,000
C Ltd profit	90,000	15,000	4,000
D Ltd profit	35,000	–	2,000
E Ltd loss	12,000	–	–

None of the above companies had any other income or gains.
You are required to

(a) Compute the corporation tax payable by each company, assuming group relief is claimed in the most efficient manner. *(15 marks)*
(b) Explain the circumstances in which a group of companies should set aside an existing group income election. *(5 marks)*

(Total: 20 marks)
CIMA

16 Corporation tax-close companies

Question 34 Maximum relevant income computation

(a) Edgar Ltd a close trading company with no associates had the following results as adjusted for taxation for the year ended 31 December 1988.

	£
Trading profits	35,000
Rental income	25,000
Bank interest	8,000
Chargeable gains	7,800
Debenture interest paid (gross)	2,000
Dividend from UK company (net)	3,750

You are required to compute the maximum relevant income for the accounting period ended 31 December 1988. *(9 marks)*

(b) State the types of company which are expressly exempted from being classified as 'close' even though they may be controlled by five or fewer participators or participator directors. (*11 marks*)

(*Total 20 marks*)

ACCA

17 Corporation tax – overseas aspects

Question 35 Controlled foreign companies

P Ltd, a company resident in the UK, owns 90% of Q (USA) Inc, a company resident in America. The directors of P Ltd are considering changing the residence of Q (USA) Inc to a far eastern country where the rate of corporation tax is 5%.

You are required to draft a memorandum to the board of P Ltd concerning the taxation implications of this proposal. (*15 marks*)

CIMA

18 Tax planning for companies

Question 36 Tax differences between sole trader and limited company

Mr D is about to set up in business and is uncertain as to whether he should trade as a sole trader or form a limited company.

You are required to draft a report for Mr D, highlighting, from a taxation point of view, the various important differences which arise between the alternative styles of trading. (*20 marks*)

CIMA

19 Capital gains tax – basic principles

(Covered by progress questions)

20 Capital gains tax – computations

Question 37 Part disposals

(a) Explain how capital gains or losses arising from part disposals of assets other than shares are calculated.

(b) If expenditure is incurred on improving an asset, how is the calculation of the chargeable gain affected? (*8 marks*)

Question 38 Leases

J owns a leasehold flat acquired for £40,000 in November 1983 when the lease had 45 years to run. He sold it in May 1988 for £80,000. Legal expenses on the sale were £600 and estate agent's fees £1,600. The flat is not his main residence. Compute the chargeable gain on the sale.

(*10 marks*)

Question 39 Pooling

Vector Limited, which makes up its accounts to 31 March each year, acquired 2,000 shares in Steep Limited in August 1983 for £5,000. Since that date the company's transactions in Steep Limited shares have been:

April 1985	Took up rights issue 1 for 4 at £2 per share
May 1986	Sold 1,000 shares at £3 each
June 1987	Received bonus issue 1 for 3
May 1988	Sold 1,000 shares at £4 each

Compute the gains arising on the two sales. (*12 marks*)

Question 40 Takeover

Culator Limited owned 10,000 shares in Victim Limited which had cost £30,000 in April 1970. The shares were quoted at 415p – 435p on 31 March 1982, and Culator had elected under s. 96 FA 1988 for all gains on assets acquired before 31 March 1982 to be computed by reference to their market value on that date.

In May 1988, there was a successful takeover bid from Predator Limited as a result of which Culator Limited received, for each share in Victim Limited:

Cash £1
3 ordinary shares in Predator Limited
£1 Predator Limited 10% loan stock

On the first dealing day after the takeover the market quotations were:

Predator Limited ordinary shares	195p–215p
Predator Limited 10% loan stock	79p–83p

Explain and compute the effect of the takeover on Culator Limited.

(*12 marks*)

22 Capital gains tax – reliefs

Question 41 Retirement relief

Basil resigned as a full-time working director in Broom and Brush Ltd on 1 June 1989 (his 64th birthday), to become part-time non-executive chairman of the company. He had joined the Company on 1 January 1983 and had acquired 28% of the company's ordinary shares on the same date. These shares were sold to existing members of the company at the time of Basil's resignation from full-time duties. Basil made a capital gain of £104,350 on the disposal of the shares (after indexation).

Current Valuations extracted from the Company's Balance Sheet at 31 May 1989 were:

	£
Freehold land and buildings	795,000
Goodwill	250,000
Quoted securities	35,000
Shares in a subsidiary company	27,500
Plant and machinery (cost £1,500,000)	1,100,000
Fixtures and fittings (cost £500,000)	350,000
Stock and work-in-progress	384,000
Debtors	728,000
Cash	2,500
Bank	(115,000)

No individual item of plant or fixtures cost more than £3,000.

You are required to calculate the capital gain for 1989/90 after any claim Basil could make. *(8 marks)*

ACCA

Question 42 Roll-over relief

JC Limited, who commenced trading in 1968, makes up its accounts annually to 31 March. In May 1988 the company sold a building which had cost £40,000 in May 1983 for £100,000.

Calculate the amount of the gain on the disposal and explain its treatment in the following four situations, claiming all available reliefs:

(a) The building is not replaced within three years by another asset qualifying for roll-over relief
(b) The building is replaced by another costing £120,000
(c) The building is replaced by another costing £60,000
(d) The building is replaced by a leasehold building with 40 years of the lease to run and costing £100,000 *(14 marks)*

23 Capital gains tax – group aspects

Question 43 Shareholding requirements

(a) What shareholding link is required for companies in the same group to transfer assets on a 'no gain no loss' basis? What is the important tax advantage of being able to do this?
(b) How does the shareholding requirement for (a) differ from the requirement for group loss relief under ss. 402–413 ICTA 1988? You are not required to consider consortia. *(8 marks)*

24 Capital gains tax – planning

Question 44 Tax benefits from planning capital transactions

Intelligent planning of capital transactions may reduce a company's tax liability. Explain three ways in which this may be possible.

(*12 marks*)

25 Value added tax

Question 45 Penalties, appeals, VAT return

(a) You are required to outline the current state of the law in respect of VAT as to:

(i) financial penalties, and
(ii) appeals to VAT tribunals. (*10 marks*)

(b) A VAT-registered business had the following transactions for the year ended 31 March 1989:

	£
Sales at standard rate	172,500
Sales at zero rate	50,000
Exempt sales	75,000
Purchases at standard rate	115,575
Purchases at zero rate	7,200
Exempt payments	66,500
Purchased new motor car	10,150
Purchased second-hand motor car	4,500

All the above amounts are inclusive of VAT where this is applicable.

You are required to calculate the amount of VAT to be accounted for to HM Customs and Excise for the year ended 31 March 1989.

(*5 marks*)
(*Total: 15 marks*)
CIMA

Question 46 Registration, VAT returns, records

You have recently received a request from the management of a newly-created business requesting your help with matters concerning value added tax. The following is an extract from their letter:

(i) We understand that some businesses are registered for VAT whilst others are not registered. We have only recently commenced trading and consider that it will take us about five years to reach full potential of sales, which we envisage will rise from £20,000 to £100,000 in that period. Could you please advise us of the position regarding registration?

(ii) How should the VAT content of our income and expenditure be reflected in our budgets and 'final accounts' at the year end?
(iii) When and how is the amount of VAT to be accounted for to the Customs and Excise, and what is the position if we should 'pay out' more VAT than we 'charge'?
(iv) What records must be kept by us in order to satisfy the regulations?

You are required to prepare a tabulated report in response to the above requests.

Note: A substantial number of marks will be awarded for the style and presentation of your report. *(15 marks)*

CIMA

Question 47 Tax invoices, difference between zero rating and exemption

With regard to value added tax:

(a) Outline the different effects where a person makes supplies which are:
  (i) Zero rated only
  (ii) Exempt only
  (iii) A mixture of zero rated and exempt *(10 marks)*
(b) State the items which must be contained in a tax invoice where the value of the taxable supply exceeds £50. *(10 marks)*

(Total: 20 marks)

ACCA

Revision questions

Question 48

G has been in business for several years and has recently been experiencing a very successful period of trading. A limited company, in the same trade, has made a very attractive cash offer for the business, which G has decided to accept.

The sale is to take place some time during the spring of 1989 and the following information relating to G's recent profits, as agreed for tax purposes, is available:

	£
Year ended 31 December 1985	8,000
Year ended 31 December 1986	24,000
Year ended 31 December 1987	36,000
Year ended 31 December 1988	48,000

G estimates that the profits for the next few months will be:

	£
Three months to 31 March 1989	6,000
One month to 30 April 1989	1,000

You are required to

(a) Advise G as to whether he should dispose of the business at 31 March 1989 or 30 April 1989. Your advice should be supported by computations of the income assessable under Schedule D Case I for all of the tax years concerned under each alternative *(16 marks)*

(b) Advise G on the capital gains tax implications of the sale of the business *(4 marks)*

Note: Make all calculations in months **not** days. *(Total: 20 marks)*
CIMA

Question 49

FD Ltd commenced trading in February 1970 and had always prepared accounts to 31 March in each year. However, in 1988 it decided to change its permanent accounting date to 30 September, to assist the management by bringing the accounting date in line with that of two associated companies in which it owns more than 75% of the share capital.

The profit for the eighteen-month period ended 30 September 1988 amounted to £59,000 after charging:

	£	£
Depreciation		24,415
Debenture interest paid (gross sum):		
31 July 1987	3,195	
31 January 1988	3,195	
31 July 1988	3,195	
		9,585
and after crediting:		
Dividends received from UK companies (inclusive of tax credits):		
30 September 1987	4,000	
30 June 1988	5,000	
		9,000

The written-down value of the plant 'pool' for tax purposes at 1 April 1987 was £76,200. Acquisitions and disposals of plant during the period were:

Acquisitions:
- 30 April 1988: 3 motor lorries, cost £10,000 each
- 30 June 1988: new plant, cost £80,000

Disposals:
- 30 September 1987: plant sold for £10,000 (original cost £24,000)

The company paid a dividend on 30 June in 1987 and 1988 of £3,500 and £3,550 respectively.

You are required to

(a) Compute the amounts of advance corporation tax and mainstream corporation tax payable in respect of the accounting periods ended 30 September 1988 *(20 marks)*
(b) Advise FD Ltd of the consequences if it were to sell an investment property on 30 September 1988 at an anticipated capital gain of £50,000 (after indexation allowance) – you are *not* required to re-calculate the corporation tax payable but only to advise on the taxation consequences of such a transaction *(3 marks)*
(c) Advise FD Ltd as to possible benefits in respect of the potential transaction in (b) above, in circumstances where one of its subsidiary companies is about to sell an asset which will result in a capital loss in excess of £100,000 *(2 marks)*

(Total: 25 marks)
CIMA

Question 50

Discuss briefly the facts, issues, decisions and legal principles involved in any FOUR of the following cases:

(i) *Cape Brandy Syndicate* v. *IRC* (1921) 12 TC 358.
(ii) *Sharkey* v. *Wernher* (1955) 36 TC 275.
(iii) *Ricketts* v. *Colquhoun* (1926) 10 TC 118.
(iv) *Heaton* v. *Bell* (1969) 46 TC 211.
(v) *Law Shipping Co. Ltd.* v. *IRC* (1924) 12 TC 621.
(vi) *Strong and Co. of Romsey Ltd.* v. *Woodifield* (1906) 5 TC 215.

(20 marks)
ACCA

Question 51

Quantock plc is a large listed company with an 80 per cent subsidiary, Mendip Ltd, a manufacturing company which started trading in 1982. Mendip's profit and loss account for the year ended 31st March 1989 (before taking corporation tax into account) was as follows.

		£	£
Net profit on trading			81,500
After charging:	Depreciation	29,500	
	Directors' remuneration	16,000	
	Loan interest (*Note (b)*)	4,500	
	Auditors' remuneration	2,500	
	Interest on bank overdraft	7,200	
		59,700	

	£	£
Investment income: Listed investment (*Note (a)*)		10,000
Unlisted companies (gross dividends)		3,000
Profits for the year		94,500
Profits b/f from previous years		27,400
		121,900
Dividends paid on ordinary shares:		
to Quantock plc (under group election)	40,000	
to minority shareholders	10,000	50,000
Undistributed profits c/f		71,900

Notes

(a) Income from listed investments consisted of:

	Gross £
Interest on loan stock in UK company	6,000
Interest on 9 per cent Treasury stock	3,000
Dividend on minority holding in Cotswold plc, a UK listed company	1,000
	10,000

(b) Mendip Ltd had issued £60,000 10 per cent loan stock on 30th June 1988 with interest payable half-yearly on 1 January and 1 July.

(c) Apart from the amounts shown on the face of the accounts, the following items of expenditure had also been charged in arriving at the net profit on trading:

	£
Increase in general provision for doubtful debts	1,340
Increase in specific provision for doubtful debts	870
Improvements to office building	1,200
Entertaining UK customers	2,370
Entertaining overseas suppliers	1,510
	7,290

(d) On 3 May 1988 Mendip Ltd had purchased new machinery for £24,000 and wishes to claim the maximum capital allowances available. All other capital expenditure has been fully written off for tax purposes.

You are required to compute the corporation tax payable by Mendip Ltd in respect of the year ended 31 March 1989 and state the due date of payment. *(25 marks)*

SCCA

Question 52

Briefly explain ten tax changes introduced in the Finance Act 1988. *(15 marks)*

Question 53

Advise the management of a limited company as to the consequences for corporation tax purposes of the following transactions which have occurred during its last financial accounting year:

(a) Loan interest received of £500 from which the borrower has advised that tax has been deducted at the standard rate *(2 marks)*
(b) Receipt of £100,000 on sale of a factory in respect of which capital allowances had been claimed; the factory was purchased new and first used in 1960 *(4 marks)*
(c) Defalcations of cash by staff have been discovered in the sum of £8,000, of which £5,000 was attributable to junior staff and the balance to a member of the board of directors *(3 marks)*
(d) Additional retail premises acquired for £40,000, which was well below normal market value due to the dilapidated state of these premises, resulting in repairs and renewals expenditure of £60,000 having to be incurred *(4 marks)*
(e) Expenditure totalling £128,000, which was incurred in entertaining the company's own staff, customers' staff and representatives from both UK and foreign business agencies. *(2 marks)*

Note: Candidates are required to describe the consequences of the above transactions, *not* to compute the consequences. (*Total: 15 marks*)
CIMA

Answers

Question 1

See page 5, Chapter 1. (*Note*: This is one of the very few practice questions answered in this way to save unnecessary repetition.)

Question 2

(a) (i) Wages and salaries
(ii) Interest paid on most Government securities and UK company debentures
(iii) Dividends paid by UK companies

(b) Tax on wages and salaries is deducted by the employer and paid over monthly to the Revenue. The deductions allow for the employees' personal reliefs by way of a system of code numbers allocated on the basis of allowances claimed by the individuals concerned. For other items paid under deduction of tax the payer makes no allowance for personal reliefs but deducts tax at basic rate (25 per cent for 1988/89) and pays the tax over to the Revenue, quarterly in the case of companies making the payments.

(c) The taxpayer makes a return of income each year. The local Inspector of Taxes to whom the return is sent raises a tax assessment which, when agreed by the taxpayer, is paid to the Collector of Taxes.

Question 3

Six 'badges of trade' were identified by the 1955 Royal Commission Report on the Taxation of Profits and Income:

(a) *Subject matter of realization* – the nature of the item bought or sold is relevant, because it may suggest alternative reasons for the transactions. For example, a picture could provide personal enjoyment, whereas a bulk lot of whisky in bond (*CIR* v. *Fraser* 1942) or toilet rolls (*Rutledge* v. *CIR* 1929) could not.

(b) *Length of period of ownership* – in general, the longer an item is retained the less likely it will be held to be part of a trading operation.

(c) *Frequency of similar transactions* – although a single transaction could be held to be an adventure in the nature of trade (examples are the whisky and toilet rolls in (a) above), in general the less frequent the transactions the less likely it will be held that a trade is being conducted.

(d) *Supplementary work* – repair work on the goods, or breaking down a bulk lot into smaller parts, will suggest trading.

(e) *Circumstances of realization* – a special explanation for the sale, such as a sale to raise money for an unexpected emergency, would tend to negate the presumption that a trade was being conducted.

(f) *Motive* – evidence as to the motive for the purchase or sale could either support or negate the presumption of trade.

Other factors could include:

(g) *Finance* – the way in which the transactions were financed could be relevant. If the transaction was financed with borrowed money, that could suggest the intention to sell within a short time to repay the loan.

(h) *Connection with existing trade* – if a trade was already being conducted, a transaction similar to that trade would be likely to be part of that trade.

(i) *Destination of proceeds* – if the proceeds of sale are used to buy more goods for resale, that leads to a presumption of trading.

Question 4

Computation of adjusted trading profit, year ended 30 June 1989:

	£	£
	+	–
Net profit per accounts	15,721	
Bad and doubtful debts:		
increase in general provision	247	
loan to employee	200	
Depreciation	2,500	
Sundry expenses:		
subscription to political party	250	
entertaining (UK and overseas)	1,626	
new lathe	801	
Profit on sale of van		341
Interest on deposit account		760
	21,345	1,101
	1,101	
Schedule D Case I	£20,244	

Question 5

(a) The general rule governing the allowability of expenditure for Schedule D Cases I and II is in s. 74 ICTA 1988 – expenditure may not be deducted unless it is 'wholly and exclusively laid out or expended for the purposes of the trade, profession or vocation'.

(b) (i) National Insurance contributions for staff genuinely employed in the business will be allowed. Contributions by proprietors are partially allowed:

- Class 2 contributions – not allowed
- Class 4 contributions – 50 per cent allowed as a deduction in computing total income (s. 617 (5) ICTA 1988)

(ii) Repairs expenditure will normally be allowed if it relates to items used in the business and there is no element of improvement. There are two somewhat conflicting cases regarding repair costs relating to assets purchased in a dilapidated condition – *Law Shipping Co. Ltd* v. *CIR* 1923 and *Odeon Associated Theatres* v. *Jones* 1971. In the Law Shipping case it was held that such repairs were not allowable as relating to the pre-acquisition period. In the Odeon Theatres case, however, such expenditure was held to be allowable provided three conditions were met:

- Normal accounting practice would treat the expenditure as revenue
- The asset could be used without the repairs
- The state of disrepair had not reduced the purchase price

(iii) Renewal of short lease – cost of acquisition of fixed assets are not generally allowable, but the costs of *renewal* of a short lease (less than fifty years) is allowable.

(iv) Salary to the proprietor's spouse is allowable provided the amount is reasonably commensurate with the duties (*Copeman* v. *Flood* 1940).

(v) Fines imposed for breaking the law are generally disallowed since it would be contrary to public policy to allow them. Parking fines paid for employees are allowable, however.

(vi) Entertainment expenses:

- Foreign customers – on or after 15 March 1988 such expenditure is no longer allowable (FA 1988)
- Foreign suppliers – not allowed (s. 577 ICTA 1988)
- Staff – reasonable entertainment of staff (as for example, a Christmas party) is allowable.

(vii) Costs of obtaining a patent or trade mark are specifically allowed by s. 83 ICTA 1988.

(viii) Redundancy payments – redundancy payments paid by a

continuing business are allowed in full. Those paid on discontinuance are allowed up to the statutory limit (s. 579 ICTA 1988). Further payments on discontinuance up to another 3 times the statutory limit are also allowed.

(ix) Cost of obtaining loan finance is specifically allowed by s. 77 (1) ICTA 1988.

(x) Value Added Tax will not normally be allowed as it is not normally ultimately suffered by the business. In those cases where it is suffered by the business it is allowed to the extent that it relates to items allowable for income tax.

Question 6

(a) F – Schedule D Case I Assessments 1985/86 to 1988/89:

	Original			*Election under s. 62*
	£		*£*	*£*
1985/86 Actual				
10/11 × £22,000	20,000			
1986/87 1st 12 months		Actual		
£22,000 + 1/12 × £21,000	23,750	1/11 × £22,000	2,000	
		11/12 × £21,000	19,250	21,250
1987/88 1st 12 months		Actual		
as 1986/87	23,750	1/12 × £21,000	1,750	
		11/12 × £30,000	27,500	29,250
1988/89 Preceding year	21,000			

Although the assessment for 1986/87 is lower, that for 1987/88 is higher by a larger amount. F will therefore not make the election under s. 62 ICTA 1988 and the final assessments will remain as stated in the 'Original' column.

Question 7

Grace – Schedule D Case I assessments 1985/86 to 1988/89:

	Original			*Revenue Election under s. 63*
	£		*£*	*£*
1985/86 Preceding year	6,000			
1986/87 Preceding year	12,000	Actual		
		9/12 × £10,000	7,500	
		3/12 × £16,000	4,000	11,500
1987/88 Preceding year	10,000	Actual		
		9/12 × £16,000	12,000	
		3/9 × £9,000	3,000	15,000
1988/89 Actual				
6.4.88 to 30.9.88				
6/9 × £9,000	6,000			

The Revenue election in 1986/87 reduces the assessment by £500. In 1987/88 the election increases the assessment by £5,000. As the

Revenue's election must be exercised for both years or neither, the final assessments will be:

	£
1985/86	6,000
1986/87	11,500
1987/88	15,000
1988/89	6,000

Question 8

(a) Harold – Schedule D Case I assessments, 1987/88 to 1989/90:

		£
1987/88 Actual 1.1.86 to 5.4.88	3/12 × £6,000	1,500
1988/89 1st 12 months trading		6,000
1989/90 Preceding year, year ended 31.12.88		6,000

Capital allowances

	Pool £	*Motor car* £	*Total allowances* £
1987/88 (basis period 1.1.88 to 5.4.88)			
Expenditure		8,800	
WDA 25% × £8,000 (max.) × 3/12		500	500
		8,300	
1988/89 (basis period 6.4.88 to 31.12.88)			
Expenditure	8,000		
WDA 25%	2,000	2,000	4,000
	6,000	6,300	
1989/90			
WDA 25%	1,500	1,575	3,075
	4,500	4,725	

(b) Harold has two options. First of all he may elect under s. 62 ICTA 1988 to have the assessments for the second and third years (here 1988/89 and 1989/90) adjusted to actual. This will not be beneficial unless the expected increase in profits fails to materialize. Harold has seven years from the end of the second year of assessment to make the election, which must thus be made by 5 April 1996. Once made, the election may be revoked within the same time limit. The second option, which may be beneficial here, is to renounce some of the capital allowances in 1987/88, 1988/89 and 1989/90, since their effect is to reduce his income below the tax threshold in view of the level of personal allowances available (£4,095 in 1988/89 for a married man). The effect would be to increase the allowances available in 1990/91 and later years, when the profits are expected to be greater.

Question 9

Tutorial notes

The examiner's report commented that this question was extremely poorly answered, surprising in view of the standard form of the question. The poor performance possibly reflected an over-concentration on corporation tax in students' preparation.

It is necessary to compute the final assessments before doing the capital allowances, as the basis periods for capital allowances depend upon those final determined for profit purposes. The 100 per cent first year allowance on the plant available until 14 March 1984 meant that the full cost could be written off in the year of the expenditure.

The question has been carefully designed so that the advice in part (b) does not need to consider the effect on the capital allowances, which would in any case be minor.

A lot of work to do in the time, perhaps, but a very useful question to study.

(a)

	Original			*Taxpayer's election under s. 62*
	£		£	£
1982/83 Actual				
1.2.83 to 5.4.83				
2/8 × £4,000	1,000			
1983/84 1st 12 months		Actual		
£4,000 + 4/12 × £18,000	10,000	6/8 × £4,000	3,000	
		6/12 × £18,000	9,000	12,000
1984/85 As 1983/84	10,000	Actual		
		6/12 × £18,000	9,000	
(No election by taxpayer under s. 62)		6/12 × £36,000	18,000	27,000
				Revenue election under s. 63
1985/86 Preceding year	18,000			
1986/87 Preceding year	36,000	Actual		
		6/12 × £16,000	8,000	
		6/12 × £1,200	600	8,600
1987/88 Preceding year	16,000	Actual		
		6/12 × £1,200	600	
(No election by Revenue under s. 63)		6/7 × £350	300	900
1988/89 Actual				
6.4.88 to 30.4.88				
1/7 × £350	50			

Capital allowances

	Pool		*Motor car (private use 20%)*	*Allowances*
	£	£	£	£
1982/83 (basis period 1.2.83 to 5.4.83)				nil

		Pool		Motor car (private use 20%)	Allowances
		£	£	£	£
1983/84 (basis period 6.4.83 to 31.1.84)					
Expenditure				4,000	
WDA 25%				1,000 × 80%	800
				3,000	
1984/85 (basis period nil –)				750 × 80%	600
				2,250	
1985/86 (basis period 1.2.84 to 30.9.84)					
Expenditure 1.3.84		2,000			
First year allowance	100%	2,000	nil		2,000
WDA 25%			—	563 × 80%	451
			nil	1,687	2,451
1986/87 (basis period 1.10.84 to 30.9.85)					
WDA 25%				422 × 80%	337
				1,265	
1987/88 (basis period 1.10.86 to 5.4.88)					
Disposals – proceeds			300	400	
Balancing (charge)/allowance			(300)	865 × 80%	392

(b) On cessation, the profit of some period or other must escape taxation, as long as the taxpayer has traded for long enough to have got onto the preceding year basis of assessment. In this case, cessation before the end of 1987/88 would have reduced the total assessments as shown below:

Assessments with cessation (say) 31 March 1988:

	Original				Revenue election under s. 63
	£	£		£	£
1985/86					
Preceding year		18,000	Actual		
			6/12 × £36,000	18,000	
			6/12 × £16,000	8,000	26,000
1986/87					
Preceding year		36,000	Actual		
			6/12 × £16,000		
			6/12 × £1,200 (as above)		8,600
(No s. 63 election by Revenue)					
1987/88					
Actual					
6/12 × £1,200	600				
6/7 × £350	300	900			

Summary of total assessments	*Cessation at 30.4.88.*	*Cessation at 31.3.88.*
	£	£
1982/83	1,000	1,000
1983/84	10,000	10,000

Summary of total assessments	*Cessation at 30.4.88*	*Cessation at 31.3.88.*
	£	£
1984/85	10,000	10,000
1985/86	18,000	18,000
1986/87	36,000	36,000
1987/88	16,000	900
1988/89	50	
	£91,050	£75,900

There is thus a saving of tax on £15,100 (£16,000 minus £900) as a result of the revision of the 1987/88 assessment from preceding year basis to actual on cessation.

Question 10

The disappearance of first year allowances for capital expenditure from 1 April 1986 meant that plant with a short life (say three to five years) would not be written off sufficiently fast by writing down allowances alone. The Finance Act 1985 introduced an election (to be made by the taxpayer within two years of the end of the accounting period of acquisition) to exclude such assets from the pool and calculate capital allowances on them separately. On a sale within five years, a balancing charge or allowance is made. If at the end of five years the plant has not been sold, the written down value is transferred into the main pool.

The result of this treatment is that the full cost of the plant is relieved over its useful life, with a specific balancing adjustment in the year of sale rather than the deduction of sale proceeds from the pool balance.

	No election			*With election*	
	Pool	*Allowances*		*Short Life assets*	*Allowances*
	£	£		£	£
1988/89					
Expenditure	10,000			10,000	
WDA 25%	2,500	2,500		2,500	2,500
	7,500			7,500	
1989/90					
WDA 25%	1,875	1,875		1,875	1,875
	5,625			5,625	
1990/91					
Sold for	2,000			2,000	
	3,625				
WDA	907	907	Balancing allowance	3,625	3,625
	2,718	5,282			£8,000

The effect is that allowances totalling £8,000 (Cost less proceeds of sale) are obtained over the three years if the depooling election is made, whereas without the election allowances totalling only £5,282 are obtained, and the remainder will be obtained over future years.

Question 11

J – Industrial building allowance:

	£	£
1986/87		
Cost 1 January 1985		300,000
(Office accommodation included as not exceeding 25% of building cost)		
Initial allowance 50%	150,000	
Writing down allowance 4%	12,000	162,000
		138,000
1987/88 to 1990/91		
Writing down allowance 4% × 4 years		48,000
		90,000
1991/92		
Proceeds of sale (building)		375,000
Balancing charge		285,000
– limited to allowances granted		£210,000
C's cost is deemed to be:		
Residue before sale		90,000
Balancing charge		210,000
		£300,000

C will be able to write this off over the balance remaining of the twenty-five years beginning when the building was first brought into use:

Date brought into use	1 January 1981
Date of sale	31 March 1986
Period of use	$5\frac{1}{4}$ years

C will therefore receive annual writing down allowances of:

$$\frac{£300{,}000}{19\tfrac{3}{4}} = £15{,}190$$

Question 12

(a) The loss of £30,000 is available to Angus for relief under s. 380 in 1987/88, the tax year in which the accounts showing the loss ended, or 1988/89. Angus may claim under s. 380 to offset the loss against other income in either or both of these years, or he could make no claims under s. 380 and carry the whole loss forward under s. 385. The claims under s. 380 may be restricted to Angus's own other income or extended to include his own and his wife's income. The most beneficial way to claim relief for the loss would be to claim it under s. 380 against the £40,000 profit of the year ended 31 December 1986 falling to be assessed in 1987/88. This has the effect of preserving income against which personal reliefs may be claimed, and also reducing income which would otherwise be liable to higher rate tax.

(b) The assessments on Angus for the years affected, if loss relief is claimed as recommended in (a), would be:

	£	£
1985/86		30,000
1986/87		10,000
1987/88	40,000	
less: loss relief s. 380	30,000	10,000
1988/89 (loss in basis period)		nil
1989/90		20,000

(c) Relief under s. 380 must be claimed within two years of the end of the tax year in which the loss arose (here 5 April 1990).

Question 13

No information is given as to profits in years after the loss, so we must confine our computations to s. 380. The possibility of carrying the loss forward under s. 385 should also be mentioned.

The fact that a letter is to be written to the taxpayer suggests that the advice should be expressed as far as possible in non-technical language.

12 August 1988

Dear Mr Smith

Tax relief for your loss of £34,000 in year ended 30 June 1988

I have now considered the problem of optimizing the tax relief you may obtain for your loss of £34,000 in the year ended 30 June 1988.

We may use the loss to reduce your income from other sources in the tax year 1988/89, in which your profit of £20,000 falls to be assessed, or in the tax year 1989/90. These claims may be extended to the income of your wife also, or used to reduce your income only. I recommend that the claim is made against your income only, since it is desirable to retain some income for all years to ensure that personal reliefs are not wasted. The size of the loss means that it will be possible and beneficial to claim for both of these years.

Another alternative would be to use the loss in future years to reduce profits of the year ending 30 June 1989 and later. The disadvantage of this method is that it means relief is delayed, and we have no certainty of profits sufficient to relieve the loss. Also, future tax rates may be lower than those of 1988/89.

My calculations of the tax effect of the claims are set out in an Appendix to this letter.

Please contact me if you need any further information or explanations.

Yours sincerely,

Mr and Mrs Smith – tax assessments after relief for loss:

		1988/89		*1989/90*
	£	£	£	£
Mr Smith				
Schedule D Case I		20,000		nil (loss in basis period)
Investment income		8,000		8,000
		28,000		8,000
Less: Loss claim s. 380		28,000		8,000 (balance)
		nil		nil
Mrs Smith				
Schedule D Case I		7,500		8,500
		7,500		8,500
Less: Personal reliefs (1989/90 assumed to be as 1988/89)				
Married allowance	4,095			
Wife's earned income allowance	2,605	6,700		6,700
		800		1,800

Although a small taxable balance remains in each year, the whole loss has operated to eliminate income otherwise subject to tax.

Question 14

The most advantageous method of claiming loss relief is to claim under s. 381 ICTA 1988 to carry the loss back for three years against the income before the business began. Such a claim may be made against X's own income only, or extended to that of his wife. It is best to claim against X's income only, thus preserving the wife's income to enable the benefit of personal allowances to be obtained.

X's business began on 1 July 1987 – his loss available for the claim is the loss for the period 1 July 1987 to 5 April 1988:

9/12 × £42,000 = £31,500. This loss may be carried back under s. 381 against the income of the years 1984/85, 1985/86 and 1986/87.

The remainder of the loss (3/12 × £42,000 = £10,500 for the period 6 April 1988 to 30 June 1988) would be aggregated with the profit or loss for the remainder of the tax year 1988/89 and could form the basis of a further claim under s. 381 to the extent that the income of the years since 1985/86 had not been relieved by the 1987/88 s. 381 claim.

Alternatively, the unrelieved £10,500 could be carried forward under s. 171. A claim under s. 168 would not be beneficial as there is only the wife's income to offset.

Relief under s. 381 for the 1987/88 loss of £31,500 would lead to repayment of tax paid on the following income:

	1984/85	*1985/86*	*1986/87*	
	£	£	£	
Salary	14,000	14,500	15,000	
s. 381 claims	14,000	14,500	3,000	(balance)
	nil	nil	12,000	

Substantial repayments of tax paid under Schedule E would be obtained.

Question 15

AY – Adjusted loss, year ended 30 June 1988:

	£	£
	+	–
Loss per accounts		31,634
Depreciation	1,850	
Patent royalties	400	
	2,250	31,634
		2,250
Schedule D Case I loss		£29,384

Capital allowances

	Pool	*Motor car (Private use 40%)*	*Allowances*
	£	£	£
Brought forward			
6 April 1985	16,400	6,500	
1985/86			
WDA 25%	4,100	1,625 × 60% £975	5,075
	12,300	4,875	
1986/87			
WDA 25%	3,075	1,219 × 60% £732	3,807
	9,225	3,656	
1987/88			
WDA 25%	2,307	914 × 60% £549	2,856
	6,918	2,742	
1988/89			
Sale proceeds	6,000	2,000	
Balancing allowances	918	742 × 60% £446	1,364

Calculation of terminal loss – loss for year ended 30 June 1988:

	£
6 April 1988 to 30 June 1988:	
Loss 3/12 × £29,384	7,346
Capital allowances	1,364
Patent royalties paid	400
1 July 1987 to 5 April 1988:	
Loss 9/12 × £29,384	22,038
9/12 × Capital allowances 1987/88 (used against profit £15,300 assessed in that year)	–
	£31,148

Final net assessments 1985/86 to 1988/89:

	£	£
1988/89 loss in basis period		nil
s. 350 assessment		400
1987/88	15,300	
Less: Capital allowances	2,856	
	12,444	
Less: Patent royalties	700	
	11,744	
Less: Terminal loss relief	11,744	nil
1986/87	24,000	
Less: Capital allowances	3,807	
	20,193	
Less: Patent royalties	900	
	19,293	
Less: Terminal loss relief	19,293	nil
1985/86	£	£
Less: Capital allowances	18,000	
	5,075	
	12,925	
Less: Patent royalties	1,750	
	11,175	
Less: Terminal loss claim (balance)	111	11,064

Loss relief memorandum:

	£
Terminal loss	31,148
1987/88	11,744
	19,404
1986/87	19,293
	111
1985/86 (balance)	111
	–

Question 16

Dear Mr Jones

Taxation of rental income under Schedule A

In response to your request I have summarized below the details you require as to the taxation of rental income.

(a) Basis of assessment and due date for payment – The basis of assessment is rent *due* in the tax year to 5 April, less allowable expenses. The tax is due on 1 January in the year of assessment, or 30 days after the raising of the assessment if later. The fact that the tax is due during the year, before the final income can be arrived at, means that an initial assessment based on the income of the previous year has to be raised and paid during the year. An adjustment is then made as soon as the final result for the year is known.

(b) *Expenses deductible* – Deductible expenses include:

  (i) Rent and rates paid by landlord
  (ii) Repairs, including wages of maintenance staff
  (iii) Cost of services provided
  (iv) Rent collection costs
  (v) Insurance
  (vi) Bad debts for irrecoverable rent

Interest paid on loans to finance the purchase of property for renting will be allowed as a deduction from total income, not specifically as a deduction from rental income. The maximum deductible in this way is the amount of rental income for the year.

Capital allowances may be claimed on plant used for maintenance, lifts, swimming pools and other amenities.

(c) Treatment of losses – The extent of relief available for losses depends on the nature of the tenancies. For your purposes, there are two types of tenancy – the *landlord's repairing lease*, in which the landlord is responsible for some part of the repairs costs, and a *tenant's repairing lease*, in which the tenant is responsible for all repairs.

All properties let on landlord's repairing leases are 'pooled', so there is free offset of profits and losses each year. Any overall balance of loss is carried forward and may be offset against overall profits arising in later years. Losses on properties let on tenant's repairing leases may first be offset against the pool profit from landlord's repairing lease properties, then any unrelieved balance may only be offset against future profits derived from the same property.

If you need any further information or explanation, please let me know.

Yours sincerely

Question 17

It is first necessary to divide the properties into tenants' repairing leases and landlord's repairing leases and properties let at less than a full rent. The result from tenants' repairing leases is computed first, because any losses may be deducted from the pool result from the landlord's repairing lease properties.

Care is needed in arriving at the rental income – note that Shop 1, for example, has *one* quarter's rent at £1,650 per annum even though the lease expired on 29 September! Work it out!

Landlord's repairing leases

	House 1		*House 2*	
	£	£	£	£
Rent receivable				
37 × £95		3,515		
43 × £105				4,515
Expenditure				
Insurance	135		117	
Ground rent	5		6	
Repairs	246		1,935	
Accountancy	35		35	
Newspaper advertising	117		134	
Gardeners' wages	120		132	
Rates	95	753	112	2,471
		2,762		2,044
				2,762
				4,806
Less: Loss on Shop 4 (see page 359)				142
				4,664

Schedule A assessment 1987/88	£
Shop 1 } see page 359	1,815
Shop 2 } see page 359	1,229
Landlord's repairing lease properties	4,664
	£7,708

(b) The 1988/89 Schedule A assessment will initially be based on that for 1987/88 (with no deduction for the loss on Shop 4) and will be due for payment on 1 January 1989. There will be an adjustment after 5 April 1989 when the final result for the year is known.

Question 18

The rules governing the allowability of Schedule E expenses are in s. 198 ICTA 1988. Travelling expenses are allowable if incurred necessarily in the performance of the duties. Other expenses must be wholly, exclusively and necessarily incurred in the performance of the duties if they are to be allowable.

Decided cases have clarified the application of the rules. For example,

(a) Tenants' repairing leases:

	Shop 1		Shop 2		Shop 4	
	£	£	£	£	£	£
Rent receivable						
Shop 1 1 qr @ £1,650 p.a.	412					
3 qrs @ £1,350 p.a.	1,763	2,175				
Shop 2				1,500		
Shop 4 1 qr @ £4,000						1,000
Premium					1,000	
less: 2(10 – 1) %					180	820
		2,175		1,500		1,820
Expenditure						
Commission						
(10% of rent *collected*)	218		113		100	
Insurance	97		123		210	
Ground rent	20		10		100	
Repairs					1,527	
Accountancy	25	360	25	271	25	1,962
		1,815		1,229		(142)

Lease at less than full rent:

	£	£
Shop 3		
Rent receivable		100
Expenditure		
Accountancy	25	
Insurance	95	120
Loss carried forward against possible future profits from same property		(20)

in *Ricketts* v. *Colquhoun* 1925, a London barrister who was also Recorder of Portsmouth was denied relief for the cost of travel from London to Portsmouth because the travel was not 'in the performance' of the duties, which did not begin until he arrived at the Court in Portsmouth. In *Pook* v. *Owen* 1969, on the other hand, a doctor was allowed travel from his home to hospital when called out while on standby duties, because he normally gave instructions to hospital staff before leaving home, and was thus 'in the performance' of his duties at that time.

As regards club subscriptions, these were disallowed in *Brown* v. *Bullock* 1961, in which a bank manager unsuccessfully claimed the cost of the subscription to a club which he visited only to meet bank customers. The grounds for disallowance were that the expenditure was not *necessarily* incurred. In *Elwood* v. *Utitz*, however, the managing director of a Northern Ireland company successfully claimed the cost of a subscription to a London club which he joined in order to obtain cheaper accommodation while in London. The subscription was held to be allowable because it saved his company money.

In *Lupton* v. *Potts* 1969, examination fees paid by an articled clerk for sitting the Law Society's examinations were not allowed, on the predictable grounds that the expenditure was not 'in the performance of the duties'.

Question 19

Schedule E income 1988/89:

	£	£	£
(a) *Salary*			14,000
(b) *Bonus* (as illustrated on page 87 of Chapter 7, there are three ways of calculating the assessable amount of a bonus based on profits. In the absence of instructions the 'strict' method should be used)			
9/12 × £3,600			2,700
(c) *Expenses allowance*		2,500	
Less: allowable expenses			
Business travel		1,800	700
(Entertainment of foreign customers now disallowed by FA 1988)			
(d) *Benefits*			
Hi-fi equipment £800 × 20%			160
The assessable value of assets made available for a director's use is taken as 20 per cent of the market value when made available.			

	£	£	£
Medical insurance (disallowed except if relating to work overseas)			300
New suits. The assessable value of assets given to a director is the cost to the company			400
			18,260
Accommodation			
£3,380 limited to 10 per cent of £18,260. As the director has no shareholding in the company, and the accommodation is necessary for the performance of his duties, it qualifies as 'job-related' accommodation. No assessment is therefore made on the value of the accommodation itself, but expenses connected with the accommodation, up to a limit of 10 per cent of the income including all other benefits, is assessable.			1,826
			£20,086

Question 20

(a) Private house – The measure of the benefit is the annual value plus an additional amount if the value of the property exceeds £75,000. A variable percentage (given in the question as 12 per cent) is applied to the excess. The P11D benefit will therefore be:

	£
Annual value	2,000
12% × (£80,000 – £75,000)	600
	2,600
less: Director's contribution	1,500
	£1,100

(b) Asset made available now taken over.

	£
The assessable benefit is the higher of:	
(i) Market value less amount paid: £600 – £400	200
(ii) Cost less amounts assessed in previous years, less amount paid	
Cost	1,500
Previously assessed:	
1985/86 to 1987/88 3 years @ 20%	900
	600
Less: Amount paid	400
	£ 200

The benefit is £200 whichever way it is calculated.

(c) As the loan is for a qualifying purpose, there will be no assessable benefit. The form P11D requires a statement that the loan has been made.

(d) The benefit is the cost to the company of providing the dishwasher – £280.

(e) The benefit is again the cost to the company – £1,200.

Question 21

The opening and closing years under Schedule D Cases III, IV and V are assessed as follows:

(a) Opening years:

First year	Actual
Second year	Actual
Third year	Preceding year.

The taxpayer may elect, under s. 66 ICTA 1988, to have the third year revised to actual.

(b) Closing years:
In the year in which the source of income ceases, the assessment is based on *actual*. The Revenue may elect to have the penultimate year revised to *actual*.

Question 22

(a) See page 118 in Chapter 9.
(b) See page 120 in Chapter 9.

Question 23

(a) The taxpayer must appeal in writing within thirty days from the date of issue of the assessment, stating the grounds for the appeal. If the taxpayer wishes also to postpone payment of the tax, written application for this must be made within the same period of thirty days. If no action is taken within the specified time limits, the assessment becomes final and due for payment in full.

(b) When there has been an application for postponement, the due date for any tax not postponed is the later of:

   (i) Thirty days after the Inspector's agreement to the postponement
   (ii) The normal due date

(c) The reckonable date is the later of:

   (i) The normal due date
   (ii) Thirty days after the determination of the appeal or, if earlier, 1 July following the end of the tax year concerned

(d) As (c) above.

Question 24

The rules governing the new personal pension schemes available from 1 July 1988 are in many ways similar to the rules previously applicable to retirement annuity policies.

The rules for the new schemes are:

(a) The pension may normally commence between age fifty and seventy-five
(b) The policy must be with a UK insurance company, bank, building society or unit trust
(c) Maximum contributions are 17½ per cent of net relevant earnings, increased for taxpayers aged over fifty. ('Net relevant earnings' means income under Schedule E or Schedule D Cases I and II, including benefits and after deducting allowable expenses, capital allowances and loss relief)
(d) Relief not used in a particular year may be carried forward for up to six years
(e) Premiums paid in a particular year may be carried back into the immediately preceding tax year
(f) Premiums are paid net of basic rate income tax
(g) The employer may contribute to the scheme
(h) The Department of Health and Social Security will make a contribution to the scheme
(i) When the scheme matures, the lump sum is tax free and the annuity is taxed as earned income
(j) The Revenue must approve the scheme

Question 25

(a) (i) Make up accounts so that results for the first twelve months (which may be the basis of the first three years' assessments) are as low as possible (within the law!)
(ii) Use the taxpayer's election under s. 62 if profits fall in the second and third years
(iii) Choose an accounting date which maximizes the time interval between that date and the due date for payment of tax
(iv) Choose the date of cessation of the business so as to minimize the effect of the Revenue's election under s. 63, remembering that some income must escape taxation if the business has existed long enough to get onto the preceding year basis of assessment. The fact that the profit of the last year is assessed on the actual basis can also lead to material changes in liability depending on the tax year chosen for cessation

(b) (i) Claim so as to preserve some income in each year so as not to lose the benefit of personal reliefs. This may often be achieved by not extending a s. 380 claim to the spouse's income
(ii) Equalize income between tax years to minimize higher rate

tax, perhaps by excluding capital allowances from the loss claim
(iii) Claim when tax rates suffered are highest
(iv) Claim so as to obtain relief as quickly as possible

Question 26

Cortex Ltd
Corporation tax computation, year ended 31 March 1989

	£ +	£ −
Net profit per accounts	573,500	
Income on Government securities		500
Building society interest		1,500
Rent receivable		4,000
Depreciation	20,000	
Provision for doubtful debts	1,000	
Legal expenses	500	
Entertaining	15,000	
Interest on debentures	10,000	
Capital allowances		14,000
	620,000	20,000
	20,000	
Schedule D Case I	600,000	
Schedule D Case III:		
Interest on Government securities	500	
Building society interest (£1,500 × 100/75)	2,000	
Schedule A	4,000	
	606,500	
Less: Charges – interest paid	8,000	
	£598,500	

Question 27

(a) Income tax returns – CT61

	Rate	Tax suffered £	Tax payable £	Income tax Paid £	Income tax Refunded £	Due date
3 months ended						
31 March 1988	27%	1,350	1,620	270		14 April '88
30 June 1988	25%	625	250		270	14 July '88
30 September 1988	25%	–	–	–	–	
31 December 1988		925	150	–	–	
		2,900	2,020	270	270	
		2,020				
Deductible from MCT		£ 880				

(b) The £880 excess of tax suffered on interest received over tax payable on interest paid will be deducted from the company's mainstream corporation tax liability. The tax attributable to the building society interest £910 (£2,730 × 25/75) will also be deducted, but is excluded from the quarterly settlement arrangements.

Question 28

ACT returns – CT61

	Franked payments	*Franked investment income*	*ACT Paid*	*ACT Refunded*	*Due date*
	£	£	£	£	
3 months ended					
30 June 1988	2,500		625		14 July 1988
30 December 1988	3,500	5,600		525	14 Jan. 1988
	£6,000	5,600	625	525	

The £100 net ACT paid will be deducted from the company's corporation tax liability for the year.

Income tax returns – CT61

	Tax suffered	*Tax payable*	*Income tax Paid*	*Income tax Refunded*	*Due date*
	£	£	£	£	
3 months ended					
30 June 1988	1,250				
30 September 1988		750			
31 March 1989		750	250		14 April 1989
	£1,250	1,500	250		

As tax payable exceeds tax suffered, there will be no effect on the corporation tax computation.

H Ltd

Corporation tax computation, year ended 31 March 1989

	£	£
Adjusted trading profit		520,000
Debenture interest received		5,000
Chargeable gains	12,000	
Less: Capital losses brought forward	15,000	
Capital loss carried forward	3,000	
		525,000
Less charges: debenture interest paid		6,000
		£519,000
Corporation tax @ 35%		181,650
Less: ACT		100
Mainstream corporation tax liability due 1 January 1990		£181,550

Question 29

Andrell Ltd
Adjustment of profit, 15 months ended 30 June 1988

	£	£
	+	–
Profit per accounts	91,050	–
Bank deposit interest received		3,450
Rents receivable		1,000
Profit on sale of plant		6,000
Tax appeal	150	
Depreciation	3,000	
Bad debts	2,000	
Debenture interest	11,250	
	107,450	10,450
	10,450	
Adjusted profit	£ 97,000	

Andrell Ltd – capital allowances
Accounting period ended 31 March 1988

	Pool £	*Allowances* £
Balance brought forward	276,000	
Additions	3,000	
	279,000	
Disposals (£15,500, limited to cost)	12,000	
	267,000	
WDA 25%	66,750	66,750
Balance carried forward	£200,250	

Accounting period ended 30 June 1988

	Pool £	*Car pool* £	*Allowances* £
Balance brought forward	200,250		
Additions		96,000	
WDA 25% × 3/12	12,516	6,000	18,516
Balances carried forward	£187,734	90,000	

	Accounting periods	
	12 months to 31 March 1988 £	*3 months ended 30 June 1988* £
Adjusted profit	77,600	19,400
Capital allowances	66,750	18,516
Schedule D Case I	10,850	884
Schedule D Case III	3,050	400
Schedule A		1,000

	Accounting periods	
	12 months to 31 March 1988	*3 months ended 30 June 1988*
	£	£
Chargeable gain – sale of profit	3,500	
	17,400	2,284
Less: Charges	7,500	nil
	£ 9,900	£ 2,284
Corporation tax payable		
£9,900 @ 27%	2,673	
£2,284 @ 25%		571
Less: ACT paid (due 14 July 1988)		160
	£ 2,673	£ 411
Due dates:	1 January 1989	1 April 1989

Question 30

Stonyhurst Ltd
Corporation tax computation, year ended 31 March 1988

	£	£
	+	–
Schedule D Case I		
Net profit per accounts	272,680	
Surplus on sale of house		17,150
Debenture interest		3,250
Dividends received from UK companies (gross)		4,600
Building society interest received (net)		700
Bank deposit interest		360
Depreciation	34,650	
Subscriptions and donations		
National Trust	50	
Political party	300	
Loan interest payable	17,500	
Professional expenses		
Tax appeal	500	
New 7 year lease	500	
Architect's fees	2,340	
Entertaining		
Foreign suppliers (not allowed even in 1987/88!)	70	
UK suppliers	340	
UK customers	180	
Capital allowances		46,620
	329,110	72,680
	72,680	
Schedule D Case I	256,430	

Stonyhurst Ltd
Corporation tax computation, year ended 31 March 1988

	£ +	£ −
Debenture interest	3,250	
Building society interest £700 × 100/73	959	
Bank interest – amount received	300	
Chargeable gain	13,150	
	274,089	
Less: Charges: Loan interest paid	16,000	
Amount chargeable to CT	£258,089	

Corporation tax payable

Corporation tax @ 35%		90,331
less: Marginal small companies relief		
$1/50\ (£500{,}000 - £262{,}689)\ \frac{£258{,}089}{£262{,}689}$		4,663
		85,668
('Profit' = £258,089 + £4,600 FII)		
Less: ACT		
Dividend paid		
£18,900 × 100/73	25,890	
Dividends received	4,600	
	£21,290	
£21,290 @ 27%		5,748
		79,920
Less: Income tax relating to building society interest		259
Corporation tax due 1 January 1989		£79,661

Capital allowances

	Main pool £	*Car pool* £	*Expensive Cars* *1* £	*2* £	*Allowances* £
Brought forward	72,125	10,438	8,598	10,520	
Additions	63,210	6,500			
	135,335	16,938			
Sales	150	2,150		7,500	
	135,185	14,788			
WDA 25%	33,797	3,697	2,000(max)		39,494
Balancing allowance				3,020	3,020
Carried forward	101,388	11,091	6,598		42,514
Industrial buildings allowances (given in question)					4,106
					£46,620

Question 31

J Clark Electrical Ltd
Calculation of loss relief

	12 months to 30 June 1986	*12 months to 30 June 1987*	*6 months to 31 December 1987*	*12 months to 31 December 1988*
	£	£	£	£
Trading profit	135,000	650,000	60,000	–
Bank interest received	4,150	7,000	5,000	8,400
Debenture interest rec'd (gross)	2,000			
Chargeable gains (chargeable amount)	6,000		3,350	
Less: Loss brought forward			(2,600)	
			750	
Less: s. 393 (2)				(8,400)
s. 393 (2) + (3)		(328,500)	(65,750)	
	£147,150	328,500	nil	nil
Corporation tax @ 35%	51,625	114,975		
Less: Small companies relief				
$\frac{1}{40}$ (£250,000 – £149,950) $\frac{£147,150}{£149,950}$	2,455			
	49,170			
Less ACT – see workings	–	76,050		
	49,170			
Less: Income tax on debenture interest received	500			
Corporation tax payable	£ 48,670	£ 38,925		

Loss relief memorandum:

	£
Loss in year ended 31 December 1988	430,000
Less: s. 393 (2)	8,400
	421,600
s. 393 (2) + (3) (6 months to 31 December 1987)	65,750
	355,850
s. 393 (2) + (3) (against 6/12 of profit of year ended 30 June 1987)	328,500
Carried forward under s. 393 (1)	£ 27,350

ACT

Year ended 31 December 1988 £

Franked payments	£210,000 × 100/75	280,000	
FII	£ 3,500 × 100/75	4,667	
		275,333 × 25%	68,833

Set-off available – nil – carried back

6 months ended 31 December 1987

Franked payments	£21,000 × 100/75	28,000	
FII	£ 7,000 × 100/75	(9,333)	
		17,667 × 25%	4,417

Set-off available – nil after loss claim – carried back

			£
Year ended 30 June 1987			
Franked payments	£14,000 × 100/75	18,667	
FII	£ 3,500 × 100/75	(4,667)	
		14,000	
Surplus FII brought forward		(2,800)	
		11,200 × 25%	2,800
ACT brought back £68,833 + £4,417			73,250
Maximum offset (using 1988 rates)			76,050

25% × £328,500 = £82,125
All ACT may therefore be offset.

Year ended 30 June 1986		
Franked payments –		nil
FII	£2100 × 100/75	(2,800)
Surplus FII carried forward		(2,800)

Tutorial notes

As the company has one subsidiary, the small company limits must be halved. Thus the company has marginal relief for the year ended 30 June 1986 but not for the following year.

The question asks us to use the current rates of corporation tax, which simplifies the calculations.

Question 32

This is a terminal loss question, but the claims available under s. 393 (2) and (3) must first be made. The format used in the previous answer may again be adopted.

The loss may be carried back for three years before the beginning of the last twelve months, that is to 1 April 1984, half way through the year ended 30 September 1984.

Burlington Ltd
Terminal loss relief

	Years ended 30 September				*6 months to*
	1984	*1985*	*1986*	*1987*	*31 March 1988*
	£	£	£	£	£
Schedule D Case I	28,000	10,000	6,000		
Terminal loss relief	14,000	(7,500)			
	14,000	2,500			
Unfranked investment income	5,000	5,000	5,000	5,000	2,500
	19,000	7,500	11,000	5,000	2,500
Less: s. 393 (2)				(5,000)	(2,500)
s. 393 (2) + (3)			(10,000)		
	19,500	7,500	1,000	nil	nil
Less: Charges	(7,500)	(7,500)	(7,500)	(7,500)	(3,750)

	Years ended 31 September				*6 months to*
	1984	*1985*	*1986*	*1987*	*31 March 1988*
	£	£	£	£	£
Chargeable to CT	£ 11,500	nil	–	–	–
Charges unrelieved			6,500	7,500 (6/12 in terminal loss claim)	3,750 (In terminal loss claim)

Section 393 loss relief memorandum – year ended 30 September 1987:

	£
Loss for year	15,000
Less: s. 393 (2)	5,000
	10,000
Less: s. 393 (2) + (3) (balance)	10,000
	–

Section 393 loss relief memorandum – 6 months ended 31 March 1988:

	£
Loss for period	20,000
Less: s. 393 (2)	2,500
Available for terminal loss claim	£17,500

Calculation of terminal loss, year ended 31 March 1988:

	£
6 months ended 31 March 1988	
Loss – balance available as above	17,500
Unrelieved trade charges	3,750
6 months ended 30 September 1987	
Loss – all relieved	nil
Unrelieved trade charges	
6/12 × £7,500	3,750
	25,000
Relieved: year ended 30 September 1985	7,500
	17,500
year ended 30 September 1984	14,000 (Maximum 6/12 × £28,000)
Unrelieved	£ 3,500

Question 33

(a) It is first necessary to consider the companies eligible to receive the benefit of group loss relief. The loss of B Ltd may be surrendered to A Ltd or D Ltd. The loss of E Ltd may be surrendered to D Ltd only, since the shareholding link with A Ltd is 72 per cent only (90 per cent × 80 per cent). Next it is necessary to consider the marginal tax rates of the eligible companies to see where it is most beneficial to claim. As there are five companies in the group, the small companies limits are reduced to £100,000 and £20,000 and profits over £20,000 will be taxed at the high marginal rate. In arriving at the optimum basis of claim we shall first work to reduce the profits of A Ltd and D Ltd to £20,000, first using the loss of E Ltd because this has the least flexibility as it can only be surrendered to D Ltd.

(Remember that the claim for group loss relief is against the profit of the claiming company *after* deducting charges.)

The results become:

	A Ltd	*B Ltd*	*C Ltd*	*D Ltd*	*E Ltd*
	£	£	£	£	£
Schedule D Case I	46,000		90,000	35,000	
Case III		3,000	15,000		
	46,000	3,000	105,000	35,000	
Less: Charges	3,000	1,000	4,000	2,000	
	43,000	2,000	101,000	33,000	
Less: s. 402 relief:					
E Ltd				12,000	
B Ltd	23,000			1,000	
Chargeable to CT	20,000	2,000	101,000	20,000	nil
CT payable:					
@ 25%	5,000	500		5,000	
@ 35%			35,350		

The examiner has contrived the figures very carefully to ensure that the relief available from E Ltd and B Ltd exactly achieves the objective of reducing the profits of A Ltd and D Ltd to £20,000, the small companies limit. Also, the profit of C Ltd is just over £100,000, sparing us the trouble of a marginal small companies calculation. A very instructive question.

(b) A group income election should be set aside if the subsidiary has franked investment income, because it can only obtain relief for it by making a franked payment. All or most of this will pass to other group companies, who can in turn pay a dividend, using the benefit of the tax credit on the franked investment income to reduce their own ACT payments.

Question 34

(a) *Edgar Ltd*

Maximum relevant income computation, year ended 31 December 1988

	Trading income	*Estate income*	*Investment income*
	£	£	£
Trading income	35,000		
Estate income – Schedule A		25,000	
Bank interest – Schedule D Case III			8,000
Less: Charges paid			(2,000)
			6,000

	Trading income £	*Estate income* £	*Investment income* £
Less: Corporation tax			
3/12 @ 27%	(2,362)	(1,687)	(405)
9/12 @ 25%	(6,563)	(4,688)	(1,125)
	26,075	18,625	4,470
Dividends received (net)			3,750
			8,220
Abatements:			
Estate income			
$£75{,}000 \times \frac{£18{,}625}{£44{,}700} = £31{,}250$			
$\frac{£31{,}250 - £18{,}625}{2} =$		(6,313)	
Investment income			
Lower of:			
10% × £44,700			
£3,000			(3,000)
		£ 12,312	£ 5,220
50% × £12,312			6,156
Maximum relevant income			£ 11,376

(b) Companies exempted from being classified as 'close' are:

(i) A company which is controlled by one or more non-close companies

(ii) A company which can only be brought within the definition of 'close' by including a non-close company as one of its participators

(iii) A quoted company in which 35 per cent of more of its voting power is beneficially held by members of the public and in which there has been at least one dealing in the previous twelve months. This exception does not apply if the 'principal members' of the company hold more than 85 per cent of the voting power.

(iv) A company not resident in the UK

Question 35

To: Directors of P Limited

19 August 1988

From: Accountant

Proposal to change residence of Q (USA) to a far eastern country

The proposal to change the residence of Q (USA) to a far eastern country with a 5 per cent rate of corporation tax is superficially attractive, but there are two problems from a tax point of view.

1 Procedure for change of residence – until 15 March 1988, it was possible to change the country of residence of a UK company, but only with Treasury consent. Since that date it is not possible to do so – companies registered in the UK have permanent UK residence status. We should need to check what the USA requirements are for a change in the residential status of a company registered there.
2 Controlled foreign company (CFC) status – the Revenue have wide powers under ss. 747 to 756 ICTA 1988 to limit the activities of 'controlled foreign companies' (CFCs). A CFC is a company:
   (a) Resident outside the UK
   (b) Controlled by persons resident in the UK
   (c) Subject to a lower level of tax in the country of residence than would be the case if it were a UK company. (This condition is satisfied if the tax in the overseas country is less than 50 per cent of what it would be in the UK)

Since US tax rates are not less than half those in the UK, Q (USA) is not at the moment within the definition, but it could become so if the residence were changed as proposed. If this happened, the consequence would be that the Revenue have the power to direct that the company's profits are to be apportioned among its individual members and subjected to UK tax, thus negating the objective of the change. There are exceptions which mean that no direction for apportionment will be made. There will be no direction if:

(a) Profit of the CFC excluding capital gains does not exceed £20,000, or
(b) The CFC pursues an 'acceptable' distribution policy by paying dividends to UK residents exceeding 50 per cent of available profits (90 per cent if not a trading company), or
(c) The CFC's activities are 'exempt' – managed in and from the country of residence and not doing business in the UK, or
(d) The Revenue are satisfied that the main purpose of the CFC's existence, and its transactions, was not a reduction in the UK tax liability of any person, or
(e) The CFC is a quoted company in which not less than 35 per cent of the shares are held by the public throughout the accounting period, with voting power held by the principal members not exceeding 85 per cent.

For Q (USA) it may be possible to escape the consequences of being a CFC if any of these exceptions can be made to apply. Exceptions (a), (b) or (c) would appear to offer the best chances of success in this respect.

Question 36

19 August 1988

Dear Mr D

Report on tax factors affecting the form of your business

The choice of trading as a sole trader or as a limited company involves more than tax considerations, but this report is confined, at your request, to taxation aspects.

The main tax differences are:

(i) A sole trader is liable to income tax whereas a company is liable to corporation tax. This is important because a company continues to be taxed at 25 per cent up to a level of £100,000 profit, whereas an individual is taxed at 40 per cent as soon as income less allowances exceeds £19,300 (1988/89). However, this advantage of incorporation is lessened if it is necessary to draw out substantial sums as directors' remuneration to cover living expenses.

(ii) National Insurance contributions for sole traders are limited whereas remuneration paid by the company attracts National Insurance contributions without an upper limit. However, this disadvantage can be overcome by paying dividends out of the company instead of remuneration.
The whole of the company's contribution is allowable against corporation tax, whereas only 50 per cent of a sole trader's Class 4 contributions and none of the Class 2 contributions are allowable.

(iii) Due dates for payment of tax are generally later for sole traders. The due date for companies is in the process of being standardized at nine months after the end of the accounting period, whereas for income tax it is still possible to obtain an interval of twenty months by choosing a 30 April accounting date, and the tax is then payable in two instalments, 20 and 26 months after the accounting date.

(iv) Losses by companies can only be offset against company profits, including capital gains, whereas losses by individuals may in general be offset against all other income (excluding capital gains). The relief under s. 381 ICTA 1988 for losses in the early years of the business is only available to sole traders.

(v) If a car is used in the business and also available for private use, the benefit is determined for income tax purposes by apportioning expenses, including capital allowances, on a mileage basis, while for corporation tax purposes the benefit is assessed on a flat rate basis on the director as an employee. Although the benefit scales have been increased, there may still be a useful element of benefit enjoyed by a director in this case.

(vi) Capital gains by individuals are charged to capital gains tax at 30 per cent with an annual exemption (£5,000 for 1988/89), whereas those of companies are charged to corporation tax at 25 per cent (up to £100,000 total profit including chargeable gains) or 35 per cent (over £500,000), with no exemption band. When a company makes a capital gain, there may be a double taxation if the gain is then distributed as dividend, thus attracting tax in the hands of the members.

Conclusions
It is difficult to make a general recommendation applicable to all situations. If losses are expected in the early years, it may well pay to begin as a sole trader, forming a company only when profits start to rise above the level needed to cover generous living costs for the proprietor. Even then, non-business assets should remain outside the company to obtain the capital gains tax annual exemption.

Question 37

(a) The cost (or market value at 31 March 1982) of the whole asset is apportioned to the part sold according to the formula:

$$\frac{\text{Sale proceeds}}{\text{Sale proceeds + Market value (as at the date of disposal) of part retained.}} \times \text{Allowable cost}$$

If the asset is land, any other fair and reasonable method of allocating cost may be applied, if agreed by the Revenue.

(b) The enhancement expenditure is included with the original cost, but indexed only from the date the additional expenditure was incurred.

Question 38

	£	£
Sale proceeds	80,000	
Less: costs of sale	2,200	77,800
Less: Cost		
$£40,000 \times \frac{95.749}{98.059}$	38,938	
(The lease was sold with 40½ years remaining. The percentage applicable to remaining life on disposal is therefore: 96.041 – ½ (96.041–95.457) = 95.749)		
Indexation £38,938 × 22.5%	8,761	47,699
Chargeable gain		£30,101

Question 39

Vector Ltd

	No. of shares	*Unindexed pool value*	*Indexed pool value*
		£	£
August 1983	2,000	5,000	5,000
April 1985:			
Indexation			
£5,000 × 10.6%			530
			5,530
Rights issue	500	1,000	1,000
	2,500	6,000	6,530
May 1986			
Indexation			
£6,530 × 3.2%			209
			6,739
Sale	1,000	2,400	2,696
	1,500	3,600	4,043
June 1987			
Bonus issue	500	–	–
	2,000	3,600	4,043
May 1988			
Indexation (from May 1986)			
£4,043 × 8.5%			344
			4,387
Sale	1,000	1,800	2,194
Pool balance	£ 1,000	1,800	2,193

Computation of gains
Year ended 31 March 1987

	£
May 1986 Proceeds of sale – 1000 Steep Ltd shares	3,000
Less: Indexed cost	2,696
	£ 304

Year ended 31 March 1989

May 1988 Proceeds of sale – 1,000 Steep Ltd shares	4,000
Less: Indexed cost	2,194
	£1,806

Question 40

The 31 March 1982 value of Culator's holding of shares in Victim Ltd will be apportioned among the elements of the consideration received in May 1988 pro rata to their value immediately after the takeover:

Cash	10,000
Shares in Predator Limited	
3 × 10,000 × 220p	66,000
10% loan stock in Predator Limited	
£10,000 × 80p	8,000
	£84,000

Apportionment of cost

Cash element (disposal)	£
$\frac{£10,000}{£84,000} \times £42,000$	5,000
Shares	
$\frac{£66,000}{£84,000} \times £42,000$	33,000
Loan stock	
$\frac{£8,000}{£84,000} \times £42,000$	4,000
	£42,000

The gain on the disposal on the takeover, represented by the cash element, will accordingly be:

	£	£
Proceeds received		10,000
Less:		
31 March 1982 market value	5,000	
Indexation:		6,685
£5,000 × 33.7%	1,685	
Chargeable gain:		£ 3,315

Question 41

The gain eligible for relief is:

$$\frac{\text{Chargeable business assets}}{\text{Chargeable assets}} \times £104,350$$

$$= \frac{£795,000 + £250,000}{£795,000 + £250,000 + £35,000 + £27,500} \times £104,350$$

$$= \frac{£1,045,000}{£1,107,500} \times £104,350$$

$$= £98,461$$

Relief available is £125,000 limited because the shares have not been owned for ten years, but for six years five months only.

The calculation is therefore:

	£	£
Gain on disposal (after indexation)		£104,350
Less: Retirement relief		
$\frac{6\ 5/12}{10} \times$ £125,000	80,208	
1/2 × remaining £18,253*	9,127	89,335
Chargeable gain		£ 15,015

* Relief at the half rate would be available up to a limit of $\frac{6\ 5/12}{10}$ × £375,000 or £240,625

Question 42

		£	£
(a)	Proceeds		100,000
	Cost	40,000	
	Indexation		
	£40,000 × 25.5%	10,200	52,200
	Chargeable gain		£ 47,800

(b) No tax will be payable on the disposal, but the cost of the replacement building will be reduced by £47,800 to £72,200.

(c) As the whole of the proceeds has not been reinvested, rollover relief is limited:

Proceeds not reinvested: £100,000 – £60,000 = £40,000

Tax will be payable immediately on £40,000 and only £7,800 can be rolled over.

(d) As the replacement asset is a depreciating asset, the gain of £47,800 will be held over until the earliest of the following three events:

(i) Disposal of the replacement asset
(ii) Date the replacement asset ceases to be used for the purpose of the trade
(iii) Ten years after the purchase of the replacement asset

If within the shortest of these times a non-depreciating asset qualifying for the relief is purchased, rollover relief may be claimed on it by deducting the held-over gain from its cost.

Question 43

(a) For intra-group asset transfers the requirement is that companies with a shareholding link of 75 per cent or more may transfer assets on a no gain no loss basis. This means that in the following situation all companies may exchange losses:

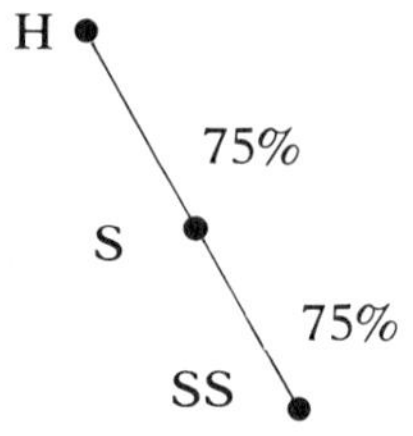

Although H only owns 56¼ per cent (75 per cent of 75 per cent) of SS, the 75 per cent shareholding link requirement is satisfied. The important tax advantage is that the ability to make no gain no loss transfers allows capital losses by one 75 per cent group company to be relieved against capital gains by another. To achieve this, the gain and the loss must both be made by the same company. An intra-group transfer on a no gain no loss basis before the sale onwards to an outsider allows this to take place.

(b) The shareholding requirement for group loss relief (trading losses etc.) differs because sub-subsidiaries are only eligible to exchange losses with their holding company if the indirect interest of the holding company is 75 per cent or more:

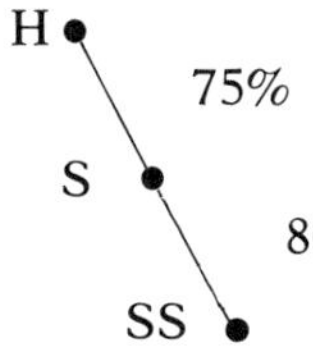

Group relief not available
(75% of 80% is only 60%)

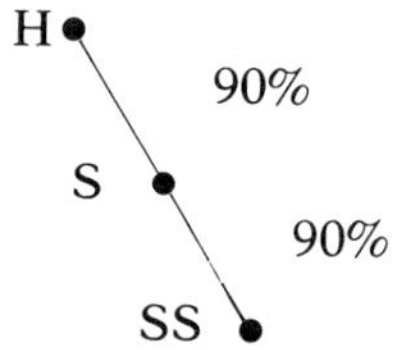

Group relief available
(90% of 90% is 81%)

Question 44

(a) By timing disposals so as to keep the company out of the marginal small companies band. For a company without associates and with no franked investment income, the tax rates for the financial year 1988 are:

Profit up to £100,000	25%
Profit £100,000 to £500,000	First £100,000 25% balance 37½%
Profit over £500,000	35%

It therefore pays a company to minimize the profits being taxed in the marginal band, and advancing or deferring disposals of chargeable assets may be a convenient way of doing this.

(b) By taking advantage of roll-over relief. When a qualifying asset is sold, the company has three years to replace it with another qualifying asset. Such a replacement has the effect of deferring payment of the tax on the first disposal until the disposal of the second asset. Replacement may also be made in the one year *before* the disposal. Even if the replacement asset is a depreciating asset (one with a life of less than sixty years), tax on the disposal may still be deferred for up to ten years.

(c) By ensuring that in a group of companies one company does not pay tax on a gain while another has unused loss relief. This is achieved by first structuring the group so that all companies are linked by a shareholding of at least 75 per cent, and then passing all disposals outside the group through one nominated company in which all gains and losses are realized and thus set off to the maximum possible extent.

Section 45

(a) (i) The VAT Act 1979 as amended by the Finance Acts 1985 and 1988 contains a number of penalty provisions:

- Default surcharge – if a trader is late with two quarterly VAT returns, Customs and Excise may issue a surcharge liability notice. If the trader is then late with another VAT return within the next year, a surcharge of 5 per cent of the VAT paid late, or £30 if greater, will be made. Every time a surcharge is made, a further surcharge liability notice is issued. If another VAT return is late, the surcharge increases to 10 per cent and on up to 30 per cent for subsequent defaults.
- Late registration – from 16 March 1988, there are penalties ranging from 10 per cent of the tax to 30 per cent of the tax if a trader is late in registering for VAT without reasonable excuse.
- Unauthorized issue of VAT invoices – a penalty of 30 per cent of the tax on the invoice is charged unless the trader can show reasonable excuse.
- Other offences – in addition to these penalty provisions there is a variety of criminal and civil offences carrying penalties, fines and even imprisonment.

(ii) Appeals to VAT tribunals – a trader may appeal to the local VAT Tribunal if he or she cannot agree the VAT liability with Customs and Excise. Notice must be given to Customs and Excise and the Tribunal's decision on a question of fact is final, though further appeal through the Courts is possible on a question of law.

(b)	£	£
Output VAT to be accounted for:		
£172,500 × 3/23		22,500
Deductible input VAT:		
£115,575 × 3/23	15,075	
Allowable		
$\frac{£50{,}000 + £150{,}000}{£50{,}000 + £150{,}000 + £75{,}000} \times £15{,}075$		10,964
Payable to Customs and Excise		£11,536

Question 46

The Board of Directors
A Limited
10 High Street
London

19 August 1988

Dear Sirs

Report on VAT matters

We have pleasure in submitting our replies to the points raised in your recent letter requesting advice on certain VAT matters.

(i) Registration
A business is required to register for VAT as soon as its taxable supplies exceed £7,500 for one quarter, or £22,100 for the year. You are also liable to register if it is clear that your turnover will exceed £22,100 for the first year. From the turnover figures you give it will therefore be necessary for you to register either immediately or in the near future. There are penalties for late registration.

(ii) VAT in budgets and annual accounts
In cash budgeting, actual cash flows are used. Sales and expenses should therefore *include* VAT, with provision for the quarterly payment or receipt of the net balance. For other budgeting and annual accounts, VAT should be excluded except when actually borne. Your business will actually bear VAT in three cases:

- VAT suffered on inputs before registration
- VAT on expenditure on cars (which will affect your annual depreciation charge)
- VAT on entertainment costs

(iii) Accounting for VAT
VAT is normally accounted for quarterly. A return of the amount due or refundable is required to be sent with payment when necessary within thirty days of the end of each quarter. A business with net refunds may elect to submit returns, and

thus receive the refunds, monthly. It is also possible, if turnover does not exceed £250,000, to have annual accounting. This does not mean that payment is deferred for a year, because payments on account must be made during the year. The election for annual accounting may only be made once the trader has been registered for one year. Another option is to elect for cash accounting rather than accounting on the basis of invoices. This method has the advantages of deferring payment of VAT until cash is actually received from customers, and giving automatic relief for bad debts.

(iv) Records

The VAT legislation requires detailed records to be kept, and retained for six years. Business records include:

- Orders and delivery notes
- Relevant business correspondence
- Purchases and sales books
- Purchase invoices and sales invoices
- Cash books and other account books
- Records of daily takings such as till rolls
- Annual accounts, including trading and profit and loss accounts
- Import and export documents
- Bank statements and paying-in slips
- VAT account
- Credit or debit notes issued or received

Please get in touch with us if there is any further information or assistance we can provide.

Yours faithfully,
B and Co.

Question 47

(a) (i) If all supplies are zero rated, a registered trader may reclaim VAT on inputs but does not charge VAT on outputs. Quarterly returns are submitted and will lead to a refund from Customs and Excise. Such a trader may elect for monthly return periods to speed up the receipt of the refunds.

(ii) If all supplies are exempt, a trader does not have to register for VAT. No VAT is charged on outputs, but VAT on inputs has to be borne as an expense.

(iii) If supplies are a mixture of zero rated and exempt, the trader will be required to register and will be able to reclaim VAT on inputs as in (i) above, to the extent that inputs relate to zero rated outputs. If exempt supplies fall below certain limits the whole of the input tax may be reclaimed. The limits are that *exempt input tax* (not exempt supplies) must be less than:

- £100 per month on average, or
- both £250 per month on average and 50 per cent of all input tax, or
- both £500 per month on average and 25 per cent of all input tax.

(b) A tax invoice must state the following information:

(i) An identifying serial number
(ii) Supplier's name, address and VAT number,
(iii) Time of supply
(iv) Customer's name and address
(v) Type of supply (sale, hire purchase, hire, etc.)
(vi) Description of goods or services supplied and quantity supplied
(vii) For each item, the charge excluding VAT and the VAT rate
(viii) Total charge made excluding VAT
(ix) Rate of any cash discount
(x) Total VAT payable

Question 48

It is necessary to do two separate sets of computations, first on the basis of cessation at 31 March 1989 with accounts made up for three months to that date showing a profit of £6,000 and second on the basis of cessation to 30 April 1989 with accounts made up for four months to that date showing a profit of £7,000.

As the profits are on a raising trend the Revenue will clearly exercise their option under s. 63, but it is probably best to show both original and final assessments to be on the safe side.

(a) (i) Cessation at 31 March 1989

		Original		*Revenue election under s. 63*	
		£		£	£
1986/87					
Year ended 31 December 1985		8,000	Actual		
			9/12 × £24,000	18,000	
			3/12 × £36,000	9,000	27,000
1987/88					
Year ended 31 December 1986		24,000	Actual		
			9/12 × £36,000	27,000	
			3/12 × £48,000	12,000	39,000
1988/89					
Actual					
9/12 × £48,000	36,000				
	6,000	42,000			

Clearly the Revenue election would be made and the final assessments would be:

	£
1986/87	27,000
1987/88	39,000
1988/89	42,000
	£108,000

(ii) Cessation at 30 April 1989

	Original		*Revenue election under s. 63*	
	£		£	£
1986/87				
Year ended 31 December 1985	8,000			
1987/88				
Year ended 31 December 1986	24,000	Actual as in (i)		39,000
1988/89				
Year ended 31 December 1987	36,000	Actual		
		9/12 × £48,000	36,000	
		3/4 × £7,000	5,250	41,250
1989/90				
Actual				
1/4 × £7,000	1,750			

The Revenue would again invoke s. 63, and the final assessments would be:

	£
1986/87	8,000
1987/88	39,000
1988/89	41,250
1989/90	1,750
	£90,000

The assessments are £18,000 less, and in addition an extra £1,000 of profit has been made. G will obviously be advised to continue until 30 April 1989.

(b) The disposal of the business will give rise to a chargeable gain based on the increase between 31 March 1982 and the date of sale, subject to indexation. As G is selling his business for cash, there is no possibility of deferring the gain as there would be if he sold for an interest of 75 per cent or more in the equity share capital of the purchasing company. However, if G reinvests in eligible assets within three years after the sale he may claim rollover relief to the extent that the gain is attributable to goodwill, land and buildings or fixed plant. If no rollover relief is available, or it is not claimed, the due date for payment will be 1 December 1989 for a sale on 31 March 1989 and 1 December 1990 for a sale on 30 April 1989. For a sale on 31 March 1989 the first £6,600 will be exempt and the remainder will be taxed at 30 per cent, while for a sale on 30 April 1989 the first £5,000 will be exempt from tax and the remainder taxed at G's marginal income tax rate (25 per cent or 40 per cent or a combination of both).

Question 49

(a) *FD Ltd*

Adjustment of profit, eighteen months ended 30 September 1988

	£	£
	+	–
Profit per accounts	59,000	
Depreciation	24,415	
Debenture interest paid	9,585	
Dividends received		9,000
	93,000	9,000
	9,000	
Adjusted profit subject to capital allowances	£ 84,000	

FD Limited – capital allowances

	Pool	*Allowances*
12 months ended 31 March 1988	£	£
Balance brought forward	76,200	
Sales (proceeds)	10,000	
	66,200	
Writing down allowance 25%	16,550	16,550
	£ 49,650	
6 months ended 30 September 1988		
Balance brought forward	49,650	
Additions	110,000	
	159,650	
Writing down allowances 25% × 6/12	19,957	19,957
	£139,693	

	12 months ended 31 March 1988	*6 months ended 30 September 1988*
	£	£
Adjusted profit as above 2:1	56,000	28,000
Capital allowances	16,550	19,957
	39,450	8,043
Less: Charges	6,390	3,195
Amount chargeable to CT	33,060	4,849
FII	4,000	5,000
'Profit'	£37,060	£ 9,849

Before calculating the CT liability, it is necessary to determine the 'small company' limits. As there are three companies in the group they are:

Lower limit	33,333	16,667
Upper limit	166,667	83,333

Small companies marginal relief thus applied for the first period only.

	£	£	£	£
Corporation tax payable				
£33,060 @ 35%		11,571		
Less: small companies marginal relief $\frac{1}{50}$ (£166,667 − £37,060) $\frac{£33,060}{£37,060}$		2,313		
		9,258		
£4,849 @ 25%				1,212
Less: ACT				
Franked payment	5,000		5,000	
FII	4,000		5,000	
	1,000 @ 27%	270	nil	
Mainstream corporation tax		£ 8,988		1,212
Due dates		1.1.89		1.7.89

(b) The gain on the sale of the investment property on 30 September 1988 would be subject to corporation tax in the 6 months ending on that date. The increase in the profit would mean that the company would enter the marginal small companies band with total amount chargeable to corporation tax of £54,849.

(c) Capital losses by one group company cannot be offset against capital gains. However, transactions between group companies with a 75 per cent shareholding link can take place on a 'no gain no loss' basis. The company about to realize the loss should first sell the asset to FD Ltd. so that the loss arises for FD. Then, when the £50,000 profit is realized by FD Ltd. it can be set off against the loss.

Question 50

(i) *Cape Brandy Syndicate* v. *IRC* 1921
A quantity of South African brandy was shipped to the UK, blended and sold in small lots over a period of about a year. It was held that the transactions amounted to a separate trading activity.

(ii) *Sharkey* v. *Wernher* 1955
The taxpayer's wife operated a stud farm assessed under Schedule D Case I and also trained and raced horses not under Schedule D Case I but as a hobby. Some horses were transferred from the stud

farm to the racing stables and the case concerned the price at which the transfer should take place. The market value of the horses considerably exceeded the cost of breeding them and maintaining them until the point of sale. It was held that the transfer should be at market value. As a result of this case the Revenue insist that items taken from the stock of any business for the proprietor's use must be at selling price, not cost.

(iii) *Ricketts* v. *Colquhoun* 1926
A taxpayer who practised as a barrister in London was also Recorder of Portsmouth. He claimed the cost of travel from London to Portsmouth as an allowable Schedule E expense. It was held that the expenses were not allowable as he was not 'in the performance of the duties' as Recorder until he actually arrived at the Court in Portsmouth.

(iv) *Heaton* v. *Bell* 1969
Lower paid employees were allowed by the employer to have the free use of a car provided they agreed to a salary reduction in return. It was held that the employees were still taxable on the full gross pay because the benefit could be turned into cash by withdrawing from the scheme.

(v) *Law Shipping Co.* v. *IRC* 1924
A ship purchased in a dilapidated state was subsequently repaired and the repair cost claimed as a Schedule D Case I expense. It was held that as the repairs related to the condition at the time of purchase it must be treated as capital expenditure and disallowed. The case must be contrasted with *Odeon Associated Theatres Ltd* v. *Jones* 1971, in which it was held that expenditure could be allowed provided three conditions were satisfied:

- Normal accounting practice would treat the expense as revenue
- The asset was capable of being used without the repairs
- The state of disrepair had not reduced the purchase price.

(vi) *Strong and Co. of Romsey Ltd* v. *Woodifield* 1906
A guest staying in a hotel was injured when a chimney fell on him. The owners of the hotel had to pay damages of £1,490 to the guest and claimed that this was a trading expense. It was held that money was not paid out 'for the purpose of earning the profits' and was thus not allowable.

Question 51

Mendip Ltd
Corporation tax computation, year ended 31 March 1989

	£	£
	+	–
Net profit per accounts	94,500	
Depreciation	29,500	

Mendip Ltd
Corporation tax computation, year ended 31 March 1989

	£	£
	+	–
Loan interest	4,500	
Investment income		13,000
Increase in general doubtful debt provision	1,340	
Improvements to office building	1,200	
Entertaining: UK customers	2,370	
Overseas suppliers	1,510	
Capital allowances		
WDA 25% × £24,000		6,000
	134,920	19,000
	19,000	
Schedule D Case I	115,920	
Schedule D Case III	9,000	
	124,920	
Less: Charge – loan interest paid	3,000	
Amount chargeable to corporation tax	£121,920	

('Profit' for small companies relief purposes is £121,920 plus franked investment income £4,000 or £125,920)

Corporation tax payable:

	£	£
£121,920 @ 35%		42,672
Less: Small companies relief		
$\frac{1}{40}$ (£250,000 – £125,920) $\frac{£121,920}{£125,920}$		3,004
		39,668
Less: ACT paid		
Franked payment £10,000 × 100/75	13,333	
FII	4,000	
	£ 9,333	
£9,333 @ 25%		2,334
		37,634
Less: Income tax on surplus UF11		
25% × (£9,000 – £3,000)		1,500
Corporation tax payable 1 January 1990		£36,134

Question 52

(a) Income tax and corporation tax:

(i) As from 15 March 1988, new deeds of covenant in favour of individuals will no longer enjoy tax relief, and income received under deed of covenant will not be taxed

(ii) Entertainment of overseas customers will no longer be an allowable expense as from 15 March 1988

(iii) Schedule B tax on commercial woodlands is abolished as from 15 March 1988, and the option to have commercial woodlands assessed under Schedule D is also abolished. As a result, cost of planting and maintenance of woodlands is no longer an allowable deduction, and the proceeds of sale of trees will be exempt from tax

(iv) Top slicing arrangements for premiums received on leases is abolished. The whole premium received, less the 2% deduction for each year of the lease after the first is taxable as part of the taxpayer's income

(v) No tax relief is to be given on new home improvement loans made on or after 6 April 1988

(b) Capital gains tax:

(i) The tax is re-based to 31 March 1982, so that gains arising before that date are no longer taxable

(ii) The amount qualifying for retirement relief is increased. For disposals on or after 6 April 1988, the first £125,000 of the gain is exempt from CGT, and half of the next £375,000 is also exempt

(iii) Satellites, space stations, spacecraft, milk quotas and potato quotas are added to the list of assets qualifying for roll-over relief

(iv) Capital gains by individuals are now to be taxed at the taxpayer's marginal income tax rate (25 per cent or 40 per cent), not 30 per cent. (The Finance (no 2) Act 1987 had already made gains by companies taxable on the same basis as income)

(c) Value added tax:

(i) The penalty provisions of the Finance Act 1985 were modified to reduce the penalties for certain offences, including those for late registration and the daily default penalties for breaches of regulations.

Question 53

(a) The gross equivalent of the loan interest received is liable to corporation tax. If £500 is the net amount the gross equivalent would be £500 × 100/75 or £666. The income tax suffered (£166) would be relieved in one of three ways:

(i) By offset in the quarterly settlement of income tax payable on interest etc. paid by the company

(ii) By deduction from the corporation tax liability of the year in which the interest was received

(iii) By refund

(b) For capital allowances purposes, a balancing charge or allowance will be computed in the period of sale by comparing the sale proceeds with the written down value. If the sale proceeds exceed the written down value there will be a balancing charge, limited to the total capital allowances granted over the period of ownership. If the proceeds exceed the valuation of the asset on 31 March 1982 there will be a chargeable gain subject to corporation tax after indexation from that date to the date of sale.

(c) Defalcations by junior staff will normally be an allowable deduction for corporation tax, provided the persons concerned were prosecuted and convicted, but defalcations by directors will not be allowable (*Bamford* v. *ATA Advertising Ltd* 1972).

(d) No capital allowances would be available on the cost of £40,000, or on any part of the £60,000 disallowed as capital. The Law Shipping case would disallow such expenditure, which is only possibly allowable if it can be brought within the criteria established in *Odeon Associated Theatres Ltd* v. *Jones*. These are:

    (i) Normal accounting practice would treat the expenditure as revenue
    (ii) The asset could be used without the expenditure
    (iii) The price was not reduced because of the expenditure

    The premises appear not to meet criterion (iii) at least, and therefore none of the expenditure would be allowable subject to possible negotiations with the Revenue on individual items.

(e) As from 15 March 1988, entertaining of foreign customers is not allowable as an expense, and entertaining UK customers and their staff has not been allowable for many years. Reasonable costs of entertaining staff would normally be allowed if relating to staff parties and the like. The Revenue have indicated a level of £50 per head as the maximum for such expenditure.

Answers to progress questions

Chapter 1

1 (a) True
  (b) False – overseas income will be liable to UK tax if enjoyed by UK residents. There may also be overseas tax on the same income, but relief is given to ensure that the taxpayer only pays, in total, the higher of the two countries' taxes.
  (c) True
  (d) False – partnerships pay income tax on their profits.

2 Cases I to V of Schedule D.

3 See Table 1, page 5.

4 See page 4.

5 See page 7.

Chapter 2

1 See pages 14–15.

2 See page 16.

3 (a) (i) True
    (ii) False – class 2 contributions are not allowable, Class 4 contributions are not allowed in computing Schedule D Case I or II profit, but 50 per cent may be deducted in computing total income from all sources.
  (b) False – depreciation is never allowable for Schedule D Cases I and II. Allowance for the loss in value of most capital assets used in the business is given by means of capital allowances (see Chapter 4).
  (c) True, provided they are incurred in the course of the trade. Writing off loans to staff or customers not allowed.

(d) True in general. Exceptions are:
  (i) Cost incurred in *renewal* of a short lease
  (ii) Costs of acquiring a patent or trade mark
(e) False – as from 15 March 1988, even entertaining of overseas customers is disallowed.

Chapter 3

1 See page 26.
2 (a) 1990/91
  (b) 1989/90
  (c) 1989/90
  (d) 1989/90
  (e) 1990/91
3

	Period	*Tax year of assessment*
(a)	1 January to 5 April 1988	1987/88
(b)	1 January to 31 December 1988	1988/89
(c)	1 January to 31 December 1988	1989/90
(d)	1 January to 31 December 1989	1990/91

4 (a) ICTA 1988 Section 62.
  (b) Assessments for both 1988/89 and 1989/90 would be based on the actual profits in those tax years, calculated by apportioning profits shown by the accounts spanning those years.

Chapter 4

1 (a) Yes
  (b) No
  (c) Yes
  (d) No
  (e) No
  (f) Yes
  (g) Yes
  (h) No
  (i) Yes
2 25 per cent writing down allowance, calculated on the reducing balance basis.
3 (a) Additions
  (b) Sale proceeds, limited to a maximum of the cost originally entering the pool
  (c) A balancing charge is made to restore the pool balance to nil from the negative figure created
4 Three from:
  (a) Cars costing up to £8,000 each (dealt with in a separate pool)
  (b) Cars costing over £8,000 each (dealt with individually)

(c) Assets with an element of private use (dealt with individually)
(d) Short life assets which are the subject of a de-pooling election. (Dealt with separately)
For detailed illustrations of the treatment of these items see pages 43–4.

5 Annual leasing or hiring costs for cars costing over £8,000 are restricted by the formula:

Allowable lease costs =

$$\text{lease costs} \times \frac{\text{£8,000} + \tfrac{1}{2}\,(\text{Cost minus £8,000})}{\text{Cost}}$$

6 Must be used for some manufacturing purpose (though other buildings can qualify).
7 See page 46.
8 ... 25 per cent ... the cost of the industrial part.
9 4 per cent writing down allowance (straight line basis). The only exception is if the expenditure is in an enterprise zone when 100 per cent of the expenditure is granted immediately.
10 A balancing charge or allowance arises. Any balancing charge cannot exceed the total allowances given over the period of ownership of the building.
11 See page 48.
12 (a) 4 per cent writing down allowance (straight line basis)
(b) 25 per cent writing down allowance (reducing balance basis)
(c) 25 per cent writing down allowance (reducing balance basis)
(d) 100 per cent allowance in year of expenditure

Chapter 5

1 Nil
2 See page 61.
3 1988/89 and 1989/90. Claim must be made within two years of 5 April 1989 – i.e. by 5 April 1991.
4 (a) True – s. 385
(b) False – s. 386 gives relief in this situation, if at least 80 per cent of the consideration is received by the person conducting the business in the form of shares, against the *income derived* by that individual from the company – salary and dividends for example.
(c) False – claims under both s. 380 and s. 385 must be made to the full extent of the available income. The only relaxation to this rule is that under s. 382 a s. 380 claim may be made against other income of the loss-making spouse only. This may have the effect of preserving the income of the other spouse to avoid loss of personal reliefs.
(d) True – s. 381
(e) False – s. 388. This statement is almost true – the only false point is that the claim is against the *profits of the same trade* in the previous three years, not against total income.

Chapter 6

1 See page 78.
2 (a) If they are improvements
  (b) If they relate to dilapidations which existed at the time the property was acquired.
  (c) If they are carried out in a void period following occupation by the landlord personally
3 See page 81.
4 Capital allowances, or 10 per cent of rents at the taxpayer's option.

Chapter 7

1 See page 87.
2 See page 88.
3 See pages 88–9.
4 Any six from those mentioned on page 91.
5 See page 92.
6 See page 98.
7 Yes, but only if:
  (a) The employee is not a director and earns not exceeding £8,500 including the value of the beneficial loan and other benefits, or
  (b) The value of the cash equivalent of the loan does not exceed £200, or
  (c) The loan is for a qualifying purpose (e.g. house purchase up to £30,000)
8 (a) See page 103.
  (b) See page 103.
  (c) See page 104.
  (d) See page 104.

Chapter 8

1 See page 109.
2 See page 110.
3 See page 113.
4 See pages 113–14.
5 See page 114.
6 See page 115.

Chapter 9

1 The Commissioners of Inland Revenue are the members of the Board of Inland Revenue responsible for the overall administration of the Revenue. The special commissioners and general commissioners

both have as their main responsibility the hearing of tax appeals. The special commissioners are full-time paid tax experts, while the general commissioners are unpaid local people. The taxpayer may choose whether to present an appeal to the special commissioners or the general commissioners.

2 See pages 119–20.

3 (a) 1 January in year of assessment and following 1 July in two equal instalments
  (b) 1 January in the year of assessment

4 (a) The due dates will be unaffected. Interest will run from the normal due dates
  (b) See pages 119–20.

5 The reckonable date is the date from which interest on overdue tax accrues.

6 See pages 122–3.

Chapter 10

1 Yes – it's tax *evasion* which isn't.

2 (a) False! It's the whole premium up to a limit of 17½ per cent of net relevant income!
  (b) False – it is *unused relief* that can be carried forward, not excess premiums.
  (c) True.

3 See page 126.

4 See page 128.

5 (a) Covenants to registered charities (if irrevocable and for a period which can exceed *three* years up to £5,000).
  (b) Covenants entered into before 15 March 1988 (if irrevocable, for a period which can exceed six years and not in favour of the taxpayer's infant unmarried child).

6 See page 130.

7 See page 131.

8 See page 133.

9 If plant is pooled, writing down allowances are obtained while it is retained, and on sale the proceeds are deducted from the pool balance. No balancing allowance can therefore arise on the sale. If the de-pooling election is made, the plant concerned is kept out of the main pool and a balancing allowance can arise on the sale. The election is beneficial for plant with a short life of (say) three to five years.

10 See page 134.

11 See page 134.

Chapter 11

1 (a) → (b)
(b) → (c)
(c) → (a)
2 Nine months after the end of the accounting period.
3 See page 143.
4 See page 143.
5 Capital gains by companies are calculated according to the rules of capital gains tax but are subjected to corporation tax at 25 per cent or 35 per cent depending on the company's profit level.
6 See page 144.

Chapter 12

1 See page 151.
2 See page 151.
3 The tax credit relating to the dividend may be deducted from ACT payments.
4 See page 152.
5 By deduction from the company's corporation tax liability of the period in which the relevant distributions were made, up to a limit found by applying the basic income tax rate to the profit chargeable to corporation tax. Any balance unrelieved may then be carried back up to six years (LIFO) or forward without time limit for offset in other years, subject to the limit described above. ACT may also be surrendered to 51 per cent subsidiaries.
6 The surplus FII is carried forward and is treated as if it were income of a later period in which distributions are sufficient to enable it to be relieved.
7 See page 155.
8 See page 159.

Chapter 13

1 (a) True
(b) False – when two accounting periods are involved, apportionment must be on the basis explained in 1(a) to 1(d) in the chapter.
(c) False – this is only necessary when the corporation tax rate changes. It is therefore not 'always' necessary.
2 See page 162.
3 See page 168.
4 Because basic profit in the marginal band is taxed at 37½ per cent (see example on page 170).

Chapter 14

1 (a) If the claim to establish the loss is not made within six years of the end of the accounting period in which the loss was made.
(b) If the ownership *and* the nature of the trade change within a three year period (ss. 768 and 769)
(c) If there is a reconstruction in which less than 75 per cent of the shares in the new company are owned by those who held the shares in the old company (ss. 343–344).

2 (a) + (b) Loss is relievable against income and capital gains before deduction of charges of the period of the loss plus, in the case of (a) 6/12 of previous 12 month period, and in the case of (b) against the whole of the previous 9 month period plus 3/12 of period before that.
(c) The loss will first be apportioned on a time basis between the two accounting periods which will cover the fifteen-month period of account (first twelve months and remaining three months). Capital allowances will be calculated separately for the two periods and added to the apportioned loss shares. The loss for the twelve month accounting period will be relieved against other income and capital gains of that period (s. 393 (2)), and any unrelieved gains of the previous twelve-month accounting period.
The loss of the three month accounting period will be relieved within that period and then carried back against 3/12 of any remaining income or capital gains of the previous period (i.e. the twelve month accounting period forming the remainder of the period of account in which the loss was made).

3 See page 179.
4 See page 183.
5 See page 184.
6 (a) (i) Loss of final accounting period
(ii) If (i) is less than twelve months, the appropriate fraction of the previous accounting period to make up twelve months
(iii) Unrelieved trade changes of period (i)
(iv) The appropriate fraction of unrelieved changes of period (ii)
(b) Three years preceding the last twelve months' trading.
(c) Trading income only
(d) Because the trade charges would otherwise become unrelieved, and there would be no trading profit of later years against which they could be relieved under s. 393 (9) because the terminal loss claim would have eliminated such profits.
(e) Yes, if there is non-trading income sufficient to cover them.

7 (a) Six years after the end of the accounting period in which the

loss arose. (It is only necessary to *establish* the claim within this period. The actual claim is against the first available profits which can be more than six years later)

(b) Two years after the end of the accounting period in which the loss arose.

(c) Six years after the date of the company's ceasing to trade.

(d) Two years after the end of the accounting period in which the loss arose, six years for claims in respect of unrelieved charges.

8 See page 191.

Chapter 15

1 (a) There must be a shareholding link of at least 75 per cent. If that is the case, losses may be exchanged by holding company, subsidiary or between fellow 75 per cent subsidiaries. A sub-subsidiary in which the holding company owns less than 75 per cent does not qualify to participate

(b) The loss is apportioned and set off against the claiming company's profits for the two years affected (see Figure 12, page 199)

2 (a) False – the maximum that can be surrendered is the lower of the surrendering company's loss and the claiming company's profit *for the current year*. Any loss which cannot be relieved by a group loss claim up to this maximum is carried forward by the *surrendering* company under s. 393 (1).

(b) False

(c) True

3 When a company is jointly owned by other companies (the consortium) so that it is not a subsidiary of any one of them but they jointly hold at least 75 per cent of the company with no member of the consortium owning less than 5 per cent.

4 (a) If it cannot obtain relief for the ACT against its own corporation tax liability and/or the subsidiary has the ability to obtain relief for it

(b) Over 50 per cent

(c) No, only ACT relating to *dividends*

(d) (i) Yes

(ii) No

(iii) Yes

(e) Surrendered ACT is offset first. The benefit is that this leaves the maximum amount of the company's own ACT available to be carried back for up to 6 years, which cannot be done with the surrendered ACT

5 (a) 75 per cent shareholding link

(b) For group asset transfer a 75 per cent subsidiary of a 75 per cent subsidiary can still transfer assets with its own holding company and with the parent company, whereas for group loss relief there must be a 75 per cent holding, direct or indirect, linking the companies concerned.

(c) (i) No corporation tax is payable on the capital gain at the time of the transfer

(ii) It facilitates the offsetting of capital gains and capital losses if all group sales and purchases of chargeable assets are channelled through one company, since capital losses cannot be surrendered as trading losses can.

Chapter 16

1 See page 209.
2 See pages 209–12.
3 See pages 214–15.
4 (a) Notify the Revenue and pay over an amount equal to ACT on the amount of the loan. (This is not ACT and cannot be offset as real ACT can be. The amount will only be refunded when the loan is repaid)
(b) The ACT cannot be refunded and the gross equivalent of the loan is treated as the income of the recipient.
(c) Yes, for loans made in the ordinary course of business or loans not exceeding £15,000 to full-time working directors not holding, with associates, more than 5 per cent of the company's ordinary share capital.
5 The cost of the benefit will be disallowed in computing the company's adjusted profit for corporation tax purposes.
6 (a) See pages 214–15.
(b) See pages 215–16.
(c) See page 218.

Chapter 17

1 A UK branch or agency.
2 No, because s. 166 FA 1988 debars it from 15 March 1988.
3 The company pays tax on its income at the higher of the tax rates involved.
4 (a) Charges may be deducted from UK income in preference to overseas income, thus maximizing DTR
(b) ACT is deducted from corporation tax after deducting DTR, thus increasing potential DTR
5 (a) Tax deducted by a country from dividends and interest paid to foreign investors
(b) Tax corresponding to corporation tax charged by a foreign country on the profits out of which dividends are paid
6 (a) See page 228.

(b) See page 228.
(c) See page 228.

Chapter 18

1 See page 231.
2 Three from:
   (a) Renouncing capital allowances in whole or part
   (b) Timing of capital expenditure
   (c) Timing of disposals realizing capital gains
   (d) Replacing specific provisions for doubtful debts (allowable) with general provisions (not allowable)
   (e) Timing of major repairs expenditure
   (f) Surrender of losses to other group companies
3 Because profits in the marginal band are taxed at approximately 37½ per cent.
4 See pages 232–3.
5 See page 233.
6 See pages 233–6.
7 See page 234.
8 See pages 234–5.

Chapter 19

1 31 March 1982
2 5 April ... on 1 December following the year of assessment or 30 days after the issue of the assessment if later ... 5,000 ... cost ... indexed ... Retail Price Index (RPI) ... 31 March 1982 ...
3 See page 240.
4 See pages 240–1.
5 See page 242.
6 See page 243.
7 (a) + (b). See page 244.
8 See page 244.
9 See page 244.

Chapter 20

1 See pages 248–9.
2 See page 249.
3 See page 251.
4 See page 252.
5 See page 254.

Chapter 21

1 See page 258.
2 See page 259.
3 See page 260.
4 See page 261.
5 See page 261.
6 See page 263.

Chapter 22

1 See page 266.
2 (a) See pages 266–7.
  (b) See page 267.
3 See page 267.
4 (a) False – a disposal by gift may give rise to a CGT charge which may be held over if both parties jointly claim for it
  (b) False – the statement is almost true but relief is not automatic – a claim must be made
  (c) False – retirement relief is claimed first, then gift relief may lead to the holding over of any balance of liability
  (d) True, as long as both were used for business purposes
  (e) True
  (f) False – you need to think about this one. It is not the *proportion* of gain, but the whole amount of the gain not reinvested. Compare the computation on page 273 with that on page 276 which *is* on a proportionate basis
  (g) True
  (h) False – they *are* allowed for CGT, *not* for income tax
  (i) True – but only just. The operative word is *may* obtain. Relief may only be obtained if the shares were originally issued directly to the shareholder by the company, the company must be a UK resident trading company and the transfer must have been at arm's length. Oh, and the claim must be made within two years

Chapter 23

1 (a) See page 282.
  (b) See page 282.
2 See page 283.

Chapter 24

1 See page 284.
2 See page 287.

Chapter 25

1 See page 292.
2 See page 293.
3 (a) See page 293.
(b) See page 293.
4 See page 294.
5 See page 295.
6 See page 295.
7 See page 296.
8 See page 297.
9 (a) + (b) see page 298.
10 See page 299.
11 See page 299.
12 (a) + (b) see page 300.
13 (a) + (b) see page 300.
14 By adopting the cash accounting scheme if turnover does not exceed £250,000, otherwise only if the debtor is formally insolvent, title in the goods has passed to the buyer and the claim to the liquidator is for the debt excluding VAT.
15 See page 301.
16 No – see page 301.
17 See page 302.
18 See page 303.
19 See page 305.

Capital gains tax – indexation factors March 1982 to May 1988

These tables show the indexation factors for movements in the Retail Price Index between March 1982 and May 1988.

To use them, first find the month of acquisition in the horizontal columns, then read down until you find the month of disposal in the vertical column below it. The figure found there is the indexation factor expressed as a percentage.

You should have familiarized yourself with the tables by using them to confirm the percentages used in illustrations in the text.

Month of disposal	*Month of acquisition 1982*											
	Jan	Feb	Mar	Apr	May	Jun	Jul	Aug	Sept	Oct	Nov	Dec
1982												
Mar	–	–	–	–	–	–	–	–	–	–	–	–
Apr	–	–	2.0	–	–	–	–	–	–	–	–	–
May	–	–	2.7	0.7	–	–	–	–	–	–	–	–
Jun	–	–	3.0	1.0	0.3	–	–	–	–	–	–	–
Jul	–	–	3.1	1.0	0.3	0.0	–	–	–	–	–	–
Aug	–	–	3.1	1.1	0.3	0.1	0.0	–	–	–	–	–
Sep	–	–	3.0	1.0	0.3	0.0	0.0	–	–	–	–	–
Oct	–	–	3.5	1.5	0.8	0.5	0.5	0.4	0.5	–	–	–
Nov	–	–	4.1	2.0	1.3	1.0	1.0	0.9	1.0	0.5	–	–
Dec	–	–	3.9	1.8	1.1	0.8	0.8	0.7	0.8	0.3	0.0	–
1983												
Jan	–	–	4.0	1.9	1.2	0.9	0.9	0.9	0.9	0.4	0.0	0.1
Feb	–	–	4.4	2.4	1.6	1.4	1.3	1.3	1.4	0.9	0.4	0.6
Mar	–	–	4.6	2.6	1.8	1.5	1.5	1.5	1.5	1.0	0.6	0.7
Apr	–	–	6.1	4.0	3.3	3.0	2.9	2.9	3.0	2.5	2.0	2.2
May	–	–	6.5	4.4	3.7	3.4	3.4	3.3	3.4	2.9	2.4	2.6
Jun	–	–	6.8	4.7	3.9	3.7	3.6	3.6	3.7	3.1	2.6	2.8
Jul	–	–	7.4	5.3	4.5	4.2	4.2	4.1	4.2	3.7	3.2	3.4
Aug	–	–	7.8	5.7	5.0	4.7	4.6	4.6	4.7	4.2	3.6	3.8

Sep	–	–	8.3	6.2	5.4	5.1	5.1	5.1	5.1	4.6	4.1	4.3
Oct	–	–	8.7	6.6	5.8	5.5	5.5	5.4	5.5	5.0	4.5	4.7
Nov	–	–	9.1	6.9	6.2	5.9	5.9	5.8	5.9	5.4	4.8	5.0
Dec	–	–	9.4	7.2	6.5	6.2	6.1	6.1	6.2	5.6	5.1	5.3
1984												
Jan	–	–	9.3	7.2	6.4	6.1	6.1	6.0	6.1	5.6	5.1	5.3
Feb	–	–	9.8	7.6	6.8	6.5	6.5	6.5	6.5	6.0	5.5	5.7
Mar	–	–	10.1	7.9	7.2	6.9	6.8	6.8	6.9	6.3	5.8	6.0
Apr	–	–	11.6	9.4	8.6	8.5	8.3	8.2	8.3	7.8	7.2	7.4
May	–	–	12.0	9.8	9.0	8.7	8.7	8.6	8.7	8.2	7.6	7.8
Jun	–	–	12.3	10.1	9.3	9.0	8.9	8.9	9.0	8.4	7.9	8.1
Jul	–	–	12.2	9.9	9.2	8.9	8.8	8.8	8.9	8.3	7.8	8.0
Aug	–	–	13.2	11.0	10.2	9.9	9.8	9.8	9.9	9.3	8.8	9.0
Sep	–	–	13.4	11.2	10.4	10.1	10.1	10.0	10.1	9.6	9.0	9.2
Oct	–	–	14.1	11.9	11.1	10.8	10.7	10.7	10.8	10.2	9.7	9.9
Nov	–	–	14.5	12.2	11.4	11.1	11.1	11.0	11.1	10.6	10.0	10.2
Dec	–	–	14.4	12.1	11.3	11.0	11.0	11.0	11.0	10.5	9.9	10.1
1985												
Jan	–	–	14.8	12.5	11.7	11.4	11.4	11.4	11.4	10.9	10.3	10.5
Feb	–	–	15.7	13.5	12.6	12.3	12.3	12.3	12.3	11.8	11.2	11.4
Mar	–	–	16.8	14.5	13.7	13.4	13.3	13.3	13.4	12.8	12.3	12.5
Apr	–	–	19.3	17.0	16.1	15.8	15.8	15.7	15.8	15.2	14.7	14.9
May	–	–	19.8	17.5	16.6	16.3	16.3	16.2	16.3	15.7	15.2	15.4
Jun	–	–	20.1	17.7	16.9	16.6	16.5	16.5	16.6	16.0	15.4	15.6
Jul	–	–	19.9	17.5	16.7	16.4	16.3	16.3	16.4	15.8	15.2	15.4
Aug	–	–	20.2	17.8	17.0	16.7	16.6	16.6	16.7	16.1	15.5	15.7
Sep	–	–	20.1	17.8	16.9	16.6	16.6	16.5	16.6	16.0	15.5	15.7
Oct	–	–	20.3	18.0	17.1	16.8	16.7	16.7	16.8	16.2	15.6	15.9
Nov	–	–	20.7	18.4	17.5	17.2	17.2	17.1	17.2	16.6	16.0	16.3
Dec	–	–	20.9	18.5	17.7	17.3	17.3	17.3	17.3	16.8	16.2	16.4
1986												
Jan	–	–	21.2	18.8	17.9	17.6	17.6	17.5	17.6	17.0	16.4	16.7
Feb	–	–	21.6	19.2	18.4	18.0	18.0	18.0	18.0	17.4	16.9	17.1
Mar	–	–	21.8	19.4	18.5	18.2	18.1	18.1	18.2	17.6	17.0	17.2
Apr	–	–	22.9	20.5	19.7	19.3	19.3	19.3	19.3	18.7	18.2	18.4
May	–	–	23.2	20.7	19.9	19.5	19.5	19.5	19.5	19.0	18.4	18.6
Jun	–	–	23.1	20.7	19.8	19.5	19.4	19.4	19.5	18.9	18.3	18.5
Jul	–	–	22.8	20.3	19.5	19.1	19.1	19.1	19.1	18.6	18.0	18.2
Aug	–	–	23.1	20.7	19.8	19.5	19.5	19.4	19.5	18.9	18.3	18.6
Sep	–	–	23.7	21.3	20.4	20.1	20.1	20.0	20.1	19.5	18.9	19.1
Oct	–	–	23.9	21.5	20.6	20.3	20.2	20.2	20.3	19.7	19.1	19.3
Nov	–	–	25.0	22.5	21.6	21.3	21.3	21.2	21.3	20.7	20.1	20.3
Dec	–	–	25.4	22.9	22.0	21.7	21.7	21.6	21.7	21.1	20.5	20.7
1987												
Jan	–	–	25.9	23.4	22.5	22.2	22.1	22.1	22.2	21.6	21.0	21.2
Feb	–	–	26.4	23.9	23.0	22.7	22.6	22.6	22.7	22.1	21.5	21.7
Mar	–	–	26.6	24.1	23.3	22.9	22.9	22.8	22.9	22.3	21.7	21.9
Apr	–	–	28.1	25.6	24.7	24.4	24.3	24.3	24.4	23.8	23.2	23.4
May	–	–	28.3	25.7	24.8	24.5	24.5	24.4	24.5	23.9	23.3	23.5
Jun	–	–	28.3	25.7	24.8	24.5	24.5	24.4	24.5	23.9	23.3	23.5

Jul	–	–	28.1	25.6	24.7	24.3	24.3	24.3	24.4	23.8	23.2	23.4
Aug	–	–	28.5	26.0	25.1	24.7	24.7	24.7	24.7	24.1	23.5	23.7
Sep	–	–	28.9	26.4	25.5	25.1	25.1	25.0	25.1	24.5	23.9	24.1
Oct	–	–	29.5	27.0	26.1	25.7	25.7	25.6	25.7	25.1	24.5	24.7
Nov	–	–	30.2	27.6	26.7	26.3	26.3	26.2	26.3	25.7	25.1	25.3
Dec	–	–	30.0	27.5	26.6	26.2	26.2	26.1	26.2	25.6	25.0	25.2
1988												
Jan	–	–	30.0	27.5	26.6	26.2	26.2	26.1	26.2	25.6	25.0	25.2
Feb	–	–	30.5	28.0	27.0	26.7	26.7	26.6	26.7	26.1	25.5	25.7
Mar	–	–	31.0	28.5	27.5	27.2	27.1	27.1	27.2	26.6	25.9	26.2
Apr	–	–	33.2	30.6	29.6	29.3	29.2	29.2	29.3	28.6	28.0	28.2
May	–	–	33.7	31.0	30.1	29.7	29.7	29.7	29.7	29.1	28.5	28.7

Month of disposal	*Month of acquisition 1983*											
	Jan	Feb	Mar	Apr	May	Jun	Jul	Aug	Sept	Oct	Nov	Dec
1983												
Jan	–	–	–	–	–	–	–	–	–	–	–	–
Feb	0.4	–	–	–	–	–	–	–	–	–	–	–
Mar	0.6	0.2	–	–	–	–	–	–	–	–	–	–
Apr	2.0	1.6	1.4	–	–	–	–	–	–	–	–	–
May	2.5	2.0	1.8	0.4	–	–	–	–	–	–	–	–
Jun	2.7	2.3	2.1	0.7	0.2	–	–	–	–	–	–	–
Jul	3.3	2.8	2.6	1.2	0.8	0.5	–	–	–	–	–	–
Aug	3.7	3.3	3.1	1.7	1.2	1.0	0.4	–	–	–	–	–
Sep	4.2	3.7	3.5	2.1	1.7	1.4	0.9	0.4	–	–	–	–
Oct	4.5	4.1	3.9	2.5	2.0	1.8	1.2	0.8	0.4	–	–	–
Nov	4.9	4.5	4.3	2.8	2.4	2.2	1.6	1.2	0.7	0.4	–	–
Dec	5.2	4.7	4.5	3.1	2.7	2.4	1.9	1.4	1.0	0.6	0.3	–
1984												
Jan	5.1	4.7	4.5	3.0	2.6	2.4	1.8	1.4	0.9	0.6	0.2	–
Feb	5.6	5.1	4.9	3.5	3.0	2.8	2.2	1.8	1.3	1.0	0.6	0.4
Mar	5.9	5.4	5.2	3.8	3.4	3.1	2.6	2.1	1.6	1.3	0.9	0.7
Apr	7.3	6.8	6.6	5.2	4.7	4.5	3.9	3.5	3.0	2.6	2.3	2.0
May	7.7	7.2	7.0	5.6	5.1	4.9	4.3	3.8	3.4	3.0	2.7	2.4
Jun	8.0	7.5	7.3	5.8	5.4	5.1	4.6	4.1	3.7	3.3	2.9	2.7
Jul	7.9	7.4	7.2	5.7	5.3	5.0	4.5	4.0	3.5	3.2	2.8	2.5
Aug	8.9	8.4	8.2	6.7	6.3	6.0	5.4	5.0	4.5	4.1	3.8	3.5
Sep	9.1	8.6	8.4	6.9	6.5	6.2	5.6	5.2	4.7	4.3	4.0	3.7
Oct	9.8	9.3	9.1	7.6	7.1	6.9	6.3	5.8	5.4	5.0	4.6	4.3
Nov	10.1	9.6	9.4	7.9	7.5	7.2	6.6	6.2	5.7	5.3	4.9	4.7
Dec	10.0	9.5	9.3	7.8	7.4	7.1	6.5	6.1	5.6	5.2	4.9	4.6
1985												
Jan	10.4	9.9	9.7	8.2	7.8	7.5	6.9	6.4	6.0	5.6	5.2	5.0
Feb	11.3	10.8	10.6	9.1	8.6	8.4	7.8	7.3	6.8	6.5	6.1	5.8
Mar	12.3	11.9	11.6	10.1	9.6	9.4	8.8	8.3	7.8	7.5	7.1	6.8
Apr	14.7	14.2	14.0	12.5	12.0	11.7	11.1	10.6	10.1	9.7	9.4	9.1
May	15.3	14.8	14.5	13.0	12.5	12.2	11.6	11.1	10.6	10.2	9.9	9.6
Jun	15.5	15.0	14.8	13.2	12.7	12.5	11.9	11.4	10.9	10.5	10.1	9.8
Jul	15.3	14.8	14.6	13.0	12.5	12.2	11.6	11.2	10.7	10.3	9.9	9.6

Aug	15.6	15.1	14.9	13.3	12.8	12.5	11.9	11.4	11.0	10.6	10.2	9.9
Sep	15.5	15.0	14.8	13.2	12.8	12.5	11.9	11.4	10.9	10.5	10.1	9.8
Oct	15.7	15.2	15.0	13.4	12.9	12.7	12.1	11.6	11.1	10.7	10.3	10.0
Nov	16.1	15.6	15.4	13.8	13.3	13.1	12.5	12.0	11.5	11.1	10.7	10.4
Dec	16.3	15.8	15.6	14.0	13.5	13.2	12.6	12.1	11.6	11.2	10.8	10.5
1986												
Jan	16.5	16.0	15.8	14.2	13.7	13.4	12.8	12.3	11.8	11.4	11.1	10.8
Feb	16.9	16.4	16.2	14.6	14.1	13.9	13.3	12.8	12.3	11.9	11.5	11.2
Mar	17.1	16.6	16.4	14.8	14.3	14.0	13.4	12.9	12.4	12.0	11.6	11.3
Apr	18.2	17.7	17.5	15.9	15.4	15.1	14.5	14.0	13.5	13.1	12.7	12.4
May	18.4	17.9	17.7	16.1	15.6	15.3	14.7	14.2	13.7	13.3	12.9	12.6
Jun	18.4	17.9	17.7	16.0	15.5	15.3	14.7	14.1	13.6	13.2	12.8	12.5
Jul	18.0	17.5	17.3	15.7	15.2	14.9	14.3	13.8	13.3	12.9	12.5	12.2
Aug	18.4	17.9	17.7	16.1	15.6	15.3	14.7	14.2	13.7	13.3	12.9	12.6
Sep	19.0	18.5	18.3	16.6	16.1	15.9	15.2	14.7	14.2	13.8	13.4	13.1
Oct	19.2	18.7	18.5	16.8	16.3	16.0	15.4	14.9	14.4	14.0	13.6	13.3
Nov	20.2	19.7	19.5	17.8	17.3	17.0	16.4	15.9	15.4	15.0	14.6	14.3
Dec	20.6	20.1	19.9	18.2	17.7	17.4	16.8	16.3	15.8	15.4	14.9	14.6
1987												
Jan	21.0	20.5	20.3	18.6	18.1	17.9	17.2	16.7	16.2	15.8	15.4	15.1
Feb	21.5	21.0	20.8	19.1	18.6	18.3	17.7	17.2	16.7	16.3	15.8	15.5
Mar	21.8	21.3	21.0	19.4	18.9	18.6	17.9	17.4	16.9	16.5	16.1	15.8
Apr	23.2	22.7	22.5	20.8	20.3	20.0	19.3	18.8	18.3	17.9	17.5	17.2
May	23.3	22.8	22.6	20.9	20.4	20.1	19.5	18.9	18.4	18.0	17.6	17.3
Jun	23.3	22.8	22.6	20.9	20.4	20.1	19.5	18.9	18.4	18.0	17.6	17.3
Jul	23.2	22.7	22.5	20.8	20.3	20.0	19.3	18.8	18.3	17.9	17.5	17.2
Aug	23.6	23.1	22.8	21.1	20.6	20.3	19.7	19.2	18.6	18.2	17.8	17.5
Sep	24.0	23.4	23.2	21.5	21.0	20.7	20.0	19.5	19.0	18.6	18.2	17.8
Oct	24.6	24.0	23.8	22.1	21.6	21.3	20.6	20.1	19.6	19.1	18.7	18.4
Nov	25.2	24.6	24.4	22.7	22.2	21.9	21.2	20.7	20.2	19.7	19.3	19.0
Dec	25.0	24.5	24.3	22.6	22.0	21.8	21.1	20.6	20.0	19.6	19.2	18.9
1988												
Jan	25.0	24.5	24.3	22.6	22.0	21.8	21.1	20.6	20.0	19.6	19.2	18.9
Feb	25.0	24.8	23.0	22.5	22.5	22.2	21.6	21.0	20.5	20.1	19.7	19.3
Mar	26.0	25.5	25.2	23.5	23.0	22.7	22.0	21.5	21.0	20.5	20.1	19.8
Apr	28.1	27.5	27.3	25.5	25.0	24.7	24.0	23.5	22.9	22.5	22.1	21.8
May	28.6	28.0	27.8	26.0	25.5	25.2	24.5	24.0	23.4	23.0	22.5	22.2

Month of disposal	*Month of acquisition 1984*											
	Jan	Feb	Mar	Apr	May	Jun	Jul	Aug	Sept	Oct	Nov	Dec
1984												
Jan	–	–	–	–	–	–	–	–	–	–	–	–
Feb	0.4	–	–	–	–	–	–	–	–	–	–	–
Mar	0.7	0.3	–	–	–	–	–	–	–	–	–	–
Apr	2.1	1.7	1.3	–	–	–	–	–	–	–	–	–
May	2.5	2.0	1.7	0.4	–	–	–	–	–	–	–	–
Jun	2.7	2.3	2.0	0.6	0.3	–	–	–	–	–	–	–
Jul	2.6	2.2	1.9	0.5	0.1	–	–	–	–	–	–	–
Aug	3.6	3.1	2.8	1.5	1.1	0.8	0.9	–	–	–	–	–

Sep	3.8	3.3	3.0	1.7	1.3	1.0	1.1	0.2	–	–	–	–
Oct	4.4	4.0	3.7	2.3	1.9	1.6	1.8	0.8	0.6	–	–	–
Nov	4.7	4.3	4.0	2.6	2.2	2.0	2.1	1.1	0.9	0.3	–	–
Dec	4.6	4.2	3.9	2.5	2.1	1.9	2.0	1.0	0.8	0.2	–	–
1985												
Jan	5.0	4.6	4.3	2.9	2.5	2.2	2.4	1.4	1.2	0.6	0.3	0.4
Feb	5.9	5.4	5.1	3.7	3.3	3.1	3.2	2.2	2.0	1.4	1.1	1.2
Mar	6.9	6.4	6.1	4.7	4.3	4.0	4.2	3.2	3.0	2.3	2.0	2.1
Apr	9.1	8.7	8.3	9.6	6.5	6.3	6.4	5.4	5.2	4.5	4.2	4.3
May	9.6	9.2	8.8	7.4	7.0	6.7	6.9	5.9	5.7	5.0	4.7	4.8
Jun	9.9	9.4	9.1	7.6	7.2	7.0	7.1	6.1	5.9	5.2	4.9	5.0
Jul	9.7	9.2	8.9	7.4	7.0	6.8	5.9	5.4	5.7	5.0	4.7	4.8
Aug	10.0	9.5	9.2	7.7	7.3	7.0	7.2	6.2	6.0	5.3	5.0	5.1
Sep	9.9	9.4	9.1	7.7	7.3	7.0	7.1	6.1	5.9	5.3	4.9	5.0
Oct	10.1	9.6	9.3	7.8	7.4	7.2	7.3	6.3	6.1	5.4	5.1	5.2
Nov	10.4	10.0	9.6	8.2	7.8	7.5	7.7	6.7	6.4	5.8	5.5	5.6
Dec	10.6	10.1	9.8	8.4	7.9	7.7	7.8	6.8	6.6	5.9	5.6	5.7
1986												
Jan	10.8	10.4	10.0	8.6	8.2	7.9	8.0	7.0	6.8	6.2	5.8	5.9
Feb	11.2	10.8	10.4	9.0	8.6	8.3	8.4	7.4	7.2	6.5	6.2	6.3
Mar	11.4	10.9	10.6	9.1	8.7	8.4	8.6	7.6	7.3	6.7	6.4	6.4
Apr	12.5	12.0	11.6	10.2	9.8	9.5	9.6	8.6	8.4	7.7	7.4	7.5
May	12.7	12.2	11.9	10.4	10.0	9.7	9.8	8.8	8.6	7.9	7.6	7.7
Jun	12.6	12.2	11.8	10.3	9.9	9.6	9.8	8.7	8.5	7.9	7.5	7.6
Jul	12.3	11.8	11.5	10.0	9.6	9.3	9.4	8.4	8.2	7.3	7.2	7.3
Aug	12.6	12.2	11.8	10.4	9.9	9.7	9.8	8.8	8.6	7.9	7.6	7.6
Sep	13.2	12.7	12.4	10.9	10.5	10.2	10.3	9.3	9.1	8.4	8.1	8.2
Oct	13.4	12.9	12.5	11.1	10.7	10.4	10.5	9.5	9.3	8.6	8.2	8.3
Nov	14.3	13.9	13.5	12.0	11.6	11.3	11.4	10.4	10.2	9.5	9.2	9.3
Dec	14.7	14.2	13.9	12.4	12.0	11.7	11.8	10.8	10.5	9.9	9.5	9.6
1987												
Jan	15.1	14.7	14.3	12.8	12.4	12.1	12.2	11.2	11.0	10.3	9.9	10.0
Feb	15.6	15.1	14.8	13.3	12.8	12.6	12.7	11.6	11.4	10.7	10.4	10.5
Mar	15.8	15.4	15.0	13.5	13.1	12.8	12.9	11.9	11.6	10.9	10.6	10.7
Apr	17.2	16.7	16.4	14.8	14.4	14.1	14.3	13.2	13.0	12.3	11.9	12.0
May	17.3	16.9	16.5	15.0	14.5	14.2	14.4	13.3	13.1	12.4	12.0	12.1
Jun	17.3	16.9	16.5	15.0	14.5	14.2	14.4	13.3	13.1	12.4	12.0	12.1
Jul	17.2	16.7	16.4	14.8	14.4	14.1	14.3	13.2	13.0	12.3	11.9	12.0
Aug	17.6	17.1	16.7	15.2	14.8	14.5	14.6	13.5	13.3	12.6	12.3	12.4
Sep	17.9	17.4	17.1	15.5	15.1	14.8	14.9	13.9	13.6	12.9	12.6	12.7
Oct	18.5	18.0	17.6	16.1	15.7	15.4	15.5	14.4	14.2	13.5	13.1	13.2
Nov	19.1	18.6	18.2	16.6	16.2	15.9	16.0	15.0	14.7	14.0	13.7	13.8
Dec	18.9	18.5	18.1	16.5	16.1	15.8	15.9	14.9	14.6	13.9	13.6	13.7
1988												
Jan	18.9	18.5	18.1	16.5	16.1	15.8	15.9	14.9	14.6	13.9	13.6	13.7
Feb	19.4	18.9	18.5	17.0	16.6	16.3	16.4	15.3	15.1	14.4	14.0	14.1
Mar	19.9	19.4	19.0	17.4	17.0	16.7	16.8	15.7	15.5	14.8	14.5	14.6
Apr	21.8	21.3	20.9	19.4	18.9	18.6	18.7	17.6	17.4	16.7	16.3	16.4
May	22.3	21.8	21.4	19.8	19.4	19.1	19.2	18.1	17.9	17.1	16.8	16.9

Month of disposal	*Month of acquisition 1985*											
	Jan	Feb	Mar	Apr	May	Jun	Jul	Aug	Sept	Oct	Nov	Dec
1985												
Jan	–	–	–	–	–	–	–	–	–	–	–	–
Feb	0.8	–	–	–	–	–	–	–	–	–	–	–
Mar	1.8	0.9	–	–	–	–	–	–	–	–	–	–
Apr	3.9	3.1	2.1	–	–	–	–	–	–	–	–	–
May	4.4	3.6	2.6	0.5	–	–	–	–	–	–	–	–
Jun	4.6	3.8	2.8	0.7	0.2	–	–	–	–	–	–	–
Jul	4.4	3.6	2.6	0.5	0.0	0.0	–	–	–	–	–	–
Aug	4.7	3.9	2.9	0.7	0.3	0.1	0.3	–	–	–	–	–
Sep	4.6	3.8	2.8	0.7	0.2	0.0	0.0	0.0	–	–	–	–
Oct	4.8	4.0	3.0	0.9	0.4	0.2	0.4	0.1	0.2	–	–	–
Nov	5.2	4.3	3.4	1.2	0.7	0.5	0.7	0.5	0.5	0.3	–	–
Dec	5.3	4.5	3.5	1.3	0.9	0.7	0.9	0.6	0.6	0.5	0.1	–
1986												
Jan	5.5	4.7	3.7	1.6	1.1	0.9	1.1	0.8	0.8	0.7	0.3	0.2
Feb	5.9	5.1	4.1	1.9	1.5	1.2	1.4	1.2	1.2	1.1	0.7	0.6
Mar	6.1	5.2	4.2	2.1	1.6	1.4	1.6	1.3	1.4	1.2	0.8	0.7
Apr	7.1	6.2	5.2	3.0	2.6	2.4	2.6	2.3	2.3	2.2	1.8	1.7
May	7.3	6.4	5.4	3.2	2.8	2.6	2.7	2.5	2.5	2.4	2.0	1.9
Jun	7.2	6.4	5.4	3.2	2.7	2.5	2.7	2.4	2.5	2.3	2.0	1.8
Jul	6.9	6.1	3.1	2.9	2.4	2.2	2.4	2.1	2.2	2.0	1.7	1.5
Aug	7.3	6.4	5.4	3.2	2.7	2.5	2.7	2.4	2.5	2.3	2.0	1.8
Sep	7.8	6.9	5.9	3.7	3.2	3.0	3.2	2.9	3.0	2.8	2.5	2.3
Oct	7.9	7.1	6.1	3.9	3.4	3.2	3.4	3.1	3.2	3.0	2.6	2.5
Nov	8.9	8.0	7.0	4.8	4.3	4.1	4.3	4.0	4.0	3.9	3.5	3.4
Dec	9.2	8.4	7.3	5.1	4.6	4.4	4.6	4.3	4.4	4.2	3.9	3.7
1987												
Jan	9.6	8.8	7.8	5.5	5.0	4.8	5.0	4.7	4.8	4.6	4.3	4.1
Feb	10.1	9.2	8.2	5.9	5.5	5.2	5.4	5.1	5.2	5.0	4.7	4.5
Mar	10.3	9.4	8.4	6.1	5.7	5.4	5.6	5.4	5.4	5.2	4.9	4.7
Apr	11.6	10.7	9.7	7.4	6.9	6.7	6.9	6.6	6.7	6.5	6.1	6.0
May	11.7	10.8	9.8	7.5	7.0	6.8	7.0	6.7	6.8	6.6	6.2	6.1
Jun	11.7	10.8	9.8	7.5	7.0	6.8	7.0	6.7	6.8	6.6	6.2	6.1
Jul	11.6	10.7	9.7	7.4	6.9	6.7	6.9	6.6	6.7	6.5	6.1	6.0
Aug	11.9	11.1	10.0	7.7	7.2	7.0	7.2	6.9	7.0	6.8	6.4	6.3
Sep	12.3	11.4	10.3	8.0	7.6	7.3	7.5	7.2	7.3	7.1	6.8	6.6
Oct	12.8	11.9	10.9	8.6	8.1	7.8	8.0	7.8	7.8	7.6	7.3	7.1
Nov	13.4	12.5	11.4	9.1	8.6	8.4	8.6	8.3	8.3	7.2	7.8	7.7
Dec	13.3	12.4	11.3	9.0	8.5	8.3	8.5	8.2	8.2	8.1	7.7	7.6
1988												
Jan	13.3	12.4	11.3	9.0	8.5	8.3	8.5	8.2	8.2	8.1	7.7	7.6
Feb	13.7	12.8	11.7	9.4	8.9	8.7	8.9	8.6	8.7	8.5	8.1	8.0
Mar	14.1	13.2	12.2	9.8	9.3	9.1	9.3	9.0	9.1	8.9	8.5	8.4
Apr	16.0	15.1	14.0	11.6	11.1	10.9	11.1	10.8	10.9	10.7	10.3	10.2
May	16.4	15.5	14.4	12.1	11.5	11.3	11.5	11.2	11.3	11.1	10.7	10.6

Month of disposal	*Month of acquisition 1986*											
	Jan	Feb	Mar	Apr	May	Jun	Jul	Aug	Sept	Oct	Nov	Dec
1986												
Jan	–	–	–	–	–	–	–	–	–	–	–	–
Feb	0.4	–	–	–	–	–	–	–	–	–	–	–
Mar	0.5	0.1	–	–	–	–	–	–	–	–	–	–
Apr	1.5	1.1	1.0	–	–	–	–	–	–	–	–	–
May	1.7	1.3	1.2	0.2	–	–	–	–	–	–	–	–
Jun	1.6	1.2	1.1	0.1	–	–	–	–	–	–	–	–
Jul	1.3	0.9	0.8	–	–	–	–	–	–	–	–	–
Aug	1.6	1.3	1.1	0.2	0.0	0.0	0.3	–	–	–	–	–
Sep	2.1	1.8	1.6	0.6	0.5	0.5	0.8	0.5	–	–	–	–
Oct	2.3	1.9	1.8	0.8	0.6	0.7	0.1	0.6	0.2	–	–	–
Nov	3.2	2.8	2.6	1.7	1.5	1.5	1.8	1.5	1.0	0.8	–	–
Dec	3.5	3.1	3.0	2.0	1.8	1.9	2.2	1.8	1.3	1.2	0.3	–
1987												
Jan	3.9	3.5	3.4	2.4	2.2	2.3	2.5	2.2	1.7	1.6	0.7	0.4
Feb	4.3	3.9	3.8	2.8	2.6	2.7	3.0	2.6	2.1	2.0	1.1	0.8
Mar	4.5	4.1	4.0	3.0	2.8	2.9	3.2	2.8	2.3	2.2	1.3	1.0
Apr	5.8	5.4	5.2	4.2	4.0	4.1	4.4	4.1	3.6	3.4	2.5	2.2
May	5.9	5.5	5.3	4.3	4.1	4.2	4.5	4.2	3.7	3.5	2.6	2.3
Jun	5.9	5.5	5.3	4.3	4.1	4.2	4.5	4.2	3.7	3.5	2.6	2.3
Jul	5.8	5.4	5.2	4.2	4.0	4.1	4.4	4.1	3.6	3.4	2.5	2.2
Aug	6.1	5.7	5.6	4.5	4.3	4.4	4.7	4.4	3.9	3.7	2.8	2.5
Sep	6.4	6.0	5.9	4.8	4.7	4.7	5.0	4.7	4.2	4.0	3.1	2.8
Oct	6.9	6.5	6.4	5.4	5.2	5.2	5.5	5.2	4.7	4.5	3.6	3.3
Nov	7.4	7.0	6.9	5.9	5.7	5.7	6.0	5.7	5.2	5.0	4.1	3.8
Dec	7.3	6.9	6.8	5.8	5.6	5.6	5.9	5.6	5.1	4.9	4.0	3.7
1988												
Jan	7.3	6.9	6.8	5.8	5.6	5.6	5.9	5.6	5.1	4.9	4.0	3.7
Feb	7.7	7.3	7.2	6.2	6.0	6.0	6.3	6.0	5.5	5.3	4.4	4.1
Mar	8.2	7.8	7.6	6.6	6.4	6.4	6.8	6.4	5.9	5.7	4.8	4.5
Apr	9.9	9.5	9.4	8.3	8.1	8.2	8.5	8.2	7.6	7.5	6.6	6.2
May	10.3	9.9	9.8	8.7	8.5	8.6	8.9	8.6	8.0	7.9	7.0	6.6

Month of disposal	*Month of acquisition 1987*											
	Jan	Feb	Mar	Apr	May	Jun	Jul	Aug	Sept	Oct	Nov	Dec
1987												
Jan	–	–	–	–	–	–	–	–	–	–	–	–
Feb	0.4	–	–	–	–	–	–	–	–	–	–	–
Mar	0.6	0.2	–	–	–	–	–	–	–	–	–	–
Apr	1.8	1.4	1.2	–	–	–	–	–	–	–	–	–
May	1.9	1.5	1.3	0.1	–	–	–	–	–	–	–	–
Jun	1.9	1.5	1.3	0.1	0.0	–	–	–	–	–	–	–
Jul	1.8	1.4	1.2	0.0	0.0	0.0	–	–	–	–	–	–
Aug	2.1	1.7	1.5	0.3	0.2	0.2	0.3	–	–	–	–	–
Sep	2.4	2.0	1.8	0.6	0.5	0.5	0.6	0.3	–	–	–	–
Oct	2.9	2.5	2.3	1.1	1.0	1.0	1.1	0.8	0.5	–	–	–
Nov	3.4	3.0	2.8	1.6	1.5	1.5	1.6	1.3	1.0	0.5	–	–
Dec	3.3	2.9	2.7	1.5	1.4	1.4	1.5	1.2	0.9	0.4	0.0	–

1988												
Jan	3.3	2.9	2.7	1.5	1.4	1.4	1.5	1.2	0.9	0.4	0.0	0.0
Feb	3.7	3.3	3.1	1.9	1.8	1.8	1.9	1.6	1.3	0.8	0.3	0.4
Mar	4.1	3.7	3.5	2.3	2.2	2.2	2.3	2.0	1.7	1.2	0.7	0.8
Apr	5.8	5.4	5.2	3.9	3.8	3.8	3.9	3.6	3.3	2.8	2.3	2.4
May	6.2	5.8	5.6	4.3	4.2	4.2	4.3	4.0	3.7	3.2	2.7	2.8

Month of disposal	*Month of acquisition 1988*											
	Jan	Feb	Mar	Apr	May	Jun	Jul	Aug	Sept	Oct	Nov	Dec
1988												
Jan	–	–	–	–	–	–	–	–	–	–	–	–
Feb	0.4	–	–	–	–	–	–	–	–	–	–	–
Mar	0.8	0.4	–	–	–	–	–	–	–	–	–	–
Apr	2.4	2.0	1.6	–	–	–	–	–	–	–	–	–
May	2.8	2.4	2.0	0.4	–	–	–	–	–	–	–	–

Index

The index is in four parts corresponding to the first four parts of the book: Income tax; Corporation tax; Capital gains tax and Value added tax

Income tax

Corporation tax

Capital gains tax

Value added tax